Angus & Robertson and the British Trade in Australian Books, 1930–1970

Anthem Australian Humanities Research Series

The **Anthem Australian Humanities Research Series** incorporates a broad range of titles on the past, present and future of Australia, comprising an excellent collection of interdisciplinary academic texts. The series aims to promote the most challenging and original work being undertaken in the field by both Australian and non-Australian scholars on Australian culture, society, politics, history and literature. Some of the most innovative research in both the traditional and new humanities today is being done by scholars in the Australian humanities, including literature, history, book history, print culture, cinema, new media and digital cultures, gender studies, cultural studies and indigenous studies.

Angus & Robertson and the British Trade in Australian Books, 1930–1970

The Getting of Bookselling Wisdom

JASON D. ENSOR

ANTHEM PRESS
LONDON • NEW YORK • DELHI

Anthem Press
An imprint of Wimbledon Publishing Company
www.anthempress.com

This edition first published in UK and USA 2013
by ANTHEM PRESS
75–76 Blackfriars Road, London SE1 8HA, UK
or PO Box 9779, London SW19 7ZG, UK
and
244 Madison Ave. #116, New York, NY 10016, USA

First published in hardback by Anthem Press in 2012

British Library Cataloguing-in-Publication Data
A catalogue record for this book is available from the British Library.

Library of Congress Cataloging-in-Publication Data
The Library of Congress has cataloged the hardcover edition as follows:
Ensor, Jason D.
Angus & Robertson and the British trade in Australian books, 1930–1970 : the getting of bookselling wisdom / Jason D. Ensor.
pages cm
Includes bibliographical references and index.
ISBN 978-0-85728-566-9
1. Angus & Robertson Publishers–History. 2. Publishers and publishing–Australia–History–20th century. 3. Booksellers and bookselling–Australia–History–20th century. 4. Australian literature–Publishing–Great Britain–History–20th century. 5. Publishers and publishing–Great Britain–History–20th century. 6. Booksellers and bookselling–Great Britain–History–20th century. 7. Book industries and trade–Australia–History–20th century. 8. Book industries and trade–Great Britain–History–20th century. 9. Australia–Foreign economic relations–Great Britain. 10. Great Britain–Foreign economic relations–Australia. I. Title.
Z533.3.A54E57 2013
070.5099409'04–dc23
2012033446

ISBN-13: 978 1 78308 058 8 (Pbk)
ISBN-10: 1 78308 058 2 (Pbk)

This title is also available as an ebook.

CONTENTS

DRAMATIS PERSONAE

Angus & Robertson, Sydney

Aubrey Cousins
Walter Cousins
George Ferguson
Paul Tracy

Angus & Robertson, London

Alec Bolton
Walter Butcher
John Ferguson
Hector MacQuarrie
Bernard Robinson
Barry Rowland
Cliff Rust
Douglas Stewart
Sam Ure Smith
Vera Wellings
Mrs Woods

Australasian Publishing Company, Sydney

Stanley Bartlett

British Publishers

John Brown (British Publishers Association)
Dwye Evans (Heinemann)
Walter Harrap (George G. Harrap & Co.)
Frank Sanders (British Publishers Association)
Stanley Unwin (George Allen & Unwin)

PREFACE

Although this book is not the first study to interrogate the extensive Mitchell Library holdings of the Angus & Robertson archives with regards to the company's business operations,[1] it is the first whose central concern is the company's production and distribution of Australian books within the United Kingdom through its London office. Often footnoted as worthy of further investigation,[2] this is an area of history which to date has only been narrowly scoped without reference to key archival volumes held by the State Library of New South Wales, Australia. Heather Rusden's interview with Alec Bolton[3] and Suzanne Lunney's interviews with George Ferguson,[4] Douglas Stewart[5] and Ernie Williams[6] provide some context but are limited due to the anecdotal nature of reminiscences. The majority of material published on Angus & Robertson, which is substantial, also records very little about the company's London operations. The best account is by Neil James in 2000, which places the London office's business within the framework of the Australian company's general overseas operations.[7] It draws on interviews conducted by James with publisher George Ferguson and former occasional London office employees John Ferguson, David Moore and Sam Ure Smith. These also take the form of reminiscences regarding operations and managers in the United Kingdom.[8] Essays appearing in the firm's own publication, *Fragment: The House Magazine of Angus & Robertson and Halstead Press* (1954–9), offer further perspective and so does commentary from Collins' Australian managing director, Ken Wilder, 'who sat on the Angus & Robertson board with a watching brief' during the 1960s.[9]

This information on the firm is concise and contributes important material for the history of exporting Australian books, but it does not afford a complete narrative and analysis of Angus & Robertson's London office. To date, much of the research and data on Australian publishing has focused on single publishing houses operating within national borders, the personality of leading publishing CEOs, or famous writers' interactions with well-known publishers. There is a significant knowledge gap, however, in the analysis of Australian publishers responding to external conditions and their international transactions. An objective of this book therefore is to fill this gap in the record: it seeks to complement existing studies on Angus & Robertson, Australian literature and other Australian publishers and to provide new insights into the historical links between the international trade in books and local transformations in the Australian publishing industry.

For its interpretative history, the research in this book draws on the documentary evidence held in volumes 18–34 of Angus & Robertson London, volumes 440–49 of Hector MacQuarrie and volumes 645–8 of Barry Rowland from the Mitchell Library's second Angus & Robertson collection, MSS 3269 ML. Together these represent nearly ten thousand documents on the subject. This restricted collection of memos, author and publisher correspondence, contracts and financial statements is supplemented by an another 4,000 documents from the archives of Angus & Robertson's subsidiary printer Halstead Press, the Publisher's Associations in Britain and Australia, and a selection of English publishers, including George G. Harrap and William Heinemann. Permission to access and digitise these documents was given by then current copyright owners of the material, HarperCollins, on 4 June 2008.

This research justifies its focus on Australian publishing by extending the argument that the production and selling of the written word mixes both cultural and profit-making agendas. It proceeds from an observation made by the Australian Productivity Commission in 2009 that books 'are a significant source of cultural value to Australia' and that the positive cultural externalities following the production of a creative work are 'significantly amplified by the broad dissemination of the ideas it contains'.[10] From that perspective, this book engages directly with the cultural capital of the nation within the context of the impact of overseas publishing on Australian literary publishing.

With books increasingly becoming the centrepiece for arguments about literary merit, national representation and commercialism, an analysis of the publishing practice can provide useful case studies that join together economic, social, cultural, political and legal tensions. This project acknowledges that the research which makes up this book, despite the empirical and archival features employed, will in some manner be a projection of contemporary historical demands: it will certainly be part of a movement that, through bibliographic and textual research, contributes to new understandings in the study of Australian publishing. In a sense, this creation of history can be collapsed into our own present demands for publishing narratives which research the shifting patterns of colonisation, trade agreement monopolies, increasingly deregulated markets, and the role of national, international and transnational publishers in Australian cultural production. In another sense, it will contribute to the building of what David Carter calls an institutional history of Australian literature: the point 'at which empirical histories become cultural or social or intellectual history, … driven in one direction down to the histories of particular texts, publishers or reading communities, and in the other direction outwards towards a history of *mentalités*, national institutions or transnational networks'.[11]

It is hoped therefore, through investigating the cultural and commercial links between books produced at home and books produced overseas – as evidenced by the experiences of Angus & Robertson – that the following chapters offer an historical primer to the contemporary transformations underway within the Australian book trade. More significantly, I hope this book contributes to a recuperation of Angus & Robertson's place in Australian cultural history as one of the nation's earliest publishers to promote the work of Australian authors in an international context.

Jason Ensor
May 2012

ACKNOWLEDGEMENTS

While it is true that only one person can research and write a monograph, it nevertheless takes an entire community to author a book. I have been very fortunate that my work has benefitted from the generous support of friends and family. For the many valuable discussions, comments and advice regarding my work, I am grateful to Glen McWilliams, Gina McWilliams (who also fed me during my various trips to Sydney and provided keen legal acumen regarding the discovery of import licensing notices), Katherine Bode, Nicholas Birns, Carol Hetherington, Shef Rogers, Tim Coronel, Paul Genoni, Ivor Indyk, Kevin Mark, Drew Whitehead, Kevin Price, Quintin Hughes, Natasha Buzzacott, Joanne Jones, Leigh Dale, Robert Dixon, Glenda Larke Noramly (for an extended discussion via Twitter regarding Australian reading habits in the early twentieth century), Paul Arthur, John Yiannakis (especially for his editorial proof of the final book manuscript), Tim Dolin, Lisa Dempster (for inviting me to host a digital session at the 2010 Emerging Writers Festival), Laurie Steed (for allowing me to wax on about Australian literature and Twitter on the SPUNC forum), Per Henningsgaard, Iva Polak, Will Smithwick (who would host a small wine bar tour of Perth following the completion of every substantial writing milestone) and Ida Smithwick. For the interstate visits that pulled me away from research and vitally reconnected me to the world beyond the screen, I owe special thanks to Chris Neilson, Shaun and Carmel O'Connor, Francis Smithwick (who sadly passed away just weeks before the completion of my research), Robyn and Phillip Simpson, and Andrew Gilbert and Brian J. Funk. When I wore my serious writing face for most of 2010 in our home office, I thank Cathy Johnston and Ian Vandeklashorst, David and Lynda Thomas, and especially Erica and Joe Mahon and Will and Ida Smithwick, for their help looking after Rana and our boys.

During the early Curtin University phase of my research, before my transfer to Murdoch University, the feedback I received from Tim Dolin was invaluable. For enabling access to the restricted second collection of the Angus & Robertson archives filed at the State Library of New South Wales, I am grateful to Arthur Easton, Jennifer Broomshead, Rosie Block, HarperCollins and Helen Benacek. Arthur Easton in particular made the process of retrieving and digitising 18,000 documents less cumbersome than it should have been. As a long-serving curator of the Angus & Robertson archives, his passing away is an incalculable loss for Australian researchers. I would also like to thank my editor at Anthem Press, Janka Romero, who has been a patient and guiding hand throughout the publishing process.

Financially, the research for this book which began as a PhD has been supported at various stages by a Curtin University of Technology Postgraduate Scholarship

(2006), an Australian Postgraduate Award (2007–10), an Australian Literary Cultures, Australian Intellectual Cultures and Western Australian Culture and History Top-Up Award (2007–10), an Association for the Study of Australian Literature Postgraduate Travel Scholarship (July 2008) and a Murdoch University PhD Completion Scholarship (2010). Funding for my two research trips to the Mitchell Library in Sydney to access archival documents was provided through Richard Nile's CI-1 ARC Discovery grant, 'Colonial Publishing and Literary Democracy in Australia: An Analysis of the Influence on Australian Literature of British and Australian Publishing'. Additionally, support for my research was supplemented with casual work from Richard Nile at the Australia Research Institute (2007–9), Tim Dolin in regards to the Australian Common Reader project (2007–9), John Yiannakis in regards to three significant publishing projects (2009–10) and Paul Arthur in Canberra (2010). Without this additional employment, my funding would not have stretched the distance with the arrival of our two sons.

Above all, my research could not have been completed without Richard Nile, Will Smithwick, Ida Smithwick and Rana Ensor. Richard I have known for over sixteen years; ever since I first hovered outside his office at the University of Queensland in 1994, curious about the possibilities of Australian studies after having just withdrawn from a Diploma in Education course the week before. Richard continues to be an inspiration for me. Throughout this project, his wisdom, guidance and encouragement has been unwavering; he always placed not only my own welfare, but also my family's welfare uppermost in every arrangement. Being someone's thesis supervisor might be the most thankless and demanding of all relationships, but it is the most important in a project of this size. To Richard, I am simply forever thankful. Similarly, I owe a great debt to Rana's family, Will and Ida Smithwick, who have been the strongest supporters of this project. These two remarkable and determined people have provided stability, especially when the going has gotten tough, and have smoothed out bumps in the road that at times seemed overwhelming. Together they helped us make Perth a home and adjust to the conflicting demands of family, work, research and writing.

Last, but certainly not least, this study is dedicated to the Ensor clan. Over the five years that I worked on this study, we quickly grew from a newly married couple to a family of four. The past few years might have been described as either raising children in an office or writing a book in a day care centre, but they were all the more fun (if not complicated) for it. I owe an indescribable amount of thanks to Rana who has not only served as a sounding board for every single page of this book, but has also been the glue between my family and research commitments. A faithful ally in the adventures that have characterised our time in Perth, Rana is my anchor in the world.

Chapter 1

THE COMPANY THAT LOVED AUSTRALIAN BOOKS

An Australian publishing company whose headquarters were based in Sydney, New South Wales, Angus & Robertson was founded by two Scots, David Mackenzie Angus and George Robertson, in January 1886 after Robertson bought a 50 per cent share in Angus' own 110 Market Street bookshop for £15.[1] The partnership was initially concerned only with the bookselling business that Angus started eighteen months earlier in June 1884. The bookshop was stocked with 'New and Second-hand Books ... purchased in the home markets on very favourable terms'[2] by a friend of Angus based in the United Kingdom, a Mr Young J. Pentland. Angus & Robertson's first entry into Australian publishing began in 1888 with a thin book of verse by H. Peden Steel titled *A Crown of Wattle* (71 pages). This was followed in the same year by *Sun and Cloud on River and Sea* (72 pages) by Ishmael Dare (a pen name for Arthur W. Jose who frequently wrote and edited for Angus & Robertson) and *Facsimile of a Proposal for a Settlement on the Coast of New South Wales* (3 pages) by Sir George Young (a work originally authored in 1785).

Angus & Robertson's modest experiments in local publishing continued into the 1890s. An expansion of its core bookselling business had required a move in 1890 to larger premises at 89 Castlereagh Street. A new ten-year partnership agreement was drafted and its starting capital was £2,331 7s 1d.[3] The year 1895 saw the beginning of regular trade publishing with the success of A. B. (Banjo) Paterson's now culturally iconic work *The Man from Snowy River and Other Verses*, considered by George Robertson to be Angus & Robertson's first bona fide book.[4] The firm swiftly followed with another two books of verse by Henry Lawson in 1896: *In the Days When the World was Wide and Other Verses* and *While the Billy Boils*. In the same year, Angus & Robertson also arranged with British company Macmillan to publish *The Man from Snowy River and Other Verses* in London in an edition of 1,140 copies.[5] Subsequent impressions were produced in Sydney and 11 impressions of Paterson's classic were published in London to 1917.[6]

The first novel published in Australia by Angus & Robertson was *Teens* by Louise Mack in 1897. The title, meant for the juvenile market, coincided with an English edition produced through Andrew Melrose. The year 1898 saw another 18 titles published into the domestic market by Angus & Robertson, one of which was *The Mutineer* by Louis Becke and Walter Jeffery. Originally an English publication handled by Unwin Bros, the British publisher supplied sheets of its London edition to Angus & Robertson, which then added its imprint.[7] Publishing an overseas title in a colonial edition was not an unfamiliar activity for Angus who had previously issued Sir Walter Scott's *Waverly Novels* and poetical works for the Australian market in 1885.[8] Angus' Colonial Editions, as the series was called, used an Edinburgh publisher to produce his Australian editions.[9] In 1899 Marcus Clarke's novel, *For the Term of His Natural Life*, was reprinted from the London and Melbourne edition originally produced in 1888 through a collaboration between British firm Richard Bentley & Son and Melbourne company George Robertson Ltd (no relation). The sheets were supplied to Angus & Robertson by Macmillan, which took ownership of Richard Bentley & Son in 1896.

Other English editions of the company's publications, which confirm Angus & Robertson's early intentions to supplement Australian sales of its titles with distribution in the British market, included: *While the Billy Boils* (Henry Lawson, London: Simpkin, Marshall, 1897), *An Emigrant's Home Letters* (Henry Parkes, London: Simpkin, Marshall, 1897), *The Coming Commonwealth* (R. R. Garran, London: Simpkin, Marshall, 1897), *At Dawn and Dusk* (V. J. Daley, London: James Bowden, 1898), and *Growth of the Empire* (A. W. Jose, London: John Murray, 1901).[10] The circumstances surrounding each title's British publication – which included Angus & Robertson paying British distributor Simpkin, Marshall a commission to carry Australian titles under its imprint – has been examined in detail by Jennifer Alison.[11] As he looked back from 1946, George Ferguson, grandson of Angus & Robertson co-founder George Robertson, observed of the late nineteenth century that 'from this time publishing on a large scale became an integral and important part of the firm's business'.[12] No doubt capitalising on the personal links afforded by its co-founders' Scottish heritage, it is clear too that the buying and selling of Australian texts, plus the exchange of reprint rights between Angus & Robertson and counterpart British firms, was a component in the company's commercial practice from the very beginning.

Due to his ill health, Angus sold his share in the partnership to his original bookshop assistant Fred Wymark and another employee Richard Thomson before returning to Scotland where he died in 1901 at the age of 36. The former partnership was succeeded by a public company, which incorporated on 4 February 1907 and re-registered on 21 September 1920. In the decade and a half in-between this transition, which also saw the First World War, Angus & Robertson published May Gibbs' *Gumnuts* (1910), C. J. Dennis' *The Songs of a Sentimental Bloke* (1915) and Norman Lindsay's *The Magic Pudding* (1918). In non-fiction, the 1920s and 1930s witnessed the first edition of the ten-volume *Australian Encyclopaedia* edited by A. W. Jose and Herbert James Carter and a twelve-volume authoritative war history edited by C. E. W. Bean titled *The Official History of Australia in the War of 1914–1918*.

Such landmark publications served to consolidate Angus & Robertson's reputation as a culturally significant publisher of Australian writing, and over time it became 'one of the largest copyright holders in Australian literature'.[13] Caroline Vera Jones has analysed the substantial 'influence which early Angus & Robertson books have had on an Australian history of ideas and even on the writing of Australian history itself'.[14] Jennifer Alison has examined the partnership's first 12 years within the context that 'Angus & Robertson holds a premier position in the history of the Australian book trade'[15] and that 'the story of Australian publishing cannot be told without the story of Angus & Robertson'.[16] Neil James has studied the firm's business from 1930 to 1970 and concluded that Angus & Robertson's output helped Australian 'culture to shape a sense of self.

It cemented the national-historical archetypes of the bush and the Australian landscape, of social democracy and the fair-go, of the grand narratives of Australian history, of distinctive Australian values and identity'.[17] And Richard Nile has interrogated the politics of Australian literary production and argued that Angus & Robertson's 'success as a publisher and bookseller was dependent entirely upon a set of commercial relations that were indifferent to any claims of nationalism'.[18] Within these accounts, an analysis of Angus & Robertson's business is an analysis of the production and distribution of a certain view of Australian culture, and it does not contradict Laura J. Miller's argument that 'commerce is culturally marked: the way it is understood and practiced depends on specific historical and cultural contexts'.[19] That is, economic outcomes influence cultural identity and vice versa.[20]

From a business perspective, Angus & Robertson's publishing activities continued to expand with the addition of Eagle Press' print facilities to the firm's operations in 1923. In its first year, Eagle Press manufactured 300,000 copies of Angus & Robertson's publications, but at the start of the Great Depression it was declared bankrupt. On 20 June 1929, George Robertson's controlling interest in Eagle Press was purchased by Angus & Robertson's subsidiary, Halstead Press Ltd,[21] solidifying the company's diversification into the three main areas of book trade business: bookselling, publishing and printing. On the bookselling side, which relied heavily on imports, Angus & Robertson's bookshop had grown its customer base to over 25,000 readers and its catalogue listed 100,000 titles by 1940.[22]

Angus & Robertson's London agency was established in 1913 after previously negotiating overseas editions through its English agent Pentland. Henry George, who acted on commission for the Sydney office, superintended the agency. The London agency was known for 25 years as the Australian Book Company and in 1937 was purchased outright by Angus & Robertson. George Ferguson visited London in 1938 to supervise the change of ownership and the agency was rebranded as 'Angus & Robertson Ltd., Publishers & Exporters'. After it was placed under the management of Hector MacQuarrie at 48 Bloomsbury Street, it was henceforth simply known as the 'London office'.

Walter Cousins succeeded George Robertson as the director of Angus & Robertson after the co-founder's death on 27 August 1933 at the age of 73. Signalling a new chapter in the company's mission, Cousins announced that Angus & Robertson could '[take] book publishing right to the heart of the industry by marketing Australian books in London'.[23] In 1932, 18 months before his death, Robertson claimed 'there [were] no British sales for Australian books'[24] and that the difficulty in sending books to London, regardless of the work to catalogue and ship them, was the 'tremendous offence to those authors whose books [Angus & Robertson] did not send'.[25] But Cousins held a different interpretation than Robertson's. Cousins cited the successful sale of Angus & Robertson's British and American rights in Frank Dalby Davison's Australian novel *Man-Shy* (1931) as a template for the company to follow in future negotiations with overseas publishers. British publisher Eyre & Spottiswood produced an English edition of Angus & Robertson's *Man-Shy* in 1934 and Chicago-based Cadmus Books published its American edition in 1935. Trade in Angus & Robertson's overseas rights for the title *Conflict* by E. V. Timms soon followed and Cousins concluded that '[he did] not think there will be any difficulty in managing publication in at least three countries for any good Australian book'.[26] He was 'determined to market Australian novels successfully in Australia as well as England and the USA'.[27]

With this confident outlook Angus & Robertson slowly developed its business overseas during the ensuing decades that also saw the Second World War. In 1936, an English edition of Vance Palmer's socially conscious novel, *The Swayne Family*, was published under the imprint of Angus & Robertson's London agency, The Australian Book Company.[28] A series of Australian titles were also marketed in London. The series was an eclectic mix that offered Marcus Clarke's *For the Term of His Natural Life* alongside Ion Idriess' *Cattle King*, J. H. Niau's *Phantom Paradise*, Albert Ellis' *Adventures in the Coral Sea*, K. Langford-Smith's *Sky Pilot in Arnhem Land*, H. Findlayson's *The Red Centre*, Keith McKoewn's *Spider Wonders of Australia* and William Hatfield's *Australia Through the Windscreen*.[29] Sales figures for this period are absent, but Hector MacQuarrie recalled in 1949 that during the 1930s The Australian Book Company sold on average 'one book per day'[30] until it was later converted into the London office. In 1951 a bookstall was set up in Australia's High Commission in London: Australia House. In 1954 new premises were purchased in London at 105 Great Russell Street with the view to further increase the sale of the firm's own publications abroad. In September of that year, original publishing by Angus & Robertson's London office commenced and continued 'with encouraging results'[31] for six years under the project name 'Operation London' until Walter Vincent Burns terminated publishing in the United Kingdom mid-1960.

Throughout the 1950s, Burns accumulated shares in Angus & Robertson and eventually attained a controlling interest. In early 1960 he was made managing director. Burns' first action was to reorganise the firm into separate retailing, publishing and printing companies, each with its own board of directors. Considerable staff dissatisfaction ensued, because Burns' interests appeared to favour increasing Angus & Robertson's real estate rather than expanding its primary business in bookselling and publishing. The result was that many long-serving personnel left Angus & Robertson within a very short period of time. Amidst the mounting pressure organised by George Ferguson, Burns resigned at the end of 1960 and sold his controlling interest to Consolidated Press. In turn, Consolidated Press sold its 30 per cent share in Angus & Robertson to a group of British publishers. Said by George Ferguson to have provided a 'stabilising influence',[32] this group consisted of William Collins, George G. Harrap and William Heinemann and for the remainder of the 1960s Angus & Robertson saw renewed growth. New retail outlets were set up in Sydney, Canberra, Wollongong, Melbourne, Perth and Newcastle. The London office too resumed operation in 1961 with Walter Butcher installed as its manager, and its activities were transferred to a new company incorporated in the United Kingdom during late 1967. On 1 January 1968, the London office started trading as 'Angus & Robertson (UK) Ltd'.

Ownership of the Angus & Robertson Ltd Group underwent further changes following the sale of William Collins' shares in the company to Tjuringa Securities in 1970. By 1971 Angus & Robertson was fully controlled by Ipec Insurance, the parent company of Tjuringa Securities, and its incumbent chairman Gordon Barton divided the Australian publisher's assets. Halstead Press was sold to another printer, John Sands Pty Ltd, and the

London office was closed after a brief attempt to strengthen its international operations. Executive director George Ferguson resigned at the end of 1970 after being 'completely marginalised'[33] and Walter Cousins left in 1972. In 1979 Angus & Robertson's bookshop division was sold to Gordon and Gotch (Australasia) Ltd and later to Whitcombe & Tombs.[34] In 1989 Angus & Robertson's publishing division was merged with Collins (Australia), where the Australian company name continues to function today as a separate (and rare) imprint of HarperCollins. In early 2011 the bookshop division comprised 164 stores and was under the ownership of REDGroup Retail until the parent company was placed into voluntary administration. Following a massive closure of the bookselling chain's outlets, former REDGroup-owned newsagency Supanews Retail acquired Angus & Robertson in late 2011 and reopened in Queensland as Angus & Robertson Book Retailing.

The London Office

Despite these upheavals in ownership over the past three decades, the name Angus & Robertson remains to date 'the most recognised book-retailing brand in Australia'.[35] In the chapters that follow I hope to establish that, through the incredible efforts of everyone involved in the operations of its London agency, for a time Angus & Robertson was also the most recognised Australian bookselling and book publishing brand in the commonwealth. That an international trade in Australian books even exists at all is due in no small part to the work initiated by those people who worked in this far-away, overtaxed office.

Besides its inception as the company's official London headquarters in 1938, little more is known about Angus & Robertson's operations based in Britain. Respected Australian historian Geoffrey Dutton, author of *Snow on the Saltbush: The Australian Literary Experience*, described the importation of Australian books into the United Kingdom by Angus & Robertson as 'a valiant effort, but never a big business, and anyone who visited the Australian bookstall at Australia House will remember what a depressing and badly stocked affair it was'.[36] In Dutton's view, selling Australian books in Britain was 'either impossible or minimal in its effect',[37] and it is unclear whether Dutton ever called on Angus & Robertson's London office while he was living in England during 1963. Dutton's comments suggest that his understanding of the company's overseas business was limited to sales made by the bookstall in Australia House. Dutton shared his conclusions with the general manager of Melbourne-based F. W. Cheshire Publishing, Andrew Fabinyi, whose company had a continuing association with Angus & Robertson. Fabinyi agreed that the bookstall was a 'difficult problem' but countered that 'in a quiet and unobtrusive way, [Angus & Robertson] have started something of a revolution … one which will give us all the best returns'.[38] But Dutton dismissed Fabinyi's defence of Angus & Robertson as 'too optimistic'.[39] While it is anecdotal view of the London office, this assessment by Dutton has retained a presence in subsequent Australian book trade histories.[40] As the following book will show, Angus & Robertson's business in London was a much larger, more successful and complicated business than has been previously recorded, subject to a set of socio-economic forces that affected any operation – be it British or Australian – which was separated from its home office by 17,000 kilometres.

Place of Publication

This book focuses on the publication of Australian books abroad. A core question that can be asked of this approach is: what does it matter who is publishing and where a book is published, reprinted or translated? Indeed, if there is general consensus that this or that novel is an 'Australian novel', what real importance does its 'place of publication' actually carry? One common-sense answer is that books are not only cultural artefacts or products of human consciousness, but also commodities produced by publishers and sold on the market at a profit. Novels are not just literary texts, but also part of a business structure that employs certain agents (authors, printers, booksellers, binders, distributors, etc.) within what Robert Darnton famously called the 'communications circuit',[41] all working together to produce a commodity sold to readers at a profit. When a novel is seen as a 'text' that is beyond market principles, a point of view not unfamiliar in literary discussions, the forces and forms of social and economic production that interrelate with its publication remain unexamined. Awareness of these forces prompts important questions for the researcher about the production of books, about the position of a publisher and about the productive relations of the time. Why are some Australian novels or books proverbially published 'over there' and not 'over here' at a particular historical moment?

A work's 'place of publication' is also connected very strongly to the value attached to books as cultural artefacts. Novels and books impute a 'presence' when thought of in a national context, and Australian literary history is documented by institutions and bibliographies devoted to assessing which novels can and cannot be thought of as 'Australian', a process that has been described as the 'the evolving nature of literary and cultural studies'.[42] Some of this is questionable from a book history point of view, such as when Bryce Courtenay and Ben Elton are considered Australian authors or D. H. Lawrence's novel *Kangaroo* as an Australian novel. Bibliographic lists of Australian novels and Australian authors vary slightly from one authority to another and each has scope policies that overlap at the core but become less focused the further one moves towards the edges. This generates anomalies between lists and there are differences, conflicts even, in the kinds of criteria used to select particular works as Australian.

There is general agreement that H. M. Green's two-volume history, while not innovative in its methods, considerably widened the definitions of what might constitute an Australian literary text. This 'widening' or 'thickening' is essentially one of the core challenges today in thinking about novels in a national context: what exactly qualifies a book to be an 'Australian' novel, projecting a link to what Raymond Williams might call the 'knowable community' of Australia?[43] In what way are specific published works authorised to take on a density, an emotional value or, as Baudrillard describes, a 'presence' known and recognised as being Australian?[44] More broadly, who does the authorising and who does the recognising? These are important questions for how books incorporate, invoke and impute structures of classification. However, questions of cultural 'ownership' can be drawn out and tested. A text's 'place of publication' (as one coordinate of textual production) can be 'framed as part of a cultural argument that defines the original situation of a published object as belonging to' a particular phase of socio-cultural relations.[45] Ayers' argument raises questions about the organisation of

Australia's literary coordinates and allows the print-cultures historian to extract meaning about publishing conditions and trends. It permits the historian to research questions of dominance with regards to specific aspects of Australian publishing within an Australian book trade that, during most of the twentieth century, was monopolised by British interests and industrial practices.

Wild Flowers in the Heart of London

This book covers the period 1930 to 1970. Because George Ferguson records in an interview that he visited London over twelve times during the course of his career at Angus & Robertson, and because he figures as the primary Sydney correspondent with British publishers and the overseas office (notwithstanding the activities of Hector MacQuarrie, Barry Rowland, Walter Butcher and Alec Bolton on the London side), the period of this book coincides with the period of Ferguson's employment at Angus & Robertson. This serves to provide a clearly defined narrative strongly linked not only with the personality of George Ferguson (who on occasion referred to the London office as 'my baby'[46] and whose resignation from Angus & Robertson at the close of 1970 signalled the end of an era), but also with the chronological reach of the current documentary holdings.

Chapters 2 and 3 describe the Australian book trade in the first half of the twentieth century within the 'framework of old imperial connections'.[47] In regards to the Tariff Board Inquiry of 1930, Chapter 2 examines the 'forces of exclusion and dominance',[48] which influenced the conditions of Australian literary production and which maximised or restricted business opportunities for Australian publishers in domestic and international markets. It suggests that an Australian company's investment in publishing was often underpinned by the income generated from the sales of international books and puts forward that 'in the matter of literature, Australia is, and must long remain, overwhelmingly a debtor or beneficiary to other nations'.[49] The episode that closes Chapter 3, regarding Angus & Robertson's co-operation with the British firm George G. Harrap, opens up the possibility of a history which goes beyond the conventional narrative of an Australian book trade grimly dominated by British publishers acting as a cartel, one in which not all overseas firms 'paid homage to the motive of achieving maximum material gain'[50] at the expense of local Australian publishing and writing. These two chapters locate this examination of Angus & Robertson's London office within the context of transnational cultural production and co-operation.

Chapters 4 to 9 trace the theoretical and practical development of Angus & Robertson's London office following the Second World War. This section focuses on the strategic if sometimes controversial disposition towards the British book trade that Angus & Robertson adopted in order to (for example) pressure English booksellers into accepting Australian titles for sale. Collectively, these chapters explore the tensions connected with running a branch office separated from its parent company by several thousand kilometres. Such tensions were common to British publishers with Australian-based franchises as Angus & Robertson was to discover through running its London office. As a result, Angus & Robertson recognised that to have any possibility of success the London office must become a part of the local circuits of production and the local cultural landscape in the United Kingdom. Chapter 7 examines the moment at which the Australian publisher confronted the problem of 'strong competition from U.K. publishers'[51] in its fullest sense by – to borrow the metaphor of Angus & Robertson's lead project 'Operation London' – 'getting in behind'.[52] A 'delicate sort of balance'[53] emerged between Angus & Robertson's London and Sydney offices, and its operations were increasingly framed by low profitability in Britain.

Popular success and Australian literary merit, it would seem, rarely coincided as the London office endeavoured to publish what the market demanded. With market conditions in London seemingly indifferent to discussions in Angus & Robertson's Sydney office, a price advantage (represented by slashing prices on Australian works) became a key component to successfully retailing Australian books in the United Kingdom. This practice was in addition to publishing 'books of a universal appeal'[54] and using the sale of popular American and British titles in the United Kingdom to catalyse the sales of Angus & Robertson's Australian books. Andrew Fabinyi claimed at the time that 'rights bought elsewhere [were] basic to the function of British publishing'.[55] Sam Ure Smith, acting as president of the Australian Book Publishers Association, similarly observed that British publishers' lists were 'strengthened'[56] by the addition of selected foreign books. This section therefore places Angus & Robertson's overseas business within the context of socio-economic pressures that compelled the Australian company to draw ever more on the British example.

Chapters 10, 11 and 12 concentrate on the firm's internal dramas that emerged challenging the importance to Angus & Robertson in having a London-based publishing department. Chapter 10 examines the breakdown in Angus & Robertson's London office after the appointment of a new director in Sydney, Walter Burns. Avoiding the well-known Sydney boardroom battles (and share-splitting tactics) that have been previously documented by Craig Munro,[57] this chapter assesses the conflicting correspondence and reports regarding the position of the overseas branch amidst ongoing pricing conflicts between books on sale in Sydney and London.

As the 'whole picture of publishing everywhere' was increasingly 'an international one',[58] by 1960 the London office became a site of conflicting visions over how to profitably join cultural and commercial agendas under the project of developing an export market for Australian publications. In Chapter 10, as Angus & Robertson re-organised itself after the costly Sydney production of the *Australian Encyclopaedia*, the London office was exposed to a raw financial assessment whose findings sustain John Feather's claim that 'the publisher who base[s] his business on a cause … always [finds] himself in commercial difficulties'.[59] However, as Chapter 10 argues at length, any assessment of Angus & Robertson in the United Kingdom by this time was quite deficient if it occurred outside the framework of mutual interdependence between Sydney and London. The London office's 'full advantages [to Angus & Robertson in Sydney] by no means appear[ed] in the London balance sheet',[60] but the overwhelmingly negative audit nevertheless set the tone for the temporary expiration of London publishing. Moreover, the criticisms implicit in the audit signalled the changes in bookselling values that challenged the London office increasingly throughout the 1960s.

After the quiet optimism of the 1950s, when the London office was 'establishing itself',[61] the 1960s was a period of self-examination in which the Sydney office re-assessed its procedures and performance regarding overseas publishing and bookselling. Chapter 11 examines the London office's identity crisis against this background as George Ferguson attempted to rebuild Angus & Robertson's business in the United Kingdom. A distinct shift in emphasis away from reprinting the works of English and American publishers occurred alongside a simultaneous move to put forward, for the first time, only Australian books in Britain. The London office became marked both with anxiety over promoting only Australian books and with a nagging awareness of commercial priority, which was articulated by the newly reorganised Angus & Robertson as a fear of lost sales potential in English language markets. The tension then between 'a London style and an Australian persona'[62] peaked around the Frankfurt Book Fair, and Angus & Robertson recognised that for any real growth in the London office a mixture of Australian, American and British titles was unavoidable. Chapter 11 reaffirms the transnational dimensions to Australian publishing and bookselling and stresses the interlocked nature of home titles and imported books (and local and foreign authors) boosting a publisher's list.

Chapter 12 brings into sharp relief the significance of the reciprocal relationship between Angus & Robertson's Sydney and London offices and argues that by 1970 the parent company could not show a positive return without deliberately leveraging London office losses in its favour. This chapter examines the way Angus & Robertson reconfigured the London office to 'gain the maximum tax relief under the [Australian] export incentive scheme'[63] and to exploit the tax benefits of exporting books manufactured in Australia to London for sale. It demonstrates the unanticipated imbalances that can result from applying government policy in a book trade context if such policy is not specifically targeted at – or configured in consultation with – the business needs of the publishing industry. As a consequence of the manner in which the scheme was implemented, like the intense attachment that British publishers' held to their overseas markets (discussed throughout this book), Chapter 12 advances the view that at the end of the 1960s Angus & Robertson had become wholly dependent on exports for the company to demonstrate profitability in its home territory. Chapter 12 places the final set of problems confronting the overseas branch within the context of Angus & Robertson becoming more focused on profitability and developing the organisational forms necessary to augment its bottom-line.

The conclusion in Chapter 13 draws together the major themes and arguments of this book and finds that the development of the sale of Australian books internationally through the London office occurred at a much greater cost to Angus & Robertson in Sydney and to the London office's executive staff than has previously been documented. The publication and sale of Angus & Robertson's books in English-language markets outside Australia could not avoid being influenced by the major British book trade practices of the time. However, because British publishers' core policy document (the British Publishers Traditional Market Agreement) organised its scope according to 'territories'[64] or cartographic approximations of nation and culture, a book's place of publication was ironically an unexpected weakness for 'the London cartel'.[65] Angus & Robertson may have been 'just boys from the bush when it [came] to publishing in London',[66] but in undertaking such business through a tiny, overtaxed office in Britain – which experienced immense success and failure in equal parts – the company could secure its place in book history as one of Australia's first transnational cultural producers.

Chapter 2

THE OVERSEAS BOOKS IN AUSTRALIAN PUBLISHING HISTORY

> [British publishers] have followed the precepts of guerrilla warfare: infiltrate the local scene; wrap yourself in righteous causes; do not neglect propaganda; organise tightly; retreat where necessary; [and] always avoid set-piece battles.[1]

The above sentiment expressed by Robert Haupt in 1988 about the presence of British publishers in Australia and, by implication, overseas or imported texts in the local book trade, echoes other sentiments recorded decades earlier and equivalent complaints are heard today. Legally and commercially across the course of the twentieth century, British trading rights pertained to exclusive English-language rights throughout the former empire.[2] Within this framework Australia was the largest export (or 'run-on')[3] market for British books to 1959, valued at its peak to be worth £4,387,810 sterling in export turnover for British publishers;[4] this value was a significant increase over Australia's estimated purchases of British books of £1.5 million sterling in 1948[5] and the second largest market for British books behind the United States after that time.[6] During this period Australian booksellers, among whom the Australian firm Angus & Robertson doubled as publishers, were able to negotiate concessions from the peak organisation, the Publishers Association of Great Britain,[7] prompting Hector MacQuarrie, managing director of Angus & Robertson's London office, to claim in 1949 that

> The [Publishers Association] P.A. in the UK are all powerful and can dictate to [their] booksellers, inflicting sanctions when their orders are ignored or disobeyed. I cannot see the UK P.A. having such success in issuing orders to Australian booksellers. There are so many diversions on the way from them to the booksellers: such as London exporters, etc.[8]

Yet fourteen years later the Book Export Development Committee[9] would accuse British publishers of direct interference in Australian publishing. In a formal complaint on behalf of the Australian book trade, Sam Ure Smith identified the British Publishers Association's key policy instrument, the British Publishers' Traditional Market Agreement, as the 'major obstacle'[10] restricting the activities of Australian publishers.

According to the Book Export Development Committee, the Traditional Market Agreement isolated Australian publishers from the international market both as importers and exporters. As importers, the agreement precluded Australian publishers from obtaining Australasian rights to reprint American books if British Empire or Commonwealth rights had been assigned to British publishers (who rarely negotiated for anything but these full market rights). As exporters, the agreement stalled the disposal of overseas rights for Australian produced titles because local publishers lacked important American contacts (and the opportunity to build them) and because British publishers often refused to purchase world rights to an Australian title if the Australian rights were not also available. The effect was to confine Australian publishers to the narrow field of books that were of local interest only and to encourage Australian authors to seek publication of their work with British publishers rather than with an Australian firm that had limited or no access to more lucrative overseas markets.

With a few exceptions, Australian publishers were being kept out of international business by market preservation mechanisms enforced by British publishers. From the point of view of British publishers, such mechanisms prevented the fragmentation of the English-language market, the protection of the Commonwealth market and, in the face of increasing competition from other English-language publishers, maintained the demand for books of British origin and for the reprints of foreign books whose rights had been acquired by British publishers.[11]

The developers of the Traditional Market Agreement, Walter Harrap, Geoffrey Faber and Wren Howard, created it to assist post-Second World War British publishers rebuild an international market for British books.[12] The Australian publisher Ure Smith, however, claimed that through the agreement British publishers were continuing a 'colonial or imperialist attitude'[13] towards the Australian book trade. Ure Smith lobbied the British Publishers Association to end the agreement and allow Australian firms to their share of trade in foreign copyright. John Brown, then president of the British Publishers Association in the United Kingdom, responded that 'modern world trade economics rather than nineteenth century politics'[14] governed both British publishers' operations and their insistence on maintaining the indivisibility of the English-language market. Dissolution of the agreement would, in Brown's view, split the market wide open for English-language books to the benefit of American publishers and adversely affect the strength of both British and Australian publishing. Privately, the association later admitted that a loss of its export markets would also critically weaken British educational, cultural and scientific influence overseas.[15] Furthermore, Brown cited the example of Angus & Robertson's London office as an Australian business whose competition was both welcomed by British publishers and indicative of the potential for other Australian publishers to have 'their lists carried in all parts of the British traditional market'.[16] Such a claim, where the single requirement for equal status between Australian and British publishers was for each firm to place its signature on the Traditional Market Agreement, supported John Feather's later assessment: 'within the British Empire there was an open market for British publishers'.[17]

Forced to Publish in London

If British publishers viewed Australia as 'a market that should be dominated and … exclusively enjoyed'[18] – an attitude which generated some resentment as reported by authors and publishers in Australian book trade inquiries – the question remains as to how London obtained such a level of importance for Australian writers and for Angus & Robertson. Indeed, why did George Ferguson defend his company's London office in 1970 with the claim that without it Angus & Robertson would 'immediately cease to count at all in Australia as publishers of adult fiction or non-fiction' and that it would be 'sheer folly' for the firm to 'vacate the most important English-speaking market'?[19] If, as Ferguson suggested in a letter to his London manager in 1953, Angus & Robertson was 'forced into publishing in London',[20] what were the conditions that led to this? What were the circumstances of bookselling and publishing in Australia immediately prior to the formal creation of Angus & Robertson's London office in 1938? To understand the issues that frequently challenged Angus & Robertson's own projects to import Australian books into the United Kingdom through its London office (and eventually originate new titles there), it is useful to understand the relationship between home and overseas titles that existed in Australia and how the production, sale and distribution of one kind was connected to the other.

Home and Overseas Books

There is an interdependent relationship between books produced at home and books imported from overseas.[21] The Australian Productivity Commission's 2009 report *Restrictions on the Parallel Importation of Books*[22] is the most recent in a long line of government attempts to understand this relationship and that of an industry that is structured by both cultural and commercial agendas. The 2009 controversy surrounding one of its core recommendations – the repealing of parallel importation restrictions on books – touched many sensitive areas in Australia, from arguments about the replacement of physical books by digital substitutes (eBooks) to multinational sales-rationalising techniques that appeared to threaten a vibrant local literary culture. This is because the production and selling of the written word is seen to cross 'the boundary between the incommensurable sacred and the marketable profane'.[23] That is, books are perceived to operate both as commodities and merchandise and as makers and markers of culture.

Describing published texts as an 'enduring and valued cultural artefact and a commodity for commercial exchange', Kathleen McLean argues it is this 'dual nature' which 'imbues the book and its production … with tensions that arise from the conflicting …, often irreconcilable goals and values of culture and commerce'.[24] In addition to their economic value for companies conducting business in the book trade, the production of certain texts and their consumption within certain markets is seen to confer symbolic value on a particular community of people.[25] Therefore, to speak of restructuring the commercial activities of Australian publishers and booksellers is to touch upon concerns about making changes to how local Australian culture is reproduced and distributed. Understandably, it becomes a highly charged discussion, which is mirrored in the impassioned debates registered by the major book trade inquiries of 2009,[26] 1995,[27] 1987,[28] 1979,[29] 1978,[30] 1973[31] and 1946.[32] The Tariff Board Inquiry conducted in 1930[33] is significant for being held at a time 'when the framework that would situate Australian publishing in relation to the global book trade was in the process of being laid down'.[34]

Avid Readers

The 2009 Productivity Commission reported that new book sales in Australia were worth approximately 2.5 billion dollars per annum[35] and that 84 per cent of Australians enjoyed reading books.[36] This finding continues a well-documented trend. Due to the 'general belief that Australians buy more books per head than other peoples',[37] Australia has historically been a market attractive to overseas publishers. As early as 1940, Vera Wellings (who would later assume a marketing role in Angus & Robertson's London office) wrote in the *Sydney Morning Herald* that '[m]ore books are bought per head of population in Australia and New Zealand than anywhere else in the English-speaking world'.[38] It was a claim repeated the following year with regards to Melbourne and Sydney where 'more books are bought, proportionately to the population, than in any other two cities of the Empire'.[39] A survey in 1953 sustained this view, concluding that Australia's national per capita expenditure on books – 21 shillings – remained the highest in the world.[40] To this were added sample sales figures from the previous two years: 75,000 Australian buyers for Nicholas Monsarrat's post-war novel *The Cruel Sea*; 60,000 for Thor Heyerdahl's *The Kon-Tiki Expedition: By Raft Across the South Seas* and 45,000 for Nevil Shute's *A Town Like Alice*. A breakdown of a 12-month record of borrowings from one Sydney municipal library accompanied the publication of the survey's results to confirm Australian readers' large appetite for the printed word: books in the genre of fiction had a total of 83,449 loans; history, travel and biography 17,646 loans; fine arts 5,273 loans; useful arts 5,759 loans; literature 4,064 loans; science 1,629 loans; and sociology 1,699 loans.[41] A month later the *Argus* in Melbourne reported from the same survey that sales of Ion Idriess titles often exceeded 50,000 copies and that Alan Marshall's autobiographical travel book, *These Are My People*, had achieved over 40,000 sales.[42] Exceeding these totals, the top-selling book produced in Australia was Neville Cayley's *What Bird is That? A Guide to the Birds of Australia*, first published by Angus & Robertson in 1931.[43]

During the second half of the 1950s, the Australian book trade depended on Britain for 80 per cent of its stock,[44] and Britain depended on Australia to absorb an average 15 per cent of its total book exports.[45] It is not surprising therefore that for much of the twentieth century Australia was perceived to be the 'special preserve' of British publishers,[46] a description coined by Walter Harrap who was critical of the attitude of some English firms towards Australia. At various times, prominent Australian authors, including Miles Franklin, Katharine Susannah Prichard, Henry Lawson and Vance Palmer, lamented the effects of this market framework upon Australian culture, criticising the British publishing establishment (aka 'Paternoster Row machine') during those periods when it wasn't printing their manuscripts. Each author expressed their own contradictory attitude towards Sydney and London, dissatisfied with the plight of the Australian book trade even as Australian authors sought and achieved publication in Britain. During his preparations for a journey to London, Henry Lawson remarked to a potential literary patron that 'the position of purely Australian literature is altogether hopeless in Australia – there is no market. The oldest and wealthiest Daily in Australia fills its columns with matter clipped from English and American magazines. Nothing "goes" well here that does not come from or through England'.[47] In 1946 the Australian Journalists Association, displeased at the displacement of local talent by the widespread (then prohibited) practice of publishing syndicated content from overseas, summarised the leading issue by asking

"Why is Australia the only English-speaking country which must go overseas to obtain the overwhelming bulk of its literary and artistic matter?"[48]

In the context of such statements, booksellers and publishers were seen to act as cultural gatekeepers; therefore, the question of which visions and representations were being marketed became important if the images of a community were ultimately produced – and originated from – overseas. For the vast majority of Australian authors, international publication during the first half of the twentieth century meant primarily publication into the British domestic and colonial markets by British publishers.[49] London's 'mythologised literary centre'[50] appeared before Australian writers as the capital of English-language publishing where British publishers often demonstrated the 'warmest of warm welcomes'[51] if a manuscript showed promise, and Australian authors believed their books 'carried more force'[52] if they were produced by a British rather than an Australian publisher. The British Book Publishers' Representatives Association of Australia and New Zealand, speaking for 50 British publishers, certainly did not discourage this view. 'As far as Australian authors are concerned', announced Horace Newman at the 1930 Tariff Board Inquiry,

> we submit that it must be obvious, in order to give the best chance of success to a world-wide sale, and, after all, authors write for the world, that a book must be published in the Empire's literary centre, which is, undoubtedly, London.[53]

George Robertson of Angus & Robertson added that 'London is the natural centre for Empire authors whose work appeals to either the very many or the comparatively few'.[54] It was a view that his grandson, George Ferguson, would repeat throughout his career at Angus & Robertson as a justification for the continued operation of its London office.

This message about the importance of London to Australian writing, which was repeated by other prominent Australian and British publishers, reinforced a situation within which Australian fiction was an imported literature obtained in limited 'colonial' editions. These editions sold at a price between six to ten shillings while Australian bookshops were well stocked with 'meretricious fiction in gay wrappers'[55] available for one or two shillings. The term 'colonial edition' did not necessarily signal an alternative edition as it once might have been, but rather it referred to the contemporary 'practice of selling the ordinary English edition at considerably reduced rates for export purposes'[56] to Australian booksellers. (Graeme Johanson has closely examined the pricing structure of colonial editions and its effect on the Australian market.)[57] With these copies being sold cheaper than home editions of the same novel by way of this price advantage, marking down the price of export editions for sale in a foreign territory was a practice that Angus & Robertson would eventually be forced to repeat through its London office.

Mass-Market Fiction

Given the preferential status accorded by booksellers and readers to cheap fiction, the concern over the quality of imported literature took on a moral dimension in the

1930s and 1940s. Throughout this period, this moral argument frequently overwhelmed the economic argument occurring simultaneously, which claimed the nation's import regulations had a vital bearing on the availability and price of books bought by the Australian public and also had a significant impact on the relative success or failure of an Australian publisher. In testimony before the 1946 Tariff Board Inquiry, the president of the Fellowship of Australian Writers George Farwell did not think that a diet of American books with an 'accent on crime', a 'loose attitude to spending big money', an 'emphasis on physical violence' and an 'ever-present atmosphere of excitement' would stimulate educational and cultural standards in Australia. Instead, he concluded that the 'continual reading of the American viewpoint' would invite contempt for things Australian.[58] This view found support from published Australian authors. Katharine Susannah Prichard widened the criticism to include British publications and saw the 'preference for the sensational and sentimental inanity of much English and American fiction'[59] as wholly antagonistic to the development of a national consciousness. Frank Clune, whose autobiographical, travel and historical titles encountered less competition from overseas publications, favoured a ban on imported cheap fiction and reading material classified as 'pulp'.[60] Jean Devanny feared that the pressure to produce for an American market would ultimately force Australian writers to eschew 'some of their truly national character'.[61] The catalyst for a tariff that could weaken the flow of overseas books into Australia was not therefore entirely economic.

Farwell, Prichard, Clune and Devanny articulated sentiments similar to those expressed a decade earlier by the Cultural Defence Committee that in 1935 published a pamphlet entitled *Mental Rubbish from Overseas: A Public Protest.* The Committee, also founded by the Fellowship of Australian Writers of which Clune was Chairman at the time, saw as its public duty the need to 'protest against the permeation of Australian life by a set of ideas not only foreign but in essence degenerate and socially dangerous'.[62] Similar to other debates regarding imported material, the committee centred its nationalistic and moralising anxiety on the 'travesty of American ideas and culture'.[63] However, changes to Australia's import licensing controls, initiated at the start of the Second World War and expanded in the late 1940s and early 1950s, did not automatically lead to the oft-anticipated local revival of the Australian literary genre and certainly not a renewal in literary fiction. In fact, domestic pulp publishers like the Sydney firms of Cleveland and Horwitz were able to derive a disproportionate benefit from local market conditions and public demand that publishers of other genres failed to obtain (see Stacked Area Graph A in the Figures and Tables). This outcome, however, was reasonably predicted in 1930 by Charles Harold Peters, general manager of Robertson & Mullens: '[T]here are some unworthy books which are held out of Australia by Customs censorship and prohibition. With a reduced competition from imported lines, an attempt would be made to produce them here, with, unfortunately, because of their base nature, a chance for sales'.[64] Like the Cultural Defence Committee, in less sensationalist terms, Peters believed that Australia could 'not build a nation on such base books'.[65] It is clear however that some Australian publishers could build an exceptionally strong trade in pulp or mass-market fiction under post-war conditions that restricted the importation of specific classes of writing from overseas sources.

Obtaining an estimate on the number of mass-market fiction works sold in post-war Australia is difficult. The majority of data is bibliographic and relates to books originated in Australia by Australian authors. While sales figures for each book are not available, a quantitative analysis of AustLit publication data in 2007 does reveal that mass-market fiction produced by Cleveland and Horwitz alone accounted for approximately 42 per cent of all first edition Australian novels – and 51 per cent of all manifestations – published in Australia during 1900–2000. However, as discussed elsewhere,[66] there are important issues over the definition of an Australian author and an Australian novel that affect an analysis of the fiction component of the Australian book market. Thus, if we exclude the output of these two publishers and limit the definition of an Australian novel to only those entities which did not fall under the category of pulp, a picture emerges regarding the measure of British companies in the publication of Australian fiction.

From 1940 to 1956 Australian companies remained the principal publishers of Australian novels (see Stacked Area Graph B). Prior to this period, British publishers were the dominant producers of Australian novels, a situation that also coincided with their enjoyment of a price advantage in the Australian market for imported British books. Although British publishers would eventually acknowledge that 'the economic and political climate of opinion after the Second World War was much less tolerant of price-fixing, collective boycott and … resale price maintenance than it had been in the thirties',[67] the idea for a tariff on imported British and American books, which would potentially bring about profitable structural changes within the Australian publishing and printing industries, originates with the 1930 government inquiry. This inquiry, charged with investigating the 'Proposal of Duty on Books, Magazines and Fashion Plates', exposed issues which continue to characterise debates in the Australian book trade today.

Tariff Board Inquiry, 1930

Australia's first *Customs Tariff Act* was passed in 1902. From colonial times the tariff had been deployed as a political and macroeconomic device for developing independence within a national industry. Despite the conventional wisdom that 'free trade represents the optimal policy regime for small open economies',[68] tariffs are applied to enable the redistribution of economic wealth within the tradeable goods sector from buyers of commodities to owners of commodities. The tariff 'cushions domestic industries from exposure to international competitive pressure'.[69] It is also a 'core tenet of official economic nationalism' and a 'main source of revenue' for the federal government.[70] Historically, tariff protections were applied to major consumer goods like passenger motor vehicles, blankets and beer. With the exception of the 'period of comprehensive import licensing'[71] which characterised 1939–1960, tariffs have by and large 'provided the bulk of the protection for Australian import-competing producers'.[72] The 1930 Inquiry, however, was the first time the tariff was debated in the context of its advantages or disadvantages for the Australian book trade.

Print culture studies historian Jenny Lee has described tariff protection as 'far too blunt [an] instrument to assist knowledge-intensive industries such as book publishing' and Tariff Board hearings as 'an unlikely venue for discussing the development of Australian literature'.[73] But the application of a tariff to the book trade makes some sense in that authors and publishers are conventionally embraced as 'cultural producers',[74] which is to say they are makers of original creative works that are seen to benefit a community's sense of self. The Australian Society of Authors argued during the 2009 Inquiry that writers 'and publishers are as important to [Australia's] national interest as our primary producers'.[75] Though distinct from physical property, their intellectual work, whether it concludes in a book of fiction or non-fiction, is protected by copyright. Through intellectual property rights or copyright, the power to 'control who may use their work gives authors and publishers the ability to trade [profitably on] their intellectual property'[76] and on the finished physical product which embodies this intellectual work. '[I]n the cold light of economic considerations', S. F. Ferguson, director of the Australian Association of British Manufacturers, testified in 1946 that books

> are merchandise … [and] have to be manufactured, bought and sold, in the same way as any other commodity. Their production involves the use of labour and raw materials, and contributes to the industrial activity of their country of origin in precisely the same way as the production of any other goods. Their exportation or importation affects the balance of payments of the country of origin concerned in just the same way as the exportation or importation of any other commodity.[77]

William St Clair suggests that cultural production is 'an integral part of economic production, subject to many of the same economic forces and governing structures as other forms of production' and is linked to the 'exercise of economic and political power'.[78] Although tariffs generally assist manufacturing sectors, in this context a duty on books arriving at the nation's border would redistribute wealth from importers of overseas copyright to owners and producers of Australian copyrights. Specifically, the tariff would hypothetically reorientate the trade towards Australian authors and Australian publishers. It would also bolster the production of fiction and non-fiction whose 'place of publication' was tied to an Australian state, territory or city.

Convened in Adelaide, Brisbane, Sydney and Melbourne, from 20 March to 16 April 1930, the Tariff Board Inquiry heard evidence from university vice-chancellors, professors, library and workers' associations, booksellers, distributors and the National Council of Women. Each responded to the proposal of a tariff on imported fiction and non-fiction publications according to the proclivities of their vested interests in the book trade. The application for a tariff was submitted by the Combined Printing and Allied Trades Tariff Committee,[79] which held that an increase in taxes on the importation of foreign-owned magazines, periodicals, fiction and other printed matter would dramatically weaken their respective price advantage in Australia and therefore restrain foreign-sourced competition in the Australian book trade. The Committee, as a coalition of ten New South Wales printing associations headed by ex-Labor Party member James Catts, pressed for this protective mechanism on behalf of all 'Australian printing craftsmen and the allied trades, artists, blockmakers and the rest'.[80] The debate which followed Catts' petition revealed that any protective mechanism for the book trade which modified the relationship between home and imported books would have, as Roger Osborne remarked in a study of the symbiotic relationship between imported overseas periodicals and Australian magazine culture, 'far-reaching implications'.[81]

The Failed Case Against Imported Literature

In 1928, immediately prior to the Great Depression, the Australian printing industry was worth £17,497,693 in buildings, machinery and plant. It employed 34,008 workers across 1,556 factories and paid £7,136,666 in wages, with unemployment in the printing industry then under two per cent (although it would rise to 16 per cent just three years later).[82] The fifth largest industry in Australia, it generated products valued at £20,810,370 from £8,139,535 worth of raw materials.[83] In response to the prominent display of books manufactured by overseas competitors that overshadowed the local product in newsagents and bookstalls throughout Australia, the printing industry estimated that the application of a protective tariff would increase its local production of books, advertising matter and so forth by £6 million.[84] As titles printed overseas were perceived to 'enjoy a phenomenal sale' in Australia,[85] this tariff was also expected to enhance the nation's anti-dumping legislation. The pressure created by protectionism to substitute imported products with ones printed locally would in turn create employment for over 11,000 new workers and pass benefits on to other branches of the book trade. Furthermore, it would contribute £2.5 million in wages and another £2.5 million in revenue – all 'without, as a general rule, increasing the price [of books] to the Australian consumer'.[86] But, reportedly endorsed by a hundred Australian factories, on the first day of proceedings in Adelaide no witnesses came forward to tender evidence in favour of the Combined Printing and Allied Trades' request.

The push by the printing coalition for a tariff was tied to the different price advantage existing between books produced in Australia and books imported from overseas; the latter's published price was the least expensive. Catts, who was also the single witness in favour of the tariff, described a situation at the Sydney hearings in which local manufacturers of books were required to pay freight, duty and other charges on raw materials (like printing paper, ink, type, etc), whereas the importation of a finished book arrived in Australia duty-free. Printers considered this an economic penalty; it was disadvantageous to the development of local production and talent, which importers of books were not subject to. Particular concerns were expressed about the amalgamated selling arrangements which exploited the price advantage accorded to overseas titles and which strengthened their dominance in the Australian book trade. Printers were critical of Melbourne-based bookseller and distributor Gordon & Gotch (Australasia) Ltd. It was alleged that their efficiency – in distributing on a weekly, fortnightly or monthly basis editions from over 2,500 overseas publications to nearly 5,000 Australian bookselling agencies in capital centres – bordered on monopoly and collusion. Since they held the Commonwealth and New Zealand distribution rights for many British and American publishers, it was claimed that Gordon & Gotch issued such a large volume of imported material onto the Australian market that printers believed the suggestions of the company's advertising circulars were looked upon by Australian booksellers as 'royal edicts'.[87] With a staff of

800, it was estimated that Gordon & Gotch engaged an additional 25,000 people in its business of distribution and, as a consequence of the size of its operations, exerted considerable commercial influence.

Similar to the conditions during the Second World War, a temporary hiatus in imports during the First World War enabled some growth in local production. The printing coalition argued that the renewed 'deluge of overseas competition' at war's end was 'crippling Australian advancement'.[88] Having drawn attention to Gordon & Gotch, which sought the sale of many more thousands of imported titles, Catts described the Australian market as being 'effectively closed against Australian writers'.[89] With the dominant note being that cheap remaindered fiction and back-dated periodicals 'constituted a serious menace to the trade in Australia',[90] the tariff was put forward as a protection mechanism which would encourage rights-trading and import replacement activity. However, the 35 witnesses who came before the Inquiry were generally opposed to protection, and Angus & Robertson – perhaps because it sought to terminate its business with Gordon & Gotch only 18 months earlier on account of Grace Bros. Ltd undercutting Angus & Robertson on the price of its own publications – abstained from commenting on Gordon & Gotch.[91] The Tariff Board therefore concluded that 'to place a duty upon books or periodicals would be seriously detrimental to the best interests of Australia',[92] lest the nation 'suffer very materially from her natural isolation':[93]

> Great variety is essential to meet the varying tastes, in order to maintain output. Firms already largely engaged in publishing in Australia assert that their success as publishers has been assisted rather than retarded by the sales of overseas publications.[94]

The articulation of a need to corral overseas content into import lines that are less threatening to local culture and local industry is a nationalist argument 'characteristic of a small Anglophone country which consumes a great deal more intellectual property than it produces'.[95] Within this argument are assumptions that 'local industries foster local creativity and indigenous talent which may otherwise have no expression';[96] that this expression 'would not necessarily occur without specific measures designed to promote it and ensure that it has access to local audiences';[97] and that the unregulated influx of imported matter challenges the sovereignty of local creativity which is not always satisfied by – nor reflected in – the purchasing preferences displayed by local audiences on the free market. While the main thrust of the Combined Printing and Allied Trades' application was essentially the transfer of market power from importers to primary producers, its supporting statements evinced these nationalist overtones alongside the promotion of local commercial development.

Since it was petitioned only 30 years after Australia's primary nationalist moment of Federation in 1901 – which was also dominated by debates over policy differences on tariffs – what caused the 1930 campaign to fail? Although the Tariff Board noted that opposition 'came chiefly from those entirely disinterested in the production or sale of books',[98] one major contributing factor was the lack of consensus within the printing industry in presenting its case. Henry Arthur Sinclair, speaking for all state associations of the Master Printers and Allied Trades Federation of Australia, appeared after Catts at the Sydney proceedings and strongly refuted the suggestion of any links with the Combined Printing and Allied Trades

Committee, declaring that they 'had no authority to speak'[99] on behalf of any printers in Sydney. Furthermore, he claimed 'no advantage could accrue to the printing industry by levying a duty'.[100] In an argument that would be repeated by the First World War Australian historian C. E. W. Bean during the second Tariff Inquiry in 1946 (whose work was produced by Angus & Robertson with government support), Sinclair pointed out the impossibility of the contemporary Australian population to support local writing: 'That the development of the book and magazine industry, with the present population in Australia, is impracticable, owing to an insufficient market and the consequent high cost of production'.[101] It was a view shared by Daniel Wrixon Thorpe, a significant figure in the Australian book trade who established the *Australian Stationery and Fancy Goods Journal*. Having carefully reviewed the best novels published in 1929 listed in the *London Observer*, Thorpe did 'not believe there [was] one book which would have sold in sufficient quantity to warrant publication of a separate edition in Australia'.[102] Gordon & Gotch used a similar defence to justify its import regime:

> It would be impossible to produce in Australia anything approaching the variety of fiction now available by drawing on the Home [British] market. Obviously also, because … of the large printing order originally placed in England, costs of production are reduced, whereas if the local publisher had to rely upon the Australian field entirely for circulation the production costs must, by reason of the limited demand, be considered advanced.[103]

Stephen Alomes has referred to this form of plea as the 'colonial economic cringe' whereby an apparent shortage in the 'structures of production' to support art and writing in Australia was connected with the dominance of 'structures of prestige, which placed value, and therefore also market value, on imported performers and writers'.[104] It followed that any measure to build up a local book trade at the expense of overseas books would be poorly received. Sinclair's presentation generally professed the superiority of English literature and, by implication of Australia's short history, the inferiority of Australian literature. He was not alone in prosecuting this argument. The South Australian branch of the Australian Booksellers Association objected to the tariff on the grounds that

> The younger a country is the greater is its need for the free introduction from outside of these records of knowledge and experience, and anything that is done to restrict the facilities for obtaining this knowledge would be … nothing short of a crime against the coming generations, who, as users of the English language, are entitled to share in the common heritage of English literature.[105]

In its follow-up, 'Report and Recommendation', the Tariff Board agreed with the Master Printers Association's pro-British argument, concluding in favour of a duty-free open market:

> Australia is a comparatively isolated country, crude in its youthfulness, but greatly blessed in that it shares in the privileges of possessing a mother tongue which gives it access to the world's best literature. To check the flow of literature to Australia would be disastrous.[106]

Conflicts of Interest

The Master Printers Association had not always supported an open market. A letter written two years earlier by Sinclair disclosed that he was originally 'very interested in securing a duty'[107] and extended an invitation for the printing coalition to combine forces with the Master Printers Association on the tariff issue. However, following the advice of his executive, Sinclair withdrew the request,[108] sparking controversy within the coalition. In a private report to members of the Australian Publishers Federation, Catts flagged the 'importing interests such as wholesale paper houses, importers of stationery, calendars, Christmas cards and assemblers of such matter printed overseas' that – in his view – dominated the Master Printers Association and were 'the greatest obstacle to protection for the printing industry'.[109] Sinclair countered publicly that Australian printers with 'mixed interests'[110] made up only five per cent of the association's membership and generally abstained from voting on debates regarding the tariff. Despite the Master Printers Association's original attraction to a tariff, Sinclair's testimony was unfortunate for Catt's cause and the Board duly recorded opposition from 'importing firms' and booksellers 'safeguarding their interests'.[111]

Catts was not without his own undeclared conflict of interest in his proposal for a tariff on paper. Born to a joiner and grocer in Wagga Wagga, New South Wales, Catts had been many things in his life, including a union secretary and, later, a controversial member of the Labor Party. He was known for his strong opinions on protectionism and for being 'a fervent Australian nationalist',[112] having once advocated for 'legislation to ensure only … [an] Australian-born could become prime minister'.[113] Catts' views on publishing and printing seemed to be similarly organised around the nation-state as a monocultural category, and he lacked a transnational, comparative or multilayered reading of the Australian book trade. Catts was also a businessman at the time of the Inquiry. With the help of his second wife, Dorothy Marguerite Catts, the former union secretary had established a profitable printing and publishing agency called Associated Business Services. This company published the *Australian Home Budget* magazine – which became Australia's first large-scale paper-pattern ordering service – as well as several other suburban papers, and it became Australia's first large-scale paper-pattern ordering service. An average edition of *Australian Home Budget* comprised 52 pages of the 'latest knitting and crochet' designs, several short fiction stories, advice on embroidery, modes and fashions, celebrity essays on 'What the Stars are Wearing', commentary on a dramatic performance in a local theatre and 'Directions to make Front Cover Free Patterns'.[114] Placing a duty on imported matter therefore, as Roger Osborne noted, 'would benefit Associated Business Services by protecting the Australian market for paper clothing patterns'[115] and would weaken the competition posed by equivalent titles produced by foreign sources. The Catts perhaps experienced the resistance by the Master Printers to a tariff as opposition to their own private commercial interests.

It was not uncommon however for members of the book trade to identify their 'own interests with those of the national culture'.[116] The opposition by the Masters Printers to an import duty pre-figured the association's response to future Inquiries. When the newly organised Australian paper mills in Tasmania filed an application for a duty on all papers in 1939, Angus & Robertson reassured its main London supplier of Antique

Wove, C. Townsend Hook & Company, that the request was 'being strenuously opposed by the [Australian] paper importers, master printers, and publishers' who, like Angus & Robertson and its London office, were 'keen to block this proposal'.[117] While the inclusion of specific classes of papers in the proposed tariff meant a retraction in Australian business for London suppliers, C. Townsend Hook's representative W. E. Dedrick found the prospect an 'incredible' challenge for Angus & Robertson whose 'quality of product [was] of national value'.[118]

Paper Producers and Paper Importers

Friction between paper producers and paper importers would continue unabated after the 1930 Australian hearings. This was just one aspect of the division and politics within the Australian book trade that the Tariff Board Inquiry exposed on the subject of importation. At the core of the controversy over imports were two opposing interests: the economic progress of a primary industry and the public right to access all literatures through inexpensive channels. Tensions between these two views emanated largely from the different kinds of evidence presented in the shared pursuit of improving market conditions for Australian books. On the one hand, the 'paper producer' view postulated a direct link between the commercial health of a local printing industry and the capital (both economic and cultural) that might accrue to the nation from employing local talent through local industry. Its evidence was based on the number of jobs created and the fiscal value added to the net worth of the industry. This view elevated the role of domestic structures of production through the creation of national literatures and artistic expression, and in 1930 it was supported by the questionable wisdom that 'imports and domestic products are perfect substitutes'.[119] It treated all books like merchandise and homogenised the value of each publication. Its primary source of protest was from those who argued that 'books merited a special place, [and] were different'.[120]

The 'paper importer' side appealed for unrestricted access to the world's written matter in which barriers to the exercise of this right could be challenged by the British 'tax on knowledge' thesis.[121] Books were not only different, argued this defence, as imports they were essential to Australia's development as a nation since knowledge should be 'without geographical boundaries'.[122] It was an argument that directed attention towards a conventional national narrative of Australia gradually overcoming isolation; it was 'understood as isolation from the British Isles [and] not as coming to terms with its geopolitical position' (discussed in Chapters 3 and 11).[123] It was also a model of argument that resonated with authors, educators and historians. During the 2009 Inquiry, author Frank Moorhouse submitted,

> In all countries [books] are recognised both as commodities in [a] commercial sense and are seen as social property – it is this character as social property which marks them off say from refrigerators and TVs and cars … They are given this special standing as social property – as property held in common and secured by copyright – because they are considered to be the building blocks, to a significant degree, of the other arts of our civilised life.[124]

H. M. Green typified this view in 1930 (repeated at the 1946 hearings) and implied writers were readers too:

> Australian writers, even more than Australian readers, need the stimulus of new ideas from the outside world, and also the training in literary skill and judgement which should result from wide reading. Anything which may increase the price of books or make them less easily available must be a very real handicap to Australian literary work.[125]

The New South Wales Bookstall Company – as publisher-booksellers like Angus & Robertson, which helped establish writing as a *bona fide* profession for many Australians (such as Arthur Hoey Davis or 'Steele Rudd', Norman Lindsay and Vance Palmer) – stressed that the success of its publishing department had 'been accomplished by the aid of sales of overseas publications'.[126] Furthermore, the Department of War Organisation of Industry's 1943 review on the Australian book trade during the Second World War reported that Australian culture would 'decline rapidly' if it was not 'fed and stimulated by contact with overseas ideas and minds that can only come to us in books'.[127] It was a conclusion held in common with the Australian Booksellers Association 13 years earlier. As a small population 'three months away from … the centre of culture'[128] and as users of the English language who shared in the 'common heritage of English literature',[129] the Australian Booksellers Association claimed the importation of cheap fiction from British sources into Australia was considered 'leaven … necessary to keep Australian literature healthy'.[130]

This 'leaven' was a stimulus not only for Australian creative work, but also for Australian readers who were often criticised as being 'slow to appreciate the literary merit of their own people's writings', even after Britain had given it 'deserved praise'[131] and were described as having a prejudice against Australian literature.[132] Indeed, in 1950 the *Mercury* reported that Australia literature 'has still a long way to go before prejudice against the local product is finally dissipated'.[133] Four years later, a reviewer of *Cockatoos* by Brent of Bin Bin (Miles Franklin) argued that "the typical early Australian novel is a shapeless, bulging swag, crudely packed to be unloaded somewhere under a wide sky, where time is as unlimited as the horizons'.[134] Publishers hoped for a more literate generation that might develop 'the pleasure of buying and owning books' through Australia's compulsory education system, but the book-buying habit and appreciation of local authors remained undeveloped in Australia; the Australian book trade was dependent not on the general public but instead on booksellers, wholesalers[135] and libraries (who were considered the largest purchasers of books in Australia in 1930).[136] George Ferguson, recalling in 1975 his first employment at Angus & Robertson as a bookseller during the 1930s, agreed with this assessment and maintained that

> Apart from the publications of A & R [Angus & Robertson] itself and of the handful of half a dozen or so other Australian publishers of the day, there were no Australian books to sell. And when you did offer one to a customer you were always prepared for a disdainful refusal. In those days, nothing Australian could be any good.[137]

This outlook by the Australian reader would undergo an important psychological change in the late 1940s as the Second World War infused the Australian community with a sense of national consciousness and an awareness of the special characteristics of their own country. It was a change anticipated by Vera Wellings in the December 1941 edition of *Sydney Morning Herald*[138] and is evident in the statistical analysis of bibliographic data for this period that shows a marked shift away from British publishers and towards Australian publishers in the production of Australian literature. Prior to the war 'the Australian author did not enjoy much honour in his own country',[139] with an average return of £60 for a book that might take 12 months to write. The New South Wales Publishers Association argued that 'the instinctive reaction of [Australian] book purchasers to a novel having their own country as its setting was one of indifference, if not actual distaste'.[140]

H. J. Hewett, managing director of the New South Wales Bookstall Company, claimed 'the majority of Australian readers prefer their setting for a novel to be outside Australia'.[141] Hewett recommended that Australian authors spend some time overseas in order to broaden their ability to write about other places and peoples. On this point, the New South Wales section member of the British Book Publishers' Representatives Association of Australian and New Zealand testified in 1930 that several popular Australian novelists 'would have been largely overlooked in Australia' if they had not been published in London. The authors and sample novels on the list advanced before the Tariff Board were as follows: H. Handel Richardson (*Ultima Thule*, *The Way Home*, *Richard Mahony*, *Maurice Guest*), Fred Howard (*The Emigrant*, *Return Ticket*), M. Barnard Eldershaw (*A House is Built*), Martin Mills (*The Montforts*), Katharine Susannah Prichard (for example, *Working Bullocks*), Dale Collins (for example, *Ordeal*, *The Sentimentalists*) and Marie Bjelke Petersen (for example, *Jewelled Nights*).[142]

While the member's comments could be considered speculative, it was an account variously supported by other Inquiry witnesses who held that Australian authors would 'seek publication abroad first, knowing the Australian trade would follow'[143] and that, due to Australia's small population, a more likely path to publication in the 1930s was implied by the sheer size of the Empire market over which British publishers presided:

> A book finds its way into circulation only when the combined readers of Britain and the Empire provide sufficient buyers to render possible a minimum edition to cover expenses and a little over, the publisher depending on the gamble of a bestseller appearing unexpectedly from amongst them.[144]

The witnesses who spoke in favour of this assessment included a cross-section of major stakeholders from the Australian book trade of the 1930s: George Herbert Barker (Queensland Booksellers Association), John Morley Bath (Australian Booksellers Association, South Australia), William Augustus Crew, (New South Wales Bookstall Company, Sydney), William Ernest Dunnett (Amalgamated Press Limited, Melbourne), Alexander James Donaldson Gray (Gordon & Gotch Australasia Limited, Melbourne), Henry Mackenzie Green (Australian English Association), William Harrison Moore (Robertson and Mullens Limited, Melbourne), Charles Harold Peters (Australian Booksellers Association, Victoria), George Robertson (Angus & Robertson, Sydney),

Ernest Scott (University of Melbourne) and Robert Victor Smith (Workers' Educational Association, Brisbane).

The terms of reference for the 1930 Tariff Board Inquiry did not mention cultural matters explicitly but rather 'goods admitted under Tariff Item 335 … [and] 339'.[145] The effects on Australian culture of a duty on overseas books were nevertheless a major component of the arguments put forward by the 'paper importer' side. Its primary source of protest was from those whose commentary focused on the evidentiary basis of their views. Indeed, the 2009 Inquiry into Australia's parallel importation laws described the 'cultural externalities' or cultural benefits which accrue to the consumption of books 'difficult to measure' and 'likely to operate in much more subtle, intangible and diffuse ways'.[146] They were 'not readily quantifiable'.[147] In this context, the Australian Booksellers Association pre-empted challenges during the 1930 Inquiry to its pro-import position by stating that 'bookselling is a particularly peculiar trade, and ordinary trade usage and conditions which pertain to other commercial enterprises cannot be applied in the conduct of a bookselling business'.[148] It was a successful argument, prompting the Board to conclude:

> The factor most definitely limiting the successful publishing of books in Australia is not the added cost of local production but the severely limited market available … It follows, therefore, that the number of extra books likely to be printed in Australia would be insignificant if the duty were imposed.[149]

The above review of the 1930 Tariff Board Inquiry reveals a highly contested but enduring relationship between home and overseas books in the Australian market for booksellers, printers, writers and publishers. This relationship was well ingrained at the time Angus & Robertson officially created its London office and can be summarised as follows. Australian booksellers required access to imported texts to populate their shelves with a greater variety of texts in order to meet the public's considerable and diverse appetite for fiction. Irrespective of arguments that sought its removal from circulation, mass-market fiction was an important component of book sales and underpinned the early growth of Australian literature. Popular titles enabled 'a bookseller to carry in stock worthy but slow-selling titles of small circulation but real importance'[150] – a commercial reality which was carried over into Angus & Robertson's 'Operation London' project in the 1950s when Australian books were the slow-selling but important titles. For Australian authors, the overseas works provided a template that writers could use to model their ideas or to differentiate their work from. For the vast majority of writers in the first half of the twentieth century, London was the centre of publishing, carrying cultural capital and the possibilities of international sales throughout the British Empire for any author whose manuscript was accepted by an English publisher. As late as 1970, George Ferguson continued to argue that Angus & Robertson would 'inevitably'[151] lose Australian authors if it closed its London office.

Australian publishers, on the other hand, lacked crucial international networks and forums for rights-trading in the 1930s from battling an informal arrangement that was later organised into the British Publishers' Traditional Market Agreement. Nevertheless, they saw the need for export markets if they were to sell home productions in profitable numbers. With a population nearing seven million in 1930, Australia could not easily support 'nor justify a publishing industry'.[152] Because of a limited infrastructure and a small market, costs of production were high in Australia, and the price advantage accorded to imported texts (or British and American export editions) mitigated against the sale of Australian-manufactured books, which seemed unreasonably expensive in comparison. The development of an export market for Australian books would lower production and unit costs in proportion to increases in print runs. Furthermore, there was a cultural dimension to export markets which British publishers were conscious of as 'prestige and influence'.[153] When the issue of a tariff on books was raised again in 1945 and 1946, Walter Harrap, a vocal supporter of Australian publishing throughout his career (discussed in the next chapter), concluded, 'What Australia needs more than the sale of Australian books in Australia is the sale of Australian books in other parts of the world. What is the good of a country having something to say to the world and yet being unable to communicate those ideas to the world?'[154] Harrap believed that 'culture is at once native and international. It cannot be created either by trade union embargoes or high tariffs'.[155] In 1930, it was a view which dominated responses to the Tariff Board Inquiry under the 'tax on knowledge' thesis, but which offered few examples of an Australian publisher successfully bringing Australian books into the world.

In a comment that predates the transnational and comparative movement in contemporary Australian literary and print cultures studies, John Raymond Wilton observed during the 1930 hearings that 'in the matter of literature, Australia is, and must long remain, overwhelmingly a debtor or beneficiary to other nations'.[156] Wilton's use of the plural 'nations' is significant, for it implied an outlook that extended beyond the nation or at least invited a consideration of the international within the national and the ways in which the business of home and overseas books were interconnected. Members of the Australian book trade in the early twentieth century certainly seemed prepared to amply discuss how to restructure book imports to greater local commercial advantage. If, however, 'there was an open market for British publishers'[157] within the British Empire, the question remained whether an Australian publisher and bookseller like Angus & Robertson, in its efforts to export Australian titles abroad, could avoid replicating the market behaviour of British publishers in an international setting.

Chapter 3

TRIANGLES OF PUBLISHING AND OTHER STORIES

> British strategies in establishing overseas branches … Phase 1: A representative of a publisher visits a country and assesses its possibilities. Where development seems possible, he sets up a resident agent working on a commission basis. Sometimes, the agent will be shared by other firms; sometimes a local wholesaler will act as agent.[1]

Whatever might be said about the national and cultural significance of the circulation of printed products, witnesses for the 1930 Tariff Board Inquiry were essentially engaged in a debate about the proper economic balance between home and overseas (imported) books. At stake from their perspective as printers, booksellers and publishers was the best strategy for securing interest in locally manufactured products within a book trade dominated by international publishers whose business practices often enriched the sale of overseas books at the expense of Australian-made books. One solution, put forward by James Howard Catts, was the call for a tariff or a duty that would severely limit the importation of books into Australia. But, as other witnesses of the inquiry revealed, to restrict overseas books by way of an economic penalty at the border posed some challenges for the Australian book trade that could not be easily resolved. Yet, it is this economic relationship between home and overseas books that has contributed (not unreasonably) to the view that Australian writers for much of the twentieth century lacked the financial and technological means to represent Australian culture to the world.[2]

In the article 'Heaven Forbid that I Should Think of Treating with an English Publisher' (2007), a title which captures the then popular disdain towards overseas publishers, John Barnes challenges the 'model of Australian creativity and originality unappreciated and resisted by London publishers' and demonstrates the utility of questioning this history by revealing the readiness of some British publishers (like Blackwood, Duckworth and Jonathan Cape) to contribute 'significantly towards the beginnings of an [Australian] national literature'.[3] To establish his point, Barnes refers to the publishing history of Joseph Furphy's *Such is Life* by Jonathan Cape fifteen years after the author's death; Henry Lawson's personal experiences in London, particularly his positive treatment by British publishers during 1900–1902; the publication of Miles Franklin's *My Brilliant Career* by Blackwood; and the unacknowledged work of publisher's reader Edward Garnett, who introduced the Overseas Library through Duckworth.[4] Correspondingly, although British publishers as a group made the path of an Australian publisher more challenging through confirming agreements that froze out competition (especially with regards to rights trading in the American market), pre-Second World War documents reveal an attempt to create a co-operative 'axis' between Angus & Robertson in Sydney and George G. Harrap & Co. in London, with the Australasian Publishing Company in Sydney (which was considered 'a part of the Harrap organisation')[5] as sales representative to both. Their aim, to quote Walter Harrap, was to 'work closely in harmony but yet as distinct entities'.[6] The Australian market might have been perceived to be the 'special preserve' of some British publishers but in the late 1930s Walter Harrap – as director of George G. Harrap, the Australasian Publishing Company, and several British printing, binding and book distribution companies – took a broader view that Angus & Robertson could be 'used in an intelligent way as part of one huge machine whose object it is to increase the sale of books in the English language'.[7]

Conscious of how the Australian and British book trade might react, Walter Harrap, in writing to Stanley Bartlett of the Australasian Publishing Co. about his London-based discussions with Angus & Robertson publisher George Ferguson, remarked that 'a copy of this letter will be given to Mr Ferguson but it will not be seen by anyone and will be destroyed when he has read it'.[8] Copies of these personal discussions survive in the Mitchell Library,[9] and this chapter will trace Angus & Robertson's negotiations within the 'axis'. The purpose of this chapter is to build upon the established history of Australian publishers struggling to develop during the early twentieth century within 'the framework of old imperial connections'.[10] However, in setting the tone for the remainder of this study, it will examine the ways in which Angus & Robertson actively sought out 'new imperial connections' during the pre-Second World War period.

Such activity prepared the way for Angus & Robertson to 'develop the sales of Australian books in the United Kingdom to the fullest extent'[11] and 'to spread Australian books abroad'.[12] Additionally, it cultivated within the company an equivocating, even contradictory attitude towards British publishers.[13] On the one hand, Angus & Robertson was exasperated at Australia continuing after the Federation to be regarded as 'an appendage of Great Britain'[14] and, according to Martyn Lyons, 'as a huge continental extension of a typical British circulating library'.[15] On the other hand, Angus & Robertson was energised by the potential opportunities afforded through negotiating with London publishers in placing Australian books 'behind the lines'[16] and the possibilities of establishing an Australian export market. This is what Richard Nile and David Walker refer to generally as 'the complex art of owning and disowning London, of courting its influence and resenting its power'.[17]

Axis of Publishers

Like many complicated relationships, this particular story of two major publishers begins with a gift and some cordial pats on the back; in this case the 'most acceptable gift' of an Australian-made book was sent in 1938 from George Ferguson to Walter Harrap, who replied with the considered praise that 'many a book on this side is published that is not half so well produced'.[18] Sending books as gifts was an integral part of Angus & Robertson's promotional strategy that also included delivering food parcels to British publishers, printers and binders regularly welcoming Australian delicacies as a 'relief from the monotony of the average [English] everyday diet'.[19] Walter Harrap appreciated the gift and also wanted to build on a two hour talk he had with Ferguson at a London luncheon about 'the problems that are facing booksellers in Australia'.[20]

George Ferguson, who had been in the educational department of Angus & Robertson from 1931 to 1937, was sent to London in April 1938 to oversee the conversion of the Australian Book Company into a new Angus & Robertson branch that would eventually be relocated from Great Russell Street to 48 Bloomsbury Street. For many years the Australian Book Company, owned by Henry George, acted on a commissioned basis as London agent for Angus & Robertson, 'buying books from British publishers under instruction from Sydney'.[21] Henry George was aided by Hector MacQuarrie, author of *How to Live at the Front* and *We and the Baby*, who since 1933 was 'in charge of the more literary side of the Australian Book Company'.[22] He circularised British booksellers and doubled the sale of Australian books every year, particularly Angus & Robertson's *War Letters of General Monash* (1934, John Monash and F. M. Cutlack) which sold hundreds of copies in the United Kingdom. When Henry George expressed his wish to retire at 85, and there were no other offers, Angus & Robertson purchased the Australian Book Company from him and Ferguson took over all operations of the Australian Book Company. Henry George died a week after Ferguson's arrival in the United Kingdom.

The conversion of the Australian Book Company into a new branch of Angus & Robertson would continue Henry George's work in 'the movement of British books to Australia for sale' in the Angus & Robertson bookshop. Due to 'being the single biggest exporter of U.K. books [purchased] in London',[23] Angus & Robertson was considered an important bookseller by British publishers. However, Ferguson also sought to 'develop a London end to the firm's publishing …, an organisation in London which could sell the books' being produced in Australia.[24] The Australian Book Company had already been experimenting with selling the British rights for titles originally published in Australia. With the exception of *Man-Shy* by Frank Dalby Davison, it proved to be no easy matter to persuade British companies to publish Australian books whose primary market had already been exploited.[25] MacQuarrie claimed in 1936, which he would repeat decades later to George Ferguson, that '[i]t would be foolish to suggest that any old Australian book can be sold here. Sellable books must have some special appeal to the English reader'.[26]

George Ferguson believed that the great majority of Australian books would 'never make their way in the world outside Australia unless they [were] handled by Australians who [saw] something in it beyond immediate financial gain'.[27] Under the directorship of Walter G. Cousins (George Robertson's successor), Angus & Robertson strongly favoured any endeavour to secure publication overseas for suitable Australian books or, where overseas publication was not possible or warranted, to 'sell Australian-produced copies in other English-speaking countries'.[28] This London branch would eventually stock all current Angus & Robertson publications to supply their trade and retail clients throughout the United Kingdom.

George Ferguson spent most of 1938 in London learning about the British book trade, visiting a number of plants and printers, and calling upon 'nearly all the British publishers of the day' to make their acquaintance. Ferguson was characterised as a 'man with a kind heart'[29] and over time many of these publishers became Ferguson's close personal friends.[30] Later, Ferguson would describe Stanley Unwin as 'an outstanding publisher' and Jonathan Cape as 'one of the greatest publishers who ever lived'.[31] He also visited J. M. Dent & Sons, Macmillan Publishers, Oxford University Press, Cambridge University Press and William Collins. Walter Harrap of George G. Harrap & Co. eventually became the first person Ferguson telephoned or went to see every time he came to London.[32]

After learning the trade at the House of Isbister, George G. Harrap started a British publishing business in October 1901, which became active in the area of educational books and children's books and later pioneered audio-visual language courses. Harrap travelled to Australia twice and was often 'staggered' by the high price of English books in Australian shops: 'When books are beyond the reach of the majority the effect upon the development of culture must be unfortunate, but a community like the Australian that is segregated from main currents suffers disastrously'.[33] His second son, Walter Harrap, joined the company in 1912 following the completion of an apprenticeship at Ballantyne Press. He saw active duty during the First World War in Flanders and Mesopotamia, but upon his return to Harrap's in 1920 (a Limited Company since 1917) his 'tactful personality' was 'felt in every sphere of the business',[34] having formed the opinion after his war service that 'publishers worked too much in isolation'.[35] Ian Norrie described Walter Harrap as

> a man of many parts, always active in trade affairs, he also, when things got behind in his warehouse, would defy union regulations, take off his jacket and pack parcels himself. Enormously energetic, given to writing long letters to *The Bookseller* and personal correspondents, he never spared himself in promoting co-operation within the trade, and in furthering the family business.[36]

In an attempt to further the foreign and dominions trade, Walter's elder brother George Harrap Jr. established the Australasian Publishing Company in Australia in 1915 after a five-continent journey. The company was the product of Harrap's partnership with Constable & Company and Houghton Mifflin Company; however, over time, 'the bonds which joined the three parties to the venture … [became] loosened'.[37] In 1922, when George junior returned to London seeking greater opportunities, control of the firm was handed over to its then existing Australian manager Stanley L. Bartlett. Through the restructured Australasian Publishing Co., Bartlett continued to represent George G. Harrap & Co. as their Australian agent and overall the business was judged by the Fellowship of Australian Writers to be 'very considerate to authors'.[38]

Bartlett's management of the Australasian Publishing Co., though very different from the management of Angus & Robertson's London office, would have characteristics in common regarding the relationship between agents, branches and off-shore parent companies. George G. Harrap senior noted in his 1935 memoir the 'peculiar difficulties in running a branch separated from the parent tree by thirteen thousand miles of ocean',[39] a point that would find an echo 25 years later in the Sydney and London offices of Angus & Robertson. Richard Hauser, who assessed the vitality of the London branch during a controversial period of reorganisation in 1960, commented to then director Walter

Burns that 'one cannot run a branch 12,000 miles away as if it were in Woolloomooloo'. The problem for publishers who coordinated agents or branch offices located in different countries was how to meet the challenges posed by distance and how to develop the opportunities that new markets offered.

Thus, included with Walter Harrap's thanks for the food parcel that followed his first London meeting with Ferguson was a copy of a highly-confidential letter sent to Stanley Bartlett at the Australasian Publishing Co., which expounded all the details of Harrap's 'triangular proposal' on behalf of George G. Harrap & Co.[40] Bartlett was familiar with the relative dangers or advantages of Australian companies publishing in their own territory, and he was in favour of the co-operative move for three reasons: it closely resembled a similar proposition Bartlett tabled two years earlier; he was anxious other publishing houses might seize this opportunity before their plan was in place; and, in his view of their 'progressive policy' and highly successful (though universally despised) mail order business, Bartlett conceded there was 'no better organisation in Australia with whom … [they] could co-operate with than A & R [Angus & Robertson]'.[41]

Perhaps motivated by a desire to contain the competition posed by an Australian branch of this 'premier book-selling organisation'[42] (as Harrap's considered them) being established next to the British Library, Harrap wanted to reverse the steady decline of their own business with Angus & Robertson in view of the company's newly increased London buying. Walter Harrap would reveal the following year that he was simply frustrated that 'the best bookselling concern in the world' – that is, it would seem in this instance, Angus & Robertson – was 'not putting every ha'porth of its energy into the selling of Harrap books'.[43] In essence, Harrap's proposition would invite Angus & Robertson to publish, under a joint imprint, any of Harrap's general books that they were inclined to produce in Australia on royalty terms that would both satisfy the author and provide Harrap's some profit on their property. In return, Angus & Robertson would undertake not to purchase direct from the copyright owners any books that Harrap sought to publish in Britain. The Australasian Publishing Co., to be appointed as independent selling agents, would receive a commission on all sales in the Australian territory beyond Angus & Robertson's shops.[44] Additionally, Harrap would obtain the right to produce an titles from Angus & Robertson's catalogue that were not published outside Australia, provided Angus & Robertson clearly showed to Harrap each book's legitimate overheads and profit to date.

As an example of what today might be labelled a business-to-business stratagem, on appearances it seemed to balance the advantages to each side fairly evenly and was generally perceived by the parties as a major step to improve relations between bookselling and publishing establishments. One of the benefits to Angus & Robertson was that 'they would only pay royalties on books actually sold'.[45] For Harrap, a primary advantage was that Angus & Robertson 'would make every endeavour, through their retail organisation, to increase the sale of Harrap books generally'.[46] And for the Australasian Publishing Co., partnership with a new agency like Angus & Robertson meant the creation of a new source of income. Ferguson also considered Harrap to be 'in the front rank of British publishers'. Harrap had 'a strong list of fiction and general literature', and he saw them as a competitor for 'new literary stars' if future Harrap titles were 'exploited and promoted throughout

Australasia to a greater extent than those of other English publishers'.[47] Similarly, Harrap reasoned that Angus & Robertson 'could very much widen the market for their [own] books, because, while so many of them … [were] not of sufficient consequence outside Australia to warrant their publication' on a large-scale basis, 'it would be possible to sell quantities ranging from 250 to 1,000 if sheets could be obtained at an economical figure'.[48] In other words, this raised the possibility of 'finding a world market for Australian authors and ideas'[49] through a trade in copyrights. It stood in contrast to previous years where Angus & Robertson had 'the greatest difficulty … obtaining hospitality to the entry of Australian books into … outside markets'[50] and, more generally, a 'limited outlet in Australia'.[51] And the Australasian Publishing Co. was well known and 'respected by Australian booksellers' whose knowledge and experience of the book trade would 'be of great value'.[52]

The plan was not without some early points of contention raised by the Australasian Publishing Co. Bartlett, though clearly supportive of the proposal, advised Walter Harrap of the 'pitfalls' and 'very grave dangers' if such an 'axis' came into operation:[53] 'I think without the shadow of a doubt we [meaning G. Harrap and the Australasian Publishing Co.] would be at once ostracized by most of the other booksellers' in Australia and that 'the success of the books' placed in the hands of Angus & Robertson would be 'at the expense of the rest of your catalogue'.[54] Bartlett explained in quite frank terms that as publisher-booksellers, Angus & Robertson was 'very unpopular' in the Australian book trade due to the 'extraordinary mail order list' it possessed and its efforts to 'gather in business' from around the whole of Australia.[55] Bartlett related a case of booksellers in Queensland whose circumstances forced it to either sell Angus & Robertson's products in order to address the demand for a competitor's catalogue or to stand by and watch the company 'encroach still further on the Brisbane market'.[56]

Disputes between Australian booksellers and Angus & Robertson over the infringement of another's sales territory have a deep history. Because Angus & Robertson doubled as publishers and booksellers, linking literary and cultural considerations with the economies of storing, selling and posting heavy objects, Perth-based Alberts' Bookshop in the 1920s was among the first to register disfavour towards the company's self-described continental thinking.[57] Though not referring to Angus & Robertson by name, in correspondence with Miles Franklin regarding *Old Blastus of Bandicoot* the Lothian Publishing Company in Melbourne questioned whether an Australian publisher that also had a retail department was in fact 'a bona fide publishing firm'.[58] Representing the London publishing houses of Longmans, Green & Co., Edward Arnold, Cobden-Sanderson, W. & R. Chambers and Cecil Palmer in the Australian market, Lothian claimed 'booksellers all over Australia and New Zealand … have a strong prejudice against books published by their retail competitors'.[59]

This was a claim Ferguson would often need to counter. In seeking to negotiate terms for drawing Angus & Robertson and British publisher William Heinemann Ltd 'closer together',[60] Ferguson explained,

> It is safe to say that the booksellers of Australia and New Zealand, with the possible exception of those right next to us in Sydney, look upon A. & R. as an Australian publishing house rather than as a rival bookseller. This is borne out by the fact that

approximately 90% of the sales of our own publications are made to the Trade and only about 10% to our own retail departments.[61]

Alberts and Bartlett would have disputed Angus & Robertson's relationship with booksellers throughout Australia had always been a 'happy one'.[62] Alberts petitioned Angus & Robertson to 'confine … [their] retail activities to NSW'.[63] However, although Perth was 'almost as far from Sydney as Moscow is from London' and would eventually become a distribution 'headache'[64] in the 1950s, Angus & Robertson 'did not expect to escape censure'[65] and continued wholesaling market books throughout the country. Bartlett disclosed that he personally had 'fought for some move that would cut across this increasing menace' from Angus & Robertson and that there seemed little in the scheme for Harrap's other than 'resentment' and 'opposition' from Australian booksellers. In fact, the Australasian Publishing Co. believed all advantages in the proposal were 'distinctly on the side of A & R because there [was] a growing feeling amongst Australian authors that first having their book published locally deprive[d] them of the possibility of overseas representation'.[66] But, in the end, he acknowledged that the Australasian Publishing Co. 'should recognise A & R as neighbours, rather than the opposition'[67] and that he would support Harrap's role. Bartlett was, however, ambivalent about pushing the proposal forward, citing that 'a good deal of water must pass under the bridge before anything … can be evolved'. [68]

With 50 years in the Australian book trade successfully behind it and in the 1930s making up almost 25 per cent of Australia's total book production,[69] Angus & Robertson responded rather self-assuredly with the view that the proposal seemed highly 'workable and profitable' and that the three organisations 'ought to be able to co-operate to their mutual benefit', judging the scheme to be more than just an 'interesting mental exercise'.[70] George Ferguson acknowledged that Bartlett would perhaps 'hear more candid expressions' of the book trade's feeling towards Angus & Robertson, but, not surprisingly, he disputed the suggestion that Australian booksellers stocked his company's books 'against their will'. Ferguson denied the existence of any unpopularity on the grounds that Angus & Robertson created the market for each book at their own expense and gave booksellers at least a 33 per cent discount, which was in addition to paying 'half the cost of freight in Australia and the total cost in New Zealand'.[71] Ferguson surmised that 'a lot of English publishers would be very happy if they could so arrange things that booksellers had to give special prominence to their books'. Angus & Robertson, he argued, was able in fact 'to create a market, within limits, for almost any book'; and should this 'alleged unpopularity' even exist, it could be reasonably discharged by having booksellers purchase direct through the Australasian Publishing Co, as per one of the proposal's recommendations.[72]

Certainly, Walter Harrap believed publishing was 'no playground for fools, nor for ideologies based on wishful thinking',[73] but he was also a 'strenuous advocate of joint co-operative methods'[74] and he rarely shied away from collaboration within the book trade.[75] In seeing this openly expressed 'enthusiasm' by Angus & Robertson after hearing Bartlett's reservations[76] and concluding that local authors might be attracted to the international joint venture, Harrap remained keen to 'work up a close companionship' with the Australian company.[77] All three firms thus emphasised the necessity of continuing the next stage of discussion in person but another ten months passed before any further progress was tabled. By then, in mid-1939, Angus & Robertson director Walter Cousins was 'heartily in favour of some form of co-operation'[78] and even Bartlett had put aside his early hesitations, looking upon the 'axis' proposal as something 'well worth discussing'.[79] But no sooner had Ferguson departed from England in 1939, leaving management of 48 Bloomsbury Street in the hands of Cambridge graduate Hector MacQuarrie (who would later wryly refer to himself as 'a jewel in A & R's London diadem'[80] and who was described by the *Sydney Morning Herald* in 1936 as 'the essence of hospitality'[81]), when the Second World War broke out. The war had long-term effects on the Australian and British book trade. These ranged from the difficulties of paper rationing to the 'wretched business of restricting the importation of Australian books' into the United Kingdom.[82] The war changed publishing practices in both countries and the term 'axis', first employed by Walter Harrap to describe the proposal, took on an unsavoury association and dropped out of use.

Because the Second World War also contributed to significant gaps in the Australian archival record, gaps which in some documentary holdings run from June 1939 to as late as October 1946, it is difficult to assess conclusively whether optimism over the 'axis' scheme would have actually translated into something more substantial and beneficial to all parties or whether it would have remained forever stalled in negotiations. In a discussion about the new London branch of Angus & Robertson, George Ferguson recalled that '[t]he War, of course, interrupted [its progress]. We had no sooner got the thing set up and working reasonably [in 1938] and I came back, and then in a matter of a few months the War was on'.[83] Soon, to the disadvantage of both the London branch and the 'axis'proposal, Ferguson was called up on duty and 'served in various areas, always in artillery' until his demobilisation towards the end of 1945.[84]

The publishing activities of Angus & Robertson during the 1940s were stretched as the war began to impact the Australian book trade, and the firm's net profit fell from £18,663 in 1937 to £13,445 in 1941 before slowly recovering a post-war peak of £30,035 in 1948.[85] Before restrictions on the use of newsprint, commercial paper and cardboard progressively set in from July 1940, the war's primary effect on the printing industry for the first two years was considered to be 'one of stimulus',[86] which encouraged technical development and innovation:

> Local manufacturers began to produce comics by scores of thousands, and to take over the printing of advertisement and manufacture of packaging for firms who had formerly relied on overseas production. The value of plant and machinery in the industry increased by over £750,000 in 1940/41.[87]

The scale of the Australian book trade's response to war-time market demand was perhaps most obvious from the increased printing of local escapist literature and children's books following a government ban estimated to reduce annual imports of American magazines, fiction and comics by £100,000 in 1940 (see Chapter 2).[88] An index of the size of the markets that Australian substitutes subsequently strived to satisfy can be interpreted from the full list of banned publications tabled in the *Sydney Morning Herald*, 12 April 1940: 41 comic strips, fictional strips and pulls; 24 love and romantic stories; 14 motion picture and radio magazines; 3 illustrated publications; all back-dated magazines and periodicals; 25 home and fashion publications; 6 classes of children's books; 59 sundry magazines and periodicals; and 95 westerns and similar fiction.[89] To accommodate the public demand for these works that would quickly 'disappear from booksellers' shelves',[90] by late 1941 Australian printers were, it was reported, producing books 'literally in [the] millions'.[91]

Sydney-based firms alone were publishing 'hundreds of thousands of fourpenny and sixpenny novelettes' or 'nasties' as they were then called.[92] Publishers churned out one title after another to satisfy a public desire for westerns, romances and thrillers, which even by 1944 could 'only be partly met';[93] one company claimed to have sold 200,000 copies of these 40,000 word novellas and that its success provided the finance to produce other better-class books.[94] Another firm reported an order for over 600,000 children's books – or 'juveniles' – with one title reprinted in an edition of 48,000 copies (a significant increase over the same title's edition of 5,000 copies the previous year in 1940).[95] Ernest Gunn, who commenced publishing in Melbourne with his firm Gunn & Taylor after the importation into Australia of children's books from non-sterling countries was prohibited, reported the production of 1.5 million juveniles in 1940 with '90 per cent of the materials used being of Australian manufacture'.[96] And local comics were selling at unprecedented levels too. Five 32-page comics created by four Australian artists achieved a circulation of 750,000 in just four months during 1941.[97]

'Nasties', 'juveniles' and comics were not the only new constituents of the Australian book trade during the Second World War. Australian subsidiaries and branches of British publishers were now also printing and binding books in Australia that were destined for the British market,[98] making English publishing houses by 1947 ironically the 'major exporters of books from this country [Australia] to the United Kingdom'.[99] British publisher Collins, for example, placed an order in 1941 for one million copies of its White Circle Pocket Novels series to be printed and bound in Sydney and Melbourne;[100] this prompted accusations during the 1946 Tariff Board Inquiry claiming that Australian books of national importance were being withheld from publication for up to a year because of production bottlenecks. Graeme Johanson in *Colonial Editions in Australia 1843–1972* noted 'between 1938 and 1945, twenty-seven per cent of all Angus & Robertson's publishing consisted of the printing of books for American or [British] publishers'.[101] With all plants operating at capacity and few new printing machines built during the war, Australian authors and publishers complained of lengthy delays, and three Australian firms waited to publish a dozen or more titles.[102] The Sydney firm Currawong Publishing suggested there would be less outcry if those books swamping binders were not 'so frothy a type'.[103] But British companies like Cassells and Collins, testified by H. L. White at the 1946 Tariff Board Inquiry, 'can publish overseas thrillers and "escape" fiction of dubious value in editions of 10,000 or more'.[104]

Irrespective of genre, authorship and producer, during the Second World War up to 75 per cent of books purchased annually had been manufactured in Australia.[105] However, the factors that spurred new growth in publishing and printing in Australia also tempered its local development post-war. When George Ferguson returned to Angus & Robertson to work full-time on the publishing side of things, pre-war book trade arrangements of supply and distribution were strained. Paper quotas (particularly problems in obtaining much-needed supplies of Mechanical Antique Wove), a sterling exchange crisis, tightened customs import regulations, congested production lines, limited international shipping space, and 'the impossibility of getting fiction and children's books into England'[106] were closely followed by a year-long ban on Australian books in Britain,[107] over-worked machinery and a shortage of skilled labour (the *Sydney Morning Herald* referred to this last as the 'real bottleneck'[108]). These issues, coupled with the inferior quality of materials associated with book production, inadequate supplies from Britain and an obligation to produce specific publications for the Australian government (that is, the Australian Pocket Library series) interfered with Angus & Robertson's ability to meet the post-war cravings of a new reading public. As with the First World War, this new reading public was gained through war-time conditions whereby demand far exceeded supply.[109] Yet even though the war later created complications for book production, Angus & Robertson's range in titles actually increased by 15 per cent during the war with Australian books accounting for 73 per cent of its total catalogue and Australian authors accounting for 70 per cent of all reprints (not including government contracts).[110] Douglas Stewart, former Angus & Robertson editor for a failed series of Australian classics called Sirius Books, explained that

> There was a big impetus to publishing during the war, partly, simply because the American army bought all the books and denuded the [Australian] book shops and more had to be published, and partly because there was this feeling of nationalism abroad and people were interested in the country.[111]

In fact, due to the sale of Australian editions in the United States, at the peak of the Second World War Angus & Robertson was able to arrange for the American publication of the following titles:

Capricornia (Xavier Herbert)
The Great Australian Loneliness (Ernestine Hill)
My Love Must Wait (Ernestine Hill)
Horrie the Wog Dog (Ion Idriess)
The Grey Gladiator (George Johnston)
The Battle of the Seaways (George Johnston)
Dingo: The Story of an Outlaw (Henry Lamond)
Brindle Royalist (Henry Lamond)
The Pea Pickers (Eve Langley)
The Cousin from Fiji (Norman Lindsay)
Now that We're Laughing (Margaret Trist)
Wings Above the Diamantina (Arthur Upfield)
Mystery of Swordfish Reef (Arthur Upfield)
Winds of Evil (Arthur Upfield)
Mr Jelly's Business (Arthur Upfield)
Bushranger of the Skies (Arthur Upfield)
Death of a Swagman (Arthur Upfield)
Green Armour (Osmar White).[112]

Circumstances for the house of George G. Harrap by contrast were less favourable. Books in the United Kingdom were declared an essential commodity after enemy action pulverised the hub of London publishing, Paternoster Row, into a 'scene of destruction so complete'.[113] Stanley Unwin would afterwards estimate that 20 million books had been destroyed from Britain's 'huge reserve of pre-war stock'[114] – one million four hundred thousand books were lost to just one bomb.[115] Although Harrap's building remained mostly intact after an incendiary attack in 1941, its confirmed losses were upwards of two hundred and fifty thousand books.[116] Recovery would be gradual and difficult. During the immediate aftermath of the war, British publishers like Harrap's would face commercial pressure within traditional markets that had become 'open to competition from new sources' while they had been away tending their wounds.[117] As Angus & Robertson's aforementioned rights trading with the United States might suggest, one new source of pressure came to be American publishers who, 'having found in Australia a most fertile soil',[118] were increasingly looked upon by British publishers with suspicion during and after the war:

> A new and serious danger is the infiltration of American editions into traditionally British overseas markets. This was inevitable when British publishers could not supply and some unscrupulous American firms could. Contracts reserving these markets have been no bulwark against American thrustfulness. Canada and South Africa in particular have been flooded with American books. Handicapped as they still are, British publishers are putting up a fight, but the Americans have tasted blood.[119]

Following his visit to the United States in 1943, Walter Harrap set in motion plans for 'a scheme to help struggling British publishers restore a viable market',[120] one whose recovery was presently dogged by a foreign exchange crisis, the loss of staff and government intervention in paper rationing (which would continue until 1949). This scheme eventually became known as the British Publishers' Traditional Market Agreement and its intent was to 'resist the growing tendency of American publishers to invade the Australian book market'[121] and to respond to the threat of competition posed by American publishers operating more broadly within the Empire market.

These unstable trade conditions encouraged '[p]ublishers who had looked abroad for markets for decades before 1939 … to revive their contacts'[122] and British companies 'began to print in Australia books that formerly they would have exported'.[123] With this in mind, there are some clues that indicate the real opportunity of the 'axis' proposal which the outbreak of war suddenly made impossible to fully realise. The first, August 1939, indicated tentative steps (initiated by Harrap) towards using a memoir as a test case: *The Country Lawyer* by Bellamy Partridge, which was published in the United States through McGraw-Hill Book Company and for which Harrap's owned the British Empire rights.[124] Though Angus & Robertson remained undecided about the suitability of the book for its catalogue, Ferguson's last letter to Harrap before the gap in documentation begins indicated that the decision revolved 'to some extent around whether we are going to have peace or war'.[125] He promised to write a more considered response when Angus & Robertson had reviewed *The Country Lawyer* and after he personally had discussed the matter with Bartlett. But there is no record of a follow-up letter. Where the documentary gap finishes in 1946, Walter Harrap signalled to the Australian book trade that

> My own firm plans to test out our Australian publications in Britain and the overseas markets by shipping Australian productions to London and distributing them through our home and export machinery. In this way British publishers with Australian branches can give Australian authors the opportunity they need to be read outside their own country. If … Australian authorship is equal to that of any other country, this reciprocal plan should be of great benefit to us all.[126]

No doubt spurred on by the precarious state of the British book trade, Harrap continued to maintain that Australian publishers and British publishers could 'work in much closer accord than hitherto'[127] and that publishers should aim at 'a reciprocal exchange of books printed in both countries'.[128] Thus, with Ferguson's return to Angus & Robertson's production and editorial departments (he would then take over as publisher following Walter Cousins' death in 1948), correspondence continued seemingly uninterrupted between Ferguson, Harrap and Bartlett for another two decades. Friendships deepened, especially in their mutual regard for the subject of cricket. With fiction 'undoubtedly in the doldrums',[129] of particular significance therefore is the record of collaboration that emerged from 1948 onwards over a series of books about cricket by one Alban George (or 'Johnnie') Moyes whose publication and distribution between all three firms reflected the ideas of the original 'axis' proposal. Ferguson remarked to Walter Harrap that 'if it were not for the fact that you and we are co-operating there would be no book at all',[130] and Harrap delighted at the opportunity of 'getting together in business'[131] with Angus & Robertson. This led Ferguson to consider Moyes, the Australian Broadcasting Commission's leading cricket commentator of the time, to be that rare breed of writer: a 'joint author'.[132] The publication record of books by Johnnie Moyes which bear the imprint 'Angus & Robertson in association with George G. Harrap', alongside publications equally divided between the companies (including the London branch of Angus & Robertson), reinforces George Ferguson's claim. The books by A. G. (Alban George / 'Johnnie') Moyes were as follows:

Bradman (London: George G. Harrap & Co., 1948)
Bradman (Sydney: George G. Harrap & Co., 1948)
Bradman (Sydney: Angus & Robertson, 1948)
A Century of Cricketers (Sydney: Angus & Robertson, 1950)
A Century of Cricketers (London: George G. Harrap & Co., 1950)
The Fight for the Ashes 1950–1951: A Critical Account of the English Tour in Australia (London: George G. Harrap & Co., 1951)
The Fight for the Ashes 1950–1951: A Critical Account of the English Tour in Australia (Sydney: Angus & Robertson, 1951)
With the West Indies in Australia, 1951–52 (Sydney: Angus & Robertson, 1952)
With the West Indies in Australia, 1951–52 (London: George G. Harrap & Co., 1952)
With the West Indies in Australia, 1951–52 (Sydney: George G. Harrap & Co., 1952)

Australian Bowlers: From Spofforth to Lindwall (Sydney: Angus & Robertson, 1953)
Australian Bowlers: From Spofforth to Lindwall (London; Sydney: Angus & Robertson in association with George G. Harrap & Co., 1953)
The South Africans in Australia, 1952–1953 (London: George G. Harrap & Co., 1953)
The South Africans in Australia, 1952–1953 (Sydney: Angus & Robertson, 1953)
Australian Batsmen: From Charles Bannerman to Neil Harvey (London; Sydney: Angus & Robertson in association with George G. Harrap & Co., 1954)
The Fight for the Ashes 1954–1955: A Critical Account of the English Tour in Australia (London: George G. Harrap & Co., 1955)
The Fight for the Ashes 1954–1955: A Critical Account of the English Tour in Australia (Sydney: Angus & Robertson, 1955)
Australian Cricket: A History (Sydney: Angus & Robertson, 1959)
Australian Cricket: A History (London: Angus & Robertson, 1959)
Benaud & Co. The Story of the Tests, 1958–1959 (London: Angus & Robertson, 1959)
With the West Indies in Australia, 1960–61 (Sydney: Angus & Robertson, 1961)
Benaud (London: Angus & Robertson, 1962)
Benaud (Sydney: Angus & Robertson, 1962)
With the M.C.C. in Australia, 1962–63: A Critical Story of the Tour (London: Angus & Robertson, 1963)
With the M.C.C. in Australia, 1962–63: A Critical Story of the Tour (Sydney: Angus & Robertson, 1963)
The Changing Face of Cricket (Sydney: Angus & Robertson, 1963)
The Changing Face of Cricket (London: George G. Harrap & Co., 1964).[133]

William Heinemann

The collaboration behind these titles would seem such a surprising feature within an intensely competitive industry like the Anglo-Australian book trade if it was the only attempt. One title by Moyes was not produced in Britain by agreement between Angus & Robertson and George G. Harrap. Instead, the 1961 edition of *With the West Indies in Australia* was published in London through William Heinemann Ltd after the arrangements between Moyes and Harrap collapsed.[134] A few years prior, Moyes suffered a coronary thrombosis which put in doubt his ability to cover the English cricket tour of Australia, a book which Angus & Robertson held exclusive rights for in the Australasian market against the remainder of Harrap's British Commonwealth rights. Ferguson 'tossed a mental penny' and resolved 'not to make arrangements with any other author but would hope against hope that Johnnie could do the job'.[135] Walter took the opposite view and, although Ferguson considered Harrap's opinion a more sober and 'wise decision',[136] Harrap estimated Moyes to be a bad risk and replaced him with ex-English cricketer Ian Peebles. A book by Peebles was subsequently published (*The Fight for the Ashes 1958–1959: The English Tour in Australia and New Zealand*) in Harrap and Angus & Robertson editions but Moyes recovered. Upset that 'Walter had written him off', he offered a manuscript of the current tour to Ferguson only and sent Harrap instead a series of 'regrettably acrimonious letters'.[137] Insulted, Harrap declined to publish Moyes, but

Angus & Robertson, feeling pressure to put something in place with regards to overseas publication, offered the next manuscript to Heinemann, which accepted it and then sold out of its edition in July 1961.[138]

The trade in Australasian and Commonwealth market rights between Angus & Robertson and William Heinemann can be traced back to the early 1930s. For example, in 1932 Angus & Robertson took copies of *Devils, Drugs and Doctors* by Howard W. Haggard from Heinemann's medical books division for the Australian market at 60 per cent off the published price.[139] Similarly, Australian rights for *Culture of the Abdomen: The Cure of Obesity and Constipation* by F. A. Hornibrook, *Companionate Marriage* by J. A. Goldsmidt and *High Blood Pressure* by Halls Dally were obtained via its London agent in the Australian Book Company. For a time, this trade was predominantly unidirectional but it took a slight deviation when Ferguson initiated negotiations for a formal agreement between the two companies in February 1948. At a London luncheon, similar to the one he had a decade earlier with Walter Harrap, Ferguson put forward a proposal to Dwye Evans and discussed 'what Angus & Robertson can do for Heinemann and what Heinemann might do for Angus & Robertson'.[140]

The contours of the Heinemann proposal resembled the former 'axis' scheme. Angus & Robertson would represent the whole of the Heinemann catalogue throughout Australia and New Zealand with the establishment of new offices in Brisbane, Melbourne and Wellington. In the post-war environment, persuaded that there would be extra books now coming out of Australia which would interest British readers, Ferguson would in return give Heinemann the first offer for publication in the United Kingdom and Europe any Australian book which Angus & Robertson produced. This would deliver to Heinemann 'a very great advantage in securing [Australian] authors' and Heinemann was additionally invited to publish any existing titles from Angus & Robertson's catalogue under a joint imprint.[141] Mutual representation and coordination between Angus & Robertson's London office and the sales department of Heinemann was a condition. This was joined by a provision that 'in the case of books originating in America … [Angus & Robertson] would co-operate fully with Heinemann in trying to obtain British Empire rights', and requested that the markets for 'Australia and New Zealand would be fully taken care of by Angus & Robertson under arrangement'.[142]

However, unlike the original 'axis' discussions, Heinemann declined the venture outright due to the progress of its own current plans for extending business in Australia. Though Heinemann was honoured by Angus & Robertson's overture to act as its agents in Australasia, the British publisher claimed to be a step further in the direction of having a company on Australian soil 'in the foreseeable future'.[143] Evans expressed regret that he personally would have enjoyed working with Angus & Robertson and reaffirmed that 'the relations between our two great firms will continue upon the sound and friendly basis that it has been in the past'.[144] Ferguson agreed that both companies were strong enough to stand on their own two feet.

Heinemann waited two and a half months before reaching a decision regarding Ferguson's proposal, citing that the scheme would be considered up until director Leslie Hall departed for Australia in May. Yet this explanation does not quite harmonise with the record of Heinemann establishing a branch office in Australia. While Ferguson acknowledged the British rejection of his idea with characteristic understanding and pledged that 'when the time comes for you to start your own company here, … any assistance or support that we can give will be most readily forthcoming',[145] Leslie Hall had in fact recruited *Meanjin* editor Clem Christesen in October the previous year to start work as Heinemann's Australian manager the following January (1948); a full month before Ferguson presented his trade agreement.[146] However, controversy surrounded Christesen's appointment with regards to an unfavourable review of a Heinemann title that appeared in *Meanjin*, and he was fired on the very day he started work. When Christesen's lawyer mounted legal action against Heinemann for breach of contract, the 'subject was never mentioned again';[147] Christesen resumed work and eventually tripled Heinemann's Australian business. It is probable therefore that Dwye Evans, in his correspondence with Ferguson, misrepresented Heinemann's timeline for setting up an Australian branch until the dispute involving Christesen was defused, leaving the option open for Heinemann to accept Angus & Robertson's bid.

What conclusions might be drawn from matching these post-war exchanges of letters with the 1930s? Stanley Unwin noted during his introduction to a report by the British Book Trade Organisation in 1939 that 'it is so much easier to try to grab someone else's business than to create a new connection; to lure away another's author rather than to develop a new idea'.[148] With Unwin's London house listed in the second volume of *A History of the Book in Australia* as co-founders of a cartel 'designed to establish [British] publishers as the major power behind the fiction industry',[149] it is reasonable to conclude that Stanley Unwin had some awareness of unethical practices within the British book trade towards Australian publishers. Yet, whenever Unwin was challenged about British publishers' prejudice towards Australian authors, he would dismiss it as 'just nonsense' and point out his own firm's publication of South Australian author William Hay.[150] Through Unwin's publishing house Allen & Unwin, Hay became recognised in the United Kingdom as a distinguished author, but he was not similarly acknowledged in Australia until many years after his death in 1945. Unwin would often cite the Australian public – not British publishers – as the group which was prejudiced against Australian authors.[151] (It is likely, however, Unwin kept to himself that a politely stated condition during early negotiations with Hay was that the sale of any South Australian book rights would prejudice Allen & Unwin's consideration of the author's work).[152]

William Hay is another unusual case of collaboration deserving closer examination – the Australian writer contributed towards the costs incurred by Allen & Unwin for publishing his books (for example, £200 for *The Escapes of Sir William Heans*[153] and £105 for *Strabane of the Mulberry Hills: The Story of a Tasmanian Lake in 1841*).[154] Stanley Unwin would refer to these contributions as 'endowments' and would later explain – not in a defensive manner as Hay's next of kin, Reverend W. B. Hay, expressed 'keen gratitude' over Allen & Unwin's treatment of his father William Hay – that

> I was proud to publish for your father and he made it easy by sharing the expense … I don't think I ever made any money out of your father's work, but on the other hand I doubt whether we ever lost a great deal thanks to his assistance. It was a co-operative undertaking in which both of us took pleasure and pride.[155]

Moyes was never required by Angus & Robertson or George G. Harrap to contribute an endowment towards the publication of his cricket manuscripts, but their eventual production nevertheless represented a co-operative undertaking by two companies on opposite sides of the world.

The history of correspondence between George Ferguson and Walter Harrap suggests that alternative forms of engagement between British and Australian publishers could occur, that alternative paths to establishing an Australian export market were negotiable, and that these need not necessarily be totally informed by the model of an aspiring colonial company appropriating the 'cultural apparatus of the imperial power' (nor vice versa).[156] Nearly fifteen years after Walter Harrap put the challenge to what he characterised as the 'policy of splendid isolation'[157] which conventionally existed between British and Australian publishers, Harrap welcomed George Ferguson with 'congratulations, brother' on the voting-in of Angus & Robertson as full members of the London-based Publishers Association in 1953, which was a significant imperial connection and rare achievement for an Australian publisher (discussed in Chapter 7).[158] Harrap, perhaps reflecting on his company's long association with Angus & Robertson, regarded friendship between British, Australian and even American publishers as being 'worth its weight in gold when you run a business' and that Ferguson's visits to London over the years had done 'nothing but good'.[159] Harrap joked to Ferguson that 'perhaps it might be a good scheme if a number of other Australian leaders … took a leaf out of your book and came over here if only to see what sort of villains we really are'.[160] Just seven years earlier, Harrap related how he had discussed the Australian situation with the Council of the Publishers Association, urging that

> nothing will be gained if we sling brickbats at each other. At our end, all that we really have to gain is the continued friendship of the Australian book trade. If, therefore we show a willingness to co-operate, then I hope no-one in Australia will be looking round the corner for some ulterior motive.[161]

Though such a statement is easily open to a modern cynical interpretation and contrasts starkly with some of the recorded activities of the Publishers Association, it is nevertheless consistent with Harrap's later views that, with Angus & Robertson's admittance to the Publishers Association, London publishers 'should know the country and the people' of Australia. Half the trouble Harrap could detect occurred 'through people misunderstanding the folk they are dealing with'.[162] Harrap didn't share the attitude of those British publishers who refused 'to admit the existence of people on the other side who see the advantages of publishing in their own territory'.[163]

How then does this apparent civic-mindedness and refined sentiment between presumably rival publishers square with the broader history of an Australian industry dominated by large British corporations? Angus & Robertson's pre-war courtship of London publishers and its post-war achievements in co-operation offer contrasts. On the one hand, Laura Miller defines the market as a thing 'governed by the imperative that participants compete with one another for relative advantage'.[164] In this view, certainly 'London publishers and the importance of the Australian market to their profit margins'[165] remains central to any history of the development of an independent Australian book trade. Yet, on the other hand, the three decades of friendly correspondence and negotiation between the firms of George G. Harrap and Angus & Robertson also offer the possibility of a parallel history which goes beyond the mere exchange or protection of copyrights for economic privileges; a history in which not all British publishers 'paid homage to the motive of achieving maximum material gain'[166] at the expense of local Australian publishing and writing.

In the final analysis, although unsuccessful with Heinemann, from early on Angus & Robertson appeared committed to building new connections with British publishers, particularly with business-to-business propositions favouring the placement of Australian texts in foreign markets.

Chapter 4

THE WORLD IS MADE OF PAPER RESTRICTIONS

> Thus we must not join the lament of the speaker who deplored the fact that Australian publishers had failed to give their books an Australian appearance, as though end-papers must always have boomerangs.[1]

The challenges of rebuilding operations between the Sydney and London offices of Angus & Robertson after the Second World War were exacerbated by the tight post-war import and export restrictions between Australian, sterling and dollar areas. Although precisely determining which restrictions altered which conditions of the Australian book trade during the 1940s and 1950s is challenging; the nature of the impact of import licensing emerges most clearly in correspondence between Australian publishers, industry organisations and the Department of Trade and Customs.

During the Second World War, the Division of Import Procurement emphasised how imperative it was that space on ships destined for Australia was 'conserved only for those commodities considered to be of primary importance to the war effort'.[2] Post-war currency shortages accentuated the need to preserve exchange reserves, and applications for licences to import fiction in paper covered editions – more specifically books in the genres of juveniles, light romance, detectives and westerns – were not made available 'under any consideration'.[3] From 1 April 1940, fictional magazines from all non-sterling countries were banned from importation into Australia and restrictions on magazines 'of little or no literary value' were tightened, many of which had already been banned as 'undesirable because of their false accentuation of sex, horror and crime'.[4] Applications to obtain other kinds of books from non-sterling (predominantly American) sources were considered on a case-by-case basis.

The Angus & Robertson archives record attempts by the company to secure authority from A. C. Moore, Minister for Trade and Customs, to import books falling into the literary, technical, medical, theological, and scientific and 'borderline'[5] subject areas. These applications were infrequently approved and the reasons offered for rejection were slight or, as the Fellowship of Australian Writers described, 'swallowed up in impenetrable silence'.[6] Routinely, the Division of Import Procurement advised applicants that 'books of a similar nature'[7] were available from sterling (British) sources and were 'not subject to licence and may be imported freely'.[8] This implied that American books could easily be substituted with British books; this questionable logic is highlighted in one rejected application by Angus & Robertson which requested the importation of 25 copies of *Sixteen Famous American Plays*.[9] Other reasons offered for refusing an import request could be oblique. For example, the Australian Booksellers Association passed its own resolution in connection with the Department of Trade and Customs' Licensing Instruction No. 290 and 1941/86. Angus & Robertson was a member of the association. In response to an application for importing what the Australian government termed 'fiction of doubtful merit published in non-sterling countries',[10] a resolution passed by the Australian Booksellers Association was quoted back to Angus & Robertson's Sydney office by the Division of Import Procurement as the primary reason for denying the firm a license to obtain *The Wisdom of China* from the United States in 1943:

> That this meeting of wholesale booksellers appreciates the action of the Government in allowing books to be freely admitted into the Commonwealth on the understanding that the importation is voluntarily restricted to books of importance such as scientific or technical books, and those reflecting current opinion. In appreciation of this concession, we undertake to give full co-operation and agree not to import fiction under the new regulation.[11]

When he was pressed for reconsideration, the Minister for Trade and Customs cautiously distanced himself from the decision of his department on *The Wisdom of China*, claiming that the last thing he wished to do was to 'get involved in discussions on the merit of [a] book'.[12] Moore softened his department's official response with a handwritten note suggesting that the book was more appropriate for 'post-war printing or importation' when it could be reasonably expected that 'exchange and shipping difficulties' would 'not be so pressing'.[13] But the restrictions faced during the war expanded after the war to include the United Kingdom. As a sterling crisis deepened, George Ferguson complained to Hector MacQuarrie in London that 'Australia has decided to begin [setting its house in order] by a limitation of imports from sterling sources ... The point is that books are now restricted by 40% (by value) of our imports'.[14] The post-war period would be a trying time for developing an export market for Australian books while concurrently, even ironically, creating ideal conditions for trade in Australian-produced pulp literature.

The following chapters document the foundational work laid by Hector MacQuarrie in the London office's 'purely English infancy',[15] his efforts to 'build up a suitable selling organisation to get rid of' Australian books[16] and the challenges he faced in making 'Operation London' financially independent of the home firm. Although MacQuarrie was occasionally comforted to know that a 'wealthy and very powerful Angus & Robertson [in] Sydney' backed his activities in the United Kingdom, he believed that if the London office came to depend on the parent company's money 'as such, we are sunk'.[17] Given the economic malaise that would eventually shut down London publishing operations in 1960 and result in MacQuarrie being replaced by Stanley Amor (see Chapter 10), this was a prescient statement. MacQuarrie continually worked to 'reach a stage when the London branch must rely on itself'[18] amidst difficulties first exposed in the employment of travelling salesman Bernard Robinson, the appointment (and sacking) of Vera Wellings as Sales Manager and in coordinating decisions with George Ferguson on London projects directed from far away in Sydney (discussed later).

Though fraught with challenges, the 1950s was a period of consistent expansion. It was the decade that Angus & Robertson (London) became a member of the UK Publishers Association (first mooted in 1950[19] and conferred in 1953)[20] and willing signatories to the controversial British Publishers' Traditional Market Agreement.[21] The dominant note of Angus & Robertson's practices throughout this period was to ensure British booksellers and publishers were not greatly offended by its various 'calculated risks[22] to extend the publication, sale and distribution of Australian books – and, increasingly, its titles – overseas. After all, the results of these 'calculated risks' could be quite extreme. In the 1951–2 financial year, the office 'lost £96 sterling on [the] A & R publishing effort in London'. However, in 1955 there were 'two great lifts in *The Shiralee* and *Away All Boats*'.[23]

Angus & Robertson's approach opened up the way for positive links with British publishers, and connections with members of the British book trade were further strengthened by the not insignificant UK export business represented by the Angus & Robertson London office. George Ferguson described the export side of business as 'the primary reason for our London office and is still as important as it ever was, if not more so'.[24] The selling of Angus & Robertson books in the United Kingdom (which Ferguson was quite determined to develop to its maximum) and its broadcasting copyright clearing service (as agents for the South African Broadcasting Corporation and the MacQuarrie Network) were seen as secondary activities. But, as we will see over the coming chapters, Angus & Robertson considered and then embraced practices that in former years were thought to be a threat to the local Australian publishing industry. This invites some preliminary conclusions regarding the model of an aspiring colonial company appropriating and redirecting the 'cultural apparatus of the imperial power' towards its own nation-building and profit-making endeavours.[25]

Paper Plans

Publishing a book in Australia during the last year of the Second World War was no simple undertaking. Paper shortages forced the Division of Import Procurement to place publishers on individual quotas. These allocations were calculated on a sliding scale with reference to each publisher's 1941 requirements that steadily reduced to 40 per cent by 1944. By 1945 booksellers could 'only import up to the value of … total purchases of all US books in 1939' (thus, Angus & Robertson's US purchases in 1939 equalled a hundred thousand Australian dollars).[26] This not only increased queues at printers and binders, creating production bottlenecks, but it also constrained publishers to turn away books they might otherwise have produced due to the delays in printing manuscripts already accepted. It was a situation Angus & Robertson director Walter Cousins described to Miles Franklin as 'getting worse'.[27] Angus & Robertson was in a double bind in that the company had agreed to print 15,000 copies of *Britain at War* and 25,000 copies of *The Battle of Egypt*, two titles from a set of seven Ministry of Information books issued by the War Office in London which Angus & Robertson was also to market in Australia. Obliged to withhold the production of its own books, Angus & Robertson had 200 titles waiting to be reprinted because 'every worthwhile Australian book … [was currently] out of print'.[28]

Reprints were also not immune to paper restrictions. The 1944 reprinting of Joseph Furphy's *Such is Life* required a special application for additional paper supported by the Fellowship of Australian Writers.[29] The Fellowship described the book to be of 'exceptional literary value', an 'important contribution to war-time morale, and a stimulus to national pride'.[30] These statements affirmed the role of fiction in the material production of national consciousness, and the release of paper for a reprint was granted. However, the Fellowship remained disturbed with 'sex, crime and western rubbish … being pulped out continuously with Australian paper'[31] – novels were promoted and popular fictions were discouraged.

When George Ferguson returned to work full-time in the publishing department after the war, one of his first projects at Angus & Robertson was to reorganise the printing schedule of its subsidiary printing company, Halstead Press. Sorting titles on a sliding scale of 'urgent' new books and reprints (categories A and B) from those of 'second priority' (categories C and D), the resultant lists illustrated that a print run of 5,000 copies was not an uncommon figure just twelve months after reprinting *Such is Life*. In the immediate post-war period, from the beginning of August to the end of November 1945, Angus & Robertson 'anticipated [the] production of 160,000 bound books'.[32]

Class A and B books included 8,000 copies of *Coast to Coast: Australian Stories 1944* edited by Vance Palmer; 10,000 copies of Osmar E. White's *Green Armour*; and 25,000 copies of C. J. Dennis' *The Songs of a Sentimental Bloke*. A. B. Paterson's *The Man from Snowy River*, H. H. Finlayson's *The Red Centre: Man and Beast in the Heart of Australia* and Henry Lawson's *On the Track, and, Over the Sliprails* made up the Australian Pocket Library Series. Class C and D books included 10,000 copies of Ion L. Idriess' *In Crocodile Land: Wandering in Northern Australia* (later reduced to 5,000 copies)[33] and another 3,000 copies of Tom Collins' *Such is Life*.

In typical business practice, Halstead would charge the parent company the following rates: for 5,000 copies of a book 220 pages long the cost was £130; for 5,000 copies of a book 332 pages long, £173; and for 5,000 copies of a book 440 pages long, £175.[34] In the pre-war period, before the Australian government began exercising control on prices and percentages of gross profit, Halstead supplied Angus & Robertson at cost and the profit on printing or sales was absorbed back into the publishing department. Neither the publishing nor the printing divisions suffered loss, even though Halstead often 'had no funds from which it could renew or extend its plant and machinery'.[35] As the sole shareholder, Angus & Robertson 'always lent the necessary funds' and reinvested each year 'to keep Halstead operating'[36] – a total of £49,371 in loans and £28,041 in capital at the war's mid-point.[37] Since 1935 Halstead had existed 'for the purpose of book production only'.[38] In 1940 the output from Halstead was divided 73 per cent for Angus & Robertson and 27 per cent for other customers. By 1943 this ratio had materially changed to 44 per cent for Angus & Robertson and 56 per cent for other clients, with an average annual net profit of £660.[39] Attempts by Halstead Press to keep this profit down to 15 per cent (a cap set during the war by the Commonwealth Prices Commissioner) resulted in higher rebates to Angus & Robertson, leaving the parent company open to 'a challenge … for showing a higher rate than in the base year 1939'.[40] This eventually led to significant revisions in the way Halstead charged – and worked with – Angus & Robertson.

The work by Halstead Press in producing books was staggering.[41] A report drawn up in early 1948 showed the monthly output of the factory when every machine and employee was engaged full-time. With averages taken from a six-month survey, 5 Linotype machines on two shifts produced 12 titles per month at 700 words per hour (based on a book of 90,000 words). Linotype machines averaged 1,500 impressions per hour or 22 titles at 4,500 copies each per month. Folding averaged 3,500 sixteen-page sections per hour, sewing 1,200 sixteen-page sections per hour and case-making 180 per hour. If all departments were operating in synchronisation, Halstead Press could produce up to 90,000 books per month. Even so, Angus & Robertson's large program necessitated the additional use of outside firms – Press Linotype Company, Harry Viles and Fleet Linotype Service – to set its books.[42]

Paper continued to present complications worldwide, from reducing the size of periodicals to creating a poor environment for book reviews.[43] In the United States, paper was 'almost an unknown quantity',[44] and in the United Kingdom, deficits in printing and writing materials required the British Board of Trade to determine (on a quarterly basis) the tonnage that could be exported to Australia.[45] Hector MacQuarrie was fully aware of the commercial impact of a restricted bookselling and publishing environment. In March 1944 he stressed the difficulty of shipping books from Britain to Australia, leaving the London office with £20,000 worth of technical and educational books awaiting dispatch to Angus & Robertson in Sydney since October 1943.[46]

In response to the lack of supplies in high-grade paper, MacQuarrie connected the London business C. Townsend Hook & Company with the Sydney office of Angus & Robertson. Townsend's papermaking mill had survived the war relatively undamaged and was gradually coming back online, operating at 50 per cent of its pre-war output (that is, half of its usual 900 tons per week) due to 'material restriction and labour shortage'.[47] Although Townsend's product did not yet equal its pre-war quality and the landed cost in Australian currency was slightly higher than the price of local paper, Ferguson considered it 'very good'.[48] Since Australian mills could not meet Angus & Robertson's requirements, a standing order of 100 tons[49] spread over 12 months in eight or nine ton allotments[50] was promptly negotiated. A further contraction in overseas industry conditions lowered the arrangement to six tons of high-grade papers over six months.[51] Later, the Board of Trade in London intervened and allowed only five tons per four months to be exported to 'recognised [Australian] importers',[52] though Townsend was occasionally able to adjust the quota after a private arrangement with the English Paper Controller.[53] It would not be until April 1950 before Angus & Robertson's paper stocks would be in a 'favourable position';[54] even so, this would last only three months.

Net Book Disagreements

Meanwhile, British publishers continued to exert their influence over the post-war Australian book trade. Having secured crucial supply channels of paper with the assistance of Hector MacQuarrie, George Ferguson resumed his advocacy for drawing the operations of the Australian book trade closer to the British template, believing 'the practice of the trade in Great Britain' should be 'very closely followed'.[55] Ferguson worked in concert with Walter Cousins (who was on the Book Trade Council) and A. A. Ritchie (who was president of the NSW Branch of the Australian Booksellers Association) and was 'determined' to avoid trade conditions which would be unacceptable to 'some of the great publishing houses in England (or in Australia, for that matter)'.[56] Amidst negotiations with William Heinemann Ltd for a formal trade agreement with Angus & Robertson, Ferguson updated Stanley Unwin in London 1948:

> The formal organisation of the Trade is proceeding fairly well. At present we are in the early stages of compiling a list of firms and individuals in Australia entitled to trade terms. Based on this list, it is the intention of Australian publishers to institute what amounts to a net book agreement for Australian books which will be operated in harmony with the net book agreement for British books.[57]

Here, Ferguson reported progress about a plan first suggested two years previously by Walter Harrap who believed 'it would be a grand gesture if the directors of Angus & Robertson met together in solemn conclave and agreed to go all out for an Australian Net Book Agreement'.[58] Harrap considered Angus & Robertson's position to be more reputable within the Australian book trade than Frederick Macmillan's publishing house was within the British equivalent, and he speculated that the Australian company could take a leadership role on the issue of an Australian Net Book Agreement much like the position Macmillan originally took in Britain during 1890.[59]

Net Book Agreements – or resale price maintenance agreements – are policies in which 'the supplier of a good' –in this case, books – 'compels those organisations (usually retailers) who resell that good to maintain a minimum, maximum or fixed price'.[60] Such agreements were fundamental to the improvement of the post-war British book trade. It was commonly held that the English language was the true victor of the Second World War, since a 'great many people [were now] interested in the market'.[61] Because 50 per cent of Britain's book production went to export markets, the 'initial sales from overseas'[62] booksellers reinforced the exclusive Commonwealth rights clauses in author contracts which in turn strengthened the position (or 'prestige and influence')[63] of British publishers against other English-language publishers which had emerged in the United States, China, Russia and Europe. British publishers also perceived the role of Net Book Agreements to be dual in nature, carrying both an opportunity as well as a responsibility. Not only were British publishers' largest export markets 'built up on the structure of local net book agreements',[64] but members of the Publishers Association (UK) also regarded these price maintenance schemes as essential for the development of local book trades because 'colonial economies were rarely able to support book publishing as an exclusive enterprise'.[65]

This perception had logic. On the one hand, any public policy regulating the scale of pricing and discounts on products ensured that firms operating within the market were *price-takers*, thereby creating a competitive industry in which firms placed priority on differentiating their brand of product from another firm's similarly-priced product. In the situation of books, this created an incentive to emphasise content over form – or cultural and textual value (that which is copyrighted) over commodity value (that which is manufactured) – where the standardised physical appearance of one book might not differ significantly from another. This incentive hinged on two factors: the impossibility of predicting the next 'bestseller in advance of actual sales' and that 'for any title there would be a number of competing alternative books satisfying the same class of need'.[66] Both were central to encouraging competition between members of the book trade and prompted British publishers to claim 'net prices were fixed by publishers in conditions of free competition'.[67]

Connected to this competitive market is the theory that 'if the industry becomes especially profitable, new firms will enter the market, increase the supply, lower the market price, and reduce the profits'.[68] Whether this was actually true or not in the situation of books was a core research question behind the 2009 Australian Productivity Commission Inquiry. The Inquiry examined the potential impact of parallel imports on bookselling and publishing or, alternatively, whether a repealing of copyright laws which prohibited overseas editions of a title to compete with locally produced editions of the same title would apply downward pressure on book pricing in Australia. The majority of responses to the 2009 Inquiry indirectly implied it would and therefore mobilised a critique of the large-scale rationalised bookselling that the repealing of parallel importation laws was expected to invite. Respondents also presented a vision of book buying which incorporated a political dimension and suggested consumers support Australian writers and Australian publishers by restraining their economic preference for 'cheaper books'.[69] As Laura Miller has argued, 'the idea that booksellers should be partially exempt from the forces of the free market demonstrates the way that books continue to be seen as a different kind of commodity'.[70]

The general understanding when the competitive market is discussed in relation to, say, farmers' markets is that 'it is not a very desirable type of market for a capitalist to be in'.[71] This seems to hold true for bookselling whose operators Miller defined as 'reluctant capitalists'.[72] However, on the other hand, the entrance of new firms or organisations with considerable commercial power leads to another kind of trade: an oligopolistic market where a small group of businesses are not *price-takers* but *price-makers*, which exert substantial control over pricing and output levels within the industry:

> [Oligopolistic markets] tend to be much more profitable, with pricing and output levels closer to a pure monopoly than to a purely competitive market. The key to having a stable oligopolistic market is that there are *barriers to entry* that make it difficult for new firms to enter these markets, even if they are extremely profitable.[73]

In this way, Net Book Agreements affirm the dominance of the book trade by Publishers Associations through fixing minimum prices and discounts (barring trade with firms who refuse to sign a standard conditions of sale) as if they were operating in an oligopolistic market. Additionally, they simultaneously guarantee competition between booksellers (shielding bookselling firms from undercutting) as if they were operating in a competitive market. In short, Net Book Agreements addressed two objectives that were essential to Frederick Macmillan's concept of a viable book trade: 'the stabilisation of prices and the regulation of profit margins to guarantee a reasonable income to both publisher and bookseller'.[74] Thus, in underpinning a structural ambivalence within the industry which simultaneously propped up commercial and cultural incentives, Net Book Agreements were essential to the interests of both British publishers and, in their view, members of local book trades; this adds support to John Feather's thesis that through the Publishers Association, British publishers 'worked together so that they could survive to compete against each other'.[75] The catch, it seemed for the twentieth-century publisher in a foreign book trade, was that you had effectively to become a British publisher.

In 1966 John Attenborough, the deputy chairman of British publisher Hodder & Stoughton, gave evidence before the Restrictive Practices Court in the United Kingdom that the 'development of the book export trade overseas follows a pattern which may be seen in three well-defined phases',[76] each underpinned by 'three bastions of British influence'.[77] Attenborough listed these three bastions as providing British publishers with material advantages over their competitors:

> (a). The full support of school and examination systems developed overseas by British educationalists and advisers and fostered by British publishers' representatives. (b). The policy of British publishers that their contracts with authors should cover exclusive market rights both in the United Kingdom and the overseas market defined as 'the British Commonwealth and [Empire] and territories under British [Trusteeship] as at 1 January 1947'. (c). The development of a soundly based distributive trade, which offers services similar to those provided by the home trade and looks to this country for its supply and its support.[78]

As mentioned in Chapter 3, which is an analogue to the pre-war actions of George Ferguson when he visited London in 1938–9, the first phase to establishing an overseas branch required a publisher's representative to visit another country and assess its potential. Where trade seems possible, the agent is then set up who works on a commission basis. Later in phase two, when business is growing, additional support is required from the parent company to offset issues connected with placing orders over great distances and to ensure the agent is not undercut by the same books being sold by another bookseller. This usually takes the form of special discounts to counter the 'greater risk entailed in buying speculative stock for a distant market'[79] and in trade agreements with overseas booksellers and publishers to coordinate orders through the overseas branch office. In phase three, the agent becomes a part of the circuits of production and a member of the cultural landscape that embodies and characterises the overseas publishing industry. Attenborough explained this final phase in detail during his defence of the British Net Book Agreement in 1962:

> When the distributive trade is well established the representatives and agents of an earlier day tend to become heads of local branches established by London publishers, with local stockholding facilities for servicing the local book trade. In some cases new companies are formed with local directors who engage in local educational and general publishing – the publishing profits returning to London. This final development is naturally dependent on the buying power and the population of the market in question.

But Australia supplies an excellent example of an overseas market which has developed this way. It could never have done so if British publishers had not taken steps to ensure the financial stability of the Australian booksellers, whose leading firms in Sydney and Melbourne cannot be surpassed in London, Paris or New York.[80]

The Post-war Anglo-Australian Book Trade

It is difficult to view Harrap's suggestion regarding an Australian Net Book Agreement as being deliberately manipulative or deceptive, particularly towards a company in which he developed enduring friendships, although it is open to such readings. In view of the above pattern of which British publishers followed through, Harrap's magnification then of the importance of Angus & Robertson to the development of an Australian Net Book Agreement was part rhetoric (employed to steer the company's activities in a specific direction that synchronised with British book trade practice) and part genuine praise. Attenborough testified before a wholly British audience that 'if you walk down Castlereagh Street [in Sydney] and go into the great bookshop of Angus & Robertson you would find a bookshop second to none in the world'.[81] Complimenting Angus & Robertson on its activities as publishers and booksellers was not always tied to its usefulness to British publishers. Additionally, Ferguson's frank admission to MacQuarrie that his 'cynical mind suspects things when *any* English publisher want[ed] to co-operate'[82] guarded against Angus & Robertson being easily misled.

While progress on an Australian Net Book Agreement since 1946 had been uneven, a 1948 conference of publishers and booksellers in Melbourne not only agreed to an Australian Schedule, but they also began the business of building an Australian Trade Register. Ferguson confided in Harrap about the fraught politics surrounding the creation of a list of Australian businesses entitled to trade or discount terms from Australian publishers, but he expected Harrap to already be well-versed in local developments. It was common practice for Stanley Bartlett of the Australasian Publishing Company to forward the minutes from important meetings, including Angus & Robertson's balance sheets.[83] The problem for Ferguson, as Harrap summarised it, was that he needed 'the agreement of British publishers' to the Australian 'list of approved booksellers'; that is, 'a three-party agreement – Australian booksellers, Australian publishers and British publishers'.[84] For example, in April 1952 when the UK Publishers Association refused recognition of a revised Australian Schedule, its secretary Frank Sanders recommended that 'it will be necessary to obtain signatures anew from all our members and it is quite obvious that these signatures will not be obtained unless the schedule makes [some] concessions'.[85]

Hinting that 'a lot of publishers of the Hodder & Stoughton, Collins and Hutchinson variety'[86] were circumventing traditional book trade channels and supplying titles to clients who would not qualify for definition as a bona fide Australian 'bookseller' on the Trade Register, Harrap's advice to Ferguson was to give 'blanket recognition to those people who up to this moment have enjoyed trade terms'.[87] In addition to chain stores and wholesalers, this would include Gordon & Gotch (Australasia) Ltd which 'might cause nothing but trouble' if Ferguson attempted to rule them out.[88] That the activity of Gordon & Gotch in Australia partially fulfilled one of the three material advantages that British publishers looked for in developing an export market – a business with a strong presence in another country's distributive trade that also looked to the United Kingdom for its supply – did not enter the conversation, and Ferguson was counselled to 'have a very generous outlook if anything is to be achieved'.[89] A blanket recognition was thus confirmed with 'general agreement'[90] reached in October 1948 and an Australian Statement of Terms was implemented on 2 May 1949.[91] Future applicants to the Trade Register would face a tighter, more regulated formula for qualifying.[92]

During his lengthy stays in the United Kingdom in 1938 and 1947, Ferguson became quite familiar with the politics of London publishing, and he observed within Australia 'trials and tribulations' similar to those experienced by members of the London book trade.[93] With negotiations on the Australian Trade Register moving forward in the 1940s and the arrangements with C. Townsend Hook & Company compensating for the present disabilities in obtaining high quality book papers locally, Ferguson believed Angus & Robertson would be ready to 'develop the sales of Australian books in the United Kingdom'[94] and be able 'to convince … British booksellers that they should stock our [Angus & Robertson] books'.[95] With Angus & Robertson registered in London as a foreign company and with premises at 48 Bloomsbury Street, Angus & Robertson was prepared to set up the necessary organisation to enable sales. Of concern to Ferguson, however, were the effects of the non-discriminatory clause of the American loan agreement with Britain that in practice made it near impossible to import fiction and children's books into London.

By the end of the war, Britain's economy was geared in war production at 55 per cent of its Gross Domestic Product, and when the United States unexpectedly ceased its Lend-Lease scheme Britain went into economic shock. The Lend-Lease scheme was a wartime agreement that allowed Britain to trade English territory for military materials from the United States and to have capital for obtaining essential consumer commodities when Britain could no longer finance its purchase using export profits. With the sudden conclusion of the Lend-Lease scheme by the United States, an American loan of £930 million in 1945 enabled Britain to retain equipment and claw back some economic stability in the immediate post-war period (it was eventually was paid off in December 2006). One of the loan's challenges for Ferguson was that Australian books were 'treated the same as American books in respect of their importation into the United Kingdom'.[96] That is, Britain could not restrict imports from the United States without the same level of restrictions applying to imports from other sources, including Australia.[97] Confronted again with a licensing system, the position in 1948 was that 'fiction and children's books may be imported into the UK up to 50% by value of the importers' 1939 quota, provided that 50% of the quantity imported is re-exported'.[98]

This provision seemed patently absurd to Ferguson, a 'virtual prohibition'[99] on Australian books, since he could not envisage under what conditions they would be imported into England for re-export. Hector MacQuarrie in the London office defined it as 'extremely annoying and a little dangerous',[100] and the Australian book trade interpreted it (rather erroneously) as a 'protectionist move by British publishers'.[101] Furthermore, the costs of raw materials for book production in 1948 were much higher than they were in 1939, and the post-war demand for 'books descriptive of Australia and the Australian way of life' in the United Kingdom was greater than ever before; an appropriate market response 'could not be measured in terms of the 1939 value' of imports.[102] Although the British Publishers Association claimed that Walter Harrap had 'fought tooth and nail to maintain its position that books should be interchangeable between peoples without the interference of quotas, duties or restrictions',[103] the Australian book trade viewed the United Kingdom 'its likeliest market, not yet exploited, largely shut off for a considerable time'.[104]

George Ferguson's 1948 letter of protest to A. J. Day at the Department of Trade and Customs in Sydney (who doubled as a member of the Inter-Departmental Committee on Publishing) petitioned for a change in quotas and contains some of the earliest recorded statements, candid in nature, on the impetus behind the building up of Angus & Robertson's London office. Ferguson believed that Australian authors could play a vital role in spreading awareness of Australia throughout the post-war world. In a private note to celebrated novelist Miles Franklin, Ferguson identified authors as 'Apostles of Culture',[105] even though this was not about writers as a group but rather the books they produced. (Ferguson believed that 'most authors completely destroy their chances of sales once they allow themselves to be seen or heard in public').[106] Ferguson's explanation, which linked the motion for an overseas branch with Australia's newly emergent post-war national consciousness, the potential impact of book exports on Australia's balance of payments, a desire to represent Australia more visibly in 'the centre of culture'[107] and a growing realisation admitted years later that 'Australia is most favourably regarded everywhere … once people know you are … not an Englishman or an American',[108] cut across the major debates of the time regarding the cultural and commercial situation of books and writers in Australia.

Ferguson argued that an export market would lower the price of Australian books in the domestic market as unit costs diminished rapidly with larger print runs. In doing so, he advanced the proposition put forward initially by Walter Harrap and S. F. Ferguson (director of the Australian Association of British Manufacturers) during the 1946 Tariff Board Inquiry. S. F. Ferguson described the development of Australian book exports as 'finding a world market for Australian authors and Australian ideas'.[109] More eloquently, Harrap professed that '[t]he words "Made in Australia" would … be viewed with affection throughout the British Commonwealth of Nations'; however, he balanced this with a sobering caution that 'they appear only on goods of quality sold at the right price'.[110] On the issue of the 'right price', it seemed George Ferguson was also alert from the very beginning to the low, even nil, profitability of the scheme to export Australian books to London, citing that an overseas branch 'for the first years would probably not pay its way'.[111] He was also acutely aware of the trade asymmetry that the Anglo-American loan created between Australian books in Britain and British books in Australia and later remarked to Harrap that

> One realises of course that even were the importation of Australian books into England completely unrestricted, we would not make our fortunes … But the present state of affairs is particularly aggravating when one knows that there is more interest about Australia in England now than ever before, and also when we here are supposed to buy as many British books as we can and place them on this market in direct competition with Australian books.[112]

In Ferguson's post-war assessment of Australia's literary output, he considered it to be superior in content and subject range compared with pre-war production. Indeed, Australian books by Australian authors were

> a most important factor in the relating of this country to the world outside, and if these books can be made available overseas the result must unquestionably be a better understanding of Australia and, no doubt, these will be a tangible result in the forms of migrants and trade generally … [T]he export market is essential if we are going to develop the publishing in this country of the more serious books for which the local demand is limited.[113]

Sharing the view of 'those in the most responsible positions in the Australian book trade'[114], Ferguson emphatically believed that British publishers were not culpable for the present situation that stalled this goal and excluded whole classes of Australian books from Britain. Instead, he blamed Britain's economic position and related his impressions of 'genuine concern'[115] and 'injustice'[116] expressed by members of the London trade whom he visited in 1947:

> In addition to opposing it on the grounds of its unfairness, several … [leading publishers] mentioned the fact that it was just plain bad business, because it could possibly end in retaliatory action being taken here [in Australia], which would damage the export to this country of British books.[117]

Fourteen years on, Attenborough recorded a similar outlook in which he maintained that British publishers were more responsive to their business relationships with Australian booksellers and publishers than had previously been acknowledged: after all, 'one does not like to have an unhappy customer who is doing £4 million worth of business'.[118] Correspondingly, Angus & Robertson was displeased that its potential volume of business in sales to London, which it estimated to be in the range of £7,000, was limited to a quota of £1,168 per year. This estimate was rather modest. Seven days later another complaint was lodged by Ferguson with regard to the steady reduction of the company's export quota to New Zealand from £9,000 to £7,533, following an unsuccessful appeal to the New Zealand government for an increase in the value of Angus & Robertson's licence to £25,000.[119] Ferguson found the attitude of New Zealand booksellers towards Australian titles 'extremely favourable' but uniformly 'hampered by the import licensing system'.[120] Nevertheless, mutual industrial difficulties and quota systems in Australia and Britain dominated the end of the 1940s. Ferguson pressed for Australian government intervention or 'some special arrangement'[121] (as did MacQuarrie in London with letters to the *Bookseller*) to improve the situation of sending books to Britain and New Zealand, but paper rationing and a prevailing 'book depression'[122] in the United Kingdom continued to frustrate book production and distribution.

The 'lifting of embargo'[123] by the British Board of Trade was eventually accomplished in late 1949, and the discontinuation of paper control in London,[124] coupled with ongoing binding issues, provided some temporary relief and new opportunities for

Angus & Robertson to offer its services to London as binders. With paper becoming 'a bit more plentiful',[125] the company negotiated via the London office to take sheets of titles in exchange for the Australasian market from British publishers, including Victor Gollancz,[126] Lothian, Oxford University Press, Allen & Unwin,[127] Macmillan,[128] Chapman and Hall,[129] Samuel French,[130] George G. Harrap, Burns Oates & Washbourne (Publishers to the Holy See)[131] and W. & R. Chambers.[132] George Ferguson's hands-on experiences in London and his open-door policy with British publishers in Australia made him pivotal to these arrangements. In an exchange with Victor Gollancz in London, Ferguson recalled,

> Before the war a visit from an English publisher was a tremendous event. Now they seem to be done up in bundles of six, but let me hasten to add that that doesn't make them any less welcome. I think a good deal of understanding has been brought about since the war by this interchange of visits.[133]

Walter Cousins passed away in 1949, just one year out from completing five decades of service to Angus & Robertson, and Ferguson took over the company's publishing and manufacturing departments. After giving Ferguson his faraway 'blessing and confidence'[134], the Walter Harrap concluded that Ferguson would 'make the grade' although he might 'have to suffer more headaches than is necessary'.[135] Ferguson was also elected president of the Australian Book Publishers Association in place of Cousins – a position Ferguson would subsequently retain for eight years – and, speculating he had 'a fairly good grip of the publishing set-up in the British world', intended to 'make Angus & Robertson fit harmoniously into it'.[136] Indeed, when pressured by the British Copyright Agency to lodge copies of books that were distributed in the United Kingdom under Angus & Robertson's London imprint, Ferguson replied, 'we should consider ourselves bound by the Copyright Act as though we were London publishers'.[137]

Hector MacQuarrie was equally gratified that Britain's import troubles were over, although he was doubtful of its immediate advantages to the London office. Even though he was pressed by the *Melbourne Herald* to advertise that 'British people … could now buy Australian fiction',[138] MacQuarrie declined on the basis that although Australian fiction had not been permitted into the United Kingdom over the previous twelve months, the time it took to obtain stock from Australia meant it would be at least another three or four months before new Australian books would be arriving in London. MacQuarrie assured the *Melbourne Herald* that when a title was published in Australia it was 'pushed under the noses of every likely publisher in the UK and given every chance' where possible.[139] However, Angus & Robertson's intention was 'to publish Australian work in London, so that Australian authors would have an excellent chance of distribution in the Home land'.[140] With the official announcement by the Australian Department of Commerce and Agriculture that books would be included in free imports from the sterling area, Angus & Robertson could finally 'make some sort of a real start'[141] in London.

Angus & Robertson editor Beatrice Davis wondered whether sending the company's 'books into England might affect the placing of them with English publishers',[142] but it was important to Ferguson 'not to give Australian authors … the impression' that

Angus & Robertson was 'too subservient to British publishers'.[143] A complete catalogue of its most 'suitable books' was being arranged to be dispatched to MacQuarrie with a circular of the company's story as part of a 'continuous softening up process on [British] booksellers',[144] offering a 33.3 per cent discount to the London trade. (The last time a complete catalogue was produced was in 1935).[145] Angus & Robertson would initially send 'safe quantities of books' to the UK, careful not to overwhelm MacQuarrie's travellers with too many titles to sell, and assured the London office that 'you can never be stuck with [a] book as you can always send it back to us here'.[146] Strong initial sales however would reverse this caution. Awakened by the 'the magic of a London imprint and how pleased most [Australian] authors would be to see it',[147] Ferguson became quite keen to have a London Angus & Robertson imprint on as many books as possible.

While MacQuarrie's work would be confined to the book trade only, a small bookshop owned and operated by Angus & Robertson would be set up to trade in London under the name of 'The Australian Bookshop'. This sales outlet would market to retail customers not only a large percentage of Angus & Robertson's own titles, but also 'books, irrespective of where published or by whom, that deal with Australia'.[148] This meant the inclusion of appropriately themed works by other Australian and English publishers and perhaps here Ferguson was applying the example that Harrap in turn had applied to Angus & Robertson – that 'although competitors, we could work together in a spirit of good comradeship'.[149]

Ferguson's choice of words for creating another bookshop in London 'devoted to things Australian'[150] is revealing. Certainly, Ferguson was attempting 'to bring Australia on to the international stage'.[151] But the special focus on products themed around a single nation regardless of their manufactured origin and authorship – that is, not Australian literature or Australian-produced titles per se but books *about* Australia – anticipates the 'rhizomic rather than historical'[152] character of national literatures in modern print culture studies. Statements made by Ferguson 25 years later continued to reflect this international perspective on publishing and yet understated the contribution of Angus & Robertson towards the development of export markets for the Australian point of view:

> I don't believe there is any great nationality about books. I think that if a book is wanted it doesn't matter where it originated or what the nationality of the author was.[153]

From London Advocate to London Bookseller

Ferguson wanted books about Australia and a place to sell them throughout the United Kingdom. Ideally located near The Strand, the Australian bookshop would blend in with several other specialised establishments in London that stocked Asian, Indian and French titles. It would angle to connect with the 'forty or fifty thousand Australians'[154] who annually visited England. (Towards the close of 1950, Ferguson would attribute some of the success of his sales in London to the migration programme).[155] Fiction by Frank Clune, William Hatfield, Ernestine Hill, Ion L. Idriess and others of the same school was not expected to make any immediate commercial impact in Britain, and

Ferguson was doubtful whether Angus & Robertson was 'up to doing fiction at all in London'.[156] But, in Ferguson's own words a quarter century later, these authors wrote 'about an aspect of Australian life and Australian environment that was known to exist but nobody knew much about'.[157] They were 'tremendously popular'[158] in Australia and a country salesman would prove similar popularity in Britain by selling 400 copies of Idriess' novels to Army Education.[159]

With post-war interest in Australia on the rise both nationally and internationally, due in great part to the food parcel scheme, Angus & Robertson would push 'a great number of important books'[160] and also begin publishing novels of a more 'universal character'.[161]

The proposal to establish an Angus & Robertson bookshop in the heart of London was met with some reservation by MacQuarrie who, often employing military metaphors in his letters, considered himself to be 'the man on the spot' duly consulted by his 'good commander'.[162] MacQuarrie was referring to his previous experience with Henry George in running a bookstall in London, which was also called The Australian Bookshop Company. It too had started with 'enormous enthusiasm' and was encouraged by the *Sydney Morning Herald*:

> It has been suggested that a shop should be established in London for the sale of books by Australian authors. The idea is opportune, and worthy of every support. The time has come for Australia to demonstrate to readers abroad that she has evolved a distinctive national literature.[163]

However, the former Australian Bookshop saw its 'dying moments' in the 1930s after selling an average 'one book per day'.[164] In MacQuarrie's view, some booksellers struggled to sell Australian titles to 'any great extent, because their customers [did] not want them to any great extent'[165]. He did, however, recognise several other booksellers had been very successful with English editions of works by Henry Handel Richardson, Eleanor Dark, Helen Simpson, Kylie Tennant, Mary Mitchell and Ruth Park. It puzzled MacQuarrie, and he balanced the success of those editions produced by local English publishers with the relative failure of Jonathan Cape who, impressed with the Australian sales of *Lassiter's Last Ride* and *Man Tracks* (both by Ion Idriess), bought the Home British rights but strived to dispose of its stock 'despite the fact that … the booksellers did their best'.[166] MacQuarrie also dismissed the specialist bookstalls as 'dusty little old shops' concentrating on antique books and pointed to the average £10 profit that Australia House on The Strand collected each month from selling Angus & Robertson books to visiting Australians. Shop space too was difficult to come by and rents had gone up 25 per cent owing to an inflated demand caused by bombing during the war.

Overall, the expenditure in setting up such a project troubled MacQuarrie, and he did not think any Australian only themed bookshop was financially viable. Too many costs worked against marketing just one class of book. For example, renting a shop front on Great Russell Street that did not include lighting and heating would average £600 per year; a more ideal location on The Strand would equal £1,200 per year if the lease was locked into seven years; and operating charges plus salaries would be no less than £2,000 per year. MacQuarrie asked Ferguson to envisage

> the idea of opening a bookshop in Sydney where there are more than a million Australians, and only selling Australian books, and books about Australia. Would such a bookshop last unless it sold fountain pens and stationery, or found some other way of keeping the wolf from the door?[167]

Ferguson acknowledged MacQuarrie's point, aware that Australian booksellers stocked their shops with titles from a variety of lists.[168] Even Angus & Robertson's own retail department fully engaged the London office to coordinate rights trading and the acquisition of British books, sometimes taking sheets[169] (or bound and unjacketed copies)[170] in exchange for sole imprint and the Australasian markets. In return, Angus & Robertson offered 'run ons' to London publishers and the British market rights when an Australian-produced title was reprinted.[171] Ferguson had observed that more and more English publishers were tending to distribute their bestsellers directly from a branch in Australia. Angus & Robertson discerned an opportunity in this practice for British companies who had not yet closed the market in Australia.[172]

This opportunity kept Hector MacQuarrie and his staff enormously busy post-war. As indicated in the previous chapter, 'the movement of British books to Australia for sale' in the Angus & Robertson bookshop raised the profile of the London office as 'the single biggest exporter of UK books [purchased] in London'.[173] Coupled with its buying and selling of broadcast rights,[174] the work of the overseas branch configured Angus & Robertson's reputation as very important booksellers for British publishers and literary agents. Ferguson therefore conceded that Angus & Robertson was obviously 'engaged in enough risks' but that the company remained determined to sell Australian books through a store in England. On account of the new post-war interest, Ferguson rejected any comparison with the Australian Bookshop of 15 years earlier as a 'waste of time'.[175] The proposal however was temporarily put 'on ice' in order to keep attention focused on the organisation of selling Angus & Robertson's books to the London trade. (It would not be considered again until one of MacQuarrie's staff suggested that Angus & Robertson might come to an arrangement with the Australia House bookstall).[176]

Moreover, already two months behind, the catalogue needed to be finalised and dispatched with 'basic stock'[177] to London. 'After all', Ferguson admitted in December 1949, 'it is a little unreasonable for any of us to expect sales when you have virtually no books to sell'.[178] MacQuarrie responded in good nature, 'relieved to know that the Robertson-Ferguson determination just isn't obstinacy'.[179]

Chapter 5

THE FIRST SALESMAN IN LONDON

> We had become convinced, as we still are, that the best way of selling Australian books in the U.K. is … to become, in effect, a small British publisher.[1]

Through the activities of one travelling salesman named Bernard Robinson, Angus & Robertson was to learn that overseas branches could not forever remain independent of local book trade politics.[2] In late February 1950, George Ferguson notified Hector MacQuarrie that the long-overdue catalogue of Angus & Robertson's titles was nearing completion and would soon be on its way to London. Though in actuality the catalogue would not be at the proof stage until July, the pressure increased for MacQuarrie to have salesmen ready to cover London, Scotland and the English provinces.[3] So too to have regular advertisements – 'as attractive as those of, say, Faber, Chatto or Jonathan Cape'[4] – start appearing in the *Bookseller* in order to 'prepare the way for … travellers'.[5]

Angus & Robertson was very enthusiastic about the cargo of books in transit and produced circulars for display in the Bank of New South Wales, located in the West End of London, and also for the Australia House on The Strand, London. But while Angus & Robertson's London office was 'enjoying considerable success in the London area', it had 'little to speak of outside the metropolitan area'.[6] It seemed there were 'frightful problem[s]'[7] enticing travellers to manage provincial sales – 'no one wanted to do it',[8] the London manager bitterly complained – and MacQuarrie had to employ salesmen from British publisher Harrap's to circulate Australian titles. MacQuarrie, however, feared the potential ire of the Australian book trade if this arrangement was ever discovered.

Soon enough, Ferguson found a solution. Bernard Robinson, who was already a subscription salesman for Angus & Robertson and interested in working in England, was appointed by Ferguson to market Angus & Robertson titles to the provincial libraries and, more generally, to meet the 'greatly developed United Kingdom interest in Australia'.[9] Robinson would arrive in April 1950 and would travel books from one province to the next on a commission of 15 per cent per sale.

It was of equal importance to Ferguson to know whether booksellers and librarians were 'interested in Australia and books about Australia'.[10] He recognised that the library trade was controlled by the British Publishers Association in which libraries obtained a 10 per cent educational discount from local booksellers via a licence, but he hoped Robinson would nevertheless 'find a way of arousing [the] interest'[11] of British libraries without 'raising Hell with the booksellers in England'.[12] MacQuarrie agreed that selling directly to libraries might 'generate a prejudice' against

Angus & Robertson when British booksellers were eventually expected to purchase quantities of stock from the London office. However, MacQuarrie was prepared to 'take a chance here and let Robinson make the attempt' as a country salesman.[13] Frank Sanders, who had been with the British Publishers Association since 1932,[14] informally advised MacQuarrie over a 'sherry and a bit of red at the Arts Theatre Club'[15] that since Angus & Robertson's books were published in Australia they technically remained free to do as they pleased, because they were not signatories to the Publishers Association's Library Agreement.

Angus & Robertson often sought advice from British publishers in their own territory. Just a month earlier, MacQuarrie had asked for a list of the 'best literary agents in the main European countries' from British publishing stalwart Stanley Unwin.[16] And so it seemed appropriate for MacQuarrie to relate to Ferguson that

> Since we are Dominion publishers, we are not bound by this agreement, and we are at perfect liberty to sell direct to the libraries at a discount of 10%. While Sanders could not possibly give an okay, he did not seem to think, personally, that we would be making any serious mistake.[17]

Ferguson agreed with Sanders' interpretation. The business of Australian books was 'just waking up'[18] and Ferguson didn't see what right the 'God Almighty Publishers Association'[19] had to interfere with Angus & Robertson's activity in London. The decision to configure Robinson's work as part reconnaissance ('information … is what we are really paying for')[20] and part direct sales was endorsed in Sydney, with unofficial tacit encouragement from a high-ranking member of the Publishers Association – at least until British booksellers were interested in Australian books. In practice, it would test the company's resolve to operate on its own terms as an independent Australian publisher in London.

Within six weeks, Bernard Robinson had raised the business of Angus & Robertson's London office, selling several hundred pounds worth of books and succeeding in 'acquainting British librarians with the fact that there are such things as Australian books'.[21] He quickly became known as Angus & Robertson's 'bombshell salesman'.[22] But, despite the necessary appointment of a travelling salesman, the overseas branch was unprepared for the sudden jump in sales that now breached £600 per month.[23] There was simply not enough stock to meet this volume of sales and a third of Robinson's orders could not be supplied.

Since a provincial salesman receives no commission on unsupplied books, Robinson was not happy. By-passing MacQuarrie, Robinson complained directly to Ferguson that the situation was 'far from satisfactory',[24] given the high expense of travelling around Britain with his wife while towing a caravan filled with Angus & Robertson's 40 best titles.[25] Robinson pressed for an expense account that included a hotel and a car, plus a salary totalling £25 per week, but Ferguson countered that there was not enough business to pay the expenses of a provincial traveller. Ferguson did concede though that Robinson had proved to him the value of keeping a salesman on the road. MacQuarrie's right-hand office worker, known only as Mrs Woods, was responsible for processing all book orders and reported to Ferguson that 'for the first time in history, a representative is carrying our range over the whole of the country and the bookshops have been skipped'.[26] Ferguson thus met Robinson's request halfway and cabled that commission would now be paid on all orders regardless of existing stock levels and whether orders could be immediately fulfilled or not. Meanwhile, the Sydney office was experiencing 'acute space problems'[27] and contemplated setting aside stock originally reserved for its local sales and shipping this instead to London.

MacQuarrie was more cautious about the sudden sales bump and the idea of sending too much stock to London. The problem as MacQuarrie saw it was the nature of the orders, which might create an uncertain dependence on Robinson for shifting reserve stock. MacQuarrie believed sending books in greater quantities than the London office could distribute would 'make a stiff fight a desperate one'.[28] (In fact, an 'avalanche of books' arriving at the London office in May 1951, to meet the impact of the Bank of New South Wales brochures, would have a depressing effect on the staff).[29] Although the majority of books handled by Robinson went to libraries in weekly sales averaging £80 to £100, they were in bundles of twos, threes and fours. Because the titles sold by Robinson were 'the cream of [Angus & Robertson's] production over the last ten years',[30] MacQuarrie foresaw an end to the current sales boom within a year,[31] believing that the office could 'not contemplate anything like a repetition of such orders'.[32]

MacQuarrie confirmed that the London office's 'progress [was] real' but counselled Ferguson that it may also be temporary; its continuation ultimately depended on factors external to Robinson: 'Progress in this market is founded on vastly improved production by you, on better books published by you and, if I may say so, the drive developed by you'.[33] Upon reflection, Ferguson agreed that the current list of Angus & Robertson titles would not support Robinson 'after he [had] given the librarians the once over'.[34] In an attempt to find alternative sources to supplement and refresh current offerings in London, the Sydney office suggested that MacQuarrie consult once again with Frank Sanders on whether he 'might know of one or two smaller British publishers who could do with representation'.[35] Titles from these British publishers would coincide with the signing on of the lists from two other Australian publishers – S. Ure Smith (founded in 1939) and F. W. Cheshire (1926) – which the London office would also represent. Ferguson believed that adding the best titles from these other publishers into the sales list of Angus & Robertson would augment the 'serious fight'[36] to sell Australian books.

Melbourne-based publisher Cheshire was largely concerned with the production of art books and Sydney-based Ure Smith confined its work to publishing school textbooks; neither published Australian fiction.[37] However, Ferguson wanted to constitute Angus & Robertson's London office as 'the *only* authority on Australian books'[38] in Britain, irrespective of which publishers' lists it actually marketed, and he emphasised new responsibilities for MacQuarrie:

> You will be representing the three leading Australian publishers when you have these two houses in addition to A. & R., and you should on all occasions and in every way try and influence the trade in England to refer all their inquiries for Australian and New Zealand books to you.[39]

The appointment of Bernard Robinson became a turning point in how the company moved towards realising this ambition. Robinson's activities would eventually foreground the need to co-operate with the local British book trade, particularly local custom, and prompt the Sydney office to reconsider its lone wolf status as an Australian publisher conducting business in the heart of the Commonwealth. MacQuarrie might have characterised Angus & Robertson as 'the poor orphans in the wind raised by the Big Rich Publishing Boys of London as they swish by in their grey Bentleys',[40] but in October 1950 he was called upon to respond to the first protest against the activities of Robinson from a bookseller in Glasgow, W. & R. Holmes. MacQuarrie's reply would set in motion important changes in Angus & Robertson's London practices and contest MacQuarrie's later assessment of the company as 'an outsider to the British book trade':[41]

> While we, as Australian publishers, believe we are in no way bound by the Library Agreement because we are not members of the UK Publishers Association and our signature to that agreement could not be given, we nevertheless wish to abide by all U.K. agreements. At the same time we dislike taking any drastic action which might discourage Mr Robinson who, travelling by car with his wife, simply has to earn adequate commission or abandon his expedition … The position bristles with difficulties but we must admit that the great interest shown by librarians in our books has been most gratifying.[42]

While distancing Angus & Robertson from the travelling salesman by describing Robinson as freelance, MacQuarrie sought to hedge Angus & Robertson's bets by claiming that the Australian publisher wanted to 'please the booksellers, the librarians and UK readers'[43] but not discourage Robinson who was obviously doing very good business. MacQuarrie described the history of the salesman's work for Angus & Robertson as a one-man 'crusade on behalf of Australian books'.[44] He laid the responsibility for Robinson's actions on British booksellers and advised that booksellers needed to demonstrate more interest in stocking Australian titles if they wished to avoid unwelcome sales techniques in the future. To Robinson, MacQuarrie immediately recommended that

> You had better work through the booksellers. If you don't, I expect there will be, shortly, a big outcry. These sort of things gather in force. On the other hand, I, personally, and most certainly for the Firm give you full marks for magnificent work … [But] I think you had better use your overwhelming personality and salesmanship on the booksellers. This would be, perhaps, of lasting benefit to us.[45]

MacQuarrie knew that if the London office was 'to put the sale of Angus & Robertson books on a firm foundation',[46] it could not afford in the long run to antagonise booksellers by risking the continuation of Robinson's sales techniques. Ferguson and MacQuarrie could reasonably defend Robinson's actions being in the nature of reconnaissance, but in the long term they could not defend their continuation. Yet because Robinson's orders were placed directly with libraries, Angus & Robertson anticipated a sizeable slump in sales after he moved on. Contrary to Sanders' early advice, W. & R. Holmes' primary complaint was that although Angus & Robertson was 'not in any way bound by the library agreement a great many Librarians to whom Mr Robinson is selling, *are*'.[47] MacQuarrie felt conflicted in the position of being 'immensely pleased while enduring some concern'[48] and, somewhat experienced with the fickle nature of book trade politics, openly admitted to Robinson:

> I'm hanged if I can speak with a clear ringing voice, telling you precisely what to do. You are 'breaking in' to a local market, crowds of interested persons will try to squash you out until you have got on top of such frustrations: after which they will elect you to the Rotary Club.[49]

After reviewing how other bookseller-publishers managed their conflicting interests by looking at the work of Basil Blackwell, H. K. Lewis and Bailliere's, Ferguson believed the answer lay perhaps in turning the London office into a licensed library supplier for Australasia in Britain, operating under the company name rather than through a traveller. On this point, Ferguson was directly addressing complaints about Robinson. The travelling salesman was not averse to librarians misunderstanding his name as Bernard *Robertson*, as the other half of the company's namesake,[50] and had on occasion misrepresented that his list was not available anywhere else.[51] Moreover, Robinson had hinted to W. & R. Holmes that 'he had authority to ignore' the Net Book Agreement, which MacQuarrie thought might undermine any future attempt by the London office to formally integrate with the local book trade.[52] At the very least, the London office could coordinate the dispatch of books to British firms that were authorised library suppliers.[53]

Thus, in a change of tone from when Robinson first arrived in May 1950, Ferguson reminded MacQuarrie that 'eventually it is the bookseller that counts, because only through him may the great British public be reached'.[54] After all, Ferguson privately believed that 'when you go into a bookshop in London as a representative, you are facing somebody who is in the box seat with a whip in his hand'.[55]

It is clear from Ferguson's subsequent correspondence with MacQuarrie that Robinson's work had proved four things that Angus & Robertson took into consideration during the development of its future plans. One, a library market now existed for Australian books in the United Kingdom. Two, the interest of booksellers in Australian titles could be (and was) aroused by the perception of lost profits accruing to rogue sales techniques. Three, low or no stock could quickly damage the company's prestige. And four, an annually revolving list of fresh books would be needed to sustain the newly established interest of British librarians and booksellers. Though tensions had temporarily arisen between British booksellers and the London office, MacQuarrie argued that Robinson's 'crusade' had not been a false move but had instead stirred things up in their favour. However, 'a strategic retreat is now called for', he recommended.[56]

Ferguson agreed and the problems (and opportunities) that Robinson provoked for the Australian publisher were joined by four responses. One, Angus & Robertson would represent other Australian publishers andadded the publications of Cheshire and Ure Smith to the London list in order to 'maintain a sufficient flow of books each year'[57] from the beginning of 1951. They were, however, to 'keep a very cold eye on Australian and New Zealand fiction' whose sales chances were 'not very good'.[58] Two, MacQuarrie should appeal to Frank Sanders for advice on 'becoming members of the Publishers Association and thus bringing [Angus & Robertson's] books under the scope of the Net Book Agreement'.[59] Sanders responded that he 'saw no reason' why the Australian firm should not join the association.[60] Three, operations in London 'must be backed up by stock as nothing could be worse … than to start a rush of people looking for Australian books and then to have no books'.[61] Even so, Ferguson would lament several years later that 'it is almost impossible to walk the tightrope between having too few and too many'.[62] And four, the London office was also to explore becoming legally 'registered as library suppliers of Australian and New Zealand books'.[63]

In short, Ferguson was 'sorry to lose Robinson',[64] but he saw 'no other way of keeping the goodwill of the British trade and thereby gradually inducing them to sell Australian books to the British public'.[65] Angus & Robertson would strive to 'work in close conformity with UK practice',[66] noting that the goodwill of library suppliers was more important to the company than Bernard Robinson.[67]

In a frank letter just six days before Christmas 1950, Ferguson explained this revised situation to Robinson:

> The truth of the matter is that A. & R. cannot risk offending the book trade in England. It has always been the policy of the firm to abide by the correct rules and usages governing the trade in the various parts of the world, and we can never depart from this. Furthermore, from the practical point of view it is essential that we do not antagonise the booksellers because if we do we can give up forever the whole idea of selling our books to the public in England, and that is what we eventually must achieve … It therefore seems quite apparent that all future library orders for our books must go through established library suppliers … and you [will] not be able to use our name or say that you [are] representing us, because to do so [will] only upset other booksellers.[68]

There was little doubt in the minds of Ferguson and MacQuarrie that Robinson had been significant to their success in the second half of 1950 and, more generally, to the increased exposure Angus & Robertson received in the British book trade. Privately, MacQuarrie and Ferguson recognised how much Angus & Robertson owed to Robinson. They were 'fully appreciative'[69] of his work even as they expected an 'anguished letter'[70] in response to their pre-Christmas reprimand. Where previous efforts had failed, Robinson had managed to 'thrust into libraries a large quantity of [Angus & Robertson] books and [stir] up stagnant waters that needed stirring'.[71] MacQuarrie eventually doubted whether anyone else could in fact move the kind of books that Robinson did; that is, 'a mass of past books, older Idriess, etc'.[72] In the sale of Angus & Robertson's books throughout the United Kingdom, Bernard Robinson was a pioneer, although he could not escape censure from the British book trade – for his prohibited methods of 'confining … attention to libraries and largely ignoring the booksellers'[73] – nor, when pressure mounted against them, from his employer Angus & Robertson.

As a travelling salesman, Robinson was unable to support himself through the more legitimate practice of obtaining a small commission from sales to booksellers only. British booksellers traditionally controlled the distribution of books to British libraries. In order for booksellers to buy stock, the difference between the price a book could be purchased for and the price it could be retailed to libraries for had to be sufficiently attractive. For Robinson, this meant that his price to booksellers had to be low but also above the minimum price set by Angus & Robertson (which needed to show profit too). The need to make the price of Angus & Robertson's books economical and therefore cheaper for booksellers applied downward pressure on Robinson's own commission, which sat somewhere between Angus & Robertson's absolute minimum price and the price British booksellers agreed to pay for a title. Therefore, by circumventing booksellers altogether and selling directly to libraries, Robinson could raise the price of his books, facilitate a higher margin in profit, and gain a larger commission by effectively 'turning himself into a bookseller'.[74]

Without doubt Robinson's strategy angered British booksellers, but such methods also played a crucial role in helping Angus & Robertson negotiate and establish a stronger position with English booksellers. Through Robinson, Angus & Robertson were able to force the British book trade to take serious notice of a colonial firm operating in London. It is not unreasonable therefore to assess Angus & Robertson's response to Robinson as somewhat harsh after – it would appear – duly using him to test the waters and gain important information about the library trade and then subsequently appropriate and redirect his findings towards the company's own nation-building and profit-making endeavours.

Robinson's modus operandi, while tacitly supported by Ferguson, MacQuarrie and even Frank Sanders of the UK Publishers Association, exposed the tensions connected with running a branch office separated from its parent company by 13,000 miles. What might work in the Australian book trade might not necessarily be acceptable in Britain. It became increasingly apparent to Ferguson and MacQuarrie that if Angus & Robertson was to succeed in London, it could not forever operate outside established channels of trade and distribution in the local book trade. With Robinson described as 'plain poison'[75] by the British booksellers whom Angus & Robertson now courted, the London office needed to promptly roll back its association with the salesman, a move that in retrospect seemed 'quite inevitable'[76] to Ferguson. Indeed, to reuse Robert Haupt's 1988 description of British publishers defending their monopoly of the Australian market for foreign titles, Angus & Robertson was in 'retreat where necessary' from any association with Bernard Robinson's activities and appeared keen to 'avoid set-piece battles' with English booksellers.[77]

Reasonable attempts were made to keep Robinson employed in a markedly reduced capacity within the work of selling Angus & Robertson's books 'under circumstances', MacQuarrie cautioned, 'we can permit',[78] but negotiations quickly broke down. MacQuarrie's final correspondence with Robinson was especially cheerless and, though targeted personally at the salesman without reference to the company's complicity regarding its part in this turn of events, it captured the conditions that forced Angus & Robertson to ultimately rethink its London office operations, notwithstanding the expression of some latent anger at being caught:

> You have been defeated, if you are defeated, by a variety of factors – the existing organisation for library supplies, Net Book Agreements plus Library-Bookseller

> Agreements, all the little blokes making a modest living in the book trade who have been dug in for years and the fact that at present our current list alone cannot, without loss to us, support you.[79]

Not surprisingly, Bernard Robinson 'ceased operations'[80] with Angus & Robertson in February 1952. The county territories of England, Ireland, Scotland and Wales were handed over to four travellers from the British company Hamish Hamilton Ltd, who would call on bookshops throughout Britain and absorb all of Robinson's activities.[81] Confident in the fact that Australian books would not 'disgrace them',[82] Angus & Robertson engaged the services of Hamish Hamilton at £750 per annum, which was paid in regular monthly instalments as 'a contribution towards the travellers' remuneration and expenses'.[83] This was in addition to Hamish Hamilton negotiating a six per cent commission on the invoiced value of all sales made in each territory, both direct and indirect.[84] Hamish Hamilton would carry three lists, including Angus & Robertson's, which took in total an hour and a quarter to go through with each bookseller.[85]

Although the company expressed genuine regret about losing Robinson – especially during a time when it needed 'above everything else … people who can sell'[86] outside London – to continue the provincial traveller 'for the sake of easy sales now bringing about a situation which it might take … years to live down'[87] underlined Angus & Robertson's 'definite intention'[88] to now coordinate the sale of its books through normal channels in the United Kingdom. In order to gain the confidence of British firms and continue the business of persuading booksellers 'that certain Australian books can be sold',[89] the activities of Bernard Robinson led Angus & Robertson to restructure its sales arrangements, revise its standing within the local book trade and explore alternative ways of selling Angus & Robertson books within the United Kingdom.

Chapter 6

THE GETTING OF BOOKSELLING WISDOM

It was a staunchly held belief of George Ferguson's that Angus & Robertson could not afford to 'neglect any reasonable chance'[1] of selling Australian books overseas, especially in London. MacQuarrie referred to this as Ferguson's 'overwhelming keenness to sell [his] literary children on this market'.[2] So when long-serving London travelling salesman Sydney A. Sewell returned from a London luncheon with the idea that, through MacQuarrie, Angus & Robertson might take over the Australia House bookstall (located on the Strand) in lieu of developing a new Australia Bookshop, Ferguson replied that he was 'absolutely all for this'.[3] Having only a 'grim' relationship with the current bookstall operator, who occasionally defaulted in paying for stock obtained on credit from the London office, MacQuarrie took the idea to C. L. Hewitt, Official Secretary for Australia in London and made a case that Angus & Robertson's management of the small store at the entrance to Australia House would be of 'immense propaganda value to the country'.[4] Moreover, it would incorporate a 'glowing display of all the best and most exciting books published in Australia, and about Australia'.[5]

As a 'lasting monument to the importance of the Commonwealth and a splendid addition to the architecture of London', built on what was formerly described as a 'rustic spot in urban surroundings'[6], Australia House was Australia's High Commission in the United Kingdom. Given the site's undeveloped origins as 'wild flowers in the heart of London',[7] Australia House seemed to MacQuarrie a fitting location for a colonial book outlet with empire-sized ambitions and later recalled Angus & Robertson's bookstall 'bringing life into [the] gloomy old morgue'.[8]

Angus & Robertson seized upon the possibility of 'one of the bays in the inner part'[9] of Australia House's ground floor that could be retained as a bookstore after restoration work to the building was complete. MacQuarrie argued that the Australian publisher would make an ideal tenant, bringing to Australia House the 'same liveliness and attractiveness'[10] that could be found in Angus & Robertson's world-famous Sydney bookshop – unlike the 'moth-eaten condition' and seven 'unsaleable Australian books'[11] that characterised the current bookstall. In its present state, MacQuarrie considered it an embarrassment for an 'up and coming country like Australia'[12] and privately described the bookstall to Ferguson as

> nothing more than an insignificant niche on the right side entrance of Australia House; where the wall becomes faintly concave, an open counter I would guess about from eight to ten feet long, stretches across this shallow cave, with just enough room behind for a

young woman to sit. There is no space for holding of any serious amount of stock … Behind it is exposed an enormous picture of a wattle tree in full golden blossom.[13]

Ferguson did not have an exaggerated idea of the commercial possibilities of a space in Australia's High Commission. In his mind, an Australia House bookstall 'means a lot more than sales[:] it means contact and prestige'.[14] Nor did Angus & Robertson neglect the propaganda potential of having a stall more appropriately located in Australia House. The plan therefore was to abandon this space in favour of one of the large bays at the far end of the ground floor. MacQuarrie, however, lacked confidence in the level of Hewitt's commitment to replace the current tenant and rejuvenate the bookstall space. He urged Ferguson to 'do a bit of prodding from [his] end'.[15]

Drawing upon on a promise initially made by Prime Minister Chifley, who guaranteed the 'fullest support of the [Australian] Government and all its departments … in the production of the new edition of the Encyclopaedia',[16] Ferguson requested Prime Minister Menzies to interest himself personally in MacQuarrie's petition for Angus & Robertson via the London office to manage the Australia House bookstall. As perhaps an indication of the company's reputation in Australia at that time, it worked. Three weeks later, the Secretary of the Prime Minister's Department in Canberra telephoned Ferguson to advise that Menzies would back Angus & Robertson's petition, that he would write to the resident Minister in London conveying his support and that 'in strictest confidence … he would be very glad if a change was made as the present lessee had always been a bit of a nuisance'.[17]

Following the procurement of Menzies' support, Angus & Robertson was 'practically certain'[18] that they would be favoured to take possession of the bookstall – or a new space – to sell books in Australia House. Consequently, the company turned its attention to debating the final rent amount and who might actually manage the sales department. MacQuarrie nominated Greta Morrison,[19] who would go on to operate the bookstall for 15 years[20] until her retirement at 65 in June 1966. After Morrison's death, the company's focus turned, more importantly, to its business identity and deciding how it would operate.

Ferguson saw the value in placing the masthead of Angus & Robertson above the new bookstall but had reservations. The recent Bernard Robinson incident, which had prohibited library sales, meant the company's activities were now under close scrutiny by the British book trade, and Angus & Robertson was not able to work around it. Ferguson expressed some reluctance about using the company name because it might alienate British booksellers and 'get us in bad with English publishers who hate the combination of bookseller-publisher':[21]

> If we use the name of Angus & Robertson we run the risk of antagonising booksellers who will say: 'What is the use of our stocking your books if you are selling them retail yourselves at Australia House?' On the other hand if we used a name such as 'The Australian Bookstall Limited' or even the old 'Australia Book Company' they could not make this charge … The only drawback about not using our own name is that it would mean something to many of the Australians.[22]

Angus & Robertson submitted a formal tender in June 1951, over a year after Sewell first raised the idea, and when Hewitt phoned MacQuarrie a month later on behalf of the Australia House, the London office was 'ready to talk business'.[23] Although the former tenant's exit required firm but delicate management, the handover went relatively smoothly and the renovated Australia House bookstall began business on 1 November 1951 after a 'sumptuous party'[24] the night before. In its new position and enlarged scope, the bookstall's overhead was 'pretty stiff'[25] at £1,000 annually (inclusive of wages), but MacQuarrie believed the 'publicity value' and 'grandeur' of the opening ceremony more than justified the £150 price tag that the evening's celebrations carried.[26] The event was not without incident however.

Angus & Robertson veteran Aubrey Cousins, who was visiting the United Kingdom for a period and assisting with the branch's post-Robinson reorganisation, gave a speech about the bookstall, after which he was approached by the *Daily Express* who politely enquired,

> We understand that Australia House is extraterritorially part of Australia. Australia has banned *Jimmy Brockett* and you are offering the book for sale on a stall in Australia House. Can you explain this?[27]

It is true that the novel of *Jimmy Brockett* was, however briefly, a banned publication in Australia. It was standard practice for customs officials to regularly detain imported copies of any publication considered suspect until such time as the Australian Commonwealth Literary Board of Censorship could assess it. (Local publications fell outside the jurisdiction of Federal Customs and were the responsibility of the States.) Penned in London by Australian Dal Stivens, the reasons for why *Jimmy Brockett* might have been considered suspect remain unclear except for a passing local media reference to the novel's close portrayal of a prominent Sydney figure.[28] The ban lasted only a few weeks and was lifted by then Customs Minister Senator O'Sullivan.[29] This, however, occurred the day after Aubrey Cousins was required to defend Angus & Robertson to the *Daily Express*:

> We are not offering *Jimmy Brockett* for sale in Australia House. Our shop does not open until tomorrow and we shall not be offering the book for sale. At the private party here, the book is on show, but not for sale.[30]

While minor, this exchange confirmed the greater degree of attention Angus & Robertson and Australian books were now attracting in London, and the Sydney office was not immune to exploiting this in other ways. Even as MacQuarrie correctly predicted that the Australian House bookstall would probably not ever bring in large visible profits nor conversely 'spell continuous loss',[31] MacQuarrie noted that 'as advertisement … for the firm it is invaluable'.[32] A year after its opening, Cousins agreed and revealed that

> Quite apart from our own satisfaction, authors [in Australia] are becoming very interested in the trade generally and have started to think about Angus & Robertson's London sales

as something legendary. They think they are much higher than they are, and we don't disillusion them.[33]

Ferguson knew though that appearances would not be enough and that it would be fatal to develop discussions he had with MacQuarrie during the late 1940s on publishing Australian books in Britain until the London office was 'equipped reasonably well on the selling side'.[34] Code-named 'Operation London', Angus & Robertson's metaphor for breaking into the London market as publishers was 'to get in behind'. It was a military concept suggested by the gardener of Hector MacQuarrie, and although the London office was working closer with the local book trade than ever before, 'getting in behind' supported the sentiment of Angus & Robertson working as outsiders or foreigners behind enemy lines.[35]

In this endeavour, similar to the rationale behind British publishing in Australia, Ferguson saw three critical stages to the entire process of proverbially getting in behind: '(a) to see in the United Kingdom [their] own publications, (b) to be able to make bids for American books with a British Empire market, [and] (c) to publish books originating in England'.[36] Production would be divided between Halstead Press in Sydney and a local firm in England. This was partly to return some profit to Angus & Robertson's subsidiary printing press, but also to keep costs down through larger print runs even as, Ferguson laboured to MacQuarrie, this method of 'keeping ahead'[37] carried the implication that 'our production must be as good as English production, book for book'.[38]

Indeed, giving the example of *Simon Black in Space* by Ivan Southall, travellers would report a year later that it only took one poorly produced Australian book 'to sour booksellers on the lot'.[39] In addition to representatives calling on booksellers, the London office would thus need to appoint a dedicated sales manager to organise travellers, direct advertising plus write blurbs, administer the Australia House bookstall and collaborate with MacQuarrie in overseeing the building up of additional export markets in 'Indonesia, South Africa, Holland, the United Kingdom or anywhere else'.[40] Dedicated to selling editions in Britain and marketing translation rights on the continent (after the creation of a Foreign Books Department in the Sydney office),[41] this new London staff member would ideally be someone who could obtain 'sales as he combats the undoubted prejudices in booksellers' minds against books published "abroad"'[42] (a moniker in 'insular English'[43] for any country outside the United Kingdom).

As far as selling Australian books on an international scale was concerned, Ferguson stressed the general principle that 'provided we do not incur an actual loss, and provided that we do not have stock all over the world on sale or return, it will pay us to do business at no profit for a while'.[44]

Configured in Ferguson's mind as a 'no-cost advertising campaign', this new sales approach was an attempt at 'educating the heathens to the fact that there are Australian books' and engendering 'some confidence in booksellers … that such books can be sold'.[45] On a practical level, it also addressed the rising labour costs in Australia by linking larger print runs of a title with the substantial savings that accrued with smaller unit costs, although Ferguson doubly recognised that the firm was 'taking a fairly considerable risk'[46] to build up London. Ferguson expected profits would come from sales in Australia and

New Zealand. However, at a commercial level, it impressed upon Angus & Robertson the need to embrace practices associated with the activities of British publishers in Australia and found objectionable by most members of the local book trade (see Chapter 4):

> Nobody could imagine for a moment that it pays British publishers to supply novels at what they call 'colonial rates' … They have done it over the years in order to capture 'colonial' markets, to increase the sphere of activity and prestige of British books throughout the world, and to increase their runnings, dumping off in the 'colonies' at low discounts whatever is surplus to their UK requirements. Their argument has been sound enough and we must do something of the same kind. It is for us to determine in each area what is the hardest bargain we can drive … [so] that we can make as much as possible out of the transaction in addition to whatever advantages accrue here from the larger runs.[47]

Yet, while Ferguson seemed willing to test the commercial limits of pushing Australian books into foreign markets by drawing on the British example, to be sure that 'no book can be damned before it has a chance',[48] the London office suffered 'sales resistance' to its catalogue and admittedly – when called upon to address the issue – some pricing resistance from the Sydney office too.[49] While still in London, Aubrey Cousins documented the local material difference between the Sydney edition of Frank Clune's *Somewhere in New Guinea: A Companion to Prowling through Papua* (1951) retailing at 25 shillings and the surplus of English books selling for 17 shillings. Observing a high retail price as a serious factor blunting the purchase of Australian books by the average British consumer, Cousins concluded that 'in the marketing of any new product, or the product of a new firm, price factor is very important, and if we had a price advantage, we would do quite well'.[50]

Six months later, the new London sales manager similarly questioned the high price of the Blue Wren book series[51] and Australian titles by Idriess or Clune, claiming that, after visiting all the booksellers in Southern England, the 'prices daunt most' of the smaller outlets.[52] By that time, having relocated back to Sydney, Cousins judged the request to reduce books priced at fifteen shillings down to ten shillings and six pence, reflecting local English pricing scales, as 'really strain[ing] the friendship'.[53] Cousins compromised and suggested the price might be reduced instead to twelve shillings six pence, arguing 'we cannot possibly work at a complete loss'.[54]

Even so, further discussion in Sydney saw two new novels (*Dust on My Shoes* by Peter Pinney and *The Ridge and the River: A Novel* by Tom Hungerford) sold in London at 10 shillings 6 pence as a test case. Thus an argument that the sales department would continue to repeat long after he left the United Kingdom, Cousins angled for cheaper book prices in his December 1951 report from London to Ferguson in Sydney. Cheaper books, it seemed, were becoming an important factor in matching the competition posed by British booksellers and publishers trading in their own territory. Such a pricing strategy is consistent with the second phase in John Attenborough's description of how British publishers developed a British book export market. That is, the overseas agent 'will ask for support from his Principals in ensuring the stability of the local bookseller', often requiring 'greater trade discounts to offset the greater risk entailed in buying speculative stock for a distant market'.[55] In this instance, the London office viewed having a price advantage as a key component to successfully selling Australian books in the British market and sought permission from the Sydney office to appropriately reduce prices.

To support the request, Cousins reported on the 'up-hill fight' to achieve publishing sales in London amounting to £1,002 for October 1951, and the one-page stock-take (dated 7 December 1951) attached to his analysis is the first clear picture of the sales of Australian books in London. Cousins' findings can be briefly summarised. Titles by Idriess, like *The Wild White Man of Badu: A Story of the Coral Sea* (published 21 August 1951), were considered 'safe' and, in this case, reflected strong sales of 672 units against 306 remaining in stock. Reprinted works like Brent of Bin Bin's *Up the Country: A Tale of the Early Australian Squattocracy* (271 sales with 204 remaining) and Clarence Benham's *Diver's Luck: A Story of Pearling Days* (likewise, 665 sales with 812 remaining) were categorised as 'old books' and were very demanding to set up, although once established they sold very nicely. Juveniles were popular too, often with stock selling out very quickly, and Bill Beatty's *This Australia: Strange and Amazing Facts* was a bestseller for a guinea at the new Australia House bookstall.[56]

However, works by Frank Clune, such as *Hands Across the Pacific: A Voyage of Discovery from Australia to the Hawaiian Islands and Canada, April to June, 1950* and *Dig: A Drama of Central Australia*, either struggled or failed entirely to find a market in London. (Later, the London office would learn that more harm is done to the cause of selling Australian books in Britain by offering a Clune title to booksellers.)[57] Similar disappointments were experienced with the Angus & Robertson editions of Hungerford's *Diseases of Poultry* and Rex Battarbee's *Modern Australian Aboriginal Art.* The failure of the latter title was due in some part, according to Cousins, to the fact that the British public was 'most consistently rude about Australian art'.[58]

Ferguson was initially philosophical about these early results and did not 'expect [the firm] to become the Oxford University Press or Jonathan Cape overnight – or ever'.[59] On the one hand, he promised Hector MacQuarrie that after Cousins departed Britain in February 1952 he would not expect the London office to 'sell hopeless books in big quantities'[60] nor would he flood the office with books that they could not possibly shift.[61] Ferguson also pointed to the speculative nature of publishing and bookselling, claiming that sometimes 'the one you thought would do well doesn't and the doubtful one … does'.[62]

At the 1930 Tariff Board Inquiry in Australia, William Moore of Robertsons & Mullens in Melbourne described this problem as a well-known condition of the Australian bookselling trade, with small markets like Australia enduring the greatest risks: 'One book is a success and another falls flat; one book is not noticed until it has been in the market for some time, and then suddenly bursts into popularity; another is a striking success in one country and a failure in another'.[63] Finding the optimal print run number was the perennial problem for publishers. The great distance between MacQuarrie and Ferguson further complicated this issue, adding an unanticipated logistical problem for Angus & Robertson in Sydney, which needed larger print runs for improved scales of economy.

Yet Angus & Robertson was unsure of just how many actual copies to produce for what in practice were two very different markets; that is, for Australian and British consumers. Ferguson complained that

> With many of our new books now we are at a loss to know what to print because, although we can make a fair sort of guess at what the sales here [in Australia] will be, we have very little idea of what the sales at your end [in London] will be. If we are over-ambitious we finish up with books that we cannot sell. If we are too cautious you are likely to send us repeat orders fairly quickly only to find the book out of print, and if we are to keep … travellers and the bookstall in England we cannot have this occurring too often.[64]

The time it took to ship books from Australia to Britain also meant that the London office was 'working so far behind'[65] the Sydney office with the perennial worry, since Bernard Robinson, that travellers might sell more books than the London office could reasonably supply in a timely fashion.[66]

Yet trade in the reverse direction, from London to Australia, was no better for British publishers who confirmed that distant markets were separated not only by space but, inevitably, by a time-frame measured according to how slowly ships crossed that space:

> If you want to establish a bookseller who is going to take the risk of holding your stock … 10,000 miles from London, he is really taking some very big risks: he is probably ordering books unseen. He is certainly going to make an order which will take him through a given period of time; for example, an Australian bookseller ordering a book published on 28 September of any given year has got to decide whether he is to supply a large part of his Christmas trade, because he is not going to have any chance of repeat shipments before Christmas.[67]

Regardless of nationality, whether it was the local bookseller or the far-away home office that controlled decisions on stock levels, stock orders for distant markets remained highly speculative. In the face of these challenges, Angus & Robertson began to analyse and push the sale of Australian books more diligently than ever before, and with an increased attention to the importance of advertising.

Over time the firm acknowledged the need to sell certain books at a cheaper price in London than in Sydney.[68] This culminated in 'two prices existing' for Angus & Robertson books: 'the Australian and the English'.[69] Furthermore, it required the company to close the market and enforce a policy that anyone in the British Isles and South Africa who wanted their books – despite the fact that the 'price from Australia would be cheaper for an English bookseller even if [they] paid post'[70] – could only order titles from the London office and not Sydney. In view of the logistical issues surrounding stock, it was a cumbersome policy to administer but nevertheless a deliberate attempt to imitate the British pattern.

The pattern was to seal off the option of ordering books directly from the publisher in the home country and to build up the strength of a local agent acting as a bookseller in the foreign dominion. This was achieved by ensuring a representative had exclusive rights to supply literary product within the foreign market. For Angus & Robertson, this meant prohibiting international orders placed directly with the Sydney office and raising the profile of its branch office on English soil as the 'centre of things'[71] for selling Australian books in other territories. With scales of economy central to the publishing paradigm, the extra copies printed for the overseas market would in turn support much-needed larger print runs back in Sydney and pass on important savings. 'If we can merely get to the point of paying our way in London', Ferguson opined, 'the extra outlet is a tremendous help to us here'.[72] It was a policy that seemed very similar to what British publishers would confess as standard practice in their defence of the Net Book Agreement before the Restrictive Trade Practices Court in 1962.

With Australia experiencing 'economic problems … reflected in the printing industry by ceiling prices and [a] lack of skilled labour',[73] Ferguson's policy implied that the health of the export trade in Australian books had a bearing, be it major or minor, on the health of Angus & Robertson back in Australia during the early 1950s.

It was of some importance then for George Ferguson to know from Hector MacQuarrie 'what kind of books [he was]selling and how many'.[74] As the original incentive behind creating an overseas branch, the uninterrupted movement of British books to the Angus & Robertson Sydney bookshop was 'still as important as ever'[75] and a 'top consideration in all … planning'.[76] With 'masses of books pouring through [the London office] en route to Sydney or Melbourne',[77] its management from Australia in coordination with Walter Butcher who oversaw the London side (known as the export department of the London office) was 'to a large extent routine'.[78]

Statistics from the export department over five years show that Butcher administered a sizeable project. In 1947, Butcher had packed books to the value of £53,316 in 337 cases and 348 bulk postbags. In 1948, the value of books packed at 48 Bloomsbury Street was £64,188 in 357 cases and 447 bulk post bags; 1949, £69,732 in 492 cases and 393 bags; 1950, £83,293 in 439 cases and 471 bags; 1951, £117,075 in 635 cases and 533 bags; and in 1952, £112,914 worth of books were packed in 602 cases and 483 bulk bags.[79] Although the London office's main object of collecting, packing and 'shipping British books as rapidly as possible to Australia'[80] had doubled in size over half a decade, the firm was determined to evolve the sale of its own books to the maximum, and it was in this area that the greatest developments were to take place if the often discussed 'Operation London' was to eventuate.

This drive to augment sales impelled a reorganisation of space at the London office. If Angus & Robertson were to make serious efforts to sell books in Britain, the 'old business' of ordering between twenty-five and fifty copies of a book would no longer remain an efficient practice for maintaining adequate supplies in London. Instead, 'reasonable stock' levels would be necessary to address the kind of demand Angus & Robertson was hoping to generate, in which there was always a book on hand for a purchase order. Certainly, the case of Bernard Robinson had revealed the need to ensure there were no lengthy delays fulfilling orders or waiting for stock to arrive from overseas: 'Australian booksellers are trained to put up with that sort of thing from British publishers', Ferguson reasoned, 'but British booksellers are not'.[81] While Ferguson had his eye on commercial needs, MacQuarrie responded with regards to practical needs and lamented, 'space is a nightmare'.[82] Eventually, the Sydney office compromised, and surplus publications were sent back to Sydney to make space in the London office for new titles. The returned stock occupied 40 cases.[83]

The British public remained as sceptical of colonial books as British booksellers. With the addition of the Cheshire and Ure Smith lists to Angus & Robertson's catalogue, plus books from other publishers being issued under the Angus & Robertson imprint (controversially with no mention of the former publisher),[84] Ferguson felt certain that the firm produced enough titles to support a full-time sales manager in London. Confident that a sufficient framework of organisation was finally in place to enable 'sales to be carried forward to ever-increasing totals',[85] Angus & Robertson was convinced this calculated risk would pay off or that losses would be limited. Ferguson advised MacQuarrie that 'the bloke appointed should come under you for his general administration, etc., but that his actual selling operations will have to be directed pretty closely from here [in Sydney]'.[86]

Anticipating MacQuarrie's rebuttal that the present run of books could not in fact support very much overhead,[87] Ferguson conceded that 'getting this selling organisation going will look a bit heavy at first'[88] but excused this setup as having the Sydney office take responsibility for 'what you may think are unprofitable adventures or waste of money'.[89] In the end, however, MacQuarrie's authority would be undermined by this arrangement. It would generate tensions in the London office and amplify issues in coordinating decisions with a distant head office.

Being 'on the spot'[90] was the frequent description for Angus & Robertson staff operating in the United Kingdom. The Sydney board of directors, mindful of the need for some autonomy, was unanimous in their decision that Aubrey Cousins (who was still in London) and Hector MacQuarrie should select a suitable person to act as the London office sales manager, rather than this decision being left entirely with the firm in Australia. Thus short-circuiting 'long exchanges and discussions'[91] between Sydney and London, Vera Wellings (who always wanted to be associated with Angus & Robertson)[92] was appointed by MacQuarrie to take over from Cousins in January 1952. Keen and enthusiastic, Wellings was to further 'the sales of Australian books in general and Angus & Robertson books in particular'.[93]

Vera Wellings began work during 'the worst time of the year for bookselling in London'.[94] It was January 1952 – the middle of a British winter when the book business was usually poor.[95] Although the movement of newspapers by Greta Morrison at the new Australia House bookstall remained 'efficient',[96] this seasonal flatness in book sales coincided with the branch changing over to a new financial system that was expected to be swifter and less arduous for C. S. Joyner, the London office accountant. For that reason, in the first few months of Wellings' appointment, it was nearly impossible for the firm to obtain a clear financial position, and it was not until the second quarter of 1952 that a picture eventually emerged.

Including titles marketed through the Australia House bookstall, by mid-April 1952 the sale of Angus & Robertson books – as opposed to the exporting of British books to the Sydney and Melbourne bookshops – necessitated an overhead of approximately £100 per week. Calculated against the 17 per cent profit margin enjoyed by the London office on Angus & Robertson books, MacQuarrie estimated the branch had in fact been operating at a loss of £170 per month.[97] However, a profit and loss statement covering twelve months of trading to March 1952 showed British sales of Angus & Robertson publications to be £9,424 sterling and costs to be £4,510 sterling, which revealed a gross profit of £4,914 sterling.[98] This too was dismissed after a while and another adjustment of expenditure would instead admit a loss to the company of over £2,000 sterling,[99] matching MacQuarrie's original estimation, until Cousins again overruled this in August 1952.

Taking into account 'our real costs', Cousins concluded that for the twelve months to March 1952 'we [had only] lost £96 sterling on [the] Angus & Robertson publishing effort in London'.[100] No further reassignments of expenditure were made to the 1951–2 profit and loss statement, and this final assessment showed, through its recorded sales of £9,424 and costs of £9,520, a resulting loss of £96 sterling. A few months later, Cousins discussed ideal totals for London sales, setting £12,000 a year as a target which would show no profit but, more importantly, show no loss either. Though unacknowledged, MacQuarrie's early assessment was very close to the implications of this target; in the sale of Angus & Robertson books from March 1951 to March 1952, the overseas branch had in fact lost an amount approaching £2,576 sterling.

Whatever the exact figure, this ambiguity and disagreement about the London office's true financial status (which frequently leaned towards loss as in this example) shadowed the successes of the overseas branch in one form or another for the entire period of its operations.

There was no question then that Australian books were selling – albeit in multiple orders of single copies[101] – but if 'the great plan'[102] did not deliver as everyone had hoped when the slow season passed it was distinctly possible that 'Operation London' would be defeated before it was even launched.

Optimistically, and sounding suspiciously like George Ferguson, Aubrey Cousins offered that in the early stages of any endeavour losses can be expected and that these profit and loss statements should be shelved away as figures for comparison, although 'from now on we should see a steady improvement'.[103] But with advertising costing the London office £1,100 for the financial year ending March 1952, Wellings and MacQuarrie clashed almost immediately over what constituted an appropriate promotional budget for improving the sale of Australian books.

Wellings dedicated herself enthusiastically to developing awareness of Angus & Robertson's London imprint that appeared on rebadged books. In addition to duties in promotion and sales, every few months Wellings selected an English region to visit and wrote up detailed reports on her personal contact with each bookseller operating in that area. From her reconnaissance, Wellings regularly concluded that in terms of product, when there was no major difference in manufacturing quality to similar items on the market and when a book was generally priced the same as its competition, attitudes towards the Angus & Robertson imprint were 'friendly and definitely improving'.[104] Feedback from booksellers frequently reinforced the need to keep prices of Australian books at a competitive level and production quality high. The Australian 'flavour' in titles was not considered a limitation but the need for uniform, reasonably priced editions was.[105] At the peak of Australia's restrictions against imports from Britain, according to Wellings' reports, booksellers also recommended the local (that is, English) printing and binding of an Australian title might help overcome the then popular bias against Australian-manufactured products on sale in London.[106] Nonetheless, MacQuarrie judged Wellings' trips and how she exercised her duties to be an extravagance the London office could not readily afford (even as her reports clearly fulfilled what Angus & Robertson initially wanted – but never fully obtained – from Bernard Robinson). 'She attempts too much', MacQuarrie complained to Ferguson, 'with a lack of prudence in spending the firm's money'.[107]

Rarely bereft of a colourful or literary description of his staff members, MacQuarrie characterised Wellings as behaving 'like a millionaire's wife let loose in a hat shop' whenever she was designing advertisements.[108] Although admitting that the new sales manager composed excellent copy and created pleasant-looking layouts, MacQuarrie found her business sense 'quite startling',[109] and in the current financial climate requested that the Sydney office 'exert control … on her spending' or at the very least instruct her to consult him before any future expenditure on advertising.[110]

Without authority, MacQuarrie felt he was just a 'frustrating influence'.[111] When no response was forthcoming a month later, MacQuarrie and even Wellings became increasingly anxious for some guidance on how much money should be allocated to each book for publicity.[112] A core frustration for Wellings was that although advertising could be tied to the London sales routine, dates of forthcoming titles for promotional copy were 'impossible to fix'[113] due to delays over finalising shipping dates or waiting for a shipment to be cleared. The distance between Sydney and London, it seemed, affected not only the availability of stock to meet the demands of the British market, but also the availability of accurate information to meet the needs of promoting new books.

Angus & Robertson confessed it was very difficult to help at such long range and concluded that the Sydney office would not be 'silly enough' to oversee advertising in London by remote control.[114] 'If you are going to sell', advised Aubrey Cousins now returned to Sydney, 'you will have to advertise and we won't be frightened to spend the money to get rid of two or three thousand books on a market which never existed previously'.[115] The challenge for Wellings, as Ferguson had experienced with stock orders, was to identify which titles would get 'the very best return for every pound outlay' and, to revisit MacQuarrie's former request, how much to spend on advertising each book.[116] The only general rule Cousins could provide was to allocate no more than 10 per cent of the sales value of each book towards promotion; any more would be extravagant.

But following this rule would be an exercise in paradoxical thinking. The speculative nature of bookselling meant Wellings had no way of knowing in advance how many copies of any particular title was actually going to sell. Even Angus & Robertson veteran George Ferguson would one day admit that he could not avoid being 'constantly struck by the false judgements' made in Sydney 'about which of our books will sell (or won't sell)' in London,[117] prompting renowned Australian editor Beatrice Davis to initiate a search for 'manuscripts suitable to both English and Australian markets'.[118] Nevertheless, if Wellings used her judgement, Cousins did not believe the annual goal was a 'terrifically difficult proposition'.[119]

The revised London balance sheets stamped with Cousin's approval indicated that to break even Wellings needed to achieve London sales of at least £12,000 sterling per year.[120] The Sydney office recommended that Wellings might balance slow periods like winter with the larger sales expected at Christmas rather than pursue £1,000 a month. But by the third quarter of 1952, Wellings was achieving just that. A September monthly return reported publishing sales of £1,437 against advertising costs of £244; with no promotional budget, the Australian House shop ticked over moderately well with £269 in the sale of books and newspapers. By comparison, the quarterly returns for July to September 1952 showed the Hamish Hamilton travellers made sales in Britain amounting to £717 with a commission of £187 while Sewell accomplished £1,004 in sales at a lower commission of £100.[121]

In the same year that Ferguson hoped the London office would 'get somewhere', with the help of 'Sewell, plus the H. H. travellers, plus the bookstall, plus Mrs Wellings and publicity of various kinds',[122] by the end of 1952 Angus & Robertson had definite evidence that Australian books – 'that is, books that measure up to the standards required in England'[123] – could be sold in the United Kingdom. Whether this was for profit or for loss, however, would remain in doubt.

Chapter 7

PREPARING FOR 'OPERATION LONDON'

> After years of pretty hard battling it seems now that the opportunity has arrived for some (I don't say all) Australian books to sell in respectable numbers in England.[1]

> A lot too much has been made of … the British Market Agreement [and it] has got to the stage of being blamed for all the ills of the book trade. It has been dragged out of shape in a most disgraceful manner. In fact it amuses me to wonder, now that there is no British Market Agreement, what are they [Australian publishers and booksellers] going to blame the troubles of the book trade on to, because they are not going to stop.[2]

The Hand that Signed the Agreement

On the back of stronger sales in 1952, January would not be a propitious start to 1953 for the London office. Due to a fire which turned the old storeroom into a 'horrid cavern' and the backyard into a 'ghastly heap of half burnt and soaking books', the present attempts to break into Britain's 'fiercely contested market'[3] with Angus & Robertson's titles was set back by £4,888 in damaged stock.[4] Although the branch had over-reached its 1952 target of £12,000 by a thousand pounds sterling, the first quarter of 1953 would be very quiet commercially while the office waited for resupplies from Sydney. Perhaps sensing a series of cutbacks due to this misfortune, Vera Wellings reinforced the importance of her role even as the office faced business loss. Wellings believed 'good publicity' matching the energy of the 'Big Boys' – that is, matching the efforts of large British publishers like Collins who were 'active already' and going 'all out to get Australian authors'[5] – was the answer.

But there was, ironically, nothing to sell. The list of books destroyed by the fire was formidable and was representative of Angus & Robertson's general stock in Australia.[6] The London office was however, as MacQuarrie would later recall, 'used to struggling … and [they would] manage very well'.[7] It was therefore indicative of Ferguson's ceaseless determination, a quality MacQuarrie observed in him long ago during times of intense difficulty, that the London office's most noteworthy developments should have emerged during this otherwise rather discouraging period.

The first step to revive the fortunes of the London office was both symbolic, controversial and involved the Publishers Association in London. Two and a half years after Angus & Robertson articulated a desire to revise the standing of its London office within the local book trade (one of many issues heightened by the case of Bernard Robinson), the secretary of the Publishers Association and friend to Angus & Robertson, Frank Sanders, finally returned with a formal response. Having made discreet enquiries about the probable fate of any application for membership that the Australian publisher might submit to the British Publishers Association, Sanders concluded that any such application would be 'unanimously accepted by the P.A. Council'.[8] George Ferguson, who was visiting the United Kingdom at the time, discussed this result privately with Sanders, and upon his return to Sydney in August 1953, agreed officially with the Board of Directors that Angus & Robertson should join the British Publishers Association.

Angus & Robertson was to officially 'infiltrate the local scene'.[9] Uncertain though of whether to emphasise the Sydney or London office in the application process, Ferguson left Hector MacQuarrie alone to complete the form with Sanders' help, who advised, given the uneven split of power and responsibilities between Sydney and London, to do all that can be reasonably done to fit the London branch into the association.[10] MacQuarrie supposed that the Publishers Association did not have 'anything like us in its bosom' and hoped Angus & Robertson would not appear to be 'at its throat' when 'Operation London' eventually got underway.[11] The completed forms were mailed back to Sydney for Ferguson to sign and were delivered in MacQuarrie's typical eloquent fashion: '[W]hen you have drawn the appropriate cheque, we shall become members of the ancient and honourable company of British publishers. I didn't think we would ever sink to that, but I suppose it will be a good idea in the end'.[12] A month later, the level of Angus & Robertson's commitment to the Publishers Association would be put to the test.

An important stage in the history of the London office was the moment Hector MacQuarrie signed the English Net Book Agreement in early December 1953 on behalf of the firm, but at the last moment he recoiled from placing his signature on the British Publishers' Traditional Market Agreement. It is clear he experienced a crisis of conscience at this decisive point; his loyalties to Angus & Robertson clashed with his public and personal views on the agreement. MacQuarrie sought last minute advice from Ferguson, underscoring how much Angus & Robertson repudiated the agreement and how often he personally had been the mouthpiece of the firm in loathing it.[13] In his impression, the agreement asked MacQuarrie and the Australian publisher 'to bite the dust',[14] and MacQuarrie naively wondered whether the Publishers Association might make an exception for this small colonial firm with large ambitions in London.

Not being an unreasonable individual nor immune from criticisms by the Publishers Association that he had 'gone Australian',[15] Sanders didn't quite understand MacQuarrie's objection, since in his view he was merely inviting Angus & Robertson to 'sign what all other members sign'[16] and that ultimately it would protect the company. Sanders added that when he had discussed the possibility of Angus & Robertson joining the association, he clearly understood from Ferguson that there would be no hesitation in signing the document despite any previously expressed opinions about the British Publishers' Traditional Market Agreement. To refuse compliance now would embarrass Sanders before the Publishers Association. MacQuarrie, covering his own ambivalence through a display of sensitivity towards the secretary's exposed situation, asked Ferguson to 'tell me what to do', conceding that

> It might have been best just to sign the thing and thus to save you a moment's bother; but I opened the battle years and years ago with some shrewd salvoes and I think it is wisest to check with you now before signing. On the whole, my advice, if it is worth anything, is to suggest that I sign the damn thing and forget it.[17]

Ferguson agreed it was ironic that Angus & Robertson should be endorsing an agreement that had been strenuously objected to by Australian publishers over the years but that the appropriate action nevertheless was 'to sign it and then forget it'.[18] Ferguson also confirmed Sanders' two points – six months earlier he had indeed privately pledged the company's future acceptance of the British Publishers' Traditional Market Agreement when the time came, and such action would in fact protect the London office 'to some extent'.[19]

Thus, with details clarified and documents subsequently authorised, Angus & Robertson entered 1954 as full members of the British Publishers Association. Ferguson's long time 'good friend',[20] British publisher Walter Harrap, welcomed the company with 'congratulations, brother'[21] and Angus & Robertson's first letter from the organisation was a members' circular about another English firm being refused the British rights on a specific book.. In short, the London office should not accept *The Florentine* published by Prentice-Hall of New York 'except on condition that they obtain all the territories required under the British Publishers' Traditional Market Agreement'.[22]

With post-Federation Australia listed on the agreement as a territory under British dominion, in practice, the British Publishers' Traditional Market Agreement restricted Australian publishers' commercial power to negotiate rights for titles produced by American publishers. This was because British publishers, operating within the much larger and therefore more lucrative English market, refused titles from the United States if American publishers sold (or desired to sell) Australian rights separately. This action applied to all 71 territories listed in an agreement that included Barbados, Burma, Egypt, Fiji, Hong Kong, Iraq, Jordon, Kenya, Northern Rhodesia, Pakistan, Sudan, and Uganda.[23]

Many of these territories were quite valuable markets in British book export turnover. For example, in 1956 New Zealand was worth £1,360,830 in export sales, India £1,639,750, South Africa £2,850,920 and Asia £1,641,770.[24] While letters such as the members' circular of January 1954 were intended to preserve rather than challenge this structure of the British book trade and therefore reinforce perceptions of British publishers as a 'cartel' regarding 'Australia merely as a market for themselves',[25] it is probable Ferguson was not too troubled by what was implied in the notices and resolutions Angus & Robertson was now receiving from the Publishers Association. In November 1953, a month before MacQuarrie signed the agreement, Angus & Robertson was very explicit in its intentions: 'We shall be after British Empire rights in future', wrote Ferguson, 'and London is the logical place from which to make such requests'.[26]

MacQuarrie remained convinced that a 'silly agreement' like that pertaining to the British Publishers' Traditional Market Agreement 'should have no weight' and that it was a 'fatuous useless kind of document'.[27] But such statements overlooked the negative attention that MacQuarrie had previously given the agreement and did not truthfully acknowledge the change in operational matters brought about by Angus & Robertson signing the agreement. The London office was now accorded a status similar to its competitors in the United Kingdom. Through its membership in the Publishers Association, Angus & Robertson was formally recognised by the local book trade as a peer, as a British publisher, and while the Sydney office would 'take things on their own merits', with regards to the British Publishers Association, the London office 'might agree' with its resolutions and notices for the sake of 'Operation London'.[28]

In this sense, analogous to the development of the British book export market as described by John Attenborough, phase three of establishing an overseas branch – in which the agent becomes a part of the circuits of production and a member of the cultural landscape that embodies and characterises the overseas publishing industry – was nearly complete.[29] Although MacQuarrie's signature on the British Empire Market Agreement has since cast uncertainty about Angus & Robertson's 'credentials as a truly indigenous operation',[30] this act can be seen in retrospect as the moment in which an Australian publisher confronted the problem of 'strong competition from UK publishers'[31] in its fullest sense by, to borrow the metaphor of 'Operation London', 'getting in behind'.[32] Unlike other Australian firms, Angus & Robertson could 'now bid for American books on a British Empire basis'.[33]

'Operation London'

The phrase 'Operation London' had been familiar to Ferguson and MacQuarrie ever since the idea was originally discussed as they 'walked about … Russell Square'[34] in the late 1940s, but by August 1953 it would begin to materialise into a practical form.

Shorthanded as 'O.L.' in internal correspondence, 'Operation London' refers to the company's core project to publish first edition books exclusively in Britain. With the chief object of the London office being 'to assist in the growing prosperity of the firm'[35] back in Sydney, in the early 1950s Ferguson's and MacQuarrie's concept was configured to address three main objectives: (a) to combat prejudice against Australian manufactured products by publishing Angus & Robertson books in English editions (fighting bias due in part to Australian licensing restrictions impacting British trade and turning public sentiment against Australian imports and in part due to a record of 'mixed production' in Australian manufactured books); (b) to generate enough turnover to underwrite the expense (and risk) of selling those Australian books that were not commercially profitable in the United Kingdom; and (c) to expand the market for Angus & Robertson's books, a market which by offering a wider distribution to the works of Australian authors would in turn attract more writers to the company. Above all, after five decades of business in Australia as publishers and two decades more as booksellers, Angus & Robertson was confident that the London office could begin producing titles in the United Kingdom, offering books of a class which might conceivably be published by British firms like Hamish Hamilton or Michael Joseph.[36]

Such tenacity foreshadowed a need to secure manuscripts that had a high probability of large sales as finished books; that is, likely bestsellers or 'books of a universal appeal'.[37] As MacQuarrie noted during his courtship of a potential English contributor to 'Operation London', Angus & Robertson proposed to publish

> in London the kind of books the better publishers would publish here [in Britain]. We think of eight such books. They have to be of a kind which booksellers will take in quantities; but their authorship, provided they are of that kind, is a matter of indifference

> to us, although we would naturally prefer our own countrymen. These eight books, we expect, will carry the overhead of those books on our list which, at the moment, are not welcome to booksellers here because of insular prejudices [to books published 'abroad']. They must be chosen with care. Their final choice is made in Sydney; but we in London naturally offer powerful advice.[38]

MacQuarrie did not think he was 'too hot at the business of picking saleable books'[39] (a view cynically shared by some of his colleagues),[40] but for any title produced by the London office Angus & Robertson would automatically enjoy exclusive rights and distribution for Australasia as well as the British Empire. With home and export markets indivisible, this allowed MacQuarrie and Ferguson to 'start without any gripping fears of disaster'.[41] In fact, both men anticipated success and expected to be 'taken very seriously by the publishing boys'[42] in London but not before some important upgrades.

The reorganisation of the London office, as the next step in reviving its fortunes, was a conspicuous feature of 1953 and 1954 and wrought changes both structurally and editorially.[43] Following Ferguson's visit to the United Kingdom, which occurred 'in an atmosphere of crisis and difficulty' after the fire,[44] a new staff member, 'a young Englishman [Barry Rowland] with considerable publishing experience',[45] was contracted to work on production in addition to sales, and a new building at 105 Great Russell Street in Bloomsbury was purchased for £18,000. Angus & Robertson, allowing MacQuarrie to keep his flat, retained 48 Bloomsbury.[46]

Under repair over several months and refitted at a cost of £3,000, with the addition of a lift plus a boiler to heat the first two floors, the renovated building in Bloomsbury was valued at around £25,000.[47] Acquiring these new premises in London might have been dispassionately disclosed in the 1954 *Report of the Directors* as extending the company's activities 'with a view of increasing sales of our publications abroad',[48] but, more importantly, this new building provided Angus & Robertson's overseas publishing operations with what Ferguson privately described as 'a home in London worthy of the dignity of the firm'.[49] Together, these changes can be seen in the broader context of the gradual professionalisation of the London office, which led to a clearer physical separation in its two arms of exporting and publishing.

New business practices were developed in consultation with Paul Tracy and Barry Rowland. In particular, Rowland travelled to the Sydney office to familiarise himself with Angus & Robertson's techniques and methods of bookselling and to learn 'something about the kinds of books we can and cannot sell'.[50] The resultant *London Publishing Procedure*[51] was considered an 'impressive document … subject to the application of common-sense in unforseen situations at both ends'.[52] Barry Rowland's 'burning desire not to fling money away with both hands'[53] put him immediately on good terms with Hector MacQuarrie, who often struggled with – and was even frightened by – the task of spending the firm's capital. Rowland was a sharp contrast to Vera Wellings who was not, ultimately, to remain an employee of the London office. Quite apart from having 'nothing to do' anymore except interview advertising professionals, Angus & Robertson did not have a place for Wellings in 'Operation London',[54] and MacQuarrie insisted the firm could no longer sustain a salary of '£12 a week for which … there [was] no return'.[55]

While it is difficult to judge to what extent this view was a continuation of an older argument, MacQuarrie had never supported increasing Wellings' salary from its original £9/5/0 [*sic*] per week. Nearly ten months after Wellings began work in January 1952, MacQuarrie was very sorry to deny her request for financial help, explaining that 'until this new crusade to distribute our books in the United Kingdom shows clearer signs of at least paying its way, your salary should not be increased'.[56] As manager, MacQuarrie expressed concern about its political effects and the potential to 'create demands from the rest of the staff'[57] should he follow through. Yet while Ferguson agreed with MacQuarrie's assessment that the results did not yet justify a wage increase and that the London manager might in fact get into 'difficulties'[58] with other staff members, Ferguson wrote to Wellings and approved her request.[59]

The action was more than just an economic penalty; MacQuarrie was displeased about the way Wellings was notified:

> It is good business practice always to accept decisions of Boards and to support them whatever you may think of them. Thus I have told Mr Joyner to pay Mrs Wellings the extra £1 per week. As an old maestro, I dare, humbly, to suggest that if you had replied to the lady's memo direct to me, and permitted me to smooth things out nicely, there would have been a lighter blow to what little authority I have.[60]

The two veterans of Angus & Robertson would quickly regain their affable footing but neither, it seemed, would completely put aside the incident. In the emerging project of 'Operation London', Ferguson reassured MacQuarrie that while the new staff member Barry Rowland was in Sydney, 'you can be absolutely certain that he will be made to realise all along that you are in charge there and I shall do all possible, personally, to build you up with him'.[61] Nevertheless, there would be times when Rowland would judge this situation as 'not expedient'.[62]

Perhaps Ferguson was aware that his support of the current London manager was not without its critics. David Moore, who assisted as a sub-editor[63] in the London office during the late 1950s after working on the company's *Australian Encyclopaedia* in Sydney,[64] questioned MacQuarrie's contribution to 'Operation London', claiming during an interview for Neil James' in depth study of Angus & Robertson that 'no one could ever understand why George Ferguson had appointed' MacQuarrie and that Rowland 'really ran the show' while 'Hector was only goosing around'.[65] But Moore's recollection differed from Ferguson's correspondence which repeatedly affirmed that MacQuarrie's judgement remained a highly valued component of the London office despite the challenges and pressures which had subsisted over the years:

> Although we are so many miles apart geographically I don't think we are ever very far apart in spirit and … you will get nothing but the fullest support from me at this end. That has been so all along, even through the bad days, and will remain.[66]

With Angus & Robertson professing 'complete confidence'[67] in the London office's management, MacQuarrie terminated Wellings' appointment in mid-September 1953 and replaced her with Sam Ure Smith[68] (who a year later relinquished the position to Desmond Briggs, also recommended by the Publishers Association).[69] Wellings was not surprised as she had already concluded 'there would be no room for [her] in the new regime'.[70] In the months preceding her departure, MacQuarrie did not permit Wellings to be identified as sales manager on official documents, preferring instead, for example, to use Barry Rowland's name on an application for membership to the British Booksellers Association. Wellings felt strongly she should have been named as such and interpreted the shift in emphasis as indicative of her future prospects with the company. As with Bernard Robinson, the Sydney office expressed earnest appreciation of Wellings' hard work, enthusiasm and perseverance in the early 'torrid'[71] days of the London office while not quite agreeing with her opinion that the 'sales of A. & R. books *are* established'[72] in the United Kingdom. Ferguson took a more cautious view that Wellings' 'battling … [would] bear fruit eventually',[73] even though MacQuarrie tentatively thought the office was 'now running at a profit'.[74]

In the final analysis, while she was a key figure in Angus & Robertson's London sales, Wellings' temperament was considered incompatible with 'Operation London', and the end of her employment signalled a revitalised focus on publishing.[75]

Chapter 8

THE SHIRALEE IN THE NORTH

In the business to create sales large enough to justify the capital costs involved in sustaining the production, sale and distribution of wholly Australian books (or what MacQuarrie described as 'books with a limited appeal'),[1] the London office sought to publish what the market demanded. That is, books not 'of the normal procession which ends with dignity in the offices of various well-established publishers' but rather 'something fresh, new … original and lively'.[2]

No doubt as a consequence of their dedication, the first two titles published (and manufactured in Britain) under the auspices of 'Operation London' were texts of American origin: *Esquire Etiquette: A Guide to Business, Sports and Social Conduct* by the editors of *Esquire Magazine* was a title first published in 1953 by Lippincott, based in Philadelphia, as was the 1950 title by Sheila MacKay Russell, *A Lamp is Heavy*.

These books were of the kind that once would likely have been refused importation into Australia direct from the United States during Australia's ongoing licensing and dollar conservation situation. They were also books in which copyright for the Australian market would conventionally have been purchased by British publishers through 'their infamous pact about American rights'.[3] It is perhaps little coincidence then that Heinemann, after losing the British Empire and Australasian rights for *Esquire Etiquette* to the London office during November 1953, in some part settled an old score. Certainly Ferguson's heart didn't bleed for his counterpart in Heinemann, Arthur Baker, who was less than satisfied with the outcome (and no doubt moderately anxious that Angus & Robertson's new premises were 'slap up against Heinemann's').[4] In his defence of the London office, Ferguson pointed to the 'forces of exclusion and dominance'[5] which had pushed Angus & Robertson to Britain in the first place:

> British publishers … knew that one of two things would have to happen to A. & R. Either we would cease to show interest in American books or we would be forced into publishing in London. Well, the latter happened and if they lose a few books to us they surely cannot blame us.[6]

MacQuarrie agreed 12 months later that Arthur Baker 'seemed to have the delightful idea that when a London publisher took a book from under the nose of an Australian publisher any kind of peevishness was absurd; but that when an Australian publisher succeeded in the same perfectly justified effort, the Australian was not really playing the game. I begged to differ'.[7]

Indeed, Angus & Robertson was 'delighted' to have acquired *A Lamp is Heavy* and *Esquire Etiquette*, which reinforced the confidence of the London office in its ability to negotiate rights to American titles for an Australian publisher.[8] Lippincott, however, contracted 'rather steep' terms on the basis that it had been 'a fight' to get these titles for the London office 'in view of other interests'.[9] In return for the rights to publish these books, Angus & Robertson made an advance of £500 for *Esquire Etiquette*, with £300 sterling of this figure an advance on the straight 10 per cent royalty for Australasian sales and £200 an advance on a rising scale of royalties for sales in all other territories. With this second condition, the royalty would be set at 10 per cent for the first 2,000 copies sold, then 12.5 per cent up to 5,000 copies and 15 per cent thereafter. *A Lamp is Heavy* carried similar conditions but with a smaller advance of £100 and 10 per cent on all sales in the United Kingdom until copies sold exceeded 3,000 whereby royalties were then paid at 12.5 per cent. Sheila MacKay Russell, the American author, would net 'somewhere around seven [US] cents a copy'.[10]

The first of these two books, *A Lamp is Heavy*, told the story of a young woman who trained to be an American nurse before the Second World War. As MacQuarrie had noted, the subject of nursing remained highly topical in Britain through addresses made by the British Broadcasting Corporation (BBC).[11] The London office opened its publishing arm with *A Lamp is Heavy* during September 1954 in an edition of 6,000, with the Sydney office taking at first 3,000 copies,[12] followed by another 2,000 in subsequent reprints.[13] (In fact, the Sydney office would rarely have the title in stock, since every shipment received from London was over-subscribed before it even arrived in Australia.)[14]

The book was an immediate success and continued to 'shine pretty fiercely',[15] lifting overall sales for September to £8,258 and pegging total turnover from April to September (excluding the Australia House Bookshop) at £21,500.[16] Over the next few weeks, the London office's new publishing department issued another three books (and the figures that follow, drawn from correspondence and profit and loss statements, differ from what has been previously recorded).[17] By November 1954, *A Lamp is Heavy* had achieved 19,500 sales. The other Lippincott title, *Esquire Etiquette*, published on 28 October, had sold 10,000 copies and was in the process of being reprinted. An Australian work, *White Coolies: A Graphic Record of Survival in World War Two* by Betty Jeffrey, opened in an edition of 3,000 originally bought from Sydney's stock of 8,000[18] and sold out in two days (including a latter London reprint of another 3,000 copies); furthermore, the Panther Books paperback edition sold 150,000 copies by October 1958 – netting the London office £1,400 in royalties split 50/50 with the author[19] – and another 150,000 paperback copies by March 1960, which sold at the rate of 8,000 a month.[20] *Lease of Life: A Novel* by popular English author Frank Baker, printed in an edition of 6,000, was down to its last five hundred.[21]

With MacQuarrie immensely cheered that overheads (often 25 per cent of the trade price)[22] could now be 'carried by those we mark out as London publishing jobs',[23] 'Operation London' for all intents and purposes had commenced and increased staff levels from 8 in February, to 17 in April,[24] and to 24 by November.[25] It was 'hopelessly crowded' in the new building at 105 Great Russell Street, and the continued prosperity of 'Operation London', as MacQuarrie knew, depended on choosing the right books:

> I expect we'll have some flops. Incidentally, no established author would consider us, and Literary Agents gave us the usual useless left-overs to consider. The books we have got, we've practically mined ourselves with no help from anyone beyond, of course, the great big help in Sydney …[26]

MacQuarrie had taken the first important steps in making 'Operation London' a reality, but they had not been without an initial 'smack on the nose'.[27] Originally commissioned to be the project's 'number one'[28] publication of the 'kind of popular stuff' Angus & Robertson wanted,[29] *The Queen in the Rain* by Jonquil[30] was reviewed by MacQuarrie (and later Rowland) to be a very poorly composed manuscript about Tonga's Queen Salote and was ultimately considered unworthy of publication. Despite a complete rewrite by MacQuarrie who commissioned the work in what he later termed 'juvenile enthusiasm'[31] and who sought to 'repair the mistake',[32] *The Queen in the Rain* never made it to press and the London office lost its then not-insignificant advance of £100 for the manuscript. The failure of *The Queen in the Rain* to materialise as a book left staff 'disappointed and discouraged';[33] they even for a time faced threats of legal action for breach of contract with the author.

Yet the remarkable progress of the four titles that followed *The Queen in the Rain* reveals how accurate Ferguson's and MacQuarrie's instincts had been with 'Operation London'. Books of a more universal appeal could tap a market in the United Kingdom which in turn might support the nobler, less commercial project of selling Australian books. Titles published under the auspices of 'Operation London' reached a vastly larger audience than any Australian book had ever achieved. The ongoing advancement of 'Operation London', however, depended on several related factors: the selection of works which passed MacQuarrie's 'tests of liveliness and sparkle and readability';[34] greater correspondence on all issues 'so that the 12,000 miles between [Sydney and London] is narrowed as much as possible';[35] adequate edition sizes to avoid the project 'being prejudiced in any way by being out of stock of good selling books' or, worse, where 'saleable books are on the ocean' and both offices are 'either out of them or embarrassed';[36] and the Sydney office taking good quantities of the project's publications.

On this fourth point, before a title was even printed in London, Angus & Robertson back in Australia would 'give … an order from three to fifteen thousand of a book',[37] prompting Ferguson to ask Rowland 'what [his] sales [were] apart from sales to [Angus & Robertson]'.[38] If indeed the Sydney office accounted for over 50 per cent (£4,400) of sales with regards to September's impressive show of turnover (£8,258),[39] Ferguson was less convinced that the London office was in fact demonstrating a profit even as 'Operation London' seemed to be 'growing at a startling speed':[40]

> Your sales to us inflate the total sales to what look like very nice figures, but of course in that particular portion you make practically nothing at all … What we ought to be aiming at is to reach as soon as possible say £50,000 of general sales quite apart from the *Simon Blacks* or *Treasuries of Science* etc, that you simply pay the printer and then charge to us, but on which you make almost no profit.[41]

Despite the concerns expressed over the London office's actual financial standing, Ferguson knew the overseas branch 'could hardly exist'[42] without the Sydney office, revealing that it was almost impossible to 'explain to anybody the delicate sort of balance which exist[ed] between A. & R. London and Sydney'.[43]

The rights to US books seem important in this regard. As discussed, American rights were secured in London which enabled sale in Australia and elsewhere. Such a setup made the London office the feeder for the Sydney office for licences secured in the United Kingdom. In turn the London office needed orders from Australia if only sometimes to 'boast of numbers' to its British peers.[44] Three months earlier, the Sydney office had assured MacQuarrie that the project was 'vitally important and must have the utmost support even at considerable cost to ourselves';[45] they were sustained by a similar guarantee in 1956 that the Sydney office 'should be able to give the works to all the "Operation London" books'.[46] Although *A Lamp is Heavy*, *Esquire Etiquette*, *White Coolies* and *Lease of Life* could command a large market, the Sydney office continued to play a crucial role in bolstering the project's sales, and Rowland recognised that it was ultimately 'Australian capital that [was] giving [them] [in London] our livelihood'.[47] The proportion of Sydney sales to market sales can be observed in the two stacked area graphs C and D in the Figures and Tables which represent the London office publishing income in £ sterling (see Chapter 12 for a closer analysis of the London office's sales to Sydney).

The success of the London office was in the end defined by the number of books it could sell in the United Kingdom, and Ferguson suggested that if 'Operation London' was going to pay its own way it needed at least six books which made over ten thousand in sales each.[48] MacQuarrie, therefore, agreed in principle that 'the business value of "Operation London" only exists in its independence, making money itself without dependence on the Home Firm'.[49] MacQuarrie acknowledged more broadly, without a sense of irony, that 'any London publisher is bound to depend to a considerable extent on sales in Australasia'.[50] But where MacQuarrie was ready to cut the lists of F. W. Cheshire and S. Ure Smith adrift from the London office, with the view that they were 'barnacles on our hull, … affect[ing] our speed',[51] Rowland remained in favour of trying to sell as many Australian books as possible, which included the 'extremely dully titles'[52] from the lists of other Australian publishers. Rowland believed, as Ferguson did a few years earlier, that it would be better for the company in the long term.

While they were obvious competitors in the retail field, both F. W. Cheshire and S. Ure Smith were 'great advocates' of Angus & Robertson books and – more importantly at least for the Sydney office – 'very good customers of Halstead Press'.[53] Moreover, Rowland ventured to say that 'if you take all the Australian books away from our list we should look very naked'.[54] According to a statistical review of sales conducted by Rowland, Australian books in general – most selling in quantities ranging from 50 to 150 per month – covered a wide variety of subjects and still provided a substantial percentage of the London office's net profits.

This was a result that pleased the Sydney office immensely. On the one hand, it proved Ferguson and MacQuarrie's theory 'that if we bait the hook with some good general books such as *A Lamp is Heavy* we can also get the fish to swallow a lot of the Australian stuff'.[55] On the other hand, as MacQuarrie would later report to Ferguson after discussing future literary candidates for the project in 1956, the sale of 'purely Australian books' at a profit in the United Kingdom was contingent on having '"Operation London" books … carry the overhead'.[56] Popular success and Australian literary merit, it would seem, rarely coincided. This is not to suggest, however, that 'Operation London' would only ever produce general books nor to 'assume that literary merit is … commercially unprofitable'.[57]

An Australian Novel in London

By 1955, the London office had fully recovered from the 1952–3 fire, an accident which in retrospect was considered a 'blessing'for Angus & Robertson's efforts in the United Kingdom.[58] Indeed, MacQuarrie was rather taken with the idea that Angus & Robertson was now a successful London publisher.

With the progress of the first four books created from 'Operation London', 1954 became 'the most successful [year] in publishing that the firm has ever had',[59] and, inevitably, this led to the project becoming 'always concerned' about bestsellers.[60] With only Hector MacQuarrie, Barry Rowland, Mrs L. Wood, and Arthur Brooker 'to keep ["Operation London"] from spilling over and getting out of control',[61] the question was what to publish next in 1955. MacQuarrie knew the success of *A Lamp is Heavy* was largely a consequence of the book being 'amusing to read'[62] and also eminently topical regarding nurses' training, even as Ferguson emphasised the 'highly necessary and highly expert "reconstruction work"'[63] that MacQuarrie brought to bear on each 'Operation London' candidate. A book's performance on the market could not be considered separate from the initial 'ghost' treatment that MacQuarrie applied to a raw manuscript's 'style and esprit'.[64] Ferguson reminded MacQuarrie that 'you are immensely essential to 'Operation London' … [A] book with a sale of 20,000 or so has been made out of that merely by that same treatment. In its original form I don't suppose between us we would have sold 4,000'.[65]

Yet the undercurrent of dependency on Australian orders amplified the pressure for MacQuarrie and Rowland to select titles that were suitable for sale in two very different markets. After all, Angus & Robertson had 'an expensive organisation [in London] that has to be paid for just the same'.[66] While Ferguson was reluctant to interfere with the decisions made by the London office and expected MacQuarrie to act as he thought right 'without fear or favour'' and whose 'judgements will always be backed',[67] the Sydney office did not need to labour the point that 'a book which excites you may leave us cold'.[68]

Although 'the steady seller is always more attractive than the risky investment',[69] Angus & Robertson's general conservatism, which seemed like a form of inertia during the immediate post-war period, was lessened somewhat in the London office by its recent achievements. Feeling adept at identifying the right kind of saleable title, MacQuarrie speculated that *The Shiralee* by Australian novelist D'arcy Niland – a work of fiction portraying an Australian swagman named Macauley 'who tramps through the back towns of New South Wales accompanied by his daughter Buster'[70] – could be another 'high spot'[71] for 'Operation London'.

Brought to MacQuarrie's attention by Niland's British literary agent Spencer Curtis Brown, *The Shiralee* was by that time in development under the guidance of

Angus & Robertson's Sydney editor Beatrice Davis who, with the author's co-operation, was in the process of pruning 'a good deal of the tough stuff out without in any way damaging the book'.[72] Ferguson anticipated this 'damn good novel'[73] doing well in Australia but did not share MacQuarrie's view that it would be a strong seller in the United Kingdom. Ferguson thought it 'might be too Australian to be any good in England'[74] and did not consider D'arcy Niland an 'Operation London' author any more than he might consider E. V. Timms, Ion L. Idriess or Frank Clune. Ferguson mused that 'if they were presented to you by some literary agent in London you would quite properly reject [them]'.[75] Nevertheless, the London office managed to sell quantities of Sydney editions of these Australian authors to the library trade in Britain, ranging from hundreds to two thousand annually.

Ferguson was convinced the book would fail in Britain, but the London manager saw a real possibility in it; he even sought to manage the book's subsidiary (film) rights.[76] MacQuarrie could not get 'un-excited' about *The Shiralee* and conjectured that 'a not-good book with a local appeal might be useless here; but a book written with talent and craftsmanship, concerned only with Pymble Lane [a reference to Ferguson's home address], will sell here as easily as it will in Pymble'.[77] The difference for MacQuarrie was that he judged *The Shiralee* not to be an Australian book per se but rather 'a great book about Australia by an Australian'.[78]

MacQuarrie drew attention to the book's 'universal character'.[79] He eventually admitted that 'no book could be more Australian [than *The Shiralee*] in the finest, truest sense',[80] but for 'Operation London' the geography or nationality of a book was less important to MacQuarrie than its universal appeal. It was an argument which proved attractive to Ferguson, and he conceded that if MacQuarrie and Rowland were to have a chance of building up sales for *The Shiralee* in London then the book would need to be manufactured in England first with the Sydney office obtaining its initial supply from the London print run. If domestic sales showed promising results, reprints of *The Shiralee* would occur thereafter in Sydney via offset printing.[81] Paul Tracey was instructed to send the manuscript to MacQuarrie in late November 1954,[82] and the Australian novel was published through 'Operation London' on 25 July 1955.[83] With pre-orders in the United Kingdom approaching 8,000 and the Sydney office taking 7,500 copies,[84] *The Shiralee* put Australia at its feet in the only way that it knew how:[85] it opened in London with an edition of 37,500 copies to reviews appearing in the *Observer*, the *Sunday Times* and the *Daily Mail*,[86] which featured it as a 'book of the month'.[87]

The Shiralee was printed by the Greycaine Book Manufacturing Company of Watford (also owned by the English book publisher Hutchinson & Company),[88] and over the six weeks they received another 3,000 orders for the novel. These orders were exclusive of Book Society sales. By August 1955, Rowland reported to Ferguson that the London office had 'the best part of 10,000 copies [remaining] to sell',[89] and indeed the novel went from strength to strength owing to what Rowland termed 'the London attack'.[90] In March 1957 *The Shiralee* was issued as a Popular Book Club edition with an estimated circulation of 50,000 readers. This edition was contracted through Odhams Press in London, which paid Angus & Robertson an advance of £625 calculated on a royalty of three pence for each copy that sold at two shillings eleven pence.[91] On 11 July 1957, a film adaption was released by Ealing Studios which, after lengthy negotiations with Hector MacQuarrie, paid the London office an advance of £1,250[92] 'on account of 1% of producers' gross receipts up to £175,000 and 2% thereafter'.[93] (Producers' gross receipts were a sum equivalent to 75 per cent of all profits received by the distributors of the film.)

The London office also handled the film and serial rights in *The Shiralee* on a 10 per cent commission basis.[94] However, in her biographical study of Beatrice Davis, Jacqueline Kent reports that the commission was instead 20 per cent and that the film rights deal arranged by MacQuarrie was 'disastrous'[95] for Niland, forcing the Australian writer to place his follow-up work *The Big Smoke* with Stanley Horwitz. (This is incorrect: *The Big Smoke* was published by the London office under the Angus & Robertson imprint during 1959 in an edition of 15,000 copies,[96] and confirms that Niland stayed with the overseas branch until at least 1962 when he made a break with the London office following its reorganisation by Walter Burns.[97]) Later in 1958, a Pan paperback edition was also arranged, with a potential circulation of 400,000, paying a royalty of nearly two pence per copy.[98] Though reportedly not much liked in Australia by its booksellers and shunned in Britain by Australians (except, that is, Western Australians),[99] domestic sales for *The Shiralee* were boosted by its selection as a Book Society Choice,[100] and the Sydney office printed its own small edition of 3,000 copies during October 1955 to tide them over while stock was in transit from London.[101]

Overall, Australian orders of the novel reached nearly 10,000, and in the United Kingdom *The Shiralee* finished 1955 as a bestseller of approximately 60,000 copies, irrespective of Panther Books, Readers' Digest and book club editions.[102] Both Rowland and Ferguson later recalled – during their defence of London publishing's relevance to Australian books – that if it were not for the London office and 'if the book had been published as just another Australian novel, without it having been initially promoted from [London], it may have been missed by reviewers, the Book Society, etc'.[103] As a paperback issued by Panther Books, it had returned £808 in royalties.[104]

It is not surprising therefore that the Sydney office was 'absolutely delighted' with the progress of the London office.[105] There may still have been 'various storms to go through'[106] (which ultimately led to the closure of the publishing department – the subject of the next chapter), but for the moment the success of *The Shiralee* marked a significant achievement in Hector MacQuarrie's foundational work – in combination with Barry Rowland and George Ferguson – to 'build up a suitable selling organisation to get rid of' Australian books overseas.[107]

'Operation London' Titles, 1955–1956

In his thesis 'Spheres of Influence: Angus and Robertson and Australian Literature From the Thirties to the Sixties', Neil James credits five books as part of 'Operation London' in 1954 by including *The Royal Visit to New Zealand*, which is a title that James records from oral interviews as fronting the display window when Angus & Robertson's new premises at Great Russell Street opened for business on 29 April 1954.[108] It is true that this book was printed in the United Kingdom and was an edition of the original title produced by A. W. Reed in Wellington. As with Angus & Robertson's own Sydney publication of

The Royal Visit to Australia of Her Majesty Queen Elizabeth II and His Royal Highness the Duke of Edinburgh, 1954, the copies of *The Royal Visit to New Zealand* made for sale by the London office were manufactured in Britain, arising out of sheets sent from Australia. After making subtle changes to captioning throughout the text[109] – edits that distinguished the London edition of *The Royal Visit to Australia* as distinct from the Sydney version – Barry Rowland ordered 15,000 copies of *The Royal Visit to Australia* and, following its publication in London on 2 June 1954,[110] dispatched 5,000 units to the Sydney office to meet the shortages in Australian stock.[111] Comparatively, Rowland ordered a print run of 4,000 copies[112] of *The Royal Visit to New Zealand*, and it was published in London on 10 May 1954.[113] Although in retrospect these titles would possibly qualify for inclusion in any discussion of 'Operation London', they are excerpted here from 1954 because they were produced several months prior to the official launch of 'Operation London' in September 1954. Moreover, while delighted with their distribution in London, which in no manner matched the 75,000 copies expected to be sold in Australia,[114] MacQuarrie did 'not look on the sale of these Royal books as symptomatic of success', nor were they representative 'of the real essence of Operation London'.[115] MacQuarrie and Rowland were still developing this project, and his comment is the only time when 'Operation London' was discussed in connection with the two books on the royal visits in New Zealand and Australia.

From a modest start with four titles in the 1954 (*A Lamp is Heavy*, *Esquire Etiquette*, *White Coolies* and *Lease of Life*), in addition to taking Sydney editions of Angus & Robertson books for sale in the United Kingdom and the success of *The Shiralee*, 'Operation London' produced another 12 books in 1955 and a further 12 books in 1956. The titles that follow have been isolated from a correspondence record of over twelve hundred letters penned during this period between Hector MacQuarrie, Barry Rowland and George Ferguson. It should be noted that in a few cases some titles do not appear in the catalogues for either the British Library or the National Library of Australia as publications of Angus & Robertson. In cases where they do appear, a couple of titles are credited as being published in Australia rather than in the United Kingdom. Both of these issues, however, are contradicted by the documentary evidence of the period which chronicles Angus & Robertson's Sydney office ordering large quantities of editions manufactured in London (often printed by Jarrolds, Hazel Watson & Vinney, Wyman & Sons, Greycaine, Billing or Purnell & Sons) for sale in Australia.

With this caveat in mind, during 1955 'Operation London' published the following:

Village Royal by P. Hopkins

The Bishop with 150 Wives: Fifty Years as a Missionary by F. X. Gsell, translated from French by MacQuarrie

How to Become a Good Dancer by Arthur Murray, an American copyright owned by Simon & Schuster that the Sydney office took in a quantity of 4,000 from London[116]

No Citation by J. Allan

Immortal Rock: The Saga of the Kensington Stone by L. G. Salverson

Away All Boats by Kenneth Dodson, which had three printings in London amounting to 31,250 copies[117] – the Sydney office easily disposed of 17,500 copies[118]

Lamp on the Snow by Mary E. Hope, which was heavily rewritten by MacQuarrie[119]
The Big Squeeze by Mark Corrigan aka Norman Lee, in a first edition of 5,000[120] even though Ferguson advised MacQuarrie to 'avoid … this tough type of detective fiction'[121]
Behind Bamboo: An Inside Story of the Japanese Prison Camps by Rohan Rivett
Bet It's a Boy by Betty Blunt
Islands of Men by Colin Simpson
Adam in Plumes by Colin Simpson

The following year, 1956, 'Operation London' published the following:

Adam in Ochre by Colin Simpson
How to Win Your Husband by N. D. Datta
Talk of the Devil by Frank Baker
The Occupying Power by G. Griffin, in which the Sydney office took 5,000 copies[122]
The Heritage of Scotland: A Collection of Forty Colour Photographs by J. Kerr
They Shall Pass Not Unseen by Ivan Southall
No Moon Tonight by D. E. Charlwood, a title originally from literary agent A. M. Heath about the air force
From the Valley I Came by Wil Jon Edwards
A Train to Catch by Anthony Rushworth
Big Boys Don't Cry by Mark Corrigan aka Norman Lee
The Great Temptation by Hans Kades, originally a German title translated into English by an American publisher and then 'de-Americanised' by MacQuarrie; after this it looked 'like a 30,000 book at least' between the Sydney and London offices[123]
Sydney for Sin by Mark Corrigan aka Norman Lee, which had grossed £176 by 1960 after it was issued in paperback by Panther Books[124]
My Crowded Solitude by J. McLaren

Chapter 9

A COMMERCIAL AND CULTURAL RELATIONSHIP

As discussed in previous chapters, there was a two-fold rationale for Angus & Robertson to setup a London office. One goal was to secure British and American titles; the other was to sell Australian books in the United Kingdom. Bearing in mind that London was the centre of a massive English-language book trade that included Australia, Ferguson was concerned that authors would leave Angus & Robertson unless it offered a 'reasonable chance of distribution in the big overseas English-speaking markets'.[1] When new Angus & Robertson managing director Walter Burns announced in 1960 that 'publishing in London was finished',[2] not surprisingly this galvanised opposition to his 'Napoleonic' management and merchandising principles (discussed further in the next chapter).[3] Just a year earlier, Angus & Robertson's Sydney office had resigned from the Australian Booksellers Association over an attempted resolution that 'no bookseller who was also a publisher could hold any executive office in the A.B.A.'[4] Given that Angus & Robertson doubled as publishers and booksellers and had staff on the committee, Ferguson dismissed the Australian Booksellers Association in the belief that it would lose most of its 'bargaining power' with British publishers following his company's resignation.[5] Yet a similar contraction of Angus & Robertson's own London office's bargaining power following Burns' announcement would once again bring into sharp relief the importance of the reciprocal relationship between the Sydney and London offices. It would suggest that one office could not exist without the other.

There was obviously a commercial dimension to the transfer of stock by either office in either direction. In the dispatch of books from London to Sydney, Angus & Robertson's interests overlapped with those of the British publishers. Even if the London office was an altogether independent publishing house, MacQuarrie surmised that like any other English publisher the economics of publishing would mean that 'Operation London' would still 'depend to a considerable extent on sales in Australasia',[6] because Australian books could not furnish sufficient income on their own in the United Kingdom. '[I]f you, for a single second', cautioned MacQuarrie, 'imagine books published in Australia by Angus & Robertson or any other Australian publishers can carry their overheads here [in Britain], except the odd book, you could not be more mistaken and you will founder'.[7] In MacQuarrie's view, it was 'wise practice' with books produced entirely in Britain for the London office to expect Sydney to take quantities and 'that cold water [should] not be thrown on our publication[s]'.[8] Like British publishers, even Barry Rowland considered Australia to be 'one of the greatest bookselling regions in the world'.[9] Yet, in the opposite direction, the dispatch of Australian books from Sydney to London meant that Angus & Robertson could exploit larger print runs for improved scales of economy.

While initially underestimating the measure of Angus & Robertson's need for a London outlet, Ferguson admitted to MacQuarrie 'you of course rather need our help more than we need yours, but at the same time your help to us has been increasingly valuable and is now really quite significant'.[10] John Attenborough had observed during his defence of the Net Book Agreement that 'a good list of titles is in itself a competitive advantage in the export market'.[11] MacQuarrie and Rowland did not overlook the fact that 'Sydney books', a category referring solely to publications by Angus & Robertson manufactured in Australia, had 'been of great value, acting in a sense like a more established publisher's back-list' even if the list had been 'designed for an Australian market' and were 'not readily taken by [British] booksellers'.[12] (Sydney books made just enough money to pay a few salaries in the London office.)[13]

As discussed in Chapters 6 and 7, the health of the export trade in Australian books had a bearing, be it major or minor, on the health of Angus & Robertson back in Australia during the 1950s, and it can be assumed in letters between Sydney and London that the company benefitted financially from the sale of 'Operation London' books. This benefit was especially apparent when the home office pushed through a period increasingly marked with economic hardship. 'If you weren't there [in Britain]', Ferguson claimed in 1956, a couple of years before the firm's financial troubles, 'we wouldn't have those books, and there would be that much less profit at this end'.[14] In July 1959 Ferguson confided in Rowland that the London office's publishing activities 'are worth more to us [in Sydney] than you may realise. You have got to the point where you are definitely affecting our printing quantities on most books for the better, with a consequent benefit to our costs and profits here'.[15] Six months later, at the peak of financial difficulty, Ferguson disclosed that the services the London office 'renders to us here are enormous'.[16] He added – an important point to carry over into the discussion of profit and loss in the next chapter – that the London office's 'full advantages by no means appear in the London balance sheet'.[17]

There was a cultural dimension as well to the relationship between Sydney and London that carried – what Stephen Alomes identifies more generally for Australian writers during the first half of the twentieth century – 'the weight of colonial deference to the imperial centre'.[18] Indeed, Ferguson admitted to Stanley Unwin, after Walter Burns forfeited his majority ownership of shares in Angus & Robertson at the end of 1960, that 'it is essential for us [in the Sydney office] to have a London branch, otherwise we cannot possibly expect to retain important authors'.[19] It seemed a London outlet was a necessary precondition for attracting Australian writers to an Australian publisher. Moreover, Ferguson envisaged himself as an 'Australian … conscious of commonwealth ties' and that these ties could be 'strengthened by a traffic in books that is not all one-way'.[20]

MacQuarrie, too, was a committed advocate of Australian publishing in Britain and often reinforced the achievement of winning fame abroad as a trademark of the Australian hero:[21] 'A really lively well-known and famous London publishing house established will be one of the greater things that have ever happened to Angus & Robertson'.[22] Such a statement betrays a sense of inferiority as well as an urge to transform the 'forces of exclusion and dominance'[23] which had compelled Angus & Robertson to initially to publish in London into a 'myth of authenticity' and achievement.[24] In bookselling terms, the exclusion of Australian publishers from the British book trade conferred on Angus & Robertson a sense of colonial alterity that could be overcome by some of Britain's 3,000 bookshops[25] taking quantities of Australian books. Although this required complicity with policies and practices that the company formerly rallied against, 'Operation London' represented a strategic relocation of Australian publishing interests whose success returned to the home office in Sydney what Attenborough referred to in the context of British publishing as a form of 'prestige and influence'.[26] In the process, it insisted on a domestic relationship between Sydney and London despite the great oceans that needed to be crossed and prolonged 'the influence of the culture of empire far beyond the period of colonial dependency'.[27]

The tension between 'a London style and an Australian persona',[28] or between Britain and the 'boys from the bush' who sought to publish there,[29] would eventually coalesce during the Frankfurt International Book Fair and find expression as identity politics during the first half of the 1960s (see Chapter 11). Towards the end of the 1950s, MacQuarrie urged Ferguson to 'keep it "English"'[30] while the London office remained committed to the 'constant search for saleable new books'.[31]

Stock Transfers and Total Sales

The scale of Angus & Robertson's support for 'Operation London' titles is perhaps most pronounced in the quantities of stock the Sydney office imported from the London office between 1955 and 1960. The titles of 'Operation London' books, in addition to the amount of stock transferred, for 1955 and 1956 have been reviewed in Chapters 7 and 8 with attention to surviving records; however, the number of copies that Angus & Robertson ordered from the United Kingdom is impossible to quantify for every single title in each year. Reference to the sales information compiled by John Ferguson and Ian Macarthur in 1960, reproduced as *Table 11* in Neil James' dissertation, is very useful as a guide but is also contradicted by information that appears in documents of the time.

For example, the 'Total UK Sales' column in *Table 11* records that 11 titles sold a combined total of 65,951 copies in 1955.[32] However, Hector MacQuarrie reported to George Ferguson on 11 October 1955 that total British-only sales for *The Shiralee* by D'Arcy Niland were nearing 60,000 copies. By this calculation, the other 10 books in *Table 11* for 1955 would have barely sold a fraction of the remaining 6,000 copies (that is, after *The Shiralee*'s 60,000 sold copies are deducted from the figure of 65,951); this amount was adequately dismissed by a stock transfer order which confirmed the London office had sold (in the same year of publication) at least 13,750 copies of *Away All Boats* (1955) by Kenneth Dodson.[33] *Table 11* and the archival record cannot both be correct. Yet this point is not to cast doubt about the integrity of James' work but rather to draw attention to the contradictions that emerge from the nature of the evidence which underlies any discussion about the London office's status. The application of either methodology, be it a form of oral history or documentary analysis, is not unproblematic. The conflicting results on the subject of 'Operation London' is indicative of a general uncertainty, even perhaps a deliberate ambiguity, within Angus & Robertson over the actual bookselling and publishing position of its London office. This ambiguity will be explored further in subsequent chapters.

'Operation London,' 1957–1958

Throughout the remainder of the 1950s 'Operation London' continued to build a catalogue of titles that the branch could call its own, strengthened by the recognition that British booksellers had 'now come to regard [A & R] with respect and as London publishers'.[34] While there were additional titles which started as sheets from other British publishers, such as *The Heritage of England in Colour* from Batsford Books,[35] according to a schedule by Paul Tracy detailing the 'Landed Costs of Angus & Robertson London Titles'[36] the London office produced at least fifteen books officially under the banner of 'Operation London' in 1957.

Some of the titles 'Operation London' published during 1957 required Hector MacQuarrie to either rewrite or translate the original manuscripts or to purchase reprint rights from other publishers. Barry Rowland, working alongside MacQuarrie, managed each title's production and sales, and their partnership led to the publication of the following:

Conflict, a British reprint of an historical fiction novel by E. V. Timms

A Fishy Tale by B. Cooke and N. Fisk, of which the Sydney office took 1,960 copies for Australia

Frogman V. C. by I. Fraser, which was rewritten by MacQuarrie,[37] selling 6,000 copies in London during January 1957 while another 7,500 were in transit to Australia[38]

Home is the Sailor by J. Whelan, with a quantity of 2,957 sent to Australia *Stranger to the Shore* by Kenneth Dodson

Glory Reflected: Sigmund Freud, Man and Father by Martin Freud, published on 15 November 1957 after a lengthy period in development as a personal project of Hector MacQuarrie's[39]

Life's Adventure by P. Gibbs, with the Sydney office taking 2,500 copies

The Story of the Walking House by Claire Simpson, a children's picture book of which 6,000 copies out of an unknown edition size were dispatched to Australia

San Demetrio by C. MacNeil, with 5,832 copies sent to Sydney

Brigalow by R. S. Porteous, the Sydney office taking 4,000 copies

Summer of the Seventeenth Doll by Raymond Lawler

Call Me When the Cross Turns Over by D'Arcy Niland, which the London office obtained through an advance of £250 against royalties[40] and sold paperback rights to Panther Books for £300;[41] the Sydney office printed its own edition in a quantity of 17,500, subscribing 10,000 copies before it was published[42]

The House of Crystal by Hans Kades, which had sold 2,811 copies by the end of January 1958[43] and 3,750 copies in Australia (though the Sydney office concluded in February 1959 that they were 'stuck' with another 3,000 units which Angus & Robertson did not expect to sell)[44]

Dumb as They Come and *The Cruel Lady* by Mark Corrigan, both published on 15 April 1957

In regard to the last two titles, Ferguson confessed he had 'a rooted objection to the author who does two books a year'.[45] Moreover, Angus & Robertson could not market thrillers very satisfactorily in Australia and would only take 1,500 copies of these and future thriller titles (if any). However, the company was willing to take on the risk of publishing an Australian play in the United Kingdom as a 'matter of prestige':[46] Lawler's *Summer of the Seventeenth Doll.*

The background to the play's first publication in London is an example of Angus & Robertson abandoning the economic principles of 'Operation London' in favour of cultural and strategic interests. Ferguson was cognisant of the fact that Lawler's play was 'stuffed full of Australian idiom, some of which will be probably unintelligible to a London audience'[47] and that there was no market for books on the theatre in Australia.[48] But, while very uncertain of the play's bookselling potential due to the nature of the text representing a 'completely new market'[49] for the London office, George Ferguson and Beatrice Davis were nevertheless undeterred in seeking separate publication for *Summer of the Seventeenth Doll* in Britain. While Lawler had provided verbal agreement for Angus & Robertson's production to coincide with the play's London performance, MacQuarrie would still need to consult with the English stage and film actor Sir Laurence Olivier for the British Empire rights.

Initially, Lawler had handed these territorial rights over to the Elizabethan Theatre which had passed them to Olivier, but Lawler was reluctant to sign a contract without the actor's consent.[50] Fortunately, negotiations were in the end straightforward. MacQuarrie and Rowland cabled their success[51] and were to produce an edition available for sale at 9/6d. The terms were a standard advance (in this instance £100) against a rising scale of royalties: 10 per cent for the first 3,000 copies, 12 per cent for the next 3,000 and 15 per cent thereafter. Furthermore, the London office was to 'pay 10% on the price received on export sales except on Australian and New Zealand sales where the royalty of 10% of the published price is payable up to 10,000 copies'.[52]

The play opened in London on 30 April 1957, and the success of Angus & Robertson's publication – placed with British printing company Purnell & Sons in May – would depend a great deal on the play's reception in the West End. (A film followed in 1959, but its pre-production did not influence Angus & Robertson's decision to publish the play in 1957.) Notwithstanding that Neil James' records that 3,000 copies of the play were sold,[53] sales figures for this title are elusive within the archival record; although it is apparent that *Summer of the Seventeenth Doll* was published in at least two London editions: a first of 4,500 copies[54] in 1957 followed by a reprint of 2,500[55] copies in 1958. The Sydney office imported 3,000 and then 2,000 copies for each print run, respectively.

As an Australian publisher, the firm continued to 'increase the proof that we do publish in London'.[56] In 1958 Angus & Robertson produced a number of titles through 'Operation London', including the following nine identified from letters:

The Doors are Closing by György Sebestyén, a Hungarian book bought by an advance of £290 against royalties,[57] with 3,000 copies dispatched to Australia[58]

London Policeman: Being Opinions, Sentiments, and Experiences of an ordinary London Policeman by Sydney C. Harvey, with the Sydney office selling its 2,000 copies by February 1958[59]

The Little King: The Book of Twenty Nights and One Night by Tamara Finch and Hector Cameron (a nom de plume for Hector MacQuarrie who rewrote most of the text), which sold for 10/6d[60]

One Man War by Hal Richardson, which was later released in a paperback edition and grossed £373 by 1960 for the London office[61]

Duet for Three Hands by Cyril Smith, with 'reconstructive'[62] work by MacQuarrie, published on 10 November, printed in an edition of 5,000, and a reprint of another 2,000 copies by Purnell & Sons,[63] delivered on 12 December

The Inside of the Cup by Alysia Wingfield

Better Golf in Five Minutes by J. V. East

Soldier Surgeon in Malaya by Thomas Hamilton, which returned £200 in paperback royalties by 1960[64]

Under the White Light: A Surgeon's Everyday Experiences by François Ody, with the Sydney office taking 3,000 copies of the memoir[65]

London Publishing, 1959–1960

For the years 1959–60, it becomes more challenging to separate out 'Operation London' books (titles published or 'originating' in Britain that the Sydney office often imported in quantities for sale in the Australasian market) from Sydney books (titles that frequently arrived in Britain as sheets which were then subsequently bound by a firm contracted by the London office).[66] Both types are documented on Angus & Robertson's 'Book Announcement' notices as new publications by the London office. Similarly, within the London office, emphasis in correspondence shifts markedly from 'Operation London' to London publishing in general. Keeping this in mind, the 1959 records show that the overseas branch produced at least twenty-three titles under the London imprint of Angus & Robertson:

The Hot Half Hour by Robert Foreman, with the Sydney office taking a quantity of 3,000[67] out of an edition of 5,000[68]

The Devil Behind Them: Nine Dedicated Drivers Who Made Motor Racing History by J. Bentley, printed by Purnell & Sons in an edition of 5,000 (2,000 for Sydney plus 3,000 for London) and priced to the public at 18 shillings[69]

Teach Yourself to Relax by Josephine Rathbone, an American popular medical title from Prentice-Hall, printed for the London office by Purnell & Sons in an edition of 4,000 split evenly between Sydney and London[70]

Kangaroos and Other Animals with Pockets by Louis Darling, with British Empire rights bought from the American publisher Morrow and the Sydney office taking 3,000 copies[71]

San Salvatore by Hans Kades, with the Sydney office taking only 2,000 copies based on the sales for Kades' previous book, *The House of Crystal*, from a London edition of 7,000[72] (the London office was down to 750 copies by July 1959)[73]

The Horn of Africa by John Buchholzer in a first edition of 3,000[74] and subsequently sold to the Adventures Book Club / Hutchinson in an edition of 10,000 at 'the magnificent sum of 4d per copy, half of which goes to the author', netting the London office £70[75]

Hector, the Stowaway Dog by Kenneth Dodson in an edition of 4,500 (3,000 to Sydney)[76]

Singapore Downbeat by Mark Corrigan, with 2,000 copies dispatched to Sydney[77]

Benaud & Co. The Story of the Tests 1958–1959 by A. G. Moyes, with sheets machined by Billings and binding by Dorstel[78]

Australian Cricket: A History also by A. G. Moyes

Patterson's Track by Eleanor Spence, a children's book reprinted from Oxford University Press

King of the Dingoes, a juvenile by Judith Wright and illustrated by Barbara Albiston, also reprinted from Oxford University Press

Spirit of Man: A Book of Adventure by Francis Joseph Allsopp and Orlando William Hunt

Simon Black Takes Over: The Strange Tale of Operation Greenleaf by Ivan Southall

The Royal Tour 1959: Canada, The United States and the St Lawrence Seaway, bought in sheets from The Ryerson Press at 95 cents a copy and sold by the London office at 21 shillings per copy, published in an edition of 1,250[79]

Doctor's Wife in New Guinea by Margaret Spencer in a small edition of 1,250

The Big Smoke by D'Arcy Niland, published in an edition of 14,500 copies (7,500 to Sydney) and sold out before publication, requiring a reprint of 3,000 copies[80] following the *Sunday Times* review that recommended Niland 'take his place beside Patrick White as an Australian writer of literary merit',[81] with paperback rights sold to Panther Books for an advance royalty of £500[82]

Insubstantial Pageant by George Molnar, with the Billing Company printing sheets and the London office publishing the finished product at 15/- net, the total production cost being 3/7d sterling per copy[83]

The Journey of Ching Lai by Eleanor Lattimore, a juvenile about a Chinese boy who longs to get to the sea, published 29 October and selling 1,500 copies by December 1957,[84] with 2,000 copies going to Sydney[85] and the New South Wales Department of Education ordering another 15,000 copies of an abridged version as a school reader[86]

Bells for a Chinese Donkey, also a juvenile by Eleanor Lattimore, published 16 November and selling 1,200 copies by December 1957,[87] with the Sydney office taking a quantity of 2,000[88]

Mr Ozzle of Withery Wood by Carol Odell and Traviss Gill, with the Sydney office ordering 1,500 copies of this English juvenile about a badger detective[89]

1960 would not be remembered as a pleasant time for Angus & Robertson, and the London office was certainly not exempt from the dramatic changes that would be implemented by Walter Burns. Although Ferguson would eventually advise Rowland in June 'not to enter into any new publishing commitments',[90] the London office, shepherded by Burns' conclusion that publishing in London was no longer necessary to support the distribution of Australian books,[91] still managed to build an industrious list which surpassed (it would appear) the output of previous years in the first six months of 1960.

Through its London imprint, Angus & Robertson published the following titles in 1960:

How to Become a Good Dancer (revised and expanded edition) by Arthur Murray, with the Sydney office taking 1,000 copies.

Conspiracy of Silence, a popular novel bought from the authors Peter Eton and James Leasor by an advance of £1,000 against royalties, with 3,000 copies dispatched to Sydney[92]

from an edition of 12,500 on sale in London for 18 shillings[93] and paperback rights sold to Panther Books against an advance of £250 on royalties[94]

Little Yellow Shoes and Other Bosnian Fairy Stories by 'Hector Cameron', with 500 copies of this title, ghost-written by Hector MacQuarrie, dispatched to Australia

The Girl from Moscow, another thriller by Mark Corrigan which the Sydney office took in a quantity of 1,250

Take This Life by Sydney Bunce, a thriller set in contemporary Sydney

He Who Rides a Tiger by Bhabani Bhattacharya in an edition of 3,000 (1,500 to Sydney), with London stock sold out by March 1960[95]

A Descant for Gossips by Thea Astley

Lunch on the Company by Ian Fellowes-Gordon, a satire on British commercial broadcasting

The Refugee by Helen Fowler

The Big Fellow by Vance Palmer, published in a small edition of 1,500

Tramps and Ladies: My Early Years in Steamers by James Bisset in an edition of 3,000, with 1,500 copies pre-ordered prior to the book's publication on 28 March[96]

The Long Dream by Richard Wright, with paperback rights sold to Panther Books for £300[97]

Sons of God by Gwyn Griffin, from New York publishers Henry Holt in an edition of 5,000 (2,750 to Sydney)[98]

In addition to the above titles, the February, March, April and May 1960 'Book Announcement' notices record the following new publications due later that year in London:

Ophthalmic Nursing by J. B. Foster
Modern English by Neile Osman
Shooting and Shooting Bushcraft by S. H. Edwards
Poems of Discovery by W. Hart-Smith
The Lighthouse and Other Poems by Nan McDonald
Fragrance and Flavour by Rosemary Hemphill
Native and Adapted Cattle by R. B. Kelly
The Blue Crane by Ian Mudie
The Riddle of a Changing World by Sir Philip Gibbs
Wake Up in Europe by Colin Simpson
Meeting Soviet Man by C. H. Manning Clark
Strike Me Lucky by Joy Cleary
Cake Icing and Decorating (revised edition) by Jean Bowring
A Wreath of Water Lilies by Pat Flower
Fear Drive My Feet by Peter Ryan
Medicine Man by F. B. McCann
The Tin Scratchers by Ion L. Idriess
Sawdust and Spangles by Majorie Clarke
Know-How in the Surf by John Bloomfield
The Drum by Sidney J. Baker
International Interiors and Design by Clive Carney
Impact of Design by Clive Carney

No Boundary Fence by Frank O'Grady
Gambols in Gastronomy by William Wallace Irwin
I Submit to No Man by Michael Mansfeld
TV Crime Drama by R. J. Thomson
Midwestern Progressive Politics by Russel B. Nye (a Michigan State University Press title)
From Main Street to the Left Bank by John A. Garraty and Walter Adams (also a Michigan State University Press title)
Three Cheers for Piggy Grunter by Noreen Shelley
Sin of Hong Kong by Mark Corrigan
Mr Brain Knows Best by Robert Burns
The Heroes by Ronald McKie

When Ferguson halted all new publishing, the London office also remained committed to an additional 12 books that had originated in London, were under contract and were currently in production:

Before and After Dinosaurs by Louis Darling
Penguins by Louis Darling
Seals and Walruses by Louis Darling
Traditional English Cooking by Helen Cox
Lady From Tokyo by Mark Corrigan
Mr Newborn Goes to France by Arthur Conte
No Sainted City by Sydney Bunce
The Shifting Heart by Richard Beynon
The Piccadilly Bushman by Ray Lawler
Three Little Chinese Girls by Eleanor Lattimore
Willow Tree Village by Eleanor Lattimore
One Rose Less by Pat Flower[99]

Another six books had signed contracts but were awaiting production:

Earthquake by Allen Andrew
Fire is their Challenge by Charles Roetter
Johannesburg: The City Where Gold Began by Robert Crisp
Of Lasting Interest: The Story of the Readers' Digest by James Playsted Wood
Norah: The Autobiography of Lady Docker by Norah Docker
Herz Auf Vier Beinen by Günther Schwab[100]

There were also another seven books in production that were contracted by, or originated from, the Sydney Head Office (not including sheet stock for 15 titles that had been ordered from Australia which were yet to be received):

Johnny Give it A Go by Elizabeth MacIntyre
Australian Animals by Sheila Hawking

Socrates and Other Poems by Francis Webb
I Swear By Apollo by Hans Kades
The Fern and the Tiki: An American View of New Zealand National Character by David Paul Ausubel
Principles and Methods of Animal Breeding by Ralph Bodkin Kelley
Sheep Management and Diseases by H. G. Belschner[101]

Although Ferguson believed that an Australian firm breaking into publishing in London was about the most difficult business he could ever have imagined,[102] one thing was certain: by 1960 Angus & Robertson's London office had equipped itself through 'Operation London' with the means of functioning as a bona fide publishing house in the United Kingdom. It is therefore an unfortunate historical moment in which genteel views of the book trade, such as Hector MacQuarrie's analysis that 'publishing is evidently not indulged in merely for profit',[103] failed to shield the London office from the processes of commercial rationalisation which were to sweep through the entire organisation and unmake any business practice judged to be unprofitable.

Chapter 10

TOMORROW, WHEN LONDON PUBLISHING ENDED

> If it was a good [Australian] book then it just had to be published, and one way or another you'd find a way of doing it, sometimes by subsidy from the Commonwealth Government, sometimes by just doing it and breaking even or losing a bit and letting some other book pay for it.[1]

> [T]he directors of Angus & Robertson were, for the most part, book people who had probably not a great deal of skill or experience in running business enterprises in what was becoming a changing world. I think you would have to say that as far as business skills were concerned, they were a pretty unsophisticated lot.[2]

Through a series of major shareholding-related manoeuvres beginning in 1958, New Zealand-born Walter Burns took up a position on the Angus & Robertson board in 1959 before being appointed managing director in February 1960. According to Craig Munro, George Ferguson 'proposed that Burns be made director'[3] when the position was made vacant by the resignation of Don Walker (who never fully recovered from a stroke the previous year).[4] Although Burns was widely acknowledged as a 'financial bloke skilled in company affairs' but 'not a publisher or a bookseller', Ferguson reasoned that 'business being the jungle it is these days, it might be well to have this kind of advice on the Board'.[5] Though the combination of Hector MacQuarrie and Barry Rowland ensured that Angus & Robertson had a 'very secure bridge-head'[6] to carry company operations in Britain and Europe, an independent audit would conclude that the London sales and publishing department was in reality costing the organisation over £11,000 sterling per year and should ultimately be reassessed as 'non revenue-producing'.[7] Additionally, the Sydney production of the now iconic *Australian Encyclopaedia* had placed Angus & Robertson overall in 'financial low water', and the Sydney office was 'badly stuck' with London titles because it had 'overestimated their sales possibilities in Australia'.[8]

By the late 1950s, Angus & Robertson in Sydney was 'more or less living from hand to mouth' until the *Australian Encyclopaedia* eventually returned the company's investment of £250,000. In part Ferguson blamed 'the tremendous amount of hire purchase business being done on television sets' which he felt undermined the book-buying market in Australia.[9] Understandably, new notes of caution and restraint were being sounded before Angus & Robertson ran into 'really serious difficulties'.[10] Even though his responsibilities were confined to publishing, Burns' appointment was viewed as a positive move and broadened Angus & Robertson's capabilities to deal with harder economic times. Ferguson advised MacQuarrie in London that 'providing we can retain the main things that the old firm has always stood for I guess we will come through all right in the end'.[11]

MacQuarrie was not so convinced. He did not believe that 'grim business men, inexperienced in publishing, will approve of this [London] show, nor will they appreciate that any ills they may isolate are produced, in effect, by the Australian invasion so powerfully organised by Heinemann, etc'.[12] This proved to be a prescient observation which would be repeated by British publisher Walter Harrap half a decade later: 'publishing is one big gamble from start to finish, and the man with an accountant's mind does not take easily to gambling'.[13] Upon his appointment, Burns described the warehousing in Sydney of unsaleable books imported from the United Kingdom as a way to 'subsidise the London branch and make the London losses appear less frightening'.[14] With 'London [publishing] in a very bad light', managing director Walter Burns would inevitably 'take drastic steps'.[15]

Price Disadvantages

It was undoubtedly the case that the recognition of Angus & Robertson by British booksellers during the second half of the 1950s, as evinced by large sales figures, created an ethos in which the London office felt it was 'on a pretty firm base'.[16] Due to its 'threshold of some reasonable success in the Old Country',[17] the overseas branch had some 'quiet optimism'[18] regarding the future. The completion of the *Australian Encyclopaedia* provided an opportunity for the company to test its international links and encouraged George Ferguson to delight for a moment in a distinctly imperial attitude, even though his company operated in an environment of restraint. In terms of marketing the *Australian Encyclopaedia*, he asked Hector MacQuarrie 'how are we to divide the world between us'?[19]

As a result, the *Australian Encyclopaedia* has an important place in the history of Angus & Robertson. This is not only for the significant cultural value that its publication marked, but also the way that a 'Sydney book' could now be marketed internationally by employing the connections built up by the London office and through 'Operation London'. The Sydney office would characteristically manage the Australasian market while the London office managed the United Kingdom and European markets; furthermore, importantly, the Ryerson Press would take care of the Canadian market and the Michigan State University Press would handle American territory. As a matter of policy, the London office paid special attention to Michigan State University Press books, often taking between 250 to 750 copies of its titles – such as *The East and West Must Meet* edited by Benjamin Houston Brow and *Bush and Backwoods: A Comparison of the Frontier in Australia and the United States* by Harry Allen[20] – and treat them the same as Sydney books.[21]

With such wide distribution a key issue for Ferguson was price uniformity, particularly between British and Australian editions since booksellers in Sydney read the same trade publication as their counterparts did in London, where the *Bookseller* was produced.[22] This furnished an opportunity for the Australian book trade to compare the published prices for two Angus & Robertson branches. Therefore, Ferguson cautioned 'it would be best to avoid complications from the outset by fixing your price at the equivalent of ours, less the rate of exchange. In other words if [ours] is to be £45 Australian then I think [yours] should be £36 Sterling'.[23] However, with apologies to Stephen Alomes, it may be the fate of those publishing houses shaped by the price advantages of other companies to produce their own price advantages in export markets.[24]

The London office continued to view having a price advantage as a key component to selling books successfully in the British market. In practice, being competitive in the United Kingdom meant that the published price of Australian books was often much lower for the English edition than the Sydney edition.[25] The issue, first raised by Vera Wellings in 1952 who petitioned for discounted trade terms on books originating from Australia in order to lower their price in Britain and increase the London office's market share, was raised again in the pricing of 'Operation London' titles. A book like *How to Become a Good Dancer* (1955), for example, retailed for 12/6 in London, whereas in Sydney it was for sale at 19/6.[26] Such gaps in prices could not be reasonably explained with reference to the *Australian Schedule of Prices*, and exchange rates provoked the ire of Australian booksellers against Angus & Robertson; thus Ferguson attempted to re-educate Rowland in the general principles of pricing books. His reasoning is worth quoting at length because of the challenges it illustrates with selling a title in two different markets, albeit within the context of mutual interdependence between the Sydney and London offices:

> We are taking 4,000 copies. If that represents, as I think it does, a very large percentage of the total printing, it would be much better for our price to be fixed first at the maximum we could get here [in Australia] for that particular book and your price [in Britain] to be then fixed with some regard to the Australian Schedule of Prices. From *our* point of view this book should be 21/- in Australia and 15/- in England and it would pay us better that way even though your sales are only 500. On the other hand if you could sell in England a number say equivalent to what we could sell here then we would be happy for you to set your price at 12/6 and we would bring ours down to 18/- if necessary although we would not be making much of a profit … [T]here are three things to be borne in mind, (a) the optimum price in England, (b) the optimum price in Australia and (c) the difference between these two prices having regard to the Schedule of Prices for English books. You must remember that all the booksellers here read *The Bookseller* and if they can see you advertising a book at 12/6 and we want to charge them say 21/- for it they will naturally object.[27]

Ferguson was exploring a preferential pricing system in that whoever took the largest quantity of stock should influence the final retail price for both markets. His comments represent a conflict of interest developing between the two sides of business that the firm conducted – publishing and bookselling – with the latter imposing terms that would enable improved profit margins.

In principle, from the point of view as publishers, MacQuarrie and Rowland recognised the merits of the London office harmonising its English prices with whatever Angus & Robertson could obtain in Australia. In a manner of speaking, they sustained

Attenborough's argument that the traditional market of British publishers at home and overseas should be indivisible.[28] But, as booksellers, MacQuarrie and Rowland anticipated an unacceptable contraction of business to result from 'Operation London' books whose success in the United Kingdom depended significantly on priced-based competition. Due to 'the hundreds and hundreds of competitors'[29] that the overseas branch contended with every day, the loss of a price advantage would quickly lead to a loss in sales confidence. '[T]he great use of O. L. in getting first class books would be killed … [A]ny attempt', explained MacQuarrie, 'to sell books even sixpence more than the prevailing prices here [in London] would ham-string us in the fight to get books'.[30]

The fact was that Angus & Robertson's export market had not been built up through observing the *Australian Schedule of Prices*, even though, in other forums, English-language publishers and booksellers were required to adhere to the *Schedule*. In the case of Angus & Robertson's books, whether an edition was produced in Sydney and exported to London or vice versa, prices could not be fixed for any imported titles without reference to local market conditions. Furthermore, titles were rarely ordered on the basis of what could be safely sold rather than what the market was estimated to be as 'the margin between success and failure [was] very thin'.[31] Ferguson later admitted that

> We must be content to take here in some cases less than we could have got for a book and hence to make less profit. On books originating here [in Sydney] you must continue to fix your price on whatever you feel you can get … [and] on books originating with you [in London] you must fix the price anyway and we shall do whatever we think best at this end.[32]

This was not a solution but an ill-timed concession continuing bookselling practices that Walter Burns would later oppose. It was not, however, out of step with English publishers who, with regards to the marketing of their editions in Australia, took a smaller margin of profit in favour of greater sales volume and lowering prices.[33]

Meanwhile, MacQuarrie recommended Ferguson 'tell the questioners in Sydney that the London House is a prestige concern making little or no profit' (not a false claim) or that Angus & Robertson should 'merely march ahead and let booksellers raise all the questions they like'.[34] The problem, however, was more fundamental to the firm's profit margin than avoiding trouble within the Australian book trade.[35] By 1959 Angus & Robertson was permitting the London office a 67 per cent discount off Sydney titles, which made the invoice price for the overseas branch close to the production cost for each copy. Add to this freight the packaging and handling charges and there was potential for the home office to incur considerable loss (or at least earn no profit) within the constrained financial setting brought about by the production of the *Australian Encyclopaedia*.

Even so, the price of bound books originating from Australia had 'jumped enormously',[36] forcing the London office to cancel some orders for Sydney titles. For example, for *Sammy Anderson: Commercial Traveller* (a 1959 novel by Henry Williamson), Rowland calculated a market of 1,500 sales if the London office retailed the book for 15 shillings or a market of 400 sales if it was available for 18 shillings. After adding binding and brass charges to the price of sheets from Australia (which were 4 shillings 11 pence), the basic cost for each finished book was a minimum 5 shillings sterling. In order to show a 'correct net margin'[37], the London office would need to retail *Sammy Anderson Commercial Traveller* at 18 shillings, which compelled Rowland to ask

> What is the policy of A. & R. Sydney? Do they want to sell as many copies of Australian produced books … in the U.K. market at prices which are competitive to other similar products published by other British publishers? Or do they only want to sell a restricted number at increased prices thereby getting A. & R. London a bad name as regards value for brass and also giving authors something to moan about[?][38]

In his usual conciliatory fashion, Ferguson explained that it was the company's recent attempts to keep local stock down that were pushing the price of Australian books up from the 'correct'[39] English price. Decreases in the size of print runs in turn increased unit costs, which amplified the final published price. Rowland, while regretful about being inflexible concerning the price situation, wanted to avoid a possibility of the London office also becoming stuck with large quantities of books that it could not sell due to titles being priced out of the British market.[40] In view of Rowland's objections, Ferguson reconfirmed that the 'policy of A. & R. Sydney is that we want to sell as many Australian books as we can in the UK market'.[41] It left the company with both a commercial problem, which was never fully resolved by the time Burns was made managing director, and with a bookselling practice that an audit (instigated by Burns) would later characterise as a form of subsidy for the London office.[42]

Profit and Loss, 1954–1960

Obtaining an accurate view of the London office's financial situation is far from easy. Official Profit and Loss statements for each year from 1954–60 are interspersed with correspondence in the first two volumes of the London office archives filed with the Mitchell Library. These statements usefully record income but document little information on expenditure (such as salaries, administration, freight, sundries, rates, outgoings, bad debts, etc.) with the exceptions of a debit line for advertising by the Australia House Bookshop, a debit line for marketing in the United Kingdom and a line for sales (stock transfers) to the Sydney Home Office. (Information on expenses exists for 1961, but this falls into the period after Richard Hauser's audit of London publishing, which is discussed below.)[43] Organised into *Table A: London office sales monthly income* and *Table B: London office sales annual income*, this data represents the first comprehensive record of turnover for the London office's publishing department during 'Operation London'. The two debit lines have been subtracted from the total revenue to show 'Actual Monthly Income' (column nine) and – in the context of Ferguson's observation that 'transfers of stock to [Sydney] … can hardly be regarded as sales as there is no profit in them whatsoever'[44] – the column documenting purchase orders by the Sydney office ('Publishing Sales SYD') is considered cost-neutral; it neither contributes to nor takes away from the London office's monthly income.

While statistics from the export department exist for 1947–52 with regard to the value of books dispatched to Sydney, no additional data is available that catalogues the recurring costs of exporting during this period or for any period thereafter. With the exception of the year 1967, it is not possible to audit income from the publishing department against expenditure by the export department for 1954–60 in any consistent or statistically valid manner in order to obtain a true picture of the London office's profit or loss result Given the infrequent mention of profit amounts that might also take into account exporting expenses, what follows is an imperfect measure of the London office's financial setting.

A Profitable Proposition

Often, the determination of a profit or a loss by the London office was worked out over several weeks in consultation with the Sydney office. This was usually well after the period in question and was subject to ongoing refinement or even reversal. To illustrate this point, on the one hand the independent financial report on Angus & Robertson in London, which assessed its operations to be 'non-revenue producing', used information 'taken from the London accounts for the year ended 31 March 1959'.[45] Yet in the course of a power struggle for control of the company in November 1960, Hector MacQuarrie – by then an ex-employee of Angus & Robertson – argued in a letter to the *Sydney Morning Herald* that the 'visible loss suffered during the six years we published [to March 1960] in London amounts to about £7,000. Statistics are often deceptive; to my mind that £7,000 is deceptive and is much more than offset by profit to the home firm'.[46]

Neil James refers to MacQuarrie's letter as the 'best indication of the London office's financial success',[47] but this overstates its significance as evidence. The next day, after the publication of MacQuarrie's letter in the *Sydney Morning Herald* and having read Walter Burns' public response in the same paper, Ferguson cautioned MacQuarrie that 'the unanimous opinion here is that your letter should not have been written and that out of the exchange Burns had undoubtedly strengthened his position in the eyes of the readers of the financial page of the *S.M.H*'.[48] MacQuarrie's counterclaim was not – at least for the political circumstances of ousting Walter Burns – supportable or convincing. On the other hand, George Ferguson contradicts both MacQuarrie's and the report's findings in a frank letter to Stanley Unwin in January 1961: 'The real problem in London is on the publishing side. We had begun to build up quite a nice little publishing business which for the twelve months ending March 31st, 1960, sold £70,000 worth of books (Sterling) and made a profit of £4,600'.[49] Whether Ferguson's claim of a profit was an accurate financial assessment of the London office or a bolstering of its appeal to a British publisher as a form of reputation management is not clear, but the figure of £70,000 presented by Ferguson correlates with the annual total for 1960 (£69,940) in *Table B: London office sales annual income.*

Over the six years prior to 1960, Hector MacQuarrie and Barry Rowland worked in various capacities to develop a British market for books with an Angus & Robertson imprint. However, as the financial troubles of the Sydney office became acute with the preparation of the *Australian Encyclopaedia* (whose investment of £250,000 had not yet returned any dividends),[50] optimism and support regarding the London office's takings gradually translated into doubt and concern about its balance of payments.

In June 1956 the profitability of the London office was a less immediate problem, because it was not in danger of being retired by its then managing director. Certainly George Ferguson, Hector MacQuarrie and Barry Rowland shared a mutual interest in seeing receipts in London exceed expenditure and hoped 'Operation London' would break even one day to 'meet the entire bill'.[51] But this carried less import than the project of physically publishing in Britain.

For example, while London publishing achieved a net profit of £3,789 for the 12 months to 31 March 1956 (from an actual turnover of £52,106) and was bracketed with an additional £2,000 in revenue derived from MacQuarrie's administration of broadcasting rights during the same period, the exporting arm of the London office had dispatched £175,000 worth of books to Sydney at a cost of approximately £8,000. This meant the branch overall was running at a loss in the neighbourhood of £2,200. Even so, this result was considered 'good' because it helped reduce exporting costs down to 5 per cent of export value (although a result of 'no loss' would have been 'pretty good' too).[52]

Ferguson was less affected by the negative balance than MacQuarrie or Rowland and encouraged the London office to keep its focus on long-term objectives. '"Operation London"', he advised, 'cannot be assessed on the result of one or two years. We have to remember that last year we had two great lifts in *The Shiralee* and *Away All Boats*'.[53] Ferguson concluded that it was always easier to obtain significant turnover when a publisher had a bestseller like *The Shiralee*, with sales augmented by the title's selection as a Book Society Choice, but 'when you can get it out of just general books of the kind which are likely to be repeated at any moment, it is much better'.[54] Indeed, the sale of Sydney books had notably progressed and that was a 'matter of fundamental importance' to Angus & Robertson.[55] If the Sydney office maintained a steady supply of books to the United Kingdom, of which the London office could consistently sell in quantities of 750 or more, then the future would continue to look promising for Australian books and for the London office too.[56]

Such optimism that the London office was 'establishing itself'[57] was followed by a period of self-examination in which the home office reassessed its procedures and performance. In June 1957 the London office announced a profit of £1,717 exclusive of broadcasting revenue.[58] The Sydney Head Office congratulated the London office on this result, although Ferguson mildly negated its success with a caveat that 'overhead plays the very devil with profit'.[59] He was conceivably projecting Angus & Robertson's financial problems with the *Australian Encyclopaedia* onto the London setting.

However, in 1958, the firm began to register even stronger concern over the inclusion of stock transfers to Sydney as sales within London office profit and loss reports,[60] and, during a visit to London, Ferguson instructed the overseas branch that these should be excluded from future gross profit assessments and processed by the Export Department instead.[61] Moreover, the value of London titles which the home office took each year fell dramatically from £18,622 in 1956, to £5,104 in 1959, and £1,994 in 1960.[62] This was the first of many contractions in Sydney business. Facing an economic crisis, Angus & Robertson favoured a tightening of budgets,[63] rather than any prescribed measure to raise capital,[64] and this decision would be the unmaking of the London office even though the value of books it sold in the United Kingdom increased steadily from £47,414 in 1956, to £54,223 in 1959, and £66,672 in 1960.[65]

Although the Sydney office had constituted a 'very important prop' for the London office to lean on in the past, the change in circumstances provided a new impetus for the overseas branch to regard Angus & Robertson in Australia 'with a sort of polite detachment as a customer, even if a good one'.[66] The reality was that by 1958 the Sydney office was stuck with London titles from 1956 like *From the Valley I Came* (by Wil Jon Edwards) and *A Train to Catch* (by Anthony Rushworth). Ferguson believed it was essential that the Sydney office 'resist sternly the temptation to take on books that *might* sell'[67] and keep its printing quantities as low as possible. He reinforced the need for interdependence between the two branches. In the future, both offices were to avoid investing money in stock that was unsaleable or slow moving and were instead to place more 'realistic' orders for each other's titles. In retrospect, the reciprocal dimension to this request was not entirely equal: Ferguson was later less than happy with the smaller volume of London orders for Sydney books, forcing Rowland to restate his argument that 'the size of our intake is so greatly governed by the price at which we can sell'.[68]

In theory, 'realistic' orders meant that quantities of London books taken by the Sydney office that formerly numbered in the range of 3,000 to 5,000 were now, through necessity, reduced to between 2,000 and 3,000 copies. In practice, the Sydney office would ultimately become 'very, very careful of all … London books because we cannot sell them to any degree'.[69] Sydney would only order background Australian books (such as natural history) in contrast to 'entertainment' books ('particularly if not Australian'), which Ferguson identified as being too risky for the local market.[70] In addition to 'play[ing] it pretty tight', this anticipated the 'refusal to reprint books which really cannot pay their way' coupled with a 'refusal to publish books for the first time which don't look pretty safe'.[71] MacQuarrie agreed with Ferguson's reservations, thinking the policy 'wise' in the Sydney office's current financial situation,[72] and understood that these changes effectively represented a revised direction for Angus & Robertson in London.

Confident with the steady sales in the United Kingdom, MacQuarrie and Rowland did not seem notably troubled by the home office's display of recession-like behaviour. They both reaffirmed the London branch's ambition to 'reach a point when our judgement on sales possibilities is good enough to allow us to look on Australasian sales as velvet'[73]. That is, both MacQuarrie and Rowland wanted 'to reach a stage when the London branch must rely on itself'.[74]

Much was contingent, however, on the London office 'getting the right books',[75] reducing overheads, revising bookseller terms ('we are giving away too much'),[76] discontinuing advances for future manuscripts[77] and lowering royalty caps in prospective author contracts by 3 per cent.[78] But the auditor's figures for 1958, assessing a total annual income of £51,983, concluded that the publishing department of the London office lost approximately £1,000 because 'sales did not increase enough to keep pace with … expenses, and in some cases expenses were unnecessarily high'.[79] The following year would see annual income rise by nearly £8,000 (boosted by British sales of the *Australian Encyclopaedia*, which accounted for £4,000, and by royalties from Panther Books paperback editions)[80] and still the 1959 figure of £59,298 would be rejected as an insufficient level of turnover to 'show much in the way of net profit'.[81] (In fact, £75,000 to £80,000 became the ideal turnover figure.) The one point that the income for 1959 did have in its favour was that it included 'genuine sales' and almost no 'stock transfers to Sydney at practically cost price'.[82]

Nevertheless, the 1959 figure demonstrated that Australian books were continuing to sell at an attractive pace in the United Kingdom. Although Ferguson's subtext suggested some growing in-house resistance to Angus & Robertson's British publishing activities, 'Operation London', he opined to Rowland more out of hope than fact that it 'might even be regarded as worthwhile from that point of view alone'.[83]

Yet, as pressures clearly mounted in Australia, with letters from Sydney to London taking on a more urgent tone, Ferguson warned that 'the two things sticking out like lighthouses in London are that we must have more turnover and we must get the overhead down'.[84] While no immediate explanation was forthcoming for what seemed like a sudden need to justify the London office in cold, objective accounting terms, a comment to MacQuarrie in December 1959 indicated Ferguson's attention was focused on the modernised business environment within which Angus & Robertson's publishing department increasingly operated: 'we do have a lot of shareholders' money invested in the company now and we've got to see that it earns its keep. We could and should be doing better on the publishing side than we are'.[85] Excluding the business interest of the Australian parent company in the activities of its subsidiary overseas branch, the London office published important books and a number of bestsellers, but it was yet to be a financially viable independent entity. It was within this context that Richard Hauser, acting under instruction from Walter Burns, would report in 1960 that the London office's publishing department 'could never possibly be a paying proposition'.[86] He added that

> this fact is emphasised even more when it is seen that out of the gross profit of 32.79% [on sales], we are paying 42% in overheads. Thus, the net loss of this department is in the vicinity of £A 3,500 p.a. However, undisclosed costs in Sydney are even greater and account for between £7,000 and £8,000 p.a. Therefore, in this department alone, the cost to the organisation as a whole is somewhere near £11,000 per year.[87]

The Reorganisation of London and Sydney

By 1960, the business interests of the firm and those of the publishing department had dramatically diverged. Even so, George Ferguson was still committed to an Australian company publishing in the United Kingdom.

Ferguson's concern for the London office's future towards the end of the 1950s can be measured in the steps he took to improve its 'profit earning power' and to 'keep it on the right side of the ledger'.[88] Less than a month after Hector MacQuarrie's partnership with Barry Rowland was praised as a 'very successful' combination in January 1958, George Ferguson announced that Rowland would be made general manager of the London office on 1 September 1958.[89] In fact, Rowland would replace MacQuarrie as London manager[90] and would be 'put in full charge of all the activities at Great Russell Street, including publishing, exporting and accounts, leaving editorial affairs, subsidiary rights (i.e., "agency" work) and broadcasting', and Hector MacQuarrie would carry on these functions from an office in 48 Bloomsbury Street (which Angus & Robertson still retained on its books).

In a surprisingly dispassionate tone for a letter between Ferguson and MacQuarrie, these staff changes were described as being 'in line with the firm's policy here, where in the last five years or so several people over sixty-five have either retired or stepped into positions of less administrative responsibility'.[91] They were also part of a renewed emphasis on publishing that was 'more technical and educational',[92] with significantly diminished enthusiasm for imaginative literature and a stronger articulation of Angus & Robertson's 'commercial or business, as opposed to the literary, side of … activities'.[93] In future, the firm 'must look to Barry',[94] persuaded as it was that Rowland was the right man to extend the London office's trade in 'books as merchandise'.[95] This was in parallel to Ferguson privately acknowledging that 'editorially MacQuarrie is a long way ahead of Barry',[96] whom he looked upon as having 'certain limitations'.[97] Although he would remain on his present salary, plus allowances, and would relocate his work to Bloomsbury Street when Rowland officially took over in September,[98] MacQuarrie's response was one of shocked assessment that this 'would produce quite a serious crisis in "Operation London"'.[99]

Underlining his lengthy employment with Angus & Robertson, which spanned a period of 25 years publishing and selling Australian books in the United Kingdom, MacQuarrie believed 'Operation London' was 'doomed' and that it would ultimately 'fade out'.[100] While MacQuarrie admitted he was overstating his personal contribution to 'Operation London', his observation would prove to be rather perceptive, although its basis in fact was not to be found entirely in staffing changes (which nevertheless played their part). Angus & Robertson would commercially reorientate after the production of the *Australian Encyclopaedia*, but the London office as a result would become exposed to financial analysis whose findings would ultimately sustain John Feather's claim that 'the publisher who based his business on a cause … always found himself in commercial difficulties'.[101]

A Quite Useless Liability

The appointment of Walter Burns to the role of managing director with duties entirely financial was by 'common consent'.[102] The London office was officially advised of this change on 5 February 1960, and the firm's former managing director, George Ferguson, in turn moved exclusively into publishing, crediting himself as 'one of the architects and not a victim of the new set-up'.[103] By the last quarter of 1959, Ferguson was convinced that the advent of 'paper backs, magazines, television, and a general shortage of money'[104] threatened Australian publishing, and he could not recall a more difficult time for Angus & Robertson. In addition to seeking improvements in efficiency,[105] Ferguson anticipated – like Angus & Robertson's Board – that Burns would add to the company's capabilities, take account of the difficult economic realities and reform the company's operations accordingly. An index of this crisis was not simply Ferguson's antecedent efforts to streamline the London office; perhaps he was certain that the whole London operation was due for a very critical look. Indeed, Burns accelerated a reorganisation of the company's overall national structure.

At the start of 1960, a parent company was created that would exercise 'financial and general policy control over [Angus & Robertson's] operating companies (or subsidiary companies)',[106] which were to be five in total: Angus & Robertson (Properties) Pty Ltd would control the firm's real estate holdings; Angus & Robertson (Bookshops) Pty Ltd would be responsible for the conduct of all retail establishments in New South Wales; Angus & Robertson (Wholesale) Pty Ltd would exist to sell books published by the firm, including any titles from other publishers obtained through the purchase of reprint rights; H. E. C. Robinson Pty Ltd would be committed to the publishing of maps, road guides and street directories; and Angus & Robertson (Publishers) Pty Ltd would be 'responsible for the publishing process from its inception in the mind of some author … until its final appearance in physical form as a book … leaving the sales side to the wholesale company'.[107]

With MacQuarrie discharged from main operations and installed in another building to administrate broadcasting rights and continue working in private on the translation of foreign books, Ferguson reassured Rowland that no one would start turning the London office upside down. But Ferguson's own labours in reorganising Angus & Robertson's international operations did not ultimately protect the London office from the effects of restructuring, and Ferguson later confessed to MacQuarrie that with the 'old-time' Angus & Robertson 'gone for good … life will be harder and not so amusing'.[108] For an overseas branch whose condition at the end of the 1950s had been less healthy than many had assumed, 1960 would be a difficult year for the London office. The reality of increasing profits was to prove very different from the dream of increasing sales, and indeed the London office would enter a dreadful period in which its 'Operation London' successes would be followed by challenges to its very existence and past achievements. The overwhelming negative audit of the London office's finances by Richard Hauser set the tone.

In February 1960 Ferguson notified the London manager that a personnel and management consultant, one Richard Hauser, would soon 'make an analysis of the functions of the departments and individuals in London with a view to integrating the whole thing properly into the new set-up'.[109] The future of the London office's side business in clearing broadcasting rights, however, would need to be reconsidered.[110] The future of London publishing was becoming clear to Ferguson, and these thoughts he shared with MacQuarrie just before requiring him to vacate his flat at 48 Bloomsbury Street (MacQuarrie's retirement was hastened by Burns' appraisal of his activities, and he left the London office on 30 June 1960, taking the broadcasting rights business with him):[111]

> Figures … are going to mean more in our lives than they have meant before, and everything now is to be done according to budgets. This will in time have its effect in London, where the amount of money to be spent will be severely controlled … chancy books must be sternly resisted … [and] the number of titles published is likely to get less.[112]

In general, the merchandising principles that Burns championed overwhelmed any other concern. Reflecting a shift in temperament away from the Sydney office being 'absolutely delighted'[113] with the progress of 'Operation London' in 1956, Ferguson's impression now was that 'so called O. L. books have contributed very little' to the London office's income[114] (an assessment reasonably defused with reference to *Table B: London office sales annual income, Table E: Sales for paperback editions of 'Operation London' titles* and an assessment which Ferguson would disown ten years later).[115] With respect to Burns' policy that 'book publishing … is to be carried on profitably',[116] it was vital that Rowland's department in London demonstrate positive financial returns.

As the London office's progenitor, Ferguson formally advised Rowland that Angus & Robertson's scene of publishing was to depart from one directed by individual personalities to one dominated by managerialism and stringent budgets. Committees of review were being established in Sydney, composed of representatives from the editorial department plus Angus & Robertson's wholesale and retail subsidiary companies, which would evaluate all the books produced in London prior to placing an order that was 'based on the expectation of sales'.[117] In turn, the overseas branch was to furnish a similar committee 'for the purpose of subjecting [both Sydney and London books] to scrutiny and criticism'[118] regardless of whether either was publishing new titles or reordering / reprinting existing titles. While it added a measure of lag in the publishing department, this solution did not lead to any tangible improvement in profitability for the London office. Angus & Robertson's operation in the United Kingdom showed immense possibilities in Hauser's view but was, in the end, condemned as a 'quite useless liability'[119] whose machinery invited pruning.

Over the passage of three months, Hauser made a complete survey of the Angus & Robertson London office, interviewing all staff, visiting publishers and other personnel as necessary.[120] He presented two accounts of his findings to Burns in May 1960.[121] The preliminary report, only four typed pages, offered the view that the branch could be made to stand on its own within six months provided one important condition was addressed. After describing Rowland as a 'good executive officer'[122] who was, it seemed, too dependent on the Sydney office and often hindered the branch from developing in an autonomous fashion, the document's core recommendation was that the London office should be made semi-independent (it was a point Hauser would also continue in his second report). With its greater editorial independence and liberty, Hauser advocated that the London office use its own business to cover costs or, failing that, 'its throat … [would be] cut".[123] Cleaving the branch into a mere 'postal section'[124] could be avoided if the overseas branch abandoned its 'old boy charm' in favour of a more business-like relationship with Sydney; a relationship founded strictly on bargaining power rather than on one business functioning as a 'private convenience'[125] or 'annexe'[126] for the other. After all, Angus & Robertson could not expect to 'run a branch 12,000 miles away as if it were in Woolloomooloo'.[127]

Hauser did not neglect the extra commercial and cultural advantages for an Australian publisher possessing a London outlet, which Ferguson and MacQuarrie regularly reinforced in their letters. 'Buying English books and selling Australian books here [in London]', Hauser argued, '… seems to me necessary to allow you [in Sydney] greater printing opportunity and more prestige with authors'.[128] But the prestige, influence and cultural benefits traditionally linked with publishing in the United Kingdom did not easily redress the London office's apparent losses. Burns would later join the debate and claim the idea that 'spiritual considerations should outweigh commercial ones [in publishing] is idealistic but unrealistic. In a public company such a viewpoint is possible only in so far as the profits of commercial publishing permit'.[129]

Attached to the first report was Hauser's Profit and Loss statement for the year ended 31 March 1959. In summary, the Australia House Bookshop traded profitably for 12 months showing a gross profit of 34.2 per cent on sales of £7,851 and a net profit of £697 sterling. The publishing department by contrast, which also incorporated the sale of Sydney and London books, achieved sales upwards of £56,766 but a net loss of £2,060. This loss was calculated after including profit from the Australia House Bookshop (£697), profit from the sale of publications to the Australia House Bookshop (£409) and income from serial / paperback royalties (£1,895). Moreover, the export department – which made no income whatsoever and was solely engaged in the exporting of British books (published by British firms) to the Angus & Robertson retail group in Australia – incurred £25,163 in expenses (of which £17,920 was paid in salaries). Distribution of this export cost was borne by the London publishing department (to an amount of £16,046) and also by the Sydney Home office (to an amount of £9,117). On this basis, combining the publishing department's net loss of £2,060 (as a result of carrying part of the export department's expenses) with charges to Angus & Robertson in Australia of £9,117 produces a total loss incurred by the London office in the year reviewed of £11,178 sterling. To this was added any other (unspecified) losses incurred by the Sydney office in supplying London.[130] In short, Hauser's initial assessment put 'London [publishing] in a very bad light'[131] (even though it is clear the publishing department helped reduce exporting costs down to a finer percentage of export value and carried the majority of expenses incurred overseas).

Although this fiscal analysis would be used as an argument for closing down Angus & Robertson's London publishing operations, the underlying economic principle of Hauser's survey was particularly diminished in his second report. Whether the new personnel and management consultant was conscious of this or not, Hauser repeated Ferguson's rationale for Angus & Robertson maintaining a branch in the United Kingdom: 'London', Hauser counselled Burns, 'is the hub of the world, even if your interests are primarily, though naturally, centred around Australia'.[132] The impetus to publish in London was no longer entirely commercial and was in fact a many-sided problem. According to Hauser, to scuttle Angus & Robertson's London endeavour now, after a total investment to date of £107,252 sterling, 'would be an acceptance of failure'.[133] Instead, echoing comments made by George Ferguson and Hector MacQuarrie in the opening years of 'Operation London', Hauser proposed that the London office should invest in six to ten best-selling books – notwithstanding the speculative nature of publishing considering 'one knows only afterwards whether it was a best seller or a poor buy'.[134] This publishing programme would be supported by the London office, which sought greater discounts from Sydney, an increase in the sales of Australian books in Britain, negotiated reprint rights for good American (and English) books, expanded trade in serialisation and campaigned for more attention to subsidiary sales. With these conditions reasonably met, Angus & Robertson might conceivably 'see London making a real success'.[135]

To obtain any real growth in the London office, it seemed to Hauser that a mixture of Australian books intertwined with American and / or British books was unavoidable. The irony was that Hauser had just described 'Operation London' in its infancy.

Hauser's second report was ignored. In the immediate aftermath, Walter Burns went to England and resolved that Angus & Robertson was no longer able to produce books in Britain. Barry Rowland promptly resigned in June 1960, after declining a reassignment to Sydney, and accepted a position at Panther Books as Chief Editor;[136] the publishing department inevitably collapsed as other staff resigned in protest at the demands of Burns, and the building at 105 Great Russell Street was sold off for £36,000 sterling.[137] Indeed, everything that George Ferguson, Hector MacQuarrie and Barry Rowland had built up in London over the course of several industrious years was in the end 'kicked to pieces'.[138]

A Reasonably Organised Show

Was London publishing a profitable proposition or 'quite [a] useless liability' as Richard Hauser described the branch in his first report?[139] Unfortunately, it remains difficult to gauge to what extent the London office operated at a profit or at a loss. This is due to fragmentary evidence combined with a poor register of overlapping receipts and expenses for 1954–60. However, one conclusion articulated in Hauser's preliminary report does demand closer scrutiny. From April 1958 to March 1959, the publishing department reduced the expenses of the export department, which for the year reviewed might have cost the Sydney Home Office approximately £25,163 rather than £9,117 if London publishing did not in fact exist. If the London office was indeed to be evaluated on its own merits as a semi-independent business capable of covering its own costs, then it seems a misguided conclusion that the department producing revenue should be the one selected for termination. Closing the export department did not appear to be an option, and a close examination of its overheads in terms of publisher's terms and packing charges is absent. (The economics of exporting from Britain would not come under review until the late 1960s whereby a case would be made for its abolition.[140] See Chapter 12.) In Angus & Robertson's broader commercial framework, where the export department generated no revenue for the London office in dispatching upwards of £175,000[141] in books to Sydney, to halt exporting would be a 'pity'.[142] This was because the benefits or 'many valuable services'[143] that accrued to Angus & Robertson (through the mark-up and sale of these books via the company's retail establishments in Australia) were not represented in any manner on the London office's balance sheets.

Allowing that the selection, packaging and dispatching of this stock originated from the London office, neither revenue nor commission from the sale of these books in Sydney showed on London Profit and Loss statements. Yet the 1959 *Report of the Directors* records a net profit of £43,931 for the whole of Angus & Robertson Ltd, described as a satisfactory result 'being higher than for the preceding year',[144] and it is not unreasonable to advance that part of this net profit would have been augmented by the sale of books dispatched from the London office's export department. With revenue from the publishing department thus subsidising its own costs and those of the export department, the import of Ferguson's disclosure – that the London office's 'full advantages by no means appear in the London balance sheet'[145] – becomes clear. An assessment of Angus & Robertson in the United Kingdom, like Hauser's, would be quite deficient if it occurred outside the context of mutual interdependence between Sydney and London.

Hauser's reports omitted many remarkable achievements by Ferguson, MacQuarrie and Rowland. For example, up until 16 March 1960, the London office had in its past few years negotiated 36 paperback sales (see *Table J*) with an average advance royalty of £250 divided 50 / 50 with authors (see *Table E*); produced at least 13 bestsellers (See *Table I*); obtained British Commonwealth rights for many books as well as American manuscripts, which was an impossible activity for other Australian publishers to undertake; successfully marketed film and television rights for Angus & Robertson publications with their serial rights in major British newspapers averaging at £250 per sale; and, using the branch in the United Kingdom as a 'very secure bridge-head'[146] to carry company operations internationally, exported Australian books to Europe, South Africa, the Middle East, Canada and the West Indies.

With 'a little quiet pride'[147] at what the London office had accomplished over the past ten years, Ferguson characterised the closure of London publishing as a strategic miscalculation in Angus & Robertson's business model. 'An Australian publisher', he shared with Stanley Unwin, 'is as entitled to be export minded as a British publisher ... Export is a common necessity for us all'.[148] Ferguson was adamant that publishing in London 'cannot be finished and [that] it must be rebuilt in some form or other'.[149]

Out of this recognition emerged the need to remove Burns as managing director, and a series of heated board-room battles, coupled with covert share-splitting tactics led by Norman Cowper, dominated the Sydney Home office during the second half of 1960 as competing bookselling and publishing interests fought for control of the company. British publishers watched on with intense interest, and Walter Harrap anticipated common sense would prevail, offering that a firm which has 'achieved as much as Angus & Robertson cannot possibly have been guided by a lot of nitwits'.[150]

Harrap's optimism and logic was not misguided. At the annual general meeting in early December 1960, Angus & Robertson's shareholders demonstrated almost no support for Burns' side and proved – to Ferguson at least – that there were 'some people left in the world who are more interested in enduring performance and the long term view rather than ... a quick quid'.[151] With his son John Ferguson subsequently installed in a new building at 54 Bartholomew Close, London, to 'hold the fort',[152] there remained quite a mess to be cleared up over the next 12 months. One thing was certain, however. The sharp rise and fall of Walter Burns had thoroughly reinvented Angus & Robertson, and the London office would never be the same again, even as it attempted to 'recreate a suitable outlook'[153] once more in the United Kingdom for the publication and sale of Australian books.

Chapter 11

A HOUSE IS REBUILT

> I hope it will not be long before the Angus & Robertson joint export apparatus reaps an export harvest for Australian publishers. I think we are well on the way to doing this because so many Australian publishers want to have a UK outlet.[1]

From the late 1940s and 1950s, the London office was characterised by Hector MacQuarrie as one of 'purely English infancy'.[2] The first half of the 1960s was marked by a maturing identity crisis. Gone was the 'old type family concern'[3] in which editorial horsepower was more important than sales or production. In its place was a modern company; a company which was more complex and heavier on the retail side and superintended large-scale shareholder investments that required dividends. Having 'rocked so violently' through the Burns' (and later Packer's) takeover episodes, Angus & Robertson was 'now fairly steady on her keel'[4] after the British publisher William Collins (along with George G. Harrap[5] and William Heinemann)[6] provided a 'stabilizing influence' through their purchase of 30 per cent of Angus & Robertson's shares.[7]

Content not to throw about its weight, Collins appeared prepared 'to lend strength to see that no more robber barons upset the place'.[8] As anti-British sentiment increased during the late 1960s, George Ferguson would often find himself defending Collins' part ownership: 'In most cases', he penned in the nation's major newspaper, 'Australian ownership would mean that the firm's attitude was Australian, but you can't assume that overseas ownership would mean an un-Australian attitude'.[9] But while Ferguson could reasonably defend Angus & Robertson's overall Australianness before its nationals, less certain was the company's sense of its London mission. In fact, Ferguson wondered whether 'national identity [was] greater than universal recognition'[10] in Angus & Robertson's business to 'fill the whole world with Australian books'.[11]

Angus & Robertson considered its 'Australianness'[12] as the company's competitive edge in the United Kingdom's 'continuing and growing market'[13] for Australian books. Ferguson suspected there was 'much readier acceptance of Australian books over there now than there used to be' and that Angus & Robertson could 'take a good deal of the credit for that'.[14] On the other hand, it was deemed a significant liability in terms of the physical placement of Angus & Robertson's stand at international book and trade fairs. Privately, Angus & Robertson understood – and were drawn to – the 'expression of feeling by Australian publishers to shake off their "Australianness" and to become part of a much greater publishing scene'.[15] However, publicly, through representing a number of Australian publishers in Britain with 'increasing success',[16] Angus & Robertson wanted to be 'known primarily as Australian publishers' in order to obtain 'the cream of the list of all Australian publishers'.[17] Yet, as the new London manager Walter Butcher pointedly asked George Ferguson, '[known] by whom?'[18]

In the London office's formative years, specifically during the Second World War, this contradictory, often equivocating attitude found expression in its dealings with British publishers. In the post Burns era, it was directed inward towards Angus & Robertson's own London image and its interaction with other publishers. For example, there was new controversy around selling the books of other Australian firms through the London office:

> There is the problem also of books rejected by us here [in Sydney] being published by other publishers and appearing as A. & R. books in London … Perhaps there ought to be closer liaison between you and us here before you agree to use our imprint on anything coming from another publisher. There could even be 'political' reasons why we would not want our name on certain books and yet you might unwittingly put it on. You can see the dangers that exist.[19]

Such issues draw attention to the transnational nature of bookselling, in which the publisher's imprint could be put to uses unrelated, even contradictory, to the reputation and cultural value it bears.

This chapter examines the London office's identity politics against the background of George Ferguson reassembling London operations after its 'hiatus'.[20] Despite a renewed rate of turnover, with Walter Butcher 'selling the kind of serious [non-fiction] Australian book which under the old regime [of MacQuarrie and Rowland] did not get much consideration',[21] a strong profit base still eluded the London office during the 1960s. Walter Burns' criticism of 'Operation London' survived his departure and continued to resonate with Angus & Robertson staff. 'The whole battle in London' consolidated around the singular struggle: 'the battle for sales'.[22] Although Burns had left the publishing scene by 1962, his economic assessment of the London office overshadowed its operations and internal correspondence for many more years. Burns' findings were repeatedly dismissed with regard to the project of publishing overseas, yet, despite his absence, there remained a campaign to prove his assessments wrong:

> [Y]our profits accrue to the publishing profit here, and your losses are subtracted from our profit. Burns of course attacked our whole London operation most bitterly, and while all the present directors have complete faith in the London end of things, and are fully committed to a policy of publishing in London, I should like to be able, naturally, to present them with a success story as soon as possible.[23]

As Ferguson set about restoring the London apparatus for distributing Australian books throughout the United Kingdom – with advice from Stanley Unwin and Walter Harrap (and perhaps, personally, more than just a little disillusioned from his clash with Walter Burns)[24] – Australia was in turn becoming 'a happy hunting ground'[25] for British publishers, which sought to establish offices or distribution warehouses in the southern hemisphere. Throughout the 1960s, the lucrative Australian market was obtaining more attention from British publishers while Britain was attempting to shift focus from the Commonwealth towards the vast market that the European Economic Community represented. While Angus & Robertson struggled in London, British publishers changed strategies by opening up branch plants in Australia. The connection between the two is not straightforward, and Angus & Robertson's reasons for being in the United Kingdom were different to the reasons for the British publishers' presence in Australia.

Closing the Market

The old colonial era of Australian booksellers indenting British books and Australian agents representing British publishers was coming to an end. This generated new tensions for Angus & Robertson's London-based export department, whose business of dispatching English books to Sydney for retailing in the company's New South Wales bookshops would be attenuated by British publishers closing the market and supplying all their Australasian trade orders themselves from offices within Australia. As booksellers, Angus & Robertson made less on books distributed in Australia by its respective publishers, but the difference in profit on indented books from its London office (40 per cent) to books supplied locally (33 per cent) was an acceptable margin.[26] Overheads, which for 1963 amounted to £11,696 in freight charges on 272 tons of books packed within 2,528 cartons,[27] invited questions regarding the effect on Angus & Robertson if the overseas export department was closed.

The Net Book Agreement generally prohibited Australian firms importing into the country titles purchased direct from a British publisher based overseas if these same titles could be obtained from an authorised supplier locally in Australia. Angus & Robertson knew well its business as a publisher and as a bookseller, and this practice was a major drive behind its London-based operations. As discussed in previous chapters, it enabled the Australian company to close its market in London and enforce a policy that anyone in the British Isles who wanted their books could only order titles from the London office and not alternatively through Sydney. This was a deliberate strategy to build up the strength of Angus & Robertson's overseas agent (acting as a bookseller or distributor of company books in the foreign dominion) by ensuring it had exclusive rights to supply product within the foreign market. In a similar fashion, the English firm Heinemann responded to a significant net loss reported by its Australian office during 1964 – reported to be in the range of £15,000 – by 'giving them some markets'.[28] The British publisher closed the supply of Heinemann books to Australia and did not permit the purchase of its books in Australia through any channel other than Heinemann's official Australian office.

As more British publishers followed Heinemann's example[29] (such as Oxford University Press),[30] Angus & Robertson's Australian-based purchasing of British books increased against a corresponding decrease in London-based purchasing. In light of this shift from overseas buying to domestic buying of new books, the economic performance of the London office would again be assessed, but, in contrast to the bias which characterised Walter Burns' administration, it was the overheads of exporting from London to Sydney that would be scrutinised.

The British publishers' preference for local production through branch plants, as opposed to maintaining an import industry, affected Angus & Robertson's trade. A reduction in the company's imports of British books was an important, if unwelcome, commercial development for the bookselling arm of Angus & Robertson. More broadly, it affected the Australian book trade as it evolved under conditions that allowed an unrestricted annual flow into the country of nearly 23,000 British titles[31] (or 13.5 million pounds of books).[32] Lloyd O'Neil, during the announcement of his retirement as managing director of the F. W. Cheshire Publishing Group in 1969, colourfully described Australia as the '"new-found Arcady", which, since the 1950s, has attracted British publishers, who, in a winter exodus, "arrive as regularly as the mutton birds from Siberia"'.[33] Although Angus & Robertson sustained close professional and personal ties with British publishers Collins, Harraps, and Batsford Books, the export side of business remained a 'primary reason for [Angus & Robertson's] London office'.[34] The weakening of this operation compelled Ferguson to bitterly revise Angus & Robertson's dependence on 'the movement of British books to Australia for sale' in the firm's bookshops:[35]

> I am not in the slightest bit interested in taking on the sales representation for English publishers or any others … To tell you the truth my heart doesn't bleed a bit if British publishers are having difficulty selling their books in Australia, and I don't feel particularly keen to help them.[36]

By 1966 the majority of Angus & Robertson's retail shops would cease to require the services of the London office's export department,[37] and its volume of business in exporting books to Australia would decrease as British publishers began routinely returning orders for British books with the advice to 'refer to our Australian house'.[38] The London office's export department would face closure 'on the grounds that it wasn't worth what it was costing'.[39]

The business practice of importing books into Australia decreased as British publishers established Australian branch plants. The significance of this was not limited to shrinking margins and heightened competition for Australian booksellers. With British publishing focused on responding to the post-war gains achieved by American publishers in English language markets,[40] British houses in London were little interested in books produced by their overseas offices if not 'indifferent even to the publishing functions of their Australian branches'.[41] For example, Frank Eyre of the Oxford University Press in Melbourne struggled to sell one hundred copies of a book on Australian painting (subsidised by the Melbourne Art Gallery) through his parent company in London. Dudley Phillips reported to Andrew Fabinyi that Pitmans 'at home'[42] refused to handle the general books he published in Australia. Penguin Books, which published a highly successful local edition of *The Australian Ugliness* (1963) by Robin Boyd, could not persuade its London branch to buy a single copy; Penguin was 'unwilling to accept any book on the strength of its Australian appeal alone'.[43] Longmans in London showed no co-operation in selling its Australian produced books. The firm of George G. Harrap, once a highly vocal supporter of the Australian book trade, were not taking quantities of books being published by Arthur Harrap in Australia.[44]

In one shape or another, Angus & Robertson had been dealing for many years as a publisher and bookseller with the issue of conducting business in differentiated markets. Through its London office and 'Operation London', Angus & Robertson had learned that Australian tastes could be particular to the Australian market and likewise with the British market. Sometimes it was not possible to obtain success with a title for sale in both markets. Penguin Australia's experience with *The Australian Ugliness* is a case in point. This was a book about Australian architecture and would have limited interest outside Australia. Yet export sales were as vital for British houses publishing in Australia as they were for local Australian companies, and, in a climate of limited options for the sale of Australian books in foreign markets, both were focusing their attention on Angus & Robertson's overseas operation. This generated opportunities for the London office to boost its catalogue with titles pulled from other publishers' lists while being careful to avoid becoming a wholesaler, which could negatively impact Angus & Robertson's reputation with authors.

Therefore, a distinct shift in emphasis away from other English publishers (coupled with a clear departure from fiction publishing because 'unless it is outstanding it just does not produce any profit at all')[45] took place alongside a parallel move to put forward, for the first time, only Australian books in Britain. Once the 'single biggest exporter of UK books [purchased] in London',[46] Ferguson envisaged Angus & Robertson's overseas branch might alternatively become 'a centre in London for Australian books'[47] and concentrated on distribution within and from the United Kingdom. During the late 1950s, publishing 'books of a universal appeal'[48] was considered the key to success in the British market by using the sales of popular titles to leaven the sales of Angus & Robertson's books.

This departure from the full-scale publication of books with British or American origins in order to be profitable represented a significant reorientation towards the handling of Australian books as the London office's core business. Ferguson had long suspected the strength of Angus & Robertson lay with its 'Australianness'[49] and wanted to test it in business. However, by participating in world book fairs, the firm's anxiety to identify the London office with Australian publishing would ironically find expression in a paving over of Angus & Robertson's geographical location. By imagining the London office as simultaneously international and yet rooted in a national character brought together by the printed word and a publisher's imprint, Angus & Robertson would promote its trading status as 'a world publisher and not as purely an Australian publisher'.[50] This would eventually reverse the London office's reorientation towards Australian books only.

What to do about London?

In the 1950s Angus & Robertson's London office was tied very closely to the personalities of Hector MacQuarrie and Barry Rowland. When MacQuarrie retired and Rowland resigned after the panic that took place around June 1960 with Walter Burns, George Ferguson's first reaction was to seek advice on how to reintroduce the London office's core activities. In January 1961 Ferguson asked his long-time friend, British publisher Walter Harrap, 'what is the best thing to do?'[51] Due to the dramatic sweeping aside of overseas publishing by Walter Burns, Ferguson faced the considerable challenge of rebuilding London operations a second time[52] and resuming the distribution of Australian books throughout Britain and continental Europe. After assessing the poor condition of the export department originally developed by the London office in the late 1940s, Ferguson confided in Harrap 'we must [again] look to the UK. If we don't we cannot continue to hold any significance as publishers and will just become the parish pump variety'.[53]

Ferguson kept faith that Angus & Robertson had much to gain by 'building A. & R. London into a sort of world centre for Australian books',[54] but he was uncertain how to undo the damage wrought by Burns' brief 'reign of terror'.[55] There was little question, however, regarding the continuing importance of export markets for the Australian publisher. Underscoring the cultural dimensions of the relationship between Sydney and London discussed in previous chapters, Ferguson knew a 'reasonable chance of distribution in the big overseas English-speaking markets' for Australian authors was fundamental to Angus & Robertson's ongoing success. On the commercial and production side was 'the fact that the longer the run the lower the unit price'.[56] From 'economical and control points of view', Angus & Robertson continued to believe that the advantages in having a London office were 'tremendous'.[57]

Ferguson did not think Angus & Robertson could respectably shop for American rights from Sydney.[58] Walter Harrap agreed. Perhaps drawing on his knowledge of the Australasian Publishing Company, which his brother helped set up in Sydney, Harrap marked Australia with having a 'geographical handicap' that mitigated against being an adequate distribution centre for the rest of the world: 'the only way you [can] get over it', he advised Ferguson, 'is to have your feet planted here [in London] as well as in Sydney'.[59] Harrap was talking about both publishing and bookselling, but Ferguson was concerned only with the latter. Certainly, Ferguson was confident that MacQuarrie and Rowland had proved during their record year of 1959[60] that Angus & Robertson could in fact retail quantities of any Australian book in the United Kingdom 'without spending too much in the selling'.[61] But, in the post Burns era, Ferguson was less convinced that the London office catalogue needed to be materially assisted by a percentage of books from Britain or America; he recognised that this would 'save it from being purely Australian'.[62]

Ferguson's primary task was to sort out the mess that was Walter Burns' legacy. As examined previously, the London office had initially defended its mission, but it was unable to withstand the demands of Burns' merchandising principles and saw its publishing infrastructure liquidated.[63] It was therefore a rare concession by Ferguson that Burns perhaps had 'brought home a few things to us that we didn't know before'.[64] The end of Walter Burns did not bring with it the end of the London office's troubles, but items which did not directly impact Angus & Robertson's Profit and Loss could be swiftly amended as the firm resumed 'a much more purposeful kind of life'.[65]

For example, the London office's distribution of Australian books published by Cheshire and Sam Ure Smith was promptly resumed after Ferguson held meetings with his Australian book trade counterparts, describing the recent events politely as a 'temporary setback'.[66] Stock for 86 titles was replenished from the Sydney warehouse, ranging in quantities of 6 (for example, *Wild Colonial Boys*, *They Came From the Sea*, *The Devil Behind Them*) to 100 (for example, *Snugglepot and Cuddlepie*, *Ned Kelly*, *The Lamp is*

Heavy).[67] Seeing these stock numbers, Ferguson was prompted to conclude, 'No wonder sales fell into a pretty poor state. Book after book that would have sold just wasn't there to sell'.[68] Stanley Amor, whom Walter Burns employed on the (now discredited) premise that Amor might secure discounts from British publishers for the export department that others previously could not, was discharged from Angus & Robertson in London 'at great expense but without unpleasantness'.[69] Cliff Rust was put in charge of the export department (securing books for Sydney at minimum terms of three months' credit before payment was due),[70] and C. Joyner would once again administrate finances. Ferguson was opposed to re-engaging Barry Rowland, who was reported to be 'extremely unpopular'[71] with staff, and he instead reappointed Walter Butcher on a three year contract at £2,000 per annum to rebuild London sales.[72] Due to his amazing capacity for detail, Butcher would oversee general office administration, all Sydney books and other Australian publishers' lists, the trade department and production.[73] George Ferguson's son, John Ferguson, would support Butcher until the younger Ferguson returned to Australia in 1962.[74]

Other items, such as marketing Australian books with comparatively low overheads while attempting little original publishing in London as possible, were more difficult to reconfigure. The crux of the situation as Harrap saw it, in his four-page reply to Ferguson, was that within clearly prescribed limits Angus & Robertson's London office needed to become an autonomous operation. In an assessment not dissimilar to the opinions of former London office managers (and later Richard Hauser), Harrap reminded Angus & Robertson's managing director that

> You must not expect to run it from Castlereagh Street, or any other address in Australia, for unless you are on the spot either here or in America or in Australia or anywhere else, you cannot keep up to date with the taste of the public and know what kind of books in which to invest … [T]he stronger the parental hand the weaker has been the child.[75]

Harrap gave the example of the Macmillan Company in New York; the company was originally a branch of the British publisher of the same name, but it was now an entirely separate concern where the only real mode of contact between the New York and London offices was financial. The 'purpose for which one founded an overseas concern'[76] should not be consigned to 'oblivion',[77] and Harrap hoped Angus & Robertson's London office might become, in effect, similar to Macmillan, Longman or Pitman in New York – controlled financially by the parent company but also a publisher in its own right, which is free to buy and sell books. Using his own house as an example, which sold books from the lists of other independent companies (such as Adlard Coles and the Fountain Press), Harrap also argued that no publishing concern could specialise only in titles connected with its home culture if the business wished to obtain noteworthy sales in markets, say, overseas from Australia. The London office would need to offer buyers 'non-Australian books … which fitted their own particular market needs'.[78]

Finally, Harrap wondered what had inspired Burns to take the actions that he did and whether the former managing director gave the London office any credit for shifting stock which might otherwise have remained unsold in Angus & Robertson's Sydney warehouse. In a review of the mutual dependencies that can exist between Australian and British publishers or offices, Harrap speculated that the Sydney house would have been selling stock to its London branch priced close to manufacturing cost, and the English sales of this stock returned low or nil profit to Angus & Robertson in Australia. An audit might claim that Sydney was in fact making a loss, with concessions to its London office appearing as a form of subsidy, but this view in Harrap's way of thinking was impractical, neglecting the improved scales of economy that larger print runs exploited:

> by selling 2,000 to London at little over cost one can print 5,000 copies instead of 3,000 copies, the all-over unit cost per copy is reduced and you make a larger margin of profit on the home sale of the 3,000 copies. Such additional profit, therefore, should really be added to the credit of your London house.[79]

Furthermore, these benefits could travel in either direction, and the London office, if properly developed, might find books suitable for the British market that were also acceptable for retail in Australian and New Zealand bookshops. The London office could then also supply Sydney with stock at a little over cost, and the office in Australia would in turn profit from their sale. By publishing larger quantities, finding books that appealed to more than one market and building into the firm's catalogue a mix of titles that addressed other cultures, Harrap suggested that an export trade in books could have a meaningful impact on the health of an Australian publisher. In displaying an undeniable, uncanny familiarity with the issues that Ferguson, MacQuarrie and Rowland had debated and at times argued over throughout the 1950s, Harrap confirmed Ferguson's conviction that 'the problems of publishers are pretty well the same all over the world':[80] publishing is a specific industry with no certainties or any special formula for good sales; the reputation of a firm's imprint is unquantifiable but absolutely important to the success of the publisher; and publishers are only as good as the books they publish and the lists they command. It was a nuanced business that the two British and Australian publishers, Harrap and Ferguson, agreed on.

Angus & Robertson understood the circumstances of its business and the rules that governed it, but it did not necessarily have command of the means by which its business could be improved. With the sales and accounting departments, staff contracts and stock shortages satisfactorily re-established at the London office,[81] Angus & Robertson remained apprehensive towards offering steep discounts for its overseas branch and maintaining price advantages in an export market. The company was equally disinclined for the London office to 'shoot off like a satellite on some orbit of its own'.[82] Harrap's advice seemed sound enough, but the parent firm in its new character appeared to be less flexible. A thorny issue for Ferguson for nearly a decade at the end of 1961was the London office's acceptance of Burns' recommendation that it would not report profit from overseas sales 'for the first year or so'.[83] On this point, Ferguson was less reasonable regarding Walter Butcher's need 'to sell *all* our books at a lower price in sterling than their published price in Australia'.[84] His son, John Ferguson, was convinced the 55 per cent discount on the Australian retail price that London purchased bound stock from Sydney was an 'unrealistic method in supplying this office'[85] if it was ever to show a profit.

Calculating overheads to be around 33 per cent, John Ferguson contended that the price should be much closer to production cost. While Angus & Robertson allowed the London office a 67 per cent discount off of Sydney books in 1959, George Ferguson defended the current practice as representing the 'lowest price we can charge'.[86] Like Rowland and MacQuarrie before him, Butcher submitted that certain books, like fiction, ought to be priced economically in the United Kingdom; that is, cheaper. 'I think there must be an appreciation of the difference between English and Australian prices, particularly with fiction. Some [256 page] books being priced at 21s. 6d Australian will not sell at more than 16s' sterling.[87]

Market conditions in London were indifferent to Ferguson's frequent attempts to negotiate leaner discount rates for Sydney titles. A price advantage continued to be a key component to successfully selling books in an export market. Ferguson agreed with some reluctance that regarding fiction – popular non-fiction and juveniles – London had in the past obtained better trade terms from Sydney but not in the case of specialised books. He contrasted a novel by Ion Idriess selling for 21/- (shillings) in Australia, which might need to retail for 15/- in order to remain competitive in the British marketplace, against a book on Australian gardening, which could sell – without objection – for 30/- in both Sydney and London.[88] It was clear that different types of books commanded different prices. The financial expectation of a customer for a novel was different to that of a would-be buyer of a gardening book. The answer for Angus & Robertson lay in the discovery of what the British market would accept. Angus & Robertson understood that prices and discounts mattered in order to enable its London office to operate at a profit but counselled that 'fiction is the last thing we are interested in really at present'.[89] Instead, the London office was advised to investigate the costs of locally printing fiction and children's books in quantities of four to seven thousand copies, since the firm 'ought to be able to publish novels at a competitive price with those published by any other British publisher'.[90]

Butcher's strong sales from September 1961 to February 1962 proved that 'a fair market exists for a lot of our books that would have been thought impossible before'.[91] Concentrating on the 'right methods of selling the right kinds of books in the right places'[92] therefore became the new blueprint for success in Britain:

> The trouble we got into with Hector and Barry were in my opinion not so much troubles brought about by a wrong basic scheme, as troubles brought about by the selection of the wrong books. We did get a number of American titles which sold quite well, for example *A Lamp is Heavy* etc., but there was too much fooling about with titles that Hector personally liked, and on which he could spend as many months as possible with editing.[93]

Australian Companies with Worldwide Interests

The desire to develop alternative export markets for Australian books underlined the rebuilding of Angus & Robertson's London office. It was hoped these new markets would counter the depressed condition of the British book trade, which was suffering under 'terrific importations coming through from the [United] States'.[94] (Although the market was always changing, the fear of American production capacities was an ongoing concern given that the United States could maintain low prices because of its huge and exclusive domestic market.) Because they were facing this challenge in a situation that was already a 'hard, tough battle',[95] the London office worked hard to rejuvenate the sale of Australian books. In January 1962, 550 export accounts were reopened in addition to another 57 accounts in Britain and 90 overseas (including 21 in America) which were added by year's end.[96] Drawing on the British Publishers Association's list and facilities for circularising the public, 18,500 catalogues were dispatched worldwide to places like South America; 1,600 catalogues were mailed to American universities; and, in addition to concentrating more on library business in Britain,[97] another 2,000 catalogues were sent to overseas libraries.

The immediate response was modest by way of 11 orders for H. M. Green's now classic *History of Australian Literature* and an order from Cuba for 25 copies of *Sheep Management and Diseases* by H. G. Belschner.[98] Producing and printing the catalogue cost £800, making advertising expenditure rather heavy for 1961, but Angus & Robertson acknowledged that 'we have to re-establish ourselves in the eyes of the world and you can't do that for nothing'.[99] Indeed, Angus & Robertson expected as usual to absorb an otherwise unavoidable loss.[100] By mid-1962 success seemed certain if still distant. Ferguson believed the London office had 'the game fairly well by the throat',[101] and sales confirmed there was a growing market once again for Australian books.

The progress of the London office, as Ferguson knew from Harrap's advice, would depend on a good list of titles. That part of the catalogue, which was previously furnished with publications from the defunct 'Operation London', could now be stocked with books by Australian publishers intent on marketing their lists internationally.[102] Confident that no other Australian firm had better knowledge of exporting books worldwide nor overseas facilities superior to 54 Bartholomew Close in London,[103] Angus & Robertson – having revived the distribution of books published by Ure Smith Ltd and F. W. Cheshire – was anxious to secure more Australian accounts. It was a matter of importance to Ferguson that Angus & Robertson 'should use its strength and resources to assist Australian publishing generally rather than merely taking a narrow view of what is best' for its own commercial interests.[104] Wrapping Angus & Robertson in 'righteous causes' (one of the tactics described by Robert Haupt regarding British publishers' activity in the Australian book trade),[105] Ferguson regarded the development of export markets for Australian publishing as 'one of the duties which [was] laid upon' the company by his late grandfather, George Robertson.[106] If the London office was to be known essentially as an Australian publisher, then according to Ferguson it should aim to carry 'the cream of the list of all … Australian publishers'.[107] Thus a key factor in negotiations with other Australian publishers would be that their titles might retail at a 'correct'[108] price. This meant buying stock in sheets or bound copies at a profitable discount.

Angus & Robertson did not want to develop a custom of continually haggling over prices nor did they want to start 'beating other Australian publishers into the ground unnecessarily'[109] for fear of losing to alternative distributors its business advantage of being the only Australian centre in London. Without 'Operation London', Angus &

Robertson alone could no longer supply a sufficient number of titles that were readily saleable in the United Kingdom.[110] The firm thus settled on a policy in which Australian-based companies could have distribution from the United Kingdom provided the London office could purchase each company's respective stock at 60 per cent off the published price (with freight and royalties pre-paid). These terms would permit Angus & Robertson a 10 per cent profit margin while ensuring the London office was not compelled to price books out of the British market. For a time these terms were deemed acceptable, and they laid the foundation for co-operation between Angus & Robertson and other Australian firms. Slowly a group of Australian booksellers and publishers accumulated. This group, which stretched to ten affiliates,[111] included: Lansdowne Press;[112] Georgian House, which used to be represented in Britain by Phoenix House and which doubled as Australian agents for J. M. Dent, Mills & Boon and the Cambridge University Press;[113] Ian Novak Publishing;[114] Barker's Bookstore; Rigby Ltd; Ure Smith Ltd; F. W. Cheshire; Green Square;[115] and Jacaranda Press.[116]

Inevitably, however, the reduction of imports from the United Kingdom wrought great changes structurally in the industry; Australian publishers, although pleased with the service Angus & Robertson's London office provided, would investigate alternative methods of boosting home sales in an industry that had 'become technically more proficient in the last 10 years'.[117] With claims of insufficient good books to go around in Australia due to 'a couple of dozen active Australian publishers'[118] now competing for manuscripts, former London office employee Sam Ure Smith, who now operated his own publishing company, wanted to incorporate overseas titles by London firms into his own Australian catalogue and offer Australian sheets to British publishers in exchange.[119]

Sam Ure Smith, who had worked with Hector MacQuarrie[120] in 1953 as part of a broader visit to the United Kingdom to gain knowledge of the publishing world,[121] was ten years later president of the Australian Book Publishers Association and proprietor of his father's Australian publishing company, Ure Smith Ltd. Ure Smith had observed that the competition for Australian manuscripts had become increasingly 'fierce' between Australian and British publishers since the late 1940s when the British Publishers' Traditional Market Agreement came into effect. As discussed, in late 1963 Ure Smith drafted a letter to John Brown, president of the British Publishers Association, and petitioned on behalf of the Australian book trade for the British Publishers Association to abolish the Traditional Market Agreement in regard to Australia.[122] Ure Smith argued that through the agreement members of the British book trade were 'attempting to prevent Australian publishers from having a legitimate share in the publishing of foreign books' at a time when Australian firms most 'need[ed] books of overseas origin to assist in maintaining a reasonable output of titles'.[123] This was particularly the case with American titles.

Although Andrew Fabinyi claimed that 'rights bought elsewhere are basic to the function of British publishing',[124] Ure Smith argued that British publishers' lists were 'strengthened' by the addition of selected foreign books and asserted that 'Australian publishing too needs this additional strength'.[125] Ure Smith pointed to the importance of reciprocal traffic where 'buying negotiations with foreign publishers [often] lead to selling negotiations'.[126] He also noted the contradiction in which Australian publishers were denied access to American titles even though it was quite in order for the Australian branch of a British publisher to continue to enjoy unrestricted access. 'We're grown up now', Ure Smith commented to the *Sydney Morning Herald* in September 1963, 'and we want the keys'.[127]

Ure Smith was sceptical about John Brown's response that Australian publishers might become signatories to the British Publishers' Traditional Market Agreement and work together at fortifying the Commonwealth market as a whole. Such a notion underlined John Feather's thesis that British publishers co-operated 'so that they could survive to compete against each other',[128] but while this arrangement had worked for Angus & Robertson Ure Smith dismissed Brown's advice. Instead, Ure Smith targeted the 50 per cent discount on fiction and juveniles that British publishers offered Australian booksellers as being especially detrimental to the creation of Australian literature (local production costs were higher and consequently profit margins were lower). Ure Smith claimed it was an anachronistic practice that continued a colonial habit of 'dumping'British books in Australia even if some of this was now done through British branch plants established locally. These British books, heavily discounted to the bookseller who calculated their final retail price in regard to the invoiced cost, acquired a price advantage in the Australian market. From the perspective of local Australian business, the price advantage made it difficult to 'compete with British fiction'.[129] As booksellers marked up their imported titles according to a fixed margin tabled in the Australian Schedule of Prices, even a small reduction of the discount would meaningfully increase the invoiced price of British books to booksellers and in turn increase the final retail price for the Australian public. A reduction therefore of the discount to 40 per cent was put forward by Ure Smith as an important step towards helping Australian publishers increase their own retail prices, accordingly improve profit margins and enable the production of smaller editions which were necessary for the publication of Australian fiction and children's books.

The response of the Publishers Association to Ure Smith's request was not dissimilar to discussions held between Angus & Robertson's own offices regarding the pricing of books in export markets and the home unit costs that export editions affected. While agreeing with criticisms of the 50 per cent discount offered by some (but not all) British publishers, juveniles and fiction represented a 'tougher'[130] business in Australia and were therefore priced according to what the market could reasonably sustain. Brown also noted that discounts varied from publisher to publisher and were set under individual economic circumstances. This was because the Restrictive Trade Practices Act (1956) in the United Kingdom prevented British publishers from coming together in any industry-wide agreement on the subject of discounts to booksellers. For these reasons alone, John Brown did not disguise the fact that the export discounts that British publishers gave to Australian booksellers would continue to be a 'tricky'[131] issue for Australian publishers. Brown consented, however, to draw wider attention to the problem within his organisation.

The exchange of letters between the Australian Book Publishers Association and the British Publishers Association also mobilised another option that would allow Australian publishers to benefit from the public demand for British titles: the development of sheet sales to Australian publishers. The advantages of unbound copies sales to both book trades, in Ure Smith's view, would be larger print-runs for British publishers and increased publishing for Australian firms. The council of the [British] Publishers Association agreed. While they were defensive regarding the British Publishers' Traditional Market Agreement, characterising it as a policy which protected British as well as Australian interests against the commercial power of American companies operating in English-language markets, the council was 'enthusiastically in favour of encouraging the sale of sheets of UK editions to Australian publishers'.[132]

The solution was warmly received as a 'novel and entirely practical'[133] answer to the Australian question of maintaining traditional markets, and the association agreed to build closer commercial relationships between British and Australian publishers. A circular was subsequently sent to all members of the British Publishers Association, calling for more serious thought on the possibility of selling rights or sheets to Australian publishers:

> Such arrangements should considerably assist the growing Australian publishing trade and would give Australian publishers a chance of acquiring American books through, and with benefit to, a British publisher. This would, of course, apply equally to titles of British origin, and in either case the British publisher would gain from the increased printing number and the resultant lower unit cost.[134]

No mention was made in the circular about Australian publishers also selling the rights or sheets of Australian books in return, but Ure Smith confirmed from his firm's private negotiations that British publishers 'rather do expect to get something back from us if we are to get something from them'.[135]

This idea gestured towards improved reciprocal traffic evolving between Australian and British companies without Angus & Robertson's London office acting as intermediary or facilitator. It is not surprising therefore that London manager Walter Butcher was not entirely supportive of Australian publishers entering into separate trade agreements with British publishers. Butcher suspected that those whom the London office now represented in the United Kingdom would offer British publishers the best from their lists while Angus & Robertson in future would be offered only their 'left-overs'.[136] In fact, Ure Smith's admission that his firm could not automatically give the London office first option on everything it published left little doubt in Butcher's mind that Ure Smith was 'going to pick out the plums to give to other publishers'.[137]

Ferguson agreed, but he also linked the continuing importance of carrying other publishers' books to the viability of the London office in its own mission to maintain a reasonable list of titles for sale in the United Kingdom. It seemed to Ferguson that Angus & Robertson was still 'hardly able to make ends meet in London even with the other Australian publishers and we wouldn't be able to make ends meet without them'.[138] Even as Ferguson publicly accepted Ure Smith's assurance that he 'shall not be trying to play both ends against the middle',[139] privately he, like Butcher, was less convinced. Yet he could see no alternative: '[F]or the time being, I think we would not want to lose them … [but] in the long run I would hope that we can get a few American books to supplement our own books, and then they can all go to hell'.[140] If 'the whole picture of publishing everywhere is an international one',[141] as Sam Ure Smith argued about the Australian book trade, then Ferguson believed the London office should focus more on expanding and becoming 'a force recognised throughout the world as an Australian company with worldwide interests'.[142]

By the late 1960s, the London office's links with other major publishing houses were being downplayed in favour of advancing its own international image. Angus & Robertson retreated significantly from its 1961 position, which noted a responsibility to carry other Australian publishers in Britain, and instead worked towards stocking in London only books marked with the company's imprint: 'We have large sums of money invested in our own publications', Ferguson remarked to Butcher, 'and our selling organisation must be devoted to shifting them, and not the books of others'.[143] The co-operation between Angus & Robertson and other Australian publishers, which was a feature of the London office's recuperation in the years immediately following Walter Burns, was slowly untangled.

From 1966 Ure Smith would make its own arrangements in London,[144] and Angus & Robertson would gradually drop the books of its counterparts and take only those few titles which 'have some real chance'.[145] Sales figures reveal that the percentage of market books not published by Angus & Robertson – which were nevertheless catalogued on the London office list – declined from 28 per cent in spring 1967 to 9 per cent in spring 1969.[146] Results from 1968 also confirm that the overseas branch was not yet in a position to ignore other Australian publishers' books, but the London office was being much more discriminating than before.[147] For the six-month period from 1 July to 31 December 1967, London office sales totalled £42,279 which included £2,835 from the sale of Lansdowne Press books, £4,143 from the sale of Rigby Ltd books and £2,124 from the sale of miscellaneous Australian publications.[148] In one form or another, Angus & Robertson would therefore continue to work with other companies but would treat its books on an entirely indifferent commercial basis. It was important to Ferguson that the London office 'become more of a publisher and less of a wholesaler'.[149]

The London office was also instructed 'not to accept anything from any other Australian publisher unless you can take a big enough quantity to warrant having A. & R.'s imprint'.[150] Although this was certainly a move to push Angus & Robertson's brand ahead of its competitors, it was coyly presented to other Australian and British publishers as an experiment to 'see whether it isn't possible on some titles to sell more copies by taking an edition with our imprint'.[151] Privately, though, the London office was interested only in books that brought Angus & Robertson 'profits or prestige or both';[152] in other words, titles that added to the firm's power to grow as British publishers. This meant obtaining books for the entire British market with 'no special effort'[153] applied to acquire Australasian rights only. Accordingly, the Sydney office dismantled its view regarding 'Australiana' being one of Angus & Robertson's core strengths as it was evaluated to encourage a view in Sydney that the 'Australian market defined the whole possible horizon' of trade.[154] In the catalogue of autumn 1968, London and Sydney titles were thus featured in a way in which their place of origin was of no consequence nor immediately obvious.

Alec Bolton, who was engaged by Angus & Robertson as the London office's editor[155] in 1966 and later as a co-director of the overseas house (see the following chapter), wanted more editorial horsepower in Sydney 'harnessed to the production of books aimed at a wider market than the Australian one'.[156] As the company entered new territories through the London office, in Bolton's view it needed to be 'more mindful of how texts will be read to non-Australian eyes'.[157] Bolton longed to specialise in the publication of universal general books rather than continuing with great effort to sell '(largely unwanted) Australian books'.[158] Consequently, from 'Australiana' emerged the idea that a business identity shaped by the company's brand and with British leanings was more beneficial in the international marketplace than foregrounding the Australian cultural theme or cultural biography of its products:

> Our feeling here is that we must go it alone as London publishers. There will probably be some uproar at this end [in Sydney] but we can handle that … In other words the 'advancement in Australian publishing' couldn't matter less at Frankfurt or anywhere else. What has to matter to us are the two things – (a) what can Angus & Robertson as British Commonwealth publishers buy at Frankfurt and (b) what can we sell? It is quite obvious that the British Commonwealth Market Agreement will not break down and frankly I don't think we would be well serviced if it did. Therefore we must operate as a British publisher in the full sense and not as an Australian one.[159]

But the London office's 'good reputation' was due not only to the attractiveness of its books, but also because its books were about Australia.[160] Like one of Stephen Alomes' ex-patriots, this would result in the London office 'neither completely possessing the nationality they have left behind, but still carry with them, nor fully acquiring that of their new place of abode'.[161] This tension between 'a London style and an Australian persona'[162] would eventually peak during Angus & Robertson's attendance at the Frankfurt Book Fair.

Frankfurt Book Fair

The Frankfurt Book Fair started in 1949 as a German book trade exhibition attended by 205 publishers displaying 8,400 books (including 2,100 new titles). In the six years preceding 1955, by which time it drew the attention of the British Publishers Association's Export Research Committee, the fair had become widely international with 1,150 booksellers from all over Europe exhibiting 36,500 books plus 12,000 new titles. Beginning modestly with two publishers managing a stall during the fair's second year, by 1955 the British Publishers Association had 180 firms representing the British book trade, and the growing presence of so many continental publishers transformed the annual exhibition into 'a market place for the sale and purchase of translation and other book rights'.[163] In 1975 Ferguson recalled that

> The purpose of the Frankfurt Book Fair of course is to make contact with publishers, editors and literary agents from other countries and to buy and sell physical books. In fact you are not allowed to sell books in Frankfurt as it is designed for the sale of the rights to publish books. Frankfurt is not only a place when one sells rights but where

> one buys rights too. You might buy a book from a German publisher for instance or a Spanish or any other publisher for sale in the English language in Australia.[164]

Ferguson located the importance of international trade fairs to publishers in the context of its benefits for authors. Exhibitions that brought together members of the book trade from around the world represented potential markets that could be tapped outside the limited range of national distribution or an audience confined to a single language:

> Every author is entitled to the best distribution he or she can get and that doesn't limit it to one language. If the rights can be sold of an Australian book in Japanese or in Hungarian or anything else, or if the rights can be sold in English in say the United States, this is all part of what a publisher ought to be doing for an author and then, of course, the publisher himself makes a profit out of it too.[165]

Angus & Robertson had been aware of the Frankfurt Book Fair since the 1950s. As part of the company's membership in the Publishers Association, year by year the London office received memorandums announcing the event and calling for participants in the British stand.[166] Occasionally, MacQuarrie would send sample copies for display.[167] According to testimony offered to the consultant Richard Hauser by then manager Barry Rowland, the London office had expressed keen interest in attending the 1960 Frankfurt Book Fair, but the Sydney office refused this request. This made no sense to Rowland since on an investment of £50 he claimed there was a possibility for the London office to make £5,000 and important contacts. Hauser, acting as a de facto representative of the Burns' management, authorised Rowland 'to go ahead'.[168] But upon hearing rumours of the impending closure of the overseas publishing department, Rowland soon resigned and work on the fair did not progress any further than Rowland's initial tentative arrangements. After Burns was voted out of the position as Angus & Robertson's managing director, Rowland's replacement, Stanley Amor, wrote to George Ferguson and suggested the London office might coordinate with the British firm W. H. Smith 'to carry our books at a fairly cheap rate … [since] it seems that we should show at this Fair'.[169] But this arrangement too never eventuated. In fact, it would not be until John Ferguson was officially installed as London manager, following the termination of Amor's employment, that Angus & Robertson would make any coordinated effort to participate in international trade fairs.

In a fashion similar to the first phase of establishing an overseas branch, John Ferguson was sent to the 1961 Frankfurt Book Fair as Angus & Robertson's representative. His mission was to assess the exhibition's potential and provide reconnaissance on 'what happens about the selling of rights'.[170] Armed with a portfolio of Australian blurbs and jackets (which, in the absence of actual books, were essential to situating texts in the market),[171] John Ferguson was cautioned by his father 'not to actually make any deals unless you are absolutely certain that the rights in question are ours to dispose of' (due to carrying a mix of publishers' titles).[172] John recorded after his attendance at the fair that it was 'essential'[173] for Angus & Robertson to be represented at the fair in 1962. He explained that

> Australia this year [1961] was significant by its absence, and I think it is important that we should have a stand to project Australia through the books displayed to this large international gathering, and to do whatever business is possible, by the selling of rights or indeed the buying of rights for our own markets.[174]

George Ferguson had suspected the fair would be 'the greatest market in the world now',[175] and he had been encouraged by the secretary of the British Publishers Association, Ron Barker, who advised him 'Frankfurt offers a singular opportunity for a publisher like yourself'.[176]

John Ferguson, travelling with his wife, two tin trunks, a pram, a tape recorder, a camp stretcher and 'a lot of books',[177] attended the 1962 fair on behalf of Angus & Robertson before travelling to the United States and returning to Australia. He expected a lot of interest in the firm's publications at the fair and was not disappointed. The event was reported to be a 'wonderful success',[178] suggesting in particular a great future for Australian children's books through European translations,[179] and led to requests for rights on a range of Angus & Robertson titles for reprinting throughout the Continent.[180] Six months earlier, the Sydney office had approached American and European publishers, inviting them to visit the Australian stand. Angus & Robertson had learned through John Ferguson's previous visit to Frankfurt that deals were rarely concluded 'on the spot' at the f; rather, the primary form of business was in making important contacts and stimulating interest in future publications. From that perspective, the company considered a show at the Frankfurt Book Fair would be invaluable, and it increased its list of 'personal friends on the Continent'.[181]

Continental Markets

The Frankfurt Book Fair was not Angus & Robertson's first attempt to reach markets outside London, but it ranked among its most successful. Ever since the Second World War there had been a constant effort by the London office to find overseas markets, especially in South East Asia, India, South Africa and Europe. Angus & Robertson canvassed each territory for book sales possibilities. South East Asia was known to be a valuable market for technical and reference books, and in 1958 Angus & Robertson enlisted Edinburgh-trained agent, Thomas Brash, to place appropriate non-fiction titles with Singapore's leading booksellers.[182] Brash also circularised the firm's books in Indonesia, Burma, Vietnam and Japan with some success. In regard to the People's Republic of China, Angus & Robertson dealt directly with an importer, Guozi Shudian, whose 'credit [was] good with the Publishers Association'.[183] Fiction, however, was impossible to sell in Far East markets, and Brash avoided books with 'pro-Red or anti-British' inclinations that consistently made them subject to confiscation. To meet the 'insatiable demand [for titles]... whatever the quality or price',[184] educational books were supplied by the Sydney office and technical titles by the London office.

Like South East Asia, India was also considered a lucrative territory for technical books;[185] although this assessment was made by George Ferguson, who travelled to India in 1958, the overseas branch turned down an offer in 1962 for representation in India by the Asia Publishing Company. This was due to the London office's then poor setup for managing what it labelled 'risky accounts'.[186] In regard to South Africa, MacQuarrie and Rowland engaged the services of Brian Lamberth who represented the firm from 1955–9;[187] his brother Rupert Lamberth assumed his territory in 1961 under an arrangement with John Ferguson.[188]

Lastly, the importance of the European Continent as a potential consumer of Australian books was recognised by MacQuarrie and Rowland when the London office employed the services of a Continental representative, Leo Beek, from 30 January 1952. Beek acted as sole agent for Angus & Robertson in Holland, Belgium, France, Italy, Western Germany, Denmark, Scandinavia and Finland[189] for a short time until he passed the bulk of the work over to Meulenhoff (Importers) who mainly operated in Holland and Western Germany.[190] Later, MacQuarrie and Rowland contracted Denis Payne who from 1 January 1959 marketed Australian books to European booksellers. In his first month Payne obtained an order for two sets of the *Australian Encyclopaedia*.[191]

It is clear then, from 1952–9, that the London office had devoted much effort in trying to obtain suitable arrangements for representation outside the United Kingdom, particularly in non-English language markets. Occasionally, while fraught by the same issues of coordinating over large distances that the Sydney and London offices were so familiar with, these resulted in sales to booksellers. But Angus & Robertson knew, as Sam Ure Smith discovered with the closing of the market in Australia for English books, that greater economic benefits accrued with selling direct to overseas firms. Once this puzzle was solved – that is, how to sell Angus & Robertson's books to international publishers – the way lay open for rights deals, unbound copies sales and other explorations of the vast European market.

The Frankfurt Book Fair symbolised one such opportunity, but the presence of Angus & Robertson physically at the next fair, in terms of an actual stand, raised in-house questions over whether the company should identify itself as a world publisher or an Australian publisher.[192] The 'battle for sales'[193] might have been the driving force behind the London office in the first half of the 1960s, but opportunities to exhibit on the international stage set the company's sense of its commercial fit with the global marketplace against the 'philosophical basis of the firm'.[194] The objectives of the London office tugged between two extremes: the market values of commodity exchange first exemplified by Walter Burns and the historical, patriotic values espoused by Ferguson's grandfather, George Robertson. Stretched between the two, the London office strived for focus: was Angus & Robertson an Australian, British, overseas or world publisher? Moreover, which identity or category stimulated book sales the most?

A British Publisher

Angus & Robertson's sense of its international identity was not easily moved away from abstract notions of national duty even while it attempted to negotiate a more commercially beneficial place in the fair – one that potentially elided its link with Australian publishing. Correspondence between Walter Butcher and George Ferguson prior to the 1964 Frankfurt Book Fair suggests that Geoffrey Blainey's classic 'tyranny of distance' thesis, as applied to the impact of Australia's geographical remoteness on its history and development, could equally fit trade show floor geography and its potential impact on shaping the identity – or perception – of a publisher:

> You will recall that the essential thinking at the recent World Book Fair was that we exhibited as part of the British scene and not as an overseas publisher. Everybody was pleased to see this, but in a few months time we shall be exhibiting as an overseas publisher at Frankfurt, and very definitely we shall be identified as such [that is, as an overseas publisher]. If our position is the same as before, we shall be near the Brazilian stand, near the Canadian stand, near the French stand, but a fair distance from the British scene; anyway sufficiently far away [enough] for us to be overlooked by any American publisher who is spending his time looking at British books only.[195]

In this context, the London office became marked with an anxiety over promoting 'Australian' publishing and with a nagging awareness of commercial priority articulated by Butcher as a fear of lost sales potential in English-language markets. He asked Ferguson, 'Are we not then doing some harm in isolating ourselves in this way?'[196] Butcher realised that at Frankfurt every country wanted to retain its national character, but he believed there was a price to be paid for doing this; emphasising the firm's Australian identity when it exhibited internationally would negatively impact rights sales. Ferguson did not disagree, for in 1964 he began to have a mounting concern that the more Australian books the London office sold, the more Angus & Robertson would be identified as solely Australian publishers. In his view, this was mirrored in agents sending manuscripts to Angus & Robertson after their second or third rejection by another publisher. (John Abernethy recalled disappointment at being confronted with a 'mediocre specimen' – John McGhee's *Cage of Mirrors* – after courting David Higham who represented 21 Australian writers.)[197] Butcher agreed and concluded that the time had come for the company to envisage itself as a 'world publisher' if it desired to 'exhibit where the return is the greatest'.[198]

This discussion between Sydney and London regarding the location of the company's stand at the Frankfurt Book Fair was very strongly anchored to commercial interests first and national boundaries second. As such, the two international faces of the London office began to emerge. On the one hand, the London office's visibility as being essentially Australian represented a new phase for colonial publishing in the international marketplace. By exhibiting independently as active makers of Australian culture in their own right and by breaking from appearances as a component of the British display, Angus & Robertson's London office challenged the entrenched hierarchy of Empire/Colony book trade history and put forward its own version of Australian publishing[199] – one in which Australian writers could achieve international distribution or world recognition through an Australian rather than British publisher. However, with trade fairs staging the layout of booths according to the world map, Australia's geographical location betrayed its distance from the world's 'literary centre which [was], undoubtedly, London'[200] and situated Angus & Robertson far from crucial English-language business. Harrap earlier referred to this as Angus & Robertson's 'geographical handicap'[201] and required the company to have operations in both Sydney and London in order to overcome and succeed trade difficulties brought about by distance. It was not commercially strategic, therefore, to be an Australian publisher in a setting organised geographically.

On the other hand, Angus & Robertson's preoccupation with placing Australian books in Europe or America could be read as 'the reflex of a threatened cultural nationalism',[202] implying that Australian publishing could only be measured in any meaningful way when held against the yard-stick of European and American publishers. At the fair this meant being sufficiently empowered to undertake trade in British, American and Continental markets. In practical terms, this meant placing Angus & Robertson 'into the centres where publishers gather' for fear of being 'left for dead'.[203]

In the end, Ferguson's decision about the Frankfurt Book Fair rejected any alternative that made the London office appear as an 'overseas' publisher. Dismissing the category because it perhaps exposed Australia to be 'awkwardly placed at the wrong end of the world' in English-language negotiations[204] – that is, with Brazil, Canada and France – Ferguson chose instead to more squarely identify Australian publishing with the British (and, by implication, the western or English) book trade: 'We here think then that we should exhibit in the British section as a British publisher taking a small stand or booth for this purpose'.[205] Like its exhibition at the 1969 Children's Book Fair in Bologna, Italy,[206] Angus & Robertson formed a part of the British Council stand organised through the Publishers Association. Although supportive of the Australian National booth in subsequent years (which also included Angus & Robertson books in its exhibition[207]), the London office's export sales and international business in rights (both buying and selling) 'increased enormously'[208] by 1967 through its association with British publishers. Furthermore, from its show at the 1964 Frankfurt Book Fair, Angus & Robertson recognised that for 'real growth' to occur it needed to follow Sam Ure Smith's example and once again internationalise its list. It eventually concluded that 'the London list of general books ought not to be cluttered up and distracted by the inclusion of books of a purely Australian nature'.[209] If Angus & Robertson wanted European and American publishers to express interest in its list then it needed to present one that was 'not overloaded with local material'.[210] Correspondingly, the London office would revert to a mixture of Australian, British and American books.

As British publishers once more, the operations of the overseas branch as it looked towards the second half of the 1960s would not be altogether unfamiliar to MacQuarrie and Rowland's operations of the 1950s.

Chapter 12

THE HIDDEN PARTS OF PUBLISHING FORTUNE

I think it is in our interests that the British Empire Rights Agreement should continue and we must continue to publish in London.[1]

At the beginning of another period of reorganisation, George Ferguson reassured Walter Butcher that the London office was 'an essential part of the [Angus & Robertson] publishing operation' and that it would be 'maintained in some form though not necessarily in its present form'.[2] With rhetoric that former London executives Hector MacQuarrie, Barry Rowland, Stanley Amor and John Ferguson would perhaps have recognised from years past, Ferguson reinforced the view that as far as general publishing was concerned the London operation was fundamental to Angus & Robertson's 'retention and attraction of [Australian] authors',[3] lest the company lose writers to the British publishers whom the London office was selling its books to. It was, in Ferguson's judgement as director of publishing, an essential part of Angus & Robertson's mission and was 'not regarded as an expendable operation'.[4] Furthermore, in response to a claim made by the new London chief editor Alec Bolton that a 'profitless prosperity'[5] was being reflected in ever higher turnovers, record months and then dismal end-of-year final analyses, Ferguson countered in February 1970 that nobody on Angus & Robertson's board actually expected the London office to make a profit. In fact, profit was 'not required' and the London office 'more than justifies its existence if it can break even'.[6] It was a statement that emphasised the London office's strategic – rather than financial – importance to Angus & Robertson in Australia.

Yet it was also a policy statement quite inconsistent with Ferguson's own views, which over the years had underscored a need for the London office to demonstrate a return (especially urgent in 1958 and 1959) or at least cover costs. As late as September 1969 Ferguson counselled that 'we have got to get to the stage where London can at least break even without having to charge back a lot of expenses to us here'.[7] Walter Butcher, as manager of the overseas branch, placed the problem of low profitability in the context of some of Angus & Robertson's decisions regarding the books it elected to publish. For Butcher, the profitability of London could not be discussed separate from the profitability of Sydney:[8] 'We are very conscious of the profitability of the company, or sometimes the lack of profitability and we see here that the company appears to be committed to projects which are not always profitable'.[9] Due to narrow margins between production cost and pricing competitively for the British market, Butcher reported the 'impossible situation'[10] of which the sale of Australian productions reduced the London office's gross profit rate. Similarly, the Australia House Bookshop experienced periods of low profitability.

Although Ferguson justified a company bookshop fronting the Strand on the basis that 'it is a valuable outlet for Australian books in London – in fact far better than any London bookshop – and also receives orders from many other countries',[11] the Australia House Bookshop strived to obtain a profit, but reported a loss of £2,100 for the financial year ending June 1970. The implication was that the London office could no longer base its trade solely on Angus & Robertson's Sydney list or Australian books only.

Ferguson responded to Butcher's concerns by confirming that the London office had made a profit in the 1950s; 'though possibly we [the Sydney office] were bearing more of the expenses then than now in hidden ways'.[12] While deliberately not acknowledging that former managing director Walter Burns had made a similar (if less temperate) assessment of Angus & Robertson's financial underwriting of the London office, pointing to practices which 'subsidise the London branch and make the London losses appear less frightening',[13] Ferguson's conclusion was in the same family of argument put forward by Richard Hauser's second audit in 1960. The core issue was not necessarily low gross profit but rather high overheads which needed to be brought under the incumbent London manager's control. Bolstered by the show of support by Angus & Robertson's board, Ferguson claimed the London office might be run more economically and, although the 'Operation London' project was not mentioned, that the London office could benefit by finding (and producing) even 'more titles of its own'.[14] The primary question then, one which by the end of the 1960s had dominated the overseas branch for nearly four decades, asked, 'how can we arrange things so that London continues to fulfil its purpose and at the same time breaks even'?[15] It was a puzzle rarely solved by former London staff to Ferguson's complete satisfaction, but as an issue which went to the very heart of the London office it was perhaps the last time Australian publishing veteran George Ferguson would be in a position to contemplate an answer.

Right up until 31 December 1970, George Ferguson remained active in his fight to substantiate Angus & Robertson's activities in Britain, and the London office continued to worry him 'more than any other part of publishing'.[16] However, Ferguson recognised that times were changing, and he saw colleagues in Angus & Robertson gradually drop out of the firm as a sign of the changing nature of publishing in the twentieth century.[17] On a personal level, Ferguson was weary of the constant battle which started in the time of Walter Burns; this struggle to prove the London office's relevance and to maintain its operations was difficult because the resolution of one problem often vacated a space for the beginnings of another. As discussed in the previous chapter, Burns' public disquiet with the London office's lack of financial vitality overshadowed its operations long after he departed from the company and it divided staff into camps. Yet Burns' criticisms signalled the changes in bookselling values that were to challenge the London office throughout the 1960s. In a letter to Lothian publishers in Melbourne, Ferguson recalled in January 1971 that 'the last ten years seem to have been all struggle, one way or another, with intervals during which one tried to do a little publishing'.[18] With a weakened sense of the cultural duty or national crusade that often characterised his earlier regard for placing Australian books in the United Kingdom, Ferguson confessed to Bolton that running the London office had become a project deprived of any joy though he still firmly believed the 'consequences of closing it down might be drastic'.[19] His belief was soon put to the test.

In 1970 Angus & Robertson's board reviewed its support for the London office and requested a report from Ferguson on the subject of publishing in Britain. Critically, Ferguson was to answer in bookselling terms the question of why Angus & Robertson needed anything at all in London.[20] Having fostered operations in the United Kingdom for over 32 years, George Ferguson presented his report with a frank admission of being 'depressed' by the London office's perceived 'bad situation'.[21] Four months later he resigned from Angus & Robertson and thereby seemingly sealed the fate of the London office. The resignation took effect on the last day of 1970. Gordon McCarthy replaced Ferguson as executive director. Publishing policy was placed in the hands of John Abernethy and Bruce Semler until March 1972 when Richard Walsh was appointed over all publishing operations.[22] Recently appointed London editor Alec Bolton was anxious that he and his partner, Australian poet Rosemary Dobson, would not be 'marooned in England'.[23] He accepted a position as director of publications at the National Library of Australia in Canberra. In his place, John Ferguson would once again manage the London office and assume the title of overseas executive director (a move that – according to the biographer of Angus & Robertson's then new majority shareholder Gordon Barton – was designed to bypass him as the publishing division's obvious heir).[24] The resignation of George Ferguson not only brought to conclusion a career in Australian publishing at Angus & Robertson, but it was also the end of an era of London publishing. Ferguson's 'impossible dream'[25] of producing and distributing Australian books abroad – a project unlike the 'purely regional, parochial sort of affair'[26] he detected in other publishers' activities – had come to an untidy end.

Ferguson's resignation took place within the context of Angus & Robertson becoming more focused on profitability and developing the organisational forms necessary to improve its bottom-line. Through the firm's office in London, modern business values first exemplified by Walter Burns nearly a decade earlier clashed with the older values once espoused by George Robertson. On the one hand, both Walter Butcher and Alec Bolton were reluctant to accept books of local Australian interest which had demonstrated limited international appeal, produced few sales and returned little profit.[27] Except for the unity of character presented by Angus & Robertson's educational titles and children's books (which for the last six months of 1967 accounted for £10,415 of the London office's total book sales in an overall turnover of £32,177),[28] the relatively small general list projected a 'disturbingly diffuse and unkempt image'[29] of the company to the world. According to Bolton, the list, as a combination of Sydney and London catalogues, was off-putting to New York editors who did not think Angus & Robertson 'could make a good job of being so many different kinds of publisher at once'.[30]

George Ferguson was acutely aware that 'low profitability may invite intervention by shareholders or others',[31] and he admitted that Angus & Robertson's status as 'something of a national institution' was 'quite out of context with the modern [internationalised] world of publishing'.[32] The Australian book trade was more internationalised than had previously been the case, and Ferguson noted there was less criticism when Angus & Robertson published books that were not in the Henry Lawson tradition.[33] Ferguson was also aware that the London office was 'being watched by a lot of people' and that it had to 'make the grade'.[34] If the London office failed, in terms of a reasonable performance on books by Angus & Robertson's best Australian authors and on books purchased from American publishers, then 'all [would] be lost'.[35] However, by maintaining the 'philosophical basis of the firm'[36] set out by his grandfather George Robertson, Ferguson felt 'bound'[37] to accept some titles that would make little sense to those who sought to restrict London's publishing program to 'books which should show a profit'.[38] It was, he confessed, 'hard to drop a policy 80 years old overboard'[39] even if, with Angus & Robertson fully integrated into the market, the pressures to focus more aggressively on profitability were extremely powerful. Ferguson's comment highlighted the continuing tension between financial necessity, his love of books and the book trade.

The British market was still the main game, but sales outside the United Kingdom accounted for between 12 and 15 per cent of the London office's total turnover. South Africa was the second largest market for Australian books and accounted for an average of 7 per cent of sales from London between 1962 and 1968, followed by Canada, Europe and the United States.[40] By 1968 the contracting business of the London office's export department – which sent British books to Australia for sale by the Angus & Robertson retail group even as most major British publishers were closing the market in Australia – was already recognised. 'Things have changed enormously', Ferguson confided to MacQuarrie, 'since your day in so far as most of the British publishers, and certainly most of the major ones, now have distribution arrangements in Australia which prevent our buying their books in England'.[41] Exports of British books from London to Sydney were diminishing at the same time as costs were rising,[42] which prompted discussions over disbanding the London office's export department[43] or downsizing it significantly.[44] With publishing activity in England bound up with the future of export,[45] Angus & Robertson attempted to meet the problem of closed markets.

One such attempt, discussed at length below, involved Angus & Robertson restructuring its London office to 'gain the maximum tax relief under the [Australian] export incentive scheme'[46] and to take advantage of the tax benefits associated with exporting Australian-produced goods to London. In part, this reconfiguration was designed to compensate for the devaluation in sterling. Faced with the biggest ever peacetime deficit, British Prime Minister Harold Wilson depreciated his nation's currency by more than 14 per cent against the American dollar in order 'to achieve an export-led growth' and consequently provoke 'a fundamental orientation of the economy in favour of the balance of payments'.[47] Although the British government expected foreign suppliers like Angus & Robertson to 'absorb some of the effect on their own profit margins in an attempt to maintain sales',[48] the devaluation in 1967 was expected to lower the demand for and increase the prices of imported goods. That meant higher landing costs and lower sales potential for books arriving from Australia. A corresponding devaluation of the branch's assets by $27,987 in 1968 had to be 'deducted from [the] accumulated profits of previous years'.[49] Under these circumstances, Ferguson's motives regarding Australian books abroad seemed out of sync with the changing bookselling demands of the time, which sought to restrict publishing programmes to profitable books only[50] and went against Alec Bolton's advice that the policies of the London office 'should be more commercial and less altruistic'.[51]

While the London office's high turnover indicated substantial success in selling Australian books in the United Kingdom and beyond, exceeding £100,000 in turnover for the first time in 1968,[52] a legacy of low or non-existent profit margins – linked to the challenges of remaining competitive against British books in their own territory – eventually overwhelmed any consideration in Australia of the London office's actual achievements. Ferguson knew that it would be unwise to be 'idealistic with someone else's money'.[53] Yet this idealism, according to Ferguson, was the 'foundation on which all Angus & Robertson's publishing ever since has been built'.[54] In the end, the London office came to mirror the division within the firm between those wanting to adapt to market forces and those desiring a continuation of family legacy and control; a clash which ultimately precipitated Ferguson's resignation.

Turning Full Circle

As discussed in the previous chapter, Angus & Robertson concluded from its exhibition at the 1964 Frankfurt Book Fair that for real growth to occur the London office must once again internationalise its list. Like the mid-to-late 1950s, the overseas branch would need to publish 'books of a universal appeal'[55] and use the marketing of these titles to influence the sales of the firm's Australian publications. Here was another lesson on the internationalisation of publishing. If Angus & Robertson wanted American or European publishers to express interest in its catalogue then the company had to present one that was 'not overloaded with local material'.[56] The firm considered managing its search for American copyrights entirely from Sydney,[57] but the experiences of the London office over the past two decades had proved that this was an unworkable strategy.[58] It was soon decided that an editorial person was necessary in the United Kingdom with both a background in Australia and a background in Angus & Robertson.[59]

Alec Bolton, a University of Sydney graduate, was initially engaged by Angus & Robertson to work on *The Australian Encyclopaedia* and John Ferguson's *Bibliography of Australia* in 1950. Trained as a copy editor under Beatrice Davis, he had a desk in the tiny attic of 89 Castlereagh Street as part of the editorial department. His office was above the bookshop, and Bolton enjoyed contact with Australian authors like Hugh McRae, Frederick Macartney, Ethel Anderson and C. E. W. Bean. Bolton recognised early on that Angus & Robertson operated under a policy initiated by founder George Robertson of 'putting things back into the community that the firm had taken out of the community'.[60] Bolton was with Angus & Robertson until October 1960 when he resigned in protest at the methods of Walter Burns who, in his view, 'wanted to carve up the firm'.[61] Bolton joined the small publishing company of Ure Smith Ltd where he stayed for six years.

In 1966 Bolton's successor at Angus & Robertson, John Abernethy, approached him over lunch to see if he was interested in becoming the editor of the London office. Having spent a lifetime seeing people off to Britain rather than going himself, Bolton found the prospect of starting an editorial department in London 'exceedingly tempting'.[62] After much deliberation, he resigned from Ure Smith Ltd, which by that time had become part of Stanley Horwitz's publishing business. Bolton was contracted as chief editor at the London office (though his £3,000[63] salary would be paid by the Sydney office)[64] and would assist in increasing the sale of Australian books in the United Kingdom.[65] An analysis of the London office's sales for the first six months of 1966 revealed that

46.6 per cent (428 titles) of its list produced 98.4 per cent of turnover in 74,091 copies sold; 491 publications sold less than ten copies and represented only 1,228 sales.[66] The tension between amplifying either business sales or literary editorial quality was an age-old argument for Ferguson,[67] and he believed that placing Alec Bolton in charge of editorial concerns and Walter Butcher in charge of sales made for 'a good team'.[68]

George Ferguson did not disguise his debt to Butcher from Bolton: 'he is loyal and hard-working and has done his utmost to get us back on the map again after the Burns debacle in 1960. That A. & R. London ever recovered at all is mainly due to Walter and this mustn't be forgotten'.[69] The appointment of Bolton, however, was a step towards renewing original publishing in Britain of the kind not seen in the six years since 'Operation London'. Its significance was not lost on George Ferguson who was 'immensely cheered' by Bolton's initial optimism towards the London office:

> As you know it has been my baby for so many years now and I've battled on over this period against a good deal of difficulty and sometimes indifference on the part of others because I feel (a) that a successful London end is essential to our publishing here, and (b) that it is not an impossible dream. In fact until Burns wrecked the show there we were going along very nicely. I know I made mistakes at this end through over eagerness in an attempt to help London. I took too many copies of some of the books they published … [which] had to be remaindered here … Yet that didn't invalidate the whole principle.[70]

Bolton quickly learned, after his arrival in London on 19 December 1966 (following a six week journey by boat),[71] that publishing in the United Kingdom was very different from publishing in Australia[72] and that 'selling Australian books in London was not an easy task'[73]. Britain was, in Bolton's view, 'not exactly a receptive market'[74] and working conditions were less than ideal. Bolton found the new premises at Bartholomew Close to be 'rather dingy and unattractive', even 'dreary and depressing',[75] and 'really out of the publishing swim'.[76] Situated close to Barts Hospital, the Church of St Bartholomew the Great and the Smithfield meat markets, it was an area of London 'where you could go into a pub for lunch and there would be white coated people there, some with blood on them'.[77] In Bolton's view this was not an area likely to attract literary novels. We 'were not in that league', he was later to record, 'so we did quite a lot of practical books'.[78]

Angus & Robertson had a long presence in London in two forms: one, as a buyer for the bookshop in Australia, often in quantities of thousands, and two, as a British distribution office for Australian books. Bolton's role was to revive the 'successful small publishing enterprise'[79] established by MacQuarrie and Rowland and to originate some Angus & Robertson books in London. The Sydney office would continue to exert editorial oversight from twelve thousand miles away and 'determin[e] … what titles we think should be produced in England'.[80] Ferguson was concerned with building up a list in London that also had sales possibilities in Australia.

Bolton's primary duty was to return the London office to the practice of releasing what in modern terms is now called a 'portfolio' of titles. This approach was intended to boost the overseas house's capability to carry the risk of selling Australian books in the United Kingdom through using revenue from best or better sellers to cover the losses on titles that did not produce profit. The underlying expectation, like that of 'Operation London', was to offset short-term losses on the prospect of future gains as Australian books in Britain became more established and commercially successful. It was a 'policy of development based on faith in the future',[81] and in a frank letter addressed to both Bolton and Butcher Ferguson described that

> The wheel has really turned full circle and in a way we are back where we were ten years ago with Hector [MacQuarrie] and Barry [Rowland] when we appreciated that our publishing in London could never be successful until it was based on a London list. Our early efforts succeeded in getting us several notable successes, but unintentionally we made the mistake of supposing that Australian books were an actual embarrassment and should be kept out of sight. Well, other times, other ideas. It might have been true then – certainly much truer than it is now. But the pitfall that it led us into was the inclusion in our Sydney list of too many 'London' titles in quantities which were too big for us to handle so that to some extent what those titles made in London was lost in Sydney and a very convenient stick was put into the hands of those who were happy to beat me with it.[82]

Exporting Books from and to Britain

Almost before Bolton could get things moving editorially, a devaluation of sterling in 1967 and a surge in the marketing of British books in Australia by English publishers created new obstacles to profitability. By 1966 Angus & Robertson perceived a pressing need to deal with the export of British books from London while inescapable facts about the marketing of British titles in Australia began to emerge. Not only was the sale of British books in Australia declining as Australian publishing increased, but those British books that were saleable tended to be 'marketed locally'[83] due to the establishment of British plants in Australia. As the costs of maintaining the export side of the London office steadily grew to 'most alarming'[84] levels, with the wages of its ten staff[85] also increasing due to a recent British Selective Employment Tax,[86] the problem for Angus & Robertson's Sydney office became a contest between the cost of obtaining British books from London and the cost of obtaining them locally.[87]

In the financial year 1965–6, the total value of books exported to Australia was nearly two hundred thousand sterling.[88] £92,864 worth of stock was dispatched to the Sydney office, £43,963 to the Melbourne firm Robertson & Mullens which Angus & Robertson had acquired, £42,840 to Alberts in Perth, £9,692 to Swains, £5,959 to Green Square, £665 to Ewins and £125 to an outlet in Wollongong.[89] This stock was bundled and freighted in 1,647 cartons, 419 cases and 142 bales.[90] In the previous financial year (1964–5) 1,482 cartons, 422 cases and 63 bales were packed and shipped,[91] indicating an increase in the physical work required to dispatch stock to Australia as well. Although the overall value of books exported was expected to decrease because of the continued movement of British publishers towards closed markets, a study by Ferguson of export costs as a percentage of value revealed expenses had risen from 5 per cent in 1959 to 9 per cent (or £18,975)[92] in 1966. This was unacceptable; any figure over 7.5 per cent meant it became 'just as cheap and much easier to buy here [in Australia]'.[93]

Debating the future of the London office's export department in terms of reducing overheads[94] did not lessen, however, the impact of Oxford, Methuen, Chapman & Hall, Cecil King, Cassell, Hodders and Heinemann closing off avenues for the Sydney office to indent (import) British books directly from London. Some British publishers like Collins were inconsistent with their closure of the market during 1967 and 1968 by forfeiting the option for some titles[95] while enforcing it for others.[96] The London office also experimented with a '"buying-round" operation'[97] that involved purchasing the closed-market titles of Oxford, Cassell and other British publishers under the name of the Australian House Bookshop. With no questions asked regarding the final destination of these orders, closed-market titles were then quietly dispatched to Australia.[98] Both Bolton and Ferguson speculated that a refusal of sale by any British publisher to the bookshop might be illegal under the British Restrictive Practices Act though they did not test this argument.[99]

The London office was cautious not to make any large-scale orders for fear of 'bust[ing] the whole thing wide open and clos[ing] our avenue for getting what books we do get now',[100] and it only briefly entertained the idea of servicing the textbook needs of Australian academics from London.[101] As a result, for the financial year 1966–7 the value in stock exported to Australia by the London office actually increased to £231,472,[102] but by 1968 Ferguson did not see very much future for the export department with its percentage cost of operation 'unacceptably high'.[103] Angus & Robertson, it became clear, was maintaining an expensive setup for a service that was becoming increasingly 'hopeless'.[104] Better value editions could be bought locally rather than indented from London. Rumours were also beginning to spread in Australia that closed-market titles could be ordered through Angus & Robertson, which led to an embarrassing encounter between the London office and the Melbourne house of Oxford University Press.

During the brief confrontation, the London office countered that any orders it received for closed-market titles published by Oxford were immediately returned 'Apply Melbourne',[105] but this was not true due to the '"buying-round" operation'.[106] Ferguson became anxious to avoid collisions with British publishers[107] and, following a personal visit to London in 1966, scaled back the export department to a 'skeleton'.[108]

Changes in the methods of supplying foreign books in Australia and in the channels of distribution within Australia were a major transformation for Angus & Robertson. It drove into marginality the London office's oldest activity,[109] and it challenged Angus & Robertson's ability to compete more effectively as booksellers and publishers in its home territory. The London office noted that the cumulative process of British publishers setting up house in Australia had a dwindling effect on market share for all Australian publishers:

> [T]here are now more publishers in Australia to share the author and sales cake, and therefore each is getting less of it. Unfortunately for us the English immigrant publisher has his backlist to give him a base … [and] he makes the bookseller subsidize his existence out there. It all adds up to a sad, sad day that U.K. publishers decided to spoil what was a wonderful book market.[110]

There were problems too with Australian books arriving in Britain. Although Sydney books would remain a mainstay of Angus & Robertson's London list, such titles had to be obtained at a price that both the Sydney and overseas branches could agree upon. The Sydney office was still operating on a scale of charges to the London office that returned little profit or caused Angus & Robertson to sell to the overseas branch at a loss. For example, during the six months ending 31 December 1968 Angus & Robertson subsidised the London office by £1,497.[111]

Ferguson was aware of the maximum price for books that Butcher and Bolton could get.[112] Unbound sheets or bound books in edition quantities marked with Angus & Robertson's London imprint were invoiced at a fraction of the London office's proposed retail price while bound books in smaller, non-edition quantities were invoiced at the Australian retail price less 60 per cent.[113] As the 1967 sterling crisis increased, the landed cost in the United Kingdom of books exported from Australia rose by over 16 per cent,[114] and the price of these books in the English market increased proportionally. Crucially, books from Australia could no longer easily obtain a price advantage in the United Kingdom without loss and soon became uncompetitive. To compensate, Angus & Robertson looked to the Australian Export Market Development Scheme for tax relief as a means to counterbalance falling profit margins. The export scheme offered an important source of government support for the distribution of Australian books abroad through the provision of double-deductions and payroll rebates. Its implementation by Angus & Robertson, however, was contentious and had dampening effects on original publishing in London.

The Export Market Development Scheme

The Export Market Development Scheme, also known as the Commonwealth Export Incentives Scheme, was established by the Department of Trade to provide tax relief for costs incurred by Australian companies in developing export markets for Australian manufactured products and to permit reductions in payroll tax liabilities connected with export earnings.[115] It was an export promotion strategy that was specifically geared towards a company's capabilities to bear export-related overheads:

> [F]or every [Australian dollar] spent on export promotion, Australian producers receive a double deduction of [two Australian dollars] from income assessable under Australian income tax. And for increases in exports over a base period, a firm receives a rebate on payroll tax depending on the labour content of the product, which … amounts to a rebate equal to anywhere from 2.5 to 15 per cent of the value of increased exports.[116]

The Australian government was keen to promote export activities and to 'inculcate an "export mentality"'[117] among Australian producers. The development of Australian export industries was perceived as an important means of addressing a trade imbalance between the nation's imports and exports. Australian publishers were minor participants in the scheme during the 1960s in regard to the Australian government funding national stands at the Frankfurt Book Fair, the American Booksellers' Fair and the New York Public Library.[118]

Although it was not explicitly developed with publishers in mind, Ferguson recognised the advantages of the scheme in 1963 when he supposed that Angus & Robertson could devote additional capital to the advertising of its books in the United Kingdom and yet not increase costs for the company.[119] Indeed, Angus & Robertson's Sydney office engaged in significant export activity, with sales (excluding London office activity) representing an average 11 per cent of turnover. In 1965 sales amounted to £138,370 in a turnover of £1,247,684. Three years later, export sales represented £190,000 in a turnover of £1,727,642. In 1968 the United Kingdom accounted for 37.3 per cent or £70,870, New Zealand 27.2 per cent or £51,680, the United States 15.6 per cent or £29,640, the Territory of Papua and New Guinea 8.8 per cent or £16,720, South East Asia and Japan 2.1 per cent or £3,990, India, Pakistan and Ceylon 2.0 per cent or £3,800 and Other 7.1 per cent or £13,490. From this, £26,755 in export royalties was earned for Angus & Robertson's authors, and £15,000 was obtained in the United Kingdom and £9,625 in the USA.[120]

From 1962–8, London office sales increased by 58 per cent.[121] These sales, in addition to those attained by the Sydney office, were attributed in part to Angus & Robertson executives visiting international publishers with the aim of selling Australian books and exchanging reprint rights. In total, four trips were made from Sydney to London and two trips from London to Sydney between 1937 and 1960. From 1960, there were five visits to the Territory of Papua and New Guinea, one visit each to Jakarta and Thailand, four visits each to Malaysia, Singapore, Hong Kong and the Philippines, three visits to Tokyo, ten visits to London, another two visits from London to Sydney, and one visit to New York that lasted a year.[122] Yet Angus & Robertson did not easily qualify for rebates over London office performance, because the transfer of goods from Sydney to London represented no real change in ownership; the firm was technically exporting to itself overseas. A book was also considered manufactured in Britain if a minimum 20 per cent of its production costs were borne in the United Kingdom. For the London office, this meant that any title with a published price over 25 shillings and any book that originated as unbound stock from Australia did not qualify for rebates.[123]

This did not prevent Angus & Robertson, however, from claiming Export Market Development Expenditure in 1967 under section 51AC of the Australian Income Tax Assessment Act. It was estimated that the London office could be relieved of at least £9,000 in expenses.[124] A subsequent audit by the firm's accountant in October 1967, Max Tennant of G. T. Hartigan & Co., alerted Ferguson to the likelihood of such claims being disallowed if they ever had to stand up to enquiry by the Australian Tax Department.[125] In order to legally gain maximum benefit from the export incentives scheme and to avoid any investigations, Tennant advised that before attempting to introduce any changes with the object of claiming greater deductions (such as placing London representatives on a salary basis charged to the Sydney office)[126] Angus & Robertson would need to 'tidy up'[127] its existing arrangements in the United Kingdom. Tennant recommended that a new company be incorporated in Britain. Under this proposal, Angus & Robertson (UK) Ltd would 'be a subsidiary of the Australian Company and [would] take over the whole of the activities at present conducted by the London branch'.[128]

Complying with the provisions of the English Companies Act meant that Angus & Robertson (UK) Ltd would have its own articles of association, executive meetings and annual meetings.[129] The Sydney office could then claim a legitimate change of ownership occurred by exporting Australian manufactured goods to a separate legal entity outside Australia.[130] It legally enabled Angus & Robertson to treat the export of Australian books to its London office 'as sales instead of stock transfers'.[131] The Sydney office was also advised to explore purchasing supplementary titles from other Australian publishers and to invoice these to its British subsidiary at a margin of profit. Such an arrangement would strengthen Angus & Robertson's position within the area of export market development and legalise claims for promotional expenses incurred in regard to this stock being merchandised in London (for example, the costs of advertising other publishers' titles in London).[132]

It was essential too that titles sold by the Sydney office to the London office should demonstrate greater profitability on the Australian side of the transaction than had previously been recorded. The London office would continue to develop its own publishing program, provided production and layout were outsourced, but the advantages of restructuring were to be shown as heavily weighted in favour of the Sydney office. These advantages included additional printing for Halstead Press, lower unit costs for an entire printed edition with benefits to the Sydney office's gross profit results on its portion of the edition (London was expected to order 1,000 or more copies),[133] and tax remissions by reason of a properly organised export system. London, however, was not to be 'deterred' by this accounting technique or 'by the fact that some individual titles might appear to be returning … too low [of a] margin of gross profit'.[134]

With insufficient time to incorporate a separate business, the London office purchased a non-operating company for £23 and re-registered its name as 'Angus & Robertson (UK) Ltd' at a further cost of £10[135] to begin trade from 1 January 1968. Up until this time, the London office had been a registered foreign business operating in London as distinct from a bona fide British company. The registration as an English firm formalised the London office's legal status as a British publisher. With £100 invested as capital,[136] Butcher, Bolton and Cliff Rust, from the export department, were appointed joint directors[137] holding £1 shares in the company. Angus & Robertson (Australia) was the majority shareholder and held the remaining £97. Ferguson, Cousins, Donald Hardy and Ernest Hyde held positions as Australian directors of the British subsidiary[138] (although Ferguson would be an 'active chairman' of the London board rather than a nominal one, because he believed the new company should be 'ridden on a somewhat shorter rein'[139]). The loss on the account from the former London office setup was carried forward to the new company to avoid British Corporation Tax.[140] The first financial year (1 July 1968 to 30 June 1969) under the scheme progressed without contest by the Australian Tax Department, and the London office officially incurred expenses previously borne by the Sydney office. These additional costs initially amounted to £13,650, and the London office absorbed them 'on behalf of Angus & Robertson'[141] in the company's formal desire to further stimulate the export of Australian manufactured goods.

This setup of 'charge-backs' was intended to benefit the Sydney office as double-deductible expenses (or expenses that can be claimed twice) under export market development expenditure in the next tax assessment cycle; it was a strategy Angus & Robertson considered by July 1969 to be 'so valuable'[142] that it was reluctant to make any changes in London which might invalidate current or future claims. For example, the appointment of London executives as directors was discovered very early in the process to be an inconvenient arrangement for export rebates and was in fact in breach of an Australian government regulation which discriminated against claiming director's salaries under the scheme. Because this placed claimable expenses of approximately £12,000 in a questionable light, Ferguson suggested a workaround in which all three staff members would be formerly demoted and restyled in the role of either manager or editor. In practice, each would continue to operate unofficially as director of the London office in their respective capacities, and the removal of titles did not indicate disapproval of the London office's collective performance. Rather Ferguson suggested the requirement reflected Angus & Robertson's 'duty to the shareholders'.[143] Staff complied and tendered their resignations as directors of Angus & Robertson (UK) Ltd, effective from 1 July 1968.[144]

Leveraging London Losses for Sydney Profits and the Commonwealth Export Incentives Scheme

On reflection Ferguson claimed Angus & Robertson '[relied] a bit too heavily on the export scheme and possibly [did] things that we certainly shouldn't have done otherwise'.[145] Yet the Commonwealth Export Incentives Scheme placed the London office in a financial position unique in its history. Because of the way in which the scheme's regulations were framed and the way by which the Sydney office utilised them, the London office was more fiscally responsible for its operations than ever before. It is perhaps indicative of just how much the Sydney office had in fact been sponsoring the overseas operation prior to its restructuring as a British company. For the first six months of the financial year 1968–9 the London office showed a profit of only £15. Walter Butcher reported to Sydney that Angus & Robertson (UK) Ltd was 'just failing to break even',[146] which suggests this was a gross profit figure or a result before deductions. Gradually, the branch would recover and show for 1969–70 a net profit of $6,630 (Australian dollar value) after charging back expenses of $20,500 to the Sydney office. In the financial year for 1970–71, net profit amounted to £7,875 sterling after charging back £18,975 in expenses. This result was also evaluated as a 'bad situation'.[147]

It is clear from a review of the few surviving profit and loss statements for 1966–70 that annual London office turnover was on the rise. From £89,175 in 1966 (with net profit at £2,953 after deducting the loss of £1,233 returned by the Australia House Bookshop)[148] to £85,906 in 1967,[149] turnover was given an enormous boost by the sale of *Self Help for Your Nerves*[150] and exceeded £100,000 in 1968.[151] By 30 June 1969, annual turnover had reached £126,000.[152] Based on a result of £40,788 for the first quarter to 31 October 1969,[153] estimates of turnover for the following financial year 1969–70 neared £160,000 and even higher thereafter.

Bolton noted during his first year in Britain that the peculiar interdependences of Angus & Robertson's separate subsidiaries worked against obtaining a price advantage *and* a profitable margin. Bolton knew how strong Ferguson's belief was that Australian printing and publishing should develop together. However, after observing how other Australian publishers took advantage of less expensive Asian printers, Bolton argued that

'Angus & Robertson's loyalty to Halstead [Press] must be nearly choking the life out of [the firm's] profitability'.[154] He called for the Sydney office to yield more of its marginally costed books to cheaper English manufacture:

> What makes it worse … is that you, needing our London quantity in order to get up to an economic printing number, must then occasionally subsidise your price to us in order that our retail price won't be right over the acceptable ceiling here. And in other cases, as you know, Walter [Butcher] takes a lower mark-up than normal for the sake of holding a tolerable retail price.[155]

Ferguson responded that Halstead Press was succeeding in diversifying its printing, showing a profit for 1968–9, and he tacitly confirmed the interdependencies between Angus & Robertson's subsidiaries by stating that 'there is really a lot of publishing profit disguised as printing profit'.[156] Yet Ferguson was not prepared for each subsidiary to 'operate strictly and severely within its own environment' and was 'unconvinced'[157] that Angus & Robertson would benefit from shifting its printing offshore. While not at this stage explicitly stated, it seemed that the object of Angus & Robertson's participation in the export incentives scheme was to reduce tax and increase net profit for the company as a whole. This in turn necessitated maintaining the export system as it was then organised. Ferguson explained:

> there is also a payroll tax rebate scheme under which rebates of payroll tax are available to companies whose export performance in any given year exceeds their performance in a base year which has been fixed by the Government. Our export performance is greatly exceeding our base year performance and increasingly so every year. And the significant thing is that the payroll exemption which we earn thereby applies to the whole payroll of Angus & Robertson Ltd. The Government recognises Angus & Robertson Ltd as a tax entity. They're not concerned with the book shop at 89 Castlereagh Street and the publishing business down in Lower George Street. We earn tax rebate on the entire payroll tax paid by Angus & Robertson and it is a mighty big concession … but it is very difficult to show it [in publishing accounts].[158]

Nevertheless, this was not without some form of operational penalty to the London office. Fulfilling the legal requirements of the export incentive scheme in a way that benefitted the Sydney office acted as a bottleneck to original London publishing, and the increased warehousing of unsaleable books exported from Australia to Britain lessened profitability. Local production in Britain would help increase the London office's gross profit margin, but only Australian manufactured books qualified for export benefits. Unsold stock quickly depreciated in value and applied significant downward pressure on the London office's annual statements. With $250,000 worth of assets[159] employed in Britain by way of stock and debtors, this inevitably caused some resentment, and most of it was directed towards the scheme. Frustrated by the increased landing costs plus the limited appeal of books arriving *en masse* from Sydney, Bolton concluded in 1969 that 'a sales organization [had] been created to exploit the Export Scheme, but insufficient material of an exportable nature [was] being fed into it'.[160] He accused the Sydney office of running the business in London 'to maximize the tax concessions instead of the profits'.[161]

The accusation that the London office's own business interests were not at the forefront of Angus & Robertson's priorities was neither unfounded nor unreasonable. Alec Bolton fully appreciated the historical and patriotic reasons that led Angus & Robertson to undertake its own manufacturing and publish books which had little chance of financial success, but he disapproved of the Australian publisher's implementation of the export incentives scheme during the late 1960s, citing it as a 'radical means'[162] for achieving company-wide profitability. Appointing full-time representatives on salary might have suited particular claims under the scheme, but it did not produce any rapid increase in turnover; despite more extensive sales coverage, a large proportion of the London office's list remained 'unsuited or overpriced for the English market'.[163] Likewise, taking Australian books in editions of 3,000 copies for London rarely resulted in 3,000 sales, because the market usually 'ran out of steam'[164] after a sale of only 1,200 copies. The export incentives scheme masked the true results of the London office's activities and forced the branch to base its operations on 'false premises',[165] which ignored the conditions of trade in the United Kingdom. Butcher and Bolton attempted to have greater say on this issue as bookmen and publishers in Britain. Both men sought to stem the flow of unsaleable books into the London office's warehouse and proposed that no future books should be accepted for publication unless each was 'costed to show a profit'.[166] Each future title had to 'find a ready market in both Australia and the United Kingdom' before it was published.[167] The London office also argued that no title should go into production without a full consultation between editors in London and Sydney with the view of evaluating the publication's likely margin of profit. If either editor concluded that sales could be negligible, Butcher believed 'there was only one answer – Reject'.[168] Under the pressure from Bolton and Butcher, Ferguson eventually agreed and pointed to similar talks held in Sydney that 'from now on every book that we accept has got to show good cause why it should be accepted'.[169] Ferguson's strategies in London had been overtaken by new financial realities.

When Ferguson presented Angus & Robertson's board with a series of proposals regarding the future of its London office, whose value to the company it seemed was 'intangible and cannot be proved or disproved in detail',[170] Ferguson described the potential loss of tax relief through closing the overseas branch as 'tantamount to taking some of the sail off the ship'.[171] However, by 1970 the accounting principle on which the London office operated had perhaps already achieved this. Certainly, the Commonwealth Export Incentives Scheme provided an opportunity for the Sydney office to strengthen the overseas branch's capacity to stand alone and use its own business to cover costs. This was a key recommendation by Richard Hauser to Walter Burns in his 1960 audit,[172] and after nearly three decades of operation its implementation within the London office might have been considered a more noteworthy event than it was. But the beginnings of independence did not bring with it the end of the London office's problems as Hauser might have anticipated. An independent government assessment by the Australian Department of Territories concluded that Australian manufacturers might profit well enough under the scheme in a way that discouraged actual investment in the destination territory.[173] That is, capital in the form of tax savings would likely be allocated towards operations within Australia rather than the development and improvement of operations internationally. In the context of the London office, the Sydney office's acceptance of valuable incentives and bonuses translated to discouraging real investment in the London office's own profitability and self-sustaining capabilities.

It is perhaps under this arrangement that we can begin to make sense of why Angus & Robertson's board in 1970 was reported to have originally said that it did not expect the London office to make a profit. Profitability from London was, in fact, 'not required',[174] because expenses as charge-backs (which affected the overseas branch more than any other subsidiary in the company)[175] demanded critical attention: 'if we can't claim them', explained Ferguson to Butcher in 1970, 'or if the claims are disallowed by our Income Tax Commissioner either in whole or in part, it could wreck our net profit'.[176] The syntax of the letter from which this statement is cited, and in light of previous comments, suggests Ferguson's use of 'our' was in reference to net profit for the entire company and not just the London office. It implied therefore that the firm's survival as a group of interdependent operations involving printing, bookselling and publishing was in question. Furthermore, with the company heavily reliant on the tax relief available under the Commonwealth Export Incentives Scheme, it suggested that Angus & Robertson was dependent on the export of its books to Britain in order to show profit in Australia.

In step with Walter Burns' determination of 'Operation London' in 1960, the warehousing of unsaleable books imported from Australia subsidised Sydney and made its losses appear less frightening to shareholders.

While the tax write-off boosted Angus & Robertson's annual profit in Australia, the accounting techniques and trade practices employed by the Sydney office to legitimise its claims and deductions eroded the London office's mission. Although the Commonwealth Export Incentives Scheme might have been seized with genuine enthusiasm as an opportunity to underwrite the export of Australian books abroad, the balance of power in Angus & Robertson had shifted by 1970. It had moved away from the kind of risk-taking publishing, which had marked the London office during the 1950s, and decisively towards business characterised by an intensified profit and loss orientation.

This orientation was, in short, a market ideology that flowed from the events of 1960. In Sydney, the adoption of this market ideology meant reassessing the worth of having a London branch which on analysis needed £14,000 in profit after 'charge-backs' of £20,000 and an asset reduction of £50,000 in order to break even.[177] In London, Bolton and Butcher's understanding of the British market meant more closely responding to commercial forces and taking into account local conditions of trade rather than the London office blindly acquiescing to its role in Australian tax avoidance.[178] This tension between accounting techniques and market intelligence between Sydney and London took its toll. The story of the London office – which had survived three decades of fluctuating fortunes as the cornerstone of Angus & Robertson's project to situate Australian publishing and Australian books in the global marketplace – would continue for just a few more years, but it would do so without George Ferguson.

Chapter 13

LEARNING FROM A DISTANCE

> As an export commodity, any cultural text must overcome the obstacle of entering an established market in which consumers have a strong understanding of their own cultural products, but a limited contextual base with which to understand the foreign commodity.[1]

> Distance is the problem … [N]o-one overseas who establishes a London publishing office readily parts with authority over the publishing policy of that office; and, books being what they are, that policy basically depends upon the decision to publish or not to publish individual manuscripts.[2]

British publisher George G. Harrap once said about the Australasian Publishing Company he helped set up in Sydney that 'it is not easy to command success for ventures of the sort in another country where much has to be learned of local customs and conditions'.[3] It can be, he concluded, an 'uphill task'.[4]

With evidence of the many uphill tasks that an Australian publisher had to overcome in order to show profit in domestic and export markets, this book has traced the material conditions of Angus & Robertson's London office when selecting works for publication, distribution and sale to British audiences. Its analysis has ranged from 1938 to 1970 – dates that describe the 32 year period of management by the London office's primary architect, George Ferguson, and the duration of communication between key individuals involved in London office operations. This book has focused on the different ways in which Angus & Robertson sought to understand, penetrate and serve the British market. Empirically, it has revealed the complex array of qualitative factors that shaped Angus & Robertson's business in London.

Social Contexts

This study underscores current research that affirms a certain idea of London as a literary influence on writing and publishing projects originating in Australia during the twentieth century. It reinforces Pierre Bourdieu's argument that literary production is the result of cultural forces operating in a 'field'[5] and that literary legitimacy cannot be separated from the material, political, legal and economic contexts of the time. Following an introduction to Angus & Robertson, Chapter 2 examines the 1930 Tariff Inquiry and reflects how profoundly the health of the Australian book trade has historically been subject to market forces and mechanisms which underpin the importation of overseas books into Australia. From the point of view of publishing and bookselling in 1930, imported books are held as a significant component in the development of the Australian book trade, and London remains fixed as the 'epicentre of Australian literary aspiration'.[6]

Moreover, this study affirms a model of print cultures research that incorporates the biographical into the relations of textual production; that is, 'the social context from which the book as material object emerge[s]'.[7] It characterises the individual as a crucial agent of change and focuses attention not only on the publisher (Walter Cousins, George Ferguson) and editor (Alec Bolton) – company roles that are often traditional sources of book history – but it also advances the importance of the country traveller or provincial salesman (Bernard Robinson), the sales or marketing manager (Vera Wellings) and the office manager (Hector MacQuarrie, Barry Rowland, John Ferguson, Walter Butcher) to the history of Australian print culture. To this is added the informal and strategic advice obtained from George Ferguson's counterparts in the British book trade (Walter Harrap, Stanley Unwin, William Collins), who contributed indirectly – but none the less significantly – to the progress of exporting Australian titles and developing original Australian publishing overseas. It becomes clear through these exchanges that the development of the sale of Australian books internationally through the London office occurred at a much greater cost – professionally, financially and personally – to Angus & Robertson in Sydney and to the London office's executive staff than has previously been acknowledged or recorded. The records of communication between these people explored in Chapters 3 to 12 illuminate critical turning points in the challenges encountered by Angus & Robertson's introduction of Australian books into the British market and beyond.

Exporting to London

This study has also examined the difficulties of an Australian company coordinating production in a foreign territory via a home office located 17,000 kilometres away in Sydney. It is a distance shown in the 1930 Tariff Board Inquiry to be measured in psychological as well as spatial terms. Yet despite the physical distance, the close cultural links between Australia and Britain – defined as both sharing educational and political systems, industrial developments, consumer cultures and the English language – meant that the United Kingdom nevertheless was a natural export destination for Australian goods and business (as was New Zealand). In this regard, London doubled as an export and literary centre for Australian publishers.

Angus & Robertson's market for Australian books in Britain was built up in stages. Its early attempts at exporting consisted in sending stock to the London office on an *ad hoc* basis. Until the late 1940s, this practice went in step with what economic studies of export behaviour call the 'sporadic exporting of surplus production'.[8] Over time this 'sporadic' transfer of books became contingent not only on products that were considered culturally significant, but also on those publications that offered strong possibilities of profit or financial return. As a result, emphasis in Angus & Robertson shifted towards export marketing and market development with the London appointment of Bernard Robinson in 1950 and Vera Wellings in 1952. Both employees were tasked with acquiring information (or market intelligence) so that the Sydney office might better understand the British market and appropriately structure its exports. What followed was 'Operation London', the brainchild of Hector MacQuarrie and George Ferguson, a key project during the 1950s in which books were published by Angus & Robertson specifically for sale in the export market. Later, more culturally distant markets such as Continental Europe were contemplated via the Frankfurt Book Fair, and efforts to penetrate them staged from London. The London office would see many changes during the next decade, but it would never fully recapture its early successes.

The Commonwealth Export Incentives Scheme

It is a discovery of this book that the London office's weakened state towards the closing years of the 1960s can be linked to the Commonwealth Export Incentives Scheme. Across the course of the 1960s, the export of British books to Australia was increasingly complemented and replaced by British books manufactured locally in Australia. Such books were produced by branch plants set up in Australia by British publishers, and, as a result, the cost of obtaining British books locally became less expensive than the cost of obtaining them from London. Although this study has demonstrated that Angus & Robertson's efforts to build up its London office closely paralleled the British pattern of book export trade development,[9] the establishment of local manufacturing facilities to service an export market was one British strategy that Angus & Robertson did not replicate in London.

Although the London office had local stockholding facilities and by 1968 was a new company 'formed with local directors'[10] – both important final steps in the third phase described by Attenborough – there were additional measures that Angus & Robertson might have explored to ensure the financial stability of its overseas branch. One measure was to engage cheaper local manufacturing facilities in London; another was to properly take into account the 'buying power and the population of the [export] market in question' in regard to the selection and quantity of Australian books being dispatched to Britain.[11] These two issues generally figured in Attenborough's pattern of book export trade development and, in the context of Australian book sales, were frequently raised by London office staff with increasing urgency between 1968 and 1970.

Angus & Robertson's heavy focus on fulfilling its requirements under the Commonwealth Export Incentives Scheme limited the company's ability to further expand London office business. Critically, Angus & Robertson could not directly invest in its overseas operation if the company continued to obtain significant tax relief in Australia. Primary correspondence from this period leads this study to conclude that Angus & Robertson's over-enthusiastic application of a government policy in a book export trade context – when such policy was not specifically targeted at nor configured in consultation with the publishing industry – resulted in a damaging imbalance between the accounting needs of the company in Australia and the business needs of its London office in Britain. Such an imbalance resulted in the poor selection and sale of Australian books appropriate to the British market, and it reduced opportunities for the London office to publish original Australian work in Britain.

Publishing in London

It is an argument of this study that a more thorough account of Australian literary production cannot occur without reference to the business circumstances that enable or confine the publication of any particular text. Throughout the 1950s and 1960s, those books that were more profitable or which generated higher turnover for the London office were also the kind of works that would be considered less culturally significant in literary terms. Yet the history of Angus & Robertson's mid-twentieth century project 'Operation London' has revealed that popular books or likely bestsellers could be tied to goals that were deemed culturally significant even if the texts employed to reach these goals were not in themselves judged to be culturally significant. For Angus & Robertson this meant a mixture of American and British titles in its London list was unavoidable if Australian books were to have any chance of success in Britain. Despite repeated attempts to move into distributing and publishing Australian titles only in London, market conditions continually reinforced the need for books of a universal nature to underwrite culturally significant goals.

In terms of print culture studies, this partly gestures towards what D. F. McKenzie refers to as 'the sociology of texts'[12] – a focus not only on the roles of all concerned with the making, distribution and reception of the physical forms of a text, but also on the business relationships within a publishing house that influence the circumstances of production for texts. In the context of Australian literary history and for other national literary histories, this invites a reconsideration of those titles, processes or relationships whose success underwrite the publication of (often though not always) less profitable literary texts. Such popular works or books of a universal nature are important as a cultural and economic phenomenon, for they provide the regular flow of capital which shapes the conditions under which the publisher may, having calculated the risk in advance, absorb the costs associated with the production, manufacture, promotion and distribution of works identified as being culturally significant. Through best or regular sellers, the publisher can invest in literary or nationally iconic texts.

In the example of Angus & Robertson, debates over which Australian title to import into the United Kingdom or what new work to publish or reissue under the London office imprint were increasingly tied to individual perceptions of local market conditions, ideas of cross-cultural rights exchange between Australian and British / Continental / American publishers, complex manufacturing relationships between the company's subsidiaries on the issue of unit costs, and in-house politics pushing for increased financial autonomy in overseas operations. It is clear that Angus & Robertson maintained a deep commitment to Australian forms of writing, publishing and printing and fixed the finished book in its correspondence as a cultural referent for the Australian community and as a professional marker of national standards in manufacturing; however, such a commitment required this aspiring Australian company to develop a list that addressed both nation-building and profit-making objectives. The experience of the London office helps therefore to explain why Angus & Robertson, having declared the culturally significant objective of 'fill[ing] the whole world with Australian books'[13], embraced practices that were perceived to question the company's 'credentials as a truly indigenous operation',[14] yet which were perhaps unavoidable in programs dedicated to achieving this objective.

Legal and Commercial Realities

This case study concludes that the development of the sale of Angus & Robertson's books in English-language markets outside Australia was indeed unavoidably influenced by British book trade practices and socio-economic factors of the time. The price advantage that British-published books enjoyed both in the United Kingdom and Australia acted as a form of commercial pressure and could be circumvented only by making the price of access to texts of Australian origin or manufacture commensurate with the cheaper British product. Economic studies in export behaviour regularly conclude that the ability of a company to export 'requires some kind of entry advantage' or 'distinct … competitive advantage' in the destination market.[15] Crucially, this business advantage must be developed in the company's domestic market before its potential can be realised in foreign markets.[16]

For Angus & Robertson this meant having a sound economic model to support the sale of cheaper books overseas. But manufacturing costs in Australia after the Second World War were high[17] as were the overheads in supporting an international branch. A price advantage in the British market, first petitioned by Vera Wellings, did not therefore automatically translate into greater profits. Instead, slashing the prices of Australian books rewarded the London office with little or no financial remuneration even as lower prices meant more Australian books were put into the hands of British readers. Over time this provided the catalyst for the London office's later complications regarding insolvency that, although not directly linked with any action by members of the British book trade, could nevertheless trace its legacy to these early unprofitable concessions. That the London office failed to find stable economic ground was partly a consequence of market conditions extraneous to the London office and partly a consequence of trade conditions in the home (Australian) economy to which it was directly tied.

Booksellers in the United Kingdom also acted as a kind of cultural barrier to the entry of new titles into the British market and, in this manner, informally controlled the circulation of texts within their jurisdictions. As George Ferguson once remarked to Hector MacQuarrie, for any publisher the British bookseller is 'in the box seat with a whip in his hand',[18] but in the end it is only through them that the great British public can be reached. Getting Australian books onto the shelves of British booksellers was not an easy task. It required Bernard Robinson to employ rogue sales techniques and singly prove the existence of a library market for Australian books in the United Kingdom. This in turn encouraged British booksellers, indignant that their (Publishers Association protected) library trade had been deliberately bypassed, to reassess Australian books in view of their own commercial interests. As a result, the London office's independence from local industry politics proved unsustainable as its business became more fully integrated into the cultural and political apparatus of the British book trade.

Furthermore, the British Publishers' Traditional Market Agreement policed English-language rights trading. As a governing structure of the book trade, it reinforced British cultural hegemony in exchange for economic and intellectual property privileges. These privileges – which advantaged texts solely published and marketed by British firms throughout the British Empire – were predominantly enjoyed by, not surprisingly, publishers based in the United Kingdom. While Australian publishers that were also physically based in Australia could only struggle under this regime to bid for the reprint rights of overseas English-language titles, the agreement's power was reasonably tempered for Angus & Robertson. Through building up an offshore publishing and marketing program in Britain, Angus & Robertson was able to alleviate (what Walter Harrap referred to as) Australia's 'geographical handicap'.[19] Because the British Publishers' Traditional Market Agreement organised its scope according to 'territories'[20] or cartographic approximations of nation and culture, a book's physical place of publication was ironically the agreement's unexpected weakness.

London was the 'logical place'[21] to make bids for British Empire rights (as Ferguson claimed) only if indeed being in London was *the* vital requirement to satisfy the agreement's formulae for participating in the trade of intellectual property to and from other international sources. The legal and commercial realities of the English book trade had thus kept British readers largely in ignorance of published goods with an Australian imprint. It was not until Angus & Robertson set up an office in London that an Australian firm could breach these barriers and that an Australian publisher could add London to its books as a place of publication.

FIGURES AND TABLES

Stacked Area Graph A

Total number of first edition Australian novels
published in Australia by Cleveland, Horwitz and other Australian publishers
from 1925 to 1975

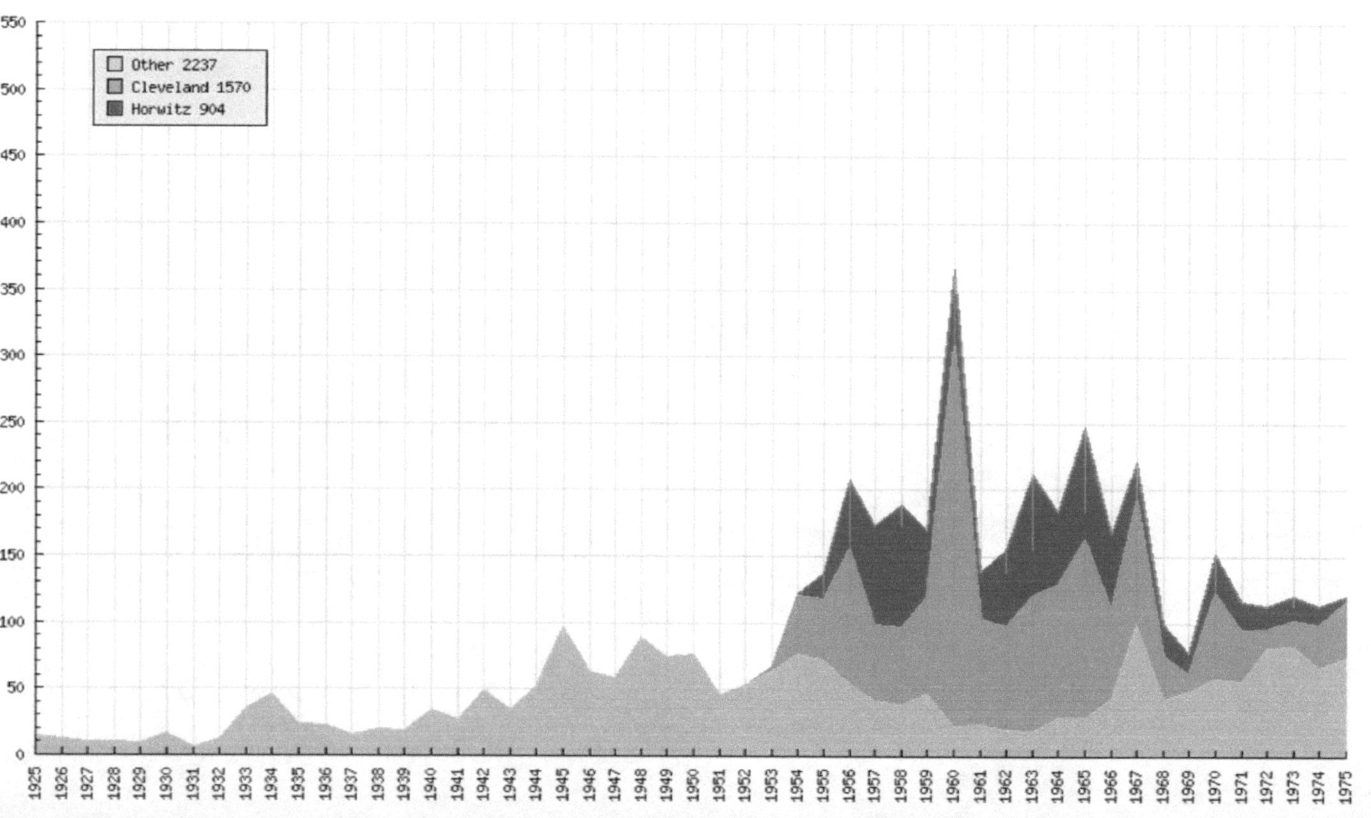

Stacked Area Graph B

Total number of first edition Australian novels
(minus the 'pulp' publications of Cleveland and Horwitz)
published in Australia and Britain only
from 1925 to 1975

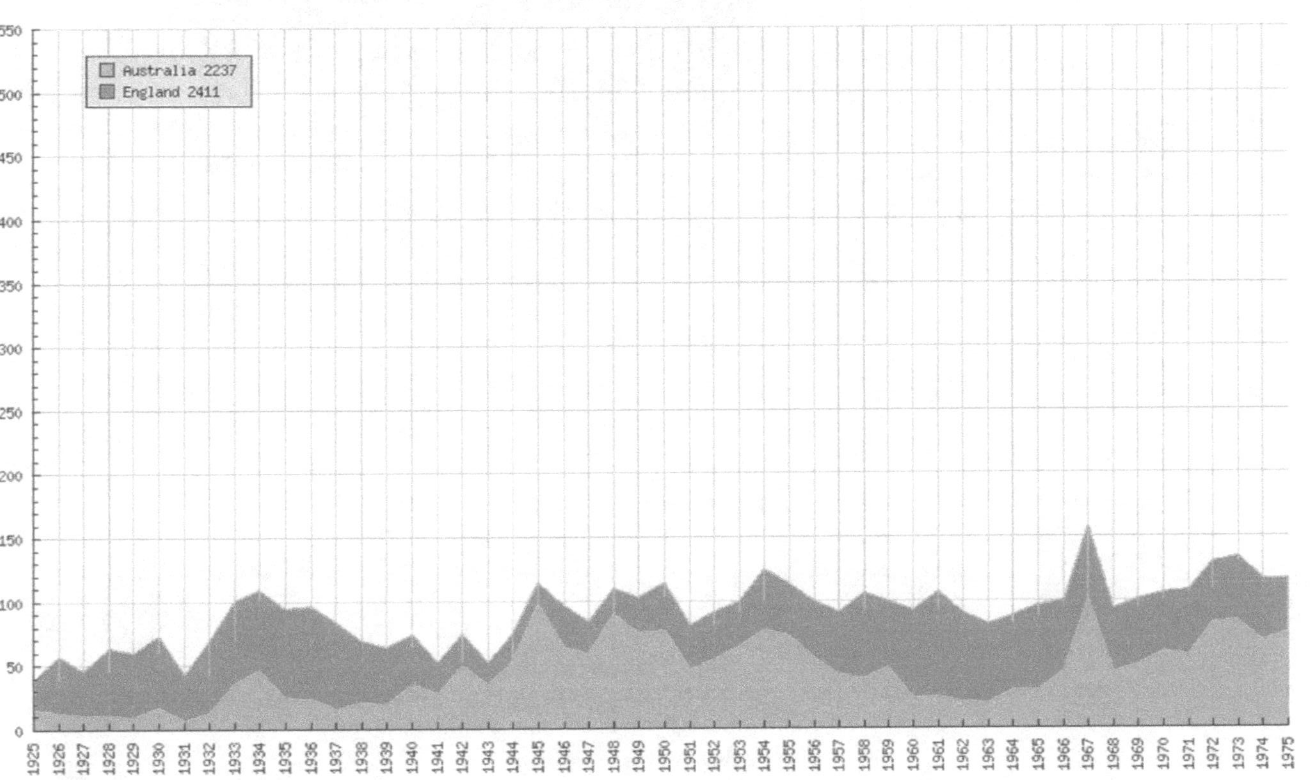

Stacked Bar Graph C

London office sales and publishing income in £ sterling

April 1954 to April 1960, MSS 3269/18-19 ML

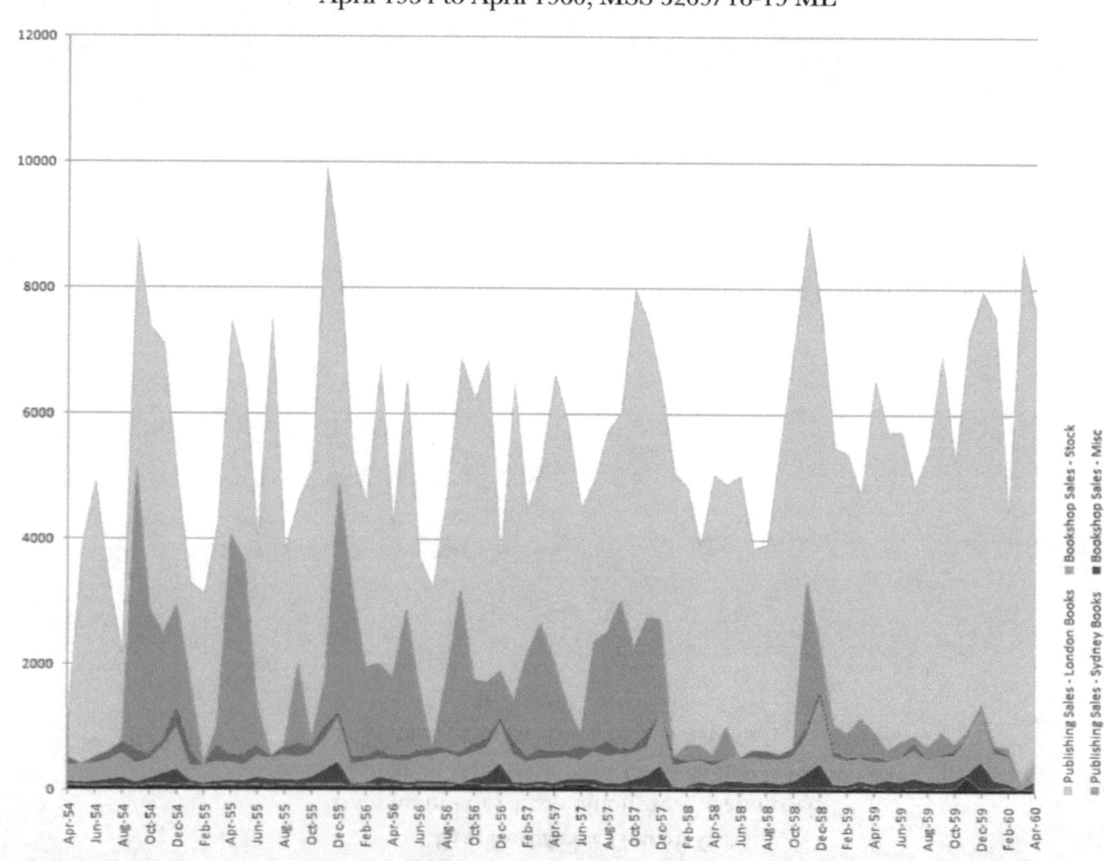

Table A

London office sales monthly income,
all amounts quoted in £ sterling (pounds) and rounded,
April 1954 to April 1960
MSS 3269/18-19 ML

	Bookshop Advertising (DEBIT)	Publishing Advertising (DEBIT)	Publishing Sales SYD (NEUTRAL)	Bookshop Sales Newspapers	Bookshop Sales Misc	Bookshop Sales Books	Publishing Sales Misc	Publishing Sales A & R London	ACTUAL MONTHLY INCOME
Apr-54	–	134	–	74	64	227	140	647	1,018
May-54	–	–	–	67	45	287	3	3,512	3,914
Jun-54	–	153	–	61	72	274	107	4,418	4,779
Jul-54	2	122	–	71	95	298	138	2,732	3,210
Aug-54	–	50	–	76	118	375	193	1,396	2,108
Sep-54	22	135	4,539	51	68	291	214	3,664	4,131
Oct-54	–	623	2,316	81	103	286	98	4,502	4,447
Nov-54	–	241	1,706	82	179	409	102	4,636	5,167
Dec-54	33	98	1,637	69	268	648	315	2,045	3,214
Jan-55	18	92	1,128	84	65	225	226	1,567	2,057
Feb-55	–	340	–	69	37	279	1	2,743	2,789
Mar-55	–	121	302	74	68	299	262	3,245	3,827
Apr-55	–	331	3,537	85	69	275	111	3,429	3,638
May-55	–	331	3,116	71	81	235	174	2,936	3,166
Jun-55	8	229	673	86	119	333	150	2,659	3,110

(Continued)

Table A Continued

	Bookshop Advertising (DEBIT)	Publishing Advertising (DEBIT)	Publishing Sales SYD (NEUTRAL)	Bookshop Sales Newspapers	Bookshop Sales Misc	Bookshop Sales Books	Publishing Sales Misc	Publishing Sales A & R London	ACTUAL MONTHLY INCOME
Jul-55	–	206	–	58	120	315	45	7,039	7,371
Aug-55	9	328	30	93	84	377	122	3,124	3,463
Sep-55	–	286	1,301	74	87	348	222	2,603	3,048
Oct-55	–	388	89	83	127	359	126	4,339	4,646
Nov-55	31	345	734	87	243	478	194	8,208	8,834
Dec-55	7	365	3,684	87	375	676	86	3,492	4,344
Jan-56	–	197	2,657	71	35	298	123	2,127	2,457
Feb-56	–	475	1,423	89	33	329	80	2,651	2,707
Mar-56	–	127	1,378	76	144	274	148	4,807	5,322
Apr-56	1	534	1,251	93	84	298	64	2,459	2,463
May-56	–	210	2,334	65	62	329	86	3,700	4,032
Jun-56	–	74	998	82	70	371	112	2,084	2,645
Jul-56	–	197	–	87	73	387	120	2,553	3,023
Aug-56	–	395	1,130	78	77	443	63	2,939	3,205
Sep-56	11	198	2,599	97	18	403	73	3,705	4,087
Oct-56	–	244	1,024	108	93	398	147	4,466	4,968
Nov-56	–	362	927	78	172	427	131	5,130	5,576
Dec-56	–	451	779	83	365	622	66	1,809	2,494
Jan-57	–	384	644	96	44	437	204	5,105	5,502

Feb-57	–	423	1,631	61	65	328	89	2,316	2,436
Mar-57	–	69	2,007	89	72	344	157	2,513	3,106
Apr-57	–	224	1,451	55	84	374	115	4,572	4,976
May-57	1	168	743	101	87	347	94	4,481	4,941
Jun-57	4	71	192	106	98	278	223	3,619	4,249
Jul-57	–	300	1,711	90	105	427	54	2,569	2,945
Aug-57	21	588	1,740	44	88	425	237	3,208	3,393
Sep-57	7	170	2,379	44	88	446	80	2,993	3,474
Oct-57	2	232	1,592	61	136	407	88	5,724	6,182
Nov-57	19	454	1,861	61	195	443	214	4,685	5,125
Dec-57	–	426	1,482	48	377	808	15	3,750	4,572
Jan-58	–	659	–	60	14	327	146	4,518	4,406
Feb-58	–	366	250	63	26	364	33	4,107	4,227
Mar-58	–	211	204	79	85	324	36	3,180	3,493
Apr-58	–	226	90	59	62	284	74	4,479	4,732
May-58	–	138	513	59	117	337	16	3,852	4,243
Jun-58	8	67	–	46	122	350	13	4,505	4,961
Jul-58	–	241	–	43	109	383	124	3,208	3,626
Aug-58	22	453	–	49	118	350	129	3,289	3,460
Sep-58	8	116	–	43	91	372	80	4,971	5,433
Oct-58	–	399	–	59	116	383	140	6,479	6,778
Nov-58	36	432	2,343	61	243	562	162	5,677	6,237
Dec-58	–	583	740	57	407	1,034	69	5,337	6,321

(Continued)

Table A Continued

	Bookshop Advertising (DEBIT)	Publishing Advertising (DEBIT)	Publishing Sales SYD (NEUTRAL)	Bookshop Sales Newspapers	Bookshop Sales Misc	Bookshop Sales Books	Publishing Sales Misc	Publishing Sales A & R London	ACTUAL MONTHLY INCOME
Jan-59	–	235	420	64	63	436	83	4,418	4,829
Feb-59	–	333	367	50	66	378	58	4,459	4,678
Mar-59	42	45	631	101	81	341	15	3,549	4,000
Apr-59	–	281	404	61	75	341	82	5,611	5,889
May-59	37	374	150	39	154	285	31	5,062	5,160
Jun-59	11	121	268	37	127	359	5	4,943	5,339
Jul-59	–	389	112	48	183	430	113	3,963	4,348
Aug-59	1	188	191	65	107	335	8	4,714	5,040
Sep-59	–	229	356	44	118	403	23	6,035	6,394
Oct-59	36	254	103	49	139	387	76	4,474	4,835
Nov-59	34	724	135	244	60	529	8	6,289	6,372
Dec-59	–	296	108	55	443	761	34	6,584	7,581
Jan-60	–	203	33	61	132	427	79	6,816	7,312
Feb-60	–	616	101	67	85	421	42	3,724	3,723
Mar-60	14	620	33	40	16	52	16	8,457	7,947
Apr-60	–	276	30	60	130	323	–	7,129	7,366

London office sales annual income,
all amounts quoted in £ sterling (pounds) and rounded,
1954 to 1960*/August 1962**
MSS 3269/18-23 ML

	Bookshop Advertising (DEBIT)	Publishing Advertising (DEBIT)	Publishing Sales SYD (NEUTRAL)	Bookshop Sales Newspapers	Bookshop Sales Misc	Bookshop Sales Books	Publishing Sales Misc	Publishing Sales A&R London	ACTUAL ANNUAL INCOME	** A&R UK Gross Profit	** A&R G.P. to Turnover
1950	–	–	–	–	–	–	–	2,266	–	–	–
1951	–	–	–	–	–	–	–	8,509	–	–	–
1952	–	–	–	–	–	–	–	9,665	–	–	–
1953	–	–	–	–	–	–	–	12,176	–	–	–
1954	–	–	–	–	–	–	–	11,444	–	–	–
1955	75	2,109	11,628	859	1,182	3,898	1,799	35,107	40,661	–	–
1956	55	3,608	18,622	960	1,517	4,297	1,581	47,414	52,106	–	–
1957	12	3,541	15,324	1,017	1,195	4,787	1,312	38,779	43,537	–	–
1958	54	3,869	13,605	812	1,383	4,970	1,335	47,406	51,983	–	–
1959	116	3,268	5,104	691	1,595	5,210	963	54,223	59,298	–	–
1960	133	4,295	1,994	810	1,639	4,730	517	66,672	69,940	–	–
** 1961	–	–	–	–	–	–	–	–	34,775	12,155	34.95%
** 1962	–	–	–	–	–	–	–	–	39,577	16,831	42.50%
** Aug 1962	–	–	–	–	–	–	–	–	29,629	12,968	43.77%

* Angus & Robertson's financial year runs from 1 April of the previous year to 31 March of the current year. For example, 1955 in the table above represents all turnover for the period 1 April 1954 to 31 March 1955; the following row for 1956 represents all turnover for the period 1 April 1955 to 31 March 1956 and so forth.

** The figures for 1961–2 are from a letter dated 23 November 1962 between Butcher and Ferguson.

Table C

London office staff annual salaries,
all amounts quoted in £ sterling (pounds) and not rounded,
1958*
MSS 3269/646 ML

Mr Rust	884	Eileen Stevens	390
Mrs Woods	572	Monica Neville	338
Mrs Howard	338	Susan Reis	260
Mr Joyner	884	Ingre Nowakowski	416
Walter Butcher	1,000	Stella Solomons	338
Greta Morrison	624	Margaret Lindsell	338
Mr Brooker	728	Anne Cox	403
Hector MacQuarrie	1,270	Oscar Schubert	469
Barry Rowland	1,600	Mr Stutchbury	351
Mr Briggs	728	Mr Smith	482
Mr Treble	676	Mr Webb	482
Mr Ratigan	520	Ingrid French	364
Miss Thornton	572	Valerie Sach	364
Kay Stocker	572	John King	312

* Combined staff salaries for 1958 amount to £16,275.

Table D

Summary of London travellers' sales and commission, all amounts quoted in £ sterling (pounds.shillings.pence) and not rounded, March 1958 to March 1960, MSS 3269/18 ML

	Mr McGarry		*Mr Snowdon		Mr Rodgers	
	Sales	**Commission**	**Sales**	**Commission**	**Sales**	**Commission**
Mar-58	189.01.05	18.18.00	1,579.03.06	39.09.07	1,964.14.05	177.06.11
Jun-58	219.11.06	21.19.01	2,771.01.01	69.05.07	2,274.05.02	187.14.09
Sep-58	238.13.09	23.12.11	1,997.03.02	49.12.06	1,751.11.01	149.05.03
Dec-58	464.08.08	46.05.08	4,283.02.00	106.15.10	3,413.17.09	310.10.01
Mar-59	296.18.04	29.08.05	1,563.10.09	38.06.08	2,139.01.02	182.13.00
Jun-59	315.06.09	31.10.08	–	–	2,475.16.06	224.06.06
Sep-59	248.17.10	24.17.08	–	–	2,626.00.01	219.15.05
Dec-59	246.00.04	24.11.11	–	–	2,886.15.01	257.05.09
Mar-60	339.08.03	33.18.09	–	–	3,153.05.07	267.09.00

	* W. Butcher		B. Lamberth		W. G. Brash	
	Sales	**Commission**	**Sales**	**Commission**	**Sales**	**Commission**
Mar-58	4,107.13.11	92.08.06	932.06.10	93.04.06	245.03.05	24.10.03
Jun-58	4,196.03.05	94.08.02	883.02.00	88.06.02	104.15.07	10.09.06
Sep-58	4,197.16.02	94.09.01	632.10.06	63.02.04	37.13.05	3.15.03
Dec-58	7,273.06.07	163.12.11	1,688.02.10	168.15.05	221.16.03	22.03.07
Mar-59	4,227.00.09	93.03.02	857.05.07	85.12.00	142.12.06	14.05.03
Jun-59	5,234.18.01	117.15.09	1,085.16.01	108.11.05	61.07.08	6.02.09
Sep-59	4,824.16.03	108.11.03	1,055.11.07	105.11.02	12.10.06	1.05.00
Dec-59	5,969.07.02	134.06.02	953.01.02	95.06.01	31.16.11	3.03.08
Mar-60	7,775.11.04	171.19.04	1,253.9.10	125.06.11	11.08.05	1.02.10

	M. F. Thum		D. Payne		K. Knowles	
	Sales	**Commission**	**Sales**	**Commission**	**Sales**	**Commission**
Mar-58	216.18.10	21.03.10	–	–	–	–
Jun-58	32.08.07	3.04.10	–	–	–	–
Sep-58	65.14.09	6.11.05	–	–	–	–
Dec-58	98.09.04	9.16.11	–	–	–	–
Mar-59	–	–	323.04.02	32.06.05	952.07.01	70.01.03
Jun-59	–	–	554.04.02	32.06.05	3,744.13.04	292.02.01
Sep-59	–	–	443.00.04	44.06.00	3,126.14.06	227.05.08
Dec-59	–	–	605.19.06	60.11.11	4,603.05.08	350.02.11
Mar-60	–	–	337.08.04	33.14.10	4,675.05.02	339.12.06

* These travellers earned a basic salary as well (not included in quarterly totals).

Table E

Panther Books,
Sales for paperback editions of 'Operation London' titles,
only royalties are quoted in £ sterling (pounds.shillings.pence) and not rounded,
sales figures are number of copies sold, 1958
MSS 3269/647 ML

Title	Author	Sales to 30 Jun 1958	Sales to 31 Dec 1958	Total Sales	* Royalties £
Away All Boats	K. Dodson	55,113	4,378	57,491	838.08.02
Big Boys Don't Cry	M. Corrigan	–	23,355	23,555	194.12.06
The Big Squeeze	M. Corrigan	18,257	915	19,172	159.15.04
The Hidden Enemy	V. H. Lloyd	–	34,210	34,210	285.01.08
No Moon Tonight	D. E. Charlwood	24,487	5,318	29,805	248.07.06
One Man War	H. Richardson	–	37,850	37,850	315.08.04
The Ridge and the River	T. A. G. Hungerford	–	24,101	24,101	20.16.10
Sydney for Sin	M. Corrigan	–	18,332	18,332	152.15.04
They Shall Not Pass Unseen	I. Southall	–	25,555	25,555	212.19.02
White Coolies	B. Jeffreys	109,074	75,764	184,838	1,732.17.01

* Total royalty amount received includes author's share, negotiated at a split of 50/50 with Angus & Robertson. Of the share that belongs to Angus & Robertson, two-thirds went to the London office and a third went to Sydney.

Table F

London office sales to overseas customers,
all amounts quoted in £ sterling (pounds.shillings.pence) and not rounded,
financial year ended 31 March 1959
MSS 3269/647 ML

Territory	Sales £
Western Europe	2,173.13.01
Africa (*Lamberth's Territory*)	4,061.00.11
Canada	1,275.13.06
India	575.07.06
Far East (*Brash's Territory*)	506.08.04
Unite States of America	371.15.02
West Indies	142.18.00
Miscellaneous *	389.18.00
TOTAL	**9,496.14.06**

* Miscellaneous includes Latin America, Ireland, Turkey, Lebanon, Nigeria, Ghana, etc.

Table G

Summary of London traveller Sydney Sewell's commission, all amounts quoted in £ sterling (pounds.shillings.pence) and not rounded, two financial years, April 1954 to March 1956
MSS 3269/447 ML

Year	Month	Commission £	Year	Month	Commission £
1954	April	22.17.09	1955	April	93.13.10
1954	May	126.02.00	1955	May	101.15.07
1954	June	53.14.00	1955	June	77.00.00
1954	July	15.04.10	1955	July	142.06.05
1954	August	46.08.06	1955	August	46.11.09
1954	September	124.01.05	1955	September	31.19.03
1954	October	149.05.04	1955	October	57.18.00
1954	November	151.13.11	1955	November	84.15.00
1954	December	69.09.03	1955	December	34.07.05
1955	January	57.14.09	1956	January	25.04.04
1955	February	101.06.05	1956	February	31.14.05
1955	March	118.04.11	1956	March	91.05.10
	TOTAL	**1,036.03.01**		**TOTAL**	**818.11.10**

Table H

Summary of London office expenses,
all amounts quoted in £ sterling (pounds) and not rounded,
April 1960 to March 1961
MSS 3269/19 ML

Item	Sales £
Travelling	350
Telephone	200
Postage	900
Stationery	700
Telegrams	10
Insurance	100
Sundry Expenses	450
Depreciation	500
Rent	2,500
Audit	200
Packing	50
Light & Heat	600
Salaries	6,800
Carriage	1,700
Travellers' Commission	3,000
Advertising / Publicity	3,000
Bad Debts	150
Professional Fees	100
TOTAL	**21,310**

Table I
London office bestsellers,
sales figures are number of copies sold,
16 March 1960,
MSS 3269/19 ML

Author Surname	Title	London	Sydney
Niland	The Shiralee	32,000	47,000
Dodson	Away All Boats	16,000	22,500
Smith	Duet for Three Hands	13,000	1,000
Eton & Leasor	Conspiracy of Silence	12,000	–
Niland	Call me When the Cross Turns Over	10,000	12,800
Niland	Big Smoke	8,500	9,000
Jeffries	White Coolies	8,500	63,000
Bowring	Cake Icing	7,000	20,000
Dodson	Stranger to the Shore	6,000	9,000
Gibbs	Life-s Adventure	6,000	2,500
Kades	San Salvatore	5,000	4,000
Simpson	Picture of Japan	4,000	25,000
Bisset	Sail Ho	3,000	4,000

Table J
London office paperback sales,
16 March 1960,
MSS 3269/19 ML

Author Surname	Title	House	Author Surname	Title	House
Bartlett	Island Victory	Digit	Bisset	Sail Ho	Mariners Lib.
Chapman	Details Enclosed	Panther	Charlwood	No Moon Tonight	Panther
Corrigan	Big Boys Don't Cry	Panther	Corrigan	Sydney for Sin	Panther
Corrigan	Dumb As They Come	Panther	Corrigan	Honolulu Snatch	Panther
Corrigan	Cruel Lady	Panther	Corrigan	Big Squeeze	Panther
Corrigan	Menace in Siam	Panther	Dodson	Away All Boats	Panther
Fowler	Shades Will Not Vanish	Readers' Digest	Fraser	Frogman V.C.	Beacon
Griffin	By the North Gate	Four Square	Hamilton	Soldier Surgeon in Malaya	World Distributors
Hungerford	Ridge and the River	Panther	Jeffrey	White Coolies	Panther
Kades	The Great Temptation	Corgi	Lawler	Summer of the 17th Doll	Fontana
Lindsay	The Magic Pudding	Puffin	Lloyd	Hidden Enemy	Panther
McKie	Proud Echo	Panther	McNeil	San Demetrio	Corgi
Niland	The Big Smoke	Panther	Niland	Call Me When the Cross Turns Over	Pan
Niland	The Shiralee	Popular Book Club & Pan	Park	A Power of Roses	Pan
Richardson	One Man Way	Panther	Russell	A Lamp is Heavy	Pan
Southall	The Shall Not Pass Unseen	Panther	Timms	The Falcon	Panther
West	Kundu	Panther	Williamson	The Sunlit Plain	Corgi
Wright	The Outsider	Panther			

NOTES

Preface

1 The previous three PhD-level studies of Angus & Robertson's business are: Jennifer Alison, 'Angus & Robertson as Publishers 1888–1900: A Business History' (PhD diss., University of New South Wales, 1997); Neil James, 'Spheres of Influence: Angus and Robertson and Australian Literature from the Thirties to the Sixties' (PhD diss., University of Sydney, 2000); and Caroline Vera Jones, 'Australian Imprint: The Influence of George Robertson on a National Narrative 1890–1935' (PhD diss., University of Sydney, 2004).
2 John Barnes, '"Heaven Forbid that I Should Think of Treating with an English Publisher": The Dilemma of Literary Nationalists in Federated Australia', in *Literary Cultures and the Material Book*, ed. Simon Eliot, Andrew Nash and Ian Willison (London: The British Library, 2007), 409.
3 Alec Bolton, interview with Heather Rusden, 11 October 1996–7 November 1996, TRC 3523, National Library of Australia.
4 George Ferguson, interview with Suzanne Lunney, 11 May 1976, TRC 452, National Library of Australia.
5 Douglas Stewart, interview with Suzanne Lunney, 1975, TRC 336, National Library of Australia.
6 Ernie Williams, interview with Suzanne Lunney, 2 December 1975, TRC 387, National Library of Australia.
7 Neil James, 'Spheres of Influence: Angus and Robertson and Australian Literature From the Thirties to the Sixties' (PhD diss., University of Sydney, 2000), 258–68.
8 James' original interview recordings were not available for this study.
9 Sam Everingham, *Gordon Barton: Australia's Maverick Entrepreneur* (Crows Nest: Allen & Unwin, 2009), 179.
10 Australian Government, *Productivity Commission, Restrictions on the Parallel Importation of Books: Productivity Commission Research Report.* (Melbourne: The Commission, 2009), 6.1.
11 David Carter, 'Structures, Networks, Institutions: The New Empiricism, Book History and Literary History', in *Resourceful Reading: The New Empiricism, eResearch and Australian Literary Culture*, ed. Katherine Bode and Robert Dixon (Sydney: Sydney University Press, 2010), 45.

Chapter 1 The Company that Loved Australian Books

1 State Library of New South Wales, 'Administrative History', *Guide to the Angus & Robertson Archives: Mitchell Library Manuscripts Guides 13* (Sydney: Library Council of New South Wales, 1990), iv–xiv.
2 D. M. Angus, 'Opening Announcement New Bookseller's Establishment', June 1884, quoted in Anthony Barker, *George Robertson: A Publishing Life in Letters* (St Lucia: University of Queensland Press, 1993), 1.
3 Anthony Barker, *George Robertson: A Publishing Life in Letters* (St Lucia: University of Queensland Press, 1993), 5.
4 George Robertson to Rudyard Kipling, 21 October 1985, MSS 3269/75 ML, quoted in Jennifer Alison, 'Angus & Robertson as Publishers 1888–1900: A Business History' (PhD diss., University of New South Wales, 1997), 35.

5 Jennifer Alison, 'Angus & Robertson as Publishers 1888–1900: A Business History' (PhD diss., University of New South Wales, 1997), 35, 54–5.
6 Alison, 'Angus & Robertson as Publishers', 129.
7 Alison, 'Angus & Robertson as Publishers', 39.
8 Caroline Vera Jones, 'Australian Imprint: The Influence of George Robertson on a National Narrative 1890–1935' (PhD diss., University of Sydney, 2004), 31.
9 Graeme Johanson, *A Study of Colonial Editions in Australia 1843–1972* (Wellington: Elibank Press, 2000), 29.
10 Alison, 'Angus & Robertson as Publishers', 54–5.
11 Alison, 'Angus & Robertson as Publishers', 54–7, 101–2, 150–55, 163–4.
12 George Ferguson, quoted in State Library of New South Wales, *Guide to the Angus & Robertson Archives: Mitchell Library Manuscripts Guides 13* (Sydney: Library Council of New South Wales, 1990), v.
13 Richard Nile, *The Making of the Australian Literary Imagination* (St Lucia: University of Queensland Press, 2002), 79.
14 Caroline Vera Jones, 'Historical Midwifery: The Editorial Birth of an Australian Narrative', *Journal of Publishing* 2 (August 2007): 27. See also: Vera Jones, 'Australian Imprint'.
15 Alison, 'Angus & Robertson as Publishers', 2.
16 Alison, 'Angus & Robertson as Publishers', 12.
17 James, 'Spheres of Influence', 296.
18 Nile, *Australian Literary Imagination*, 55.
19 Laura J. Miller, *Reluctant Capitalists: Bookselling and the Culture of Consumption* (Chicago: University of Chicago Press, 2006), 9.
20 See Jacques Olivier, Mathias Thoenig and Thierry Verdier, 'Globalisation and the Dynamics of Cultural Identity', *Journal of International Economics* 76 (2008): 356–70; George A. Akerlof and Rachel E. Kranton, 'Economics and Identity', *Quarterly Journal of Economics* 65.3 (August 2000): 715–53.
21 Nile, *Australian Literary Imagination*, 62–3.
22 Nile, *Australian Literary Imagination*, 74.
23 Nile, *Australian Literary Imagination*, 65.
24 George Robertson to Angela Thirkell, 6 January 1932, quoted in Anthony Barker, *George Robertson: A Publishing Life in Letters* (St Lucia: University of Queensland Press, 1993), 209.
25 Robertson to Thirkell quoted in Barker, *A Publishing Life in Letters*, 209.
26 Walter Cousins quoted in Richard Nile, *The Making of the Australian Literary Imagination* (St Lucia: University of Queensland Press, 2002), 67. See 65–7 for more background.
27 Cousins quoted in Nile, *Australian Literary Imagination*, 71.
28 Nile, *Australian Literary Imagination*, 71.
29 Nile, *Australian Literary Imagination*, 72.
30 Hector MacQuarrie to George Ferguson, 29 November 1949, MSS 3269/440 ML.
31 State Library of New South Wales, *Guide to the Angus & Robertson Archives: Mitchell Library Manuscripts Guides 13* (Sydney: Library Council of New South Wales, 1990), vii.
32 George Ferguson to Hector MacQuarrie, 21 March 1963, MSS 3269/449 ML.
33 Sam Everingham, *Gordon Barton: Australia's Maverick Entrepreneur* (Crows Nest: Allen & Unwin, 2009), 189.
34 Alison, 'Angus & Robertson as Publishers', 3.
35 REDGroup Retail also owns Borders, Calendar Club, Supanews and Whitcoulls. 'About Us', REDGroup Retail, http://www.arw.co.nz/about-us
36 Geoffrey Dutton, *Snow on the Saltbush: The Australian Literary Experience* (Ringwood, Victoria: Penguin, 1985), 255–6.
37 Dutton, *Snow on the Saltbush*, 255.
38 Dutton, *Snow on the Saltbush*, 256.

39 Dutton, *Snow on the Saltbush*, 256.
40 Nile, *Australian Literary Imagination*, 72–3.
41 Robert Darnton, *The Kiss of the Lamourette* (London: Faber and Faber, 1990).
42 'Scope Policy', AustLit: The Australian Literature Resource, http://austlit.edu.au/about/scopepolicy
43 Edward W. Said, *Culture and Imperialism* (London: Chatto and Windus, 1993), 85.
44 For a discussion on 'presence', see Jean Baudrillard, *Simulacra and Simulation* (United States of America: University of Michigan Press, 1994).
45 David Ayers, 'Materialism and the Book', *Poetics Today* 24.4 (2003): 759–80.
46 George Ferguson to Alec Bolton, 21 September 1967, MSS 3269/30 ML.
47 Richard Nile and David Walker, 'Marketing the Literary Imagination: Production of Australian Literature, 1915–1965', *The Penguin New Literary History of Australia, Australian Literary Studies (Special Issue)* 13.4 (October 1988): 284.
48 Bill Ashcroft, 'Home and Horizon', in *Diaspora: The Australasian Experience*, ed. Cynthia vanden Driesen and Ralph Crane (New Delhi: Prestige Books, 2006), 52.
49 John Raymond Wilton, University of Adelaide, quoted in Tariff Board Australia, *Report of Evidence at Tariff Board Inquiries into Proposal of Duty on Books, Magazines and Fashion Plates Held in Adelaide, Brisbane, Sydney and Melbourne* (Melbourne: Australian Booksellers Association, 1930), 8.
50 Miller, *Reluctant Capitalists*, 9.
51 Hector MacQuarrie to Captain Taylor, 28 August 1953, MSS 3269/444 ML.
52 James, 'Spheres of Influence', 260.
53 George Ferguson to Hector MacQuarrie, 8 November 1955, MSS 3269/446 ML.
54 Hector MacQuarrie to Stanley Rinehart, 4 November 1954, MSS 3269/445 ML.
55 Andrew Fabinyi to Sam Ure Smith, 7 October 1963, MSS 3269/106 ML.
56 Sam Ure Smith to John Brown, 18 October 1963, MSS 3269/106 ML.
57 Craig Munro, 'Case-Study: A&R's Takeover Crisis', in *A History of the Book in Australia 1946–2005: Paper Empires*, ed. Craig Munro and Robyn Sheahan-Bright (St Lucia: University of Queensland Press, 2006): 13–18.
58 Sam Ure Smith to Walter Butcher, 26 May 1964, MSS 3269/22 ML.
59 John Feather, *A History of British Publishing* (London: Routledge, 1988), 201.
60 George Ferguson to Hector MacQuarrie, 4 December 1959, MSS 3269/449 ML.
61 Hector MacQuarrie to George Ferguson, 14 November 1957, MSS 3269/448 ML.
62 Stephen Alomes, 'Colonial to Global: Paradoxes of Expatriation in Australia's Diasporic Story', in *Diaspora: The Australasian Experience*, ed. Cynthia vanden Driesen and Ralph Crane (New Delhi: Prestige Books, 2006): 137.
63 Walter Butcher to George Ferguson, 26 September 1967, MSS 3269/30 ML.
64 R. E. Barker, Members Circular, The Publishers Association (UK), 18 January 1963, MSS 3269/557 ML.
65 Robert Haupt, 'The Book Rebellion', *Age*, 5 November 1988.
66 George Ferguson to Walter Harrap, 1 December 1949, MSS 3269/440 ML.

Chapter 2 The Overseas Books in Australian Publishing History

1 Robert Haupt, 'The Book Rebellion', *Age*, 5 November 1988.
2 Russi Jal Taraporevala, *Competition and Its Control in the British Book Trade 1850–1939* (London: Pitman Publishing, 1973); Martin Lyons and John Arnold, eds, *A History of the Book in Australia 1891–1945: A National Culture in a Colonised Market* (St Lucia: University of Queensland Press, 2001).
3 Jenny Lee, 'War and Peace in the Australian Book Trade', unpublished paper, 13.
4 Data taken from 'Book Publishing Export Group Turnover Statistics: Territorial Analysis of Export Turnover', in *Books Are Different: An Account of the Defence of the Net Book Agreement before*

the Restrictive Practices Court in 1962, ed. R. E. Barker and G. R. Davis (London: Macmillan, 1966): 907.

5 'Australia is Britain's Best Market for Books', *Mercury*, 28 December 1948.

6 According to the statistics presented before the 1962 Restrictive Practices Court case, 1959 is the year that the United States overtakes Australia in export turnover. Though Australia obtains greater export value than the United States in 1960, it is again second to America in 1961. See also Richard Nile, *The Making of the Australian Literary Imagination* (St Lucia: University of Queensland Press, 2002); Paul Eggert, 'The Colonial Market, Imperial Publisher, and the Demise of the Three-Decker Novel', *Book History* 6 (2006): 127–46; and Graeme Johanson, *A Study of Colonial Editions in Australia, 1843–1972* (Wellington: Elibank Press, 2000).

7 For a more detailed background of this association see Reginald John Lethbridge Kingsford, *The Publishers Association, 1896–1946: With an Epilogue* (London: Cambridge University Press, 1970).

8 Hector MacQuarrie to George Ferguson, 26 November 1949, MSS 3269/440 ML.

9 It was a sub-committee of the Australian Book Publishers Association.

10 Sam Ure Smith, Australian Book Publishers Association (Sydney) to John Brown, Publishers Association (London), 18 October 1963, MSS 3269/106 ML.

11 R. E. Barker and G. R. Davis, eds, *Books Are Different: An Account of the Defence of the Net Book Agreement before the Restrictive Practices Court in 1962* (London: Macmillan, 1966), 463.

12 Gael Cresp, *The British Publishers' Traditional Market Agreement: A Study* (Melbourne: Royal Melbourne Institute of Technology, 1977), 4.

13 John Brown, Publishers Association (London) to Sam Ure Smith, Australian Book Publishers Association (Sydney), 1 January 1964, MSS 3269/106 ML.

14 Brown to Smith, 1 January 1964, MSS 3269/106 ML.

15 Barker and Davis, *Books Are Different*, 472.

16 Brown to Smith, 1 January 1964, MSS 3269/106 ML.

17 John Feather, *A History of British Publishing* (London: Routledge, 1988), 204.

18 George Ferguson, 'Publishing in London by Angus & Robertson Limited: A Paper for the guidance of the Board', unpublished, August 1970, MSS 3269/34 ML.

19 Ferguson, 'Publishing in London', August 1970, MSS 3269/34 ML.

20 George Ferguson to Hector MacQuarrie, 19 November 1953, MSS 3269/444 ML.

21 Barker and Davis, *Books Are Different*, 470.

22 Released on 14 July 2009 at http://www.pc.gov.au/projects/study/books/report

23 Laura J. Miller, *Reluctant Capitalists: Bookselling and the Culture of Consumption* (London: University of Chicago Press, 2006), 19.

24 Kathleen McLean, 'Culture, Commerce and Ambivalence: A Study of Australian Federal Government Intervention in Book Publishing' (PhD diss., unpublished, Monash University, 2002), ii.

25 Jacques Olivier, Mathias Thoenig and Thierry Verdier, 'Globalisation and the Dynamics of Cultural Identity', *Journal of International Economics* 76 (2008): 356–70.

26 Australian Government, Productivity Commission, *Restrictions on the Parallel Importation of Books: Productivity Commission Research Report* (Melbourne: The Commission, 2009).

27 Prices Surveillance Authority, *Inquiry into Book Prices and Parallel Imports* (Melbourne: Prices Surveillance Authority, 1995).

28 Industries Assistance Commission, *Pulp, Paper, Paper Products and Printing Industries* (Canberra: Australian Government Publishing Service, 1987).

29 Industries Assistance Commission, *The Publishing Industry* (Canberra: Australian Government Publishing Service, 1979).

30 Industries Assistance Commission report, *Products of the Printing Industry* (Canberra: Australian Government Publishing Service, 1978).

31 Tariff Board, *Tariff revision, Products of the Printing Industry* (Canberra: Australian Government Publishing Service, 1973).

32 'Tariff Board Inquiry into the Publishing Industry of Australia', *Booksellers, Stationers and Fancy Goods Journal of Australia and New Zealand* (Melbourne: DW Thorpe, January to February 1946); Tariff Board Australia, *Tariff Board's Report on Publishing Industry* (Canberra: Commonwealth Government Printer, 1946).
33 Tariff Board Australia, *Report of Evidence at Tariff Board Inquiries into Proposal of Duty on Books, Magazines and Fashion Plates Held in Adelaide, Brisbane, Sydney and Melbourne* (Melbourne: Australian Booksellers Association, 1930).
34 Lee, 'War and Peace', 1.
35 Productivity Commission, *Parallel Importation of Books*, xv.
36 Productivity Commission, *Parallel Importation of Books*, 2.7.
37 H. L. White, *The Future of Australian Publishing* (Sydney: Australian Institute of Political Science, 1946), 2.
38 Vera Wellings, 'Australians are Bookworms: Literary Influence', *Sydney Morning Herald*, 21 December 1940.
39 Neville Cardus, 'The Pen and the Sword: Perils and Pleasures of Reading', *Sydney Morning Herald*, 26 April 1941.
40 'Australia, it seems, is a Bookish Place', *Sydney Morning Herald*, 22 May 1953.
41 'Australia, it seems, is a Bookish Place', *Sydney Morning Herald*, 22 May 1953.
42 'Four in Every Ten Australians Never Read a Book', *Argus*, 20 June 1953.
43 'Four in Every Ten Australians Never Read a Book', *Argus*, 20 June 1953.
44 George Ferguson to John Bush, Victor Gollancs, London, 19 March 1952, MSS 3269/293 ML.
45 This figure is calculated with reference to the tables 'Book Publishing Export Group Turnover Statistics' and 'Territorial Analysis of Export Turnover' for the period 1956–1961, in R. E. Barker and G. R. Davis, eds, *Books Are Different: An Account of the Defence of the Net Book Agreement before the Restrictive Practices Court in 1962* (London: Macmillan, 1966), 905, 907.
46 Walter Harrap to Stanley Bartlett, 2 September 1938, MSS 3269/322 ML.
47 Henry Lawson, quoted in Stephen Alomes, *When London Calls: The Expatriation of Australian Creative Artists to Britain* (Cambridge: Cambridge University Press, 1999), 10.
48 J. C. James, Australian Journalists Association, 'Tariff Board Inquiry into the Publishing Industry in Australia', in *Ideas: Booksellers, Stationers and Fancy Goods Journal of Australia and New Zealand* (Melbourne: D. W. Thorpe, January 1946): 28.
49 Luke Trainor, 'Australian Writers, British Publishers, 1870–1902', *Australian Historical Society* 37.127 (April 2006): 140–55; Diane Brown, 'Publishing Culture: Commissioning Books in Australia, 1970–2000' (PhD diss., Victoria University, 2003).
50 Richard Nile and David Walker, 'The "Paternoster Row Machine" and the Australian Book Trade, 1890–1945', in *A History of the Book in Australia 1891–1945: A National Culture in a Colonised Market*, ed. Martyn Lyons and John Arnold (St Lucia: University of Queensland Press, 2001): 7.
51 Stanley Unwin, George Allen & Unwin to Rev. William B. Hay, 31 May 1951, Allen & Unwin AUC 20, Vol. 13, University of Reading.
52 See, for example, John Hetherington to Philip Unwin, 22 September 1944, John Hetherington AUC 194, Vol. 9, University of Reading.
53 Horace Bohmer Newman, New South Wales section, British Book Publishers' Representatives Association of Australia and New Zealand, in Tariff Board Australia, *Report of Evidence (1930)*, 56.
54 George Robertson, in Tariff Board Australia, *Report of Evidence (1930)*, 37.
55 C. S. P. Throssell (Katharine Susannah Prichard), in 'Tariff Board Inquiry', *Ideas: Booksellers, Stationers and Fancy Goods (1946)*, 59.
56 Frank Sanders, ed., *British Book Trade Organisation: A Report on the Work of the Joint Committee* (London: George Allen & Unwin, 1939), 95.
57 Graeme Johanson, *Colonial Editions in Australia 1843–1972* (Wellington: Elibank Press, 2000).
58 George Farwell, Fellowship of Australian Writers, in 'Tariff Board Inquiry', *Ideas: Booksellers, Stationers and Fancy Goods (1946)*, 43.

59 Throssell, in 'Tariff Board Inquiry', *Ideas: Booksellers, Stationers and Fancy Goods (1946)*, 59.
60 Frank Clune, in 'Tariff Board Inquiry', *Ideas: Booksellers, Stationers and Fancy Goods* (1946), 51.
61 Jean Devanny, in 'Tariff Board Inquiry', *Ideas: Booksellers, Stationers and Fancy Goods* (1946), 34.
62 Cultural Defence Committee, *Mental Rubbish from Overseas: A Public Protest* (Sydney: Cultural Defence Committee, 1935), 4.
63 Cultural Defence Committee, *Mental Rubbish*, 11.
64 Charles Harold Peters, in Tariff Board Australia, *Report of Evidence (1930)*, 80.
65 Charles Harold Peters, in Tariff Board Australia, *Report of Evidence (1930)*, 80.
66 Jason Ensor, 'Is a Picture Worth 10,175 Australian Novels?', in *Resourceful Reading: The New Empiricism, eResearch and Australian Literary Culture*, ed. Katherine Bode and Robert Dixon (Sydney: Sydney University Press, 2010): 240–73; Richard Nile and Jason Ensor, 'The Novel, the Implicated Reader and Australian Literary Cultures, 1950–2008', in *Cambridge History of Australian Literature*, ed. P. Pierce (Melbourne: Cambridge University Press, 2009), 517–48; Jason Ensor, 'Still Waters Run Deep: Empirical Methods and the Migration Patterns of Regional Publishers' Authors and Titles within Australian Literature', in *Antipodes* (December 2009): 197–208; Jason Ensor, 'Reprints, International Markets and Local Literary Taste: New Empiricism and Australian Literature', in *Journal of the Association for the Study of Australian Literature* (Special Issue 2008): 198–218.
67 Barker and Davis, *Books Are Different*, 41.
68 Productivity Commission, *Parallel Importation of Books*, 4.6.
69 Productivity Commission, *Parallel Importation of Books*, 4.6.
70 Lee, 'War and Peace', 3.
71 Peter Lloyd, '100 Years of Tariff Protection in Australia', *Australian Economic History Review* 48.2 (July 2008): 101.
72 Lloyd, '100 Years of Tariff', 101.
73 Lee, 'War and Peace', 3.
74 Australian Society of Authors, quoted in Productivity Commission, *Parallel Importation of Books*, 6.11.
75 Australian Society of Authors, quoted in Productivity Commission, *Parallel Importation of Books*, 6.11.
76 Productivity Commission, *Parallel Importation of Books*, 3.1.
77 S. F. Ferguson, Director, Australian Association of British Manufacturers, in 'Tariff Board Inquiry', *Ideas: Booksellers, Stationers and Fancy Goods (1946)*, 122.
78 William St Clair, *The Reading Nation in the Romantic Period* (New York: Cambridge University Press, 2004), 440.
79 In previous studies, it was named as the 'printers' union'.
80 James Howard Catts, in Tariff Board Australia, *Report of Evidence (1930)*, 25.
81 Roger Osborne, 'A National Interest in an International Market: The Circulation of Magazines in Australia during the 1930s', *History Australia* 5.3 (2008): 75.3.
82 J. Hagan, *Printers and Politics: A History of the Australian Printing Unions 1850–1950* (Canberra: Australian National University Press, 1966), 243.
83 These exact figures are taken from H. E. Guy, in Tariff Board Australia, *Report of Evidence (1930)*, 2. They are also summarised in Richard Nile and David Walker, 'The "Paternoster Row Machine" and the Australian Book Trade, 1890–1945', in *A History of the Book in Australia 1891–1945: A National Culture in a Colonised Market*, ed. *Martyn* Lyons and John Arnold (St Lucia: University of Queensland Press, 2001), 13–14.
84 James Howard Catts, in Tariff Board Australia, *Report of Evidence (1930)*, 20.
85 James Howard Catts, in Tariff Board Australia, *Report of Evidence (1930)*, 21.
86 H. E. Guy, in Tariff Board Australia, *Report of Evidence (1930)*, 2.
87 James Howard Catts, in Tariff Board Australia, *Report of Evidence (1930)*, 21.
88 James Howard Catts, in Tariff Board Australia, *Report of Evidence (1930)*, 21.
89 James Howard Catts, in *Australian Publishers Federation: Report*, Sydney (1930): 9. MSS 314/256 ML.

90 Tariff Board Australia, *Report of Evidence (1930)*, 26, 30.
91 Gordon & Gotch (Australasia) Ltd to Angus & Robertson, 3 February 1928, MSS 314/34 ML.
92 Tariff Board Australia, 'Tariff Board's Report and Recommendation: Tariff Revision – Fashion Plates and Books; Books, Magazines N.E.I. and Printed Matter, N.E.I. – Request for Increased Duties, 26 June 1930', *Parliamentary Papers – General Session* 1929–31, vol. 3, 11/1777.
93 Tariff Board Australia, 'Tariff Board's Report and Recommendation', 10/1776.
94 Tariff Board Australia, 'Tariff Board's Report and Recommendation', 10/1776.
95 Julian Thomas, 'CDs and the Politics of Intellectual Property', *Media and Culture Review* (July 1998): 1.
96 Gareth Grainger, 'Protection of Cultural Sovereignty in a Free-Trade Environment', *Media and Culture Review* (July 1998): 12.
97 Grainger, 'Cultural Sovereignty', 12.
98 Tariff Board Australia, quoted in Kathleen McLean, 'Culture, Commerce and Ambivalence: A Study of Australian Federal Government Intervention in Book Publishing' (PhD diss., unpublished, Monash University, 2002), 124.
99 Henry Arthur Sinclair, in Tariff Board Australia, *Report of Evidence (1930)*, 32.
100 Henry Arthur Sinclair, in Tariff Board Australia, *Report of Evidence (1930)*, 32.
101 Henry Arthur Sinclair, in Tariff Board Australia, *Report of Evidence (1930)*, 32.
102 D. W. Thorpe, in Tariff Board Australia, *Report of Evidence (1930)*, 84.
103 Alexander James Donaldson Gray, General Manager, Gordon & Gotch, in Tariff Board Australia, *Report of Evidence (1930)*, 32.
104 Stephen Alomes, 'Colonial to Global: Paradoxes of Expatriation in Australia's Diasporic Story', in *Diaspora: The Australasian Experience*, ed. Cynthia vanden Driesen and Ralph Crane (New Delhi: Prestige Books, 2006), 136.
105 John Morley Bath, South Australian branch, Australian Booksellers Association, in Tariff Board Australia, *Report of Evidence (1930)*, 11.
106 Tariff Board Australia, 'Tariff Board's Report', 9/1775.
107 Letter reprinted in *Australian Publishers Federation: Report*, (Sydney 1930), 5. MSS 314/256 ML.
108 On 4 February 1928.
109 James Howard Catts, *Australian Publishers Federation: Report*, Sydney (1930): 17. MSS 314/256 ML.
110 Henry Arthur Sinclair, in Tariff Board Australia, *Report of Evidence (1930)*, 32.
111 Tariff Board Australia, 'Tariff Board's Report', 7/1773. Quoted in Kathleen McLean, 'Culture, Commerce and Ambivalence: A Study of Australian Federal Government Intervention in Book Publishing' (PhD diss., unpublished, Monash University, 2002), 124.
112 *Australian Dictionary of Biography*, Arthur Hoyle, s.v. 'Catts, James Howard (1877–1951)'http://www.adb.online.anu.edu.au/biogs/A070600b.htm, accessed 19 January 2010.
113 *Australian Dictionary of Biography*, 'Catts, James Howard (1877–1951)', accessed 19 January 2010.
114 Associated Business Services, *Australian Home Budget* (Sydney: Deaton and Spencer, 1 September 1932).
115 Osborne, 'A National Interest', 75.3.
116 David Carter, 'Literary Canons and Literary Institutions', *Southerly* 57.3 (1997): 22.
117 George Ferguson to W E Dedrick, 12 May 1939, MSS 3269/348 ML.
118 W. E. Dedrick to George Ferguson, 24 May 1939, MSS 3269/348 ML.
119 David Merett and Simon Ville, 'Tariffs, Subsidies and Profits: A Re-Assessment of Structural Change in Australia 1901–1939' (Australian and Pacific Economic and Business History Conference, University of Sydney, Sydney, 12–14 February 2007).
120 Barker and Davis, *Books Are Different*, 48.
121 The 1930 report provides a summary of the nineteenth-century origins of this phrase on page 68.

122 Ernest Scott, Professor, History, University of Melbourne, in Tariff Board Australia, *Report of Evidence (1930)*, 71.
123 Lars Jensen, *Unsettling Australia: Readings in Australian Cultural History* (New Delhi: Atlantic, 2005), 138.
124 Copyright Restrictions on the Parallel Importation of Books, Submissions, No. 103 'Frank Moorhouse', http://www.pc.gov.au/projects/study/books/submissions, accessed 15 January 2010.
125 Henry Mackenzie Green, in Tariff Board Australia, *Report of Evidence (1930)*, 38.
126 William Augustus Crew, Manager, NSW Bookstall Company, Sydney, in Australian Tariff Board, *Report of Evidence (1930)*, 41.
127 Commonwealth of Australia, *Department of War Organisation of Industry: Book Publication Committee*, 1943.
128 Robert Victor Smith, Librarian, Workers' Educational Association, Brisbane, in Australian Tariff Board, *Report of Evidence (1930)*, 16.
129 John Morley Bath, Australian Booksellers Association, South Australia, in Australian Tariff Board, *Report of Evidence (1930)*, 11.
130 John Morley Bath, Australian Booksellers Association, South Australia, in Australian Tariff Board, *Report of Evidence (1930)*, 11.
131 Horace Bohmer Newman, British Book Publishers' Representatives Association of Australia and New Zealand, New South Wales, in Australian Tariff Board, *Report of Evidence (1930)*, 56.
132 John Reed, Reed & Harris, Publishers, Melbourne, in 'Tariff Board Inquiry', *Ideas: Booksellers, Stationers and Fancy Goods (1946)*, 143.
133 'Art was lost on the soil', *Argus*, 25 September 1954.
134 'Australian Writing and Local Prejudice', *Mercury*, 29 July 1950.
135 A. Fabinyi, in 'Tariff Board Inquiry', *Ideas: Booksellers, Stationers and Fancy Goods (1946)*, 75.
136 Tariff Board Australia, *Report of Evidence (1930)*, 66.
137 George Ferguson, quoted in The Australian Book Trade, 'Changes in the Australian Book Trade 1935–1974', in *The Report of the Australian Book Trade Working Party* (1975): 87. Cited in Caroline Kapusta, 'British Influence on the Development of the Australian Booktrade' (masters thesis, Monash University, 1983), 46.
138 Wellings, 'Australians are Bookworms': 'This war, by emphasising our national individuality, may do much towards the crystallisation of a national literature.'
139 'Bottleneck in Book Production: Publishers and Authors Miss Unique Opportunity', *Sydney Morning Herald*, 7 October 1944.
140 H. J. Hewett, New South Wales Publishers Association, in 'Tariff Board Inquiry', *Ideas: Booksellers, Stationers and Fancy Goods (1946)*, 46.
141 P. Dowling, Director, News South Wales Bookstall Company, Sydney, in 'Tariff Board Inquiry', *Ideas: Booksellers, Stationers and Fancy Goods (1946)*, 85.
142 Horace Bohmer Newman, British Book Publishers' Representatives Association of Australia and New Zealand, New South Wales, in Australian Tariff Board, *Report of Evidence (1930)*, 55.
143 Frank Tate, President, Library Association of Victoria, in Australian Tariff Board, *Report of Evidence (1930)*, 62.
144 Charles Harold Peters, President, Australian Booksellers Association, Victoria, in Australian Tariff Board, *Report of Evidence (1930)*, 77.
145 Tariff Board Australia, *Report of Evidence (1930)*, 2.
146 Productivity Commission, *Parallel Importation of Books*, 6.10.
147 Productivity Commission, *Parallel Importation of Books*, 7.3.
148 John Morley Bath, South Australian branch, Australian Booksellers Association, in Tariff Board Australia, *Report of Evidence (1930)*, 9.
149 Tariff Board Australia, 'Tariff Board's Report', 8/1774.
150 Charles Harold Peters, in Tariff Board Australia, *Report of Evidence (1930)*, 79.
151 George Ferguson, 'Publishing in London', August 1970, MSS 3269/34 ML.

152 Charles Harold Peters, in Tariff Board Australia, *Report of Evidence (1930)*, 80.
153 Barker and Davis, *Books Are Different*, 472.
154 Walter Harrap, quoted in 'Nation Uncivilised Without Publishing System', *Sydney Morning Herald*, 14 December 1945.
155 Walter Harrap, quoted in 'Culture and Customs' *Argus*, 15 December 1945.
156 John Raymond Wilton, University of Adelaide, in Tariff Board Australia, *Report of Evidence (1930)*, 8.
157 Feather, *British Publishing*, 204.

Chapter 3 Triangles of Publishing and Other Stories

1 R. E. Barker and G. R. Davies, eds, *Books are Different: An Account of the Defence of the Net Book Agreement before the Restrictive Practices Court in 1962* (London: Macmillan, 1966), 466–7.
2 An earlier version of this chapter was first published in Jason Ensor, 'A Policy of Splendid Isolation: Angus & Robertson, George G. Harrap and the Politics of Co-operation in the Australian Book Trade During the Late 1930s', *Script & Print* 34.1 (Burwood, Victoria: Bibliographical Society of Australia and New Zealand, 2010): 34–42.
3 John Barnes, '"Heaven Forbid that I Should Think of Treating with an English Publisher": The Dilemma of Literary Nationalists in Federated Australia', in *Literary Cultures and the Material Book*, ed. Simon Eliot, Andrew Nash and Ian Willison (London: The British Library, 2007), 409.
4 See also Peter Morton, 'Australia's England, 1880–1950' in Peter Pierce, ed., *The Cambridge History of Australian Literature* (Melbourne: Cambridge University, Press 2009), 255–81.
5 George Ferguson to Walter Harrap, 26 October 1938, MSS 3269/322 ML.
6 Walter Harrap to Stanley Bartlett, 2 September 1938, MSS 3269/322 ML.
7 Walter Harrap to Stanley Bartlett, 2 September 1938, MSS 3269/322 ML.
8 Walter Harrap to Stanley Bartlett, 2 September 1938, MSS 3269/322 ML.
9 All correspondence is sourced from the restricted second collection of material related to the documentary archives of Angus & Robertson, State Library of New South Wales, Sydney. Permission to access and use these records was granted by the HarperCollins Subsidiary Rights Manager, 4 June 2008.
10 Richard Nile and David Walker, 'Marketing the Literary Imagination: Production of Australian Literature, 1915–1965', *The Penguin New Literary History of Australia, Australian Literary Studies (Special Issue)* 13.4 (October 1988): 284.
11 George Ferguson to A. J. Day (Department of Commerce and Agriculture), 1 July 1948, MSS 3269/580 ML.
12 George Ferguson, 'Publishing in London by Angus & Robertson Limited: A Paper for the guidance of the Board', unpublished, August 1970, MSS 3269/34 ML.
13 See for example Hector MacQuarrie to Walter Harrap, 23 November 1949, MSS 3269/440 ML.
14 Angus & Robertson to J. P. Lippincott Company (Philadelphia), 16 June 1918, MSS 314/53 ML.
15 Martyn Lyons, 'Britain's Largest Export Market', in *A History of the Book in Australia 1891–1945: A National Culture in a Colonised Market*, ed. Martyn Lyons and John Arnold (St Lucia: University of Queensland Press, 2001), 25.
16 Angus & Robertson's actual metaphor for breaking into the London market as publishers and booksellers was 'to get in behind', a military concept suggested by the gardener of Hector MacQuarrie, which led to the company establishing a British branch, an endeavour named 'Operation London'. See Neil James, 'Spheres of Influence: Angus & Robertson and Australian Literature from the Thirties to the Sixties' (PhD diss., University of Sydney, 2000), 260.
17 Richard Nile and David Walker, 'The "Paternoster Row Machine" and the Australian Book Trade, 1890–1945', in *A History of the Book in Australia 1891–1945: A National Culture in a Colonised Market*, ed. Martyn Lyons and John Arnold (St Lucia: University of Queensland Press, 2001), 17.

18 Walter Harrap to George Ferguson, 2 September 1938, MSS 3269/322 ML.
19 H. J. Jarrold to George Ferguson, 31 January 1949, MSS 3269/364 ML. For further examples of Angus & Robertson sending food parcels to the United Kingdom, see also W. E. Dedrick to George Ferguson, 8 June 1948, MSS 3269/348 ML; Sheila Hodges to George Ferguson, 10 February 1949, MSS 3269/293 ML; and Walter Harrap to George Ferguson, 4 November 1949, MSS 3269/322 ML.
20 Walter Harrap to Stanley Bartlett, 2 September 1938, MSS 3269/322 ML.
21 George Ferguson, interview with Suzanne Lunney, 11 May 1976, TRC 452, National Library of Australia, 32.
22 Leslie Rees, 'Australian Books In London: Attacking British Apathy', *West Australian*, 2 May 1936.
23 Hector MacQuarrie to George Ferguson, 29 March 1950, MSS 3269/440 ML.
24 George Ferguson, interview with Suzanne Lunney, 11 May 1976, TRC 452, National Library of Australia, 34–5.
25 Rees, 'Australian Books In London'.
26 Hector MacQuarrie quoted in Rees, 'Australian Books In London'.
27 Ferguson, 'Publishing in London', MSS 3269/34 ML.
28 W. G. Cousins, Angus & Robertson, in 'Tariff Board Inquiry into the Publishing Industry in Australia', *Ideas: Booksellers, Stationers and Fancy Goods Journal of Australia and New Zealand* (Melbourne: D. W. Thorpe, January 1946), 38.
29 Walter Harrap to George Ferguson, 4 October 1954, MSS 3269/322 ML.
30 George Ferguson, interview with Suzanne Lunney, 11 May 1976, TRC 452, National Library of Australia, 34.
31 George Ferguson, interview with Suzanne Lunney, 11 May 1976, TRC 452, National Library of Australia, 35. For more background on George Ferguson, see Neil James, '"The Fountainhead": George Ferguson and Angus & Robertson', *Publishing Studies* 7 (Autumn 1999): 6–16; and Neil James, '"Basically We Thought About Books" – An Interview with George Ferguson', *Publishing Studies* 5 (Spring 1997): 8–16.
32 George Ferguson to Ian Harrap on the sudden death of Walter Harrap, 21 April 1967, MSS 3269/322 ML.
33 George G. Harrap, *Some Memories, 1901–1935: A Publisher's Contribution to the History of Publishing* (London: Harrap, 1935), 98.
34 Harrap, *Some Memories*, 42.
35 Ian Norrie, *Mumby's Publishing and Bookselling in the Twentieth Century* (London: Bell & Hyman, 1982), 58.
36 Norrie, *Mumby's Publishing*, 142–3.
37 Harrap, *Some Memories*, 144–5.
38 George Farwell, Fellowship of Australian Writers, in 'Tariff Board Inquiry', *Ideas: Booksellers, Stationers and Fancy Goods(1946)*, 61.
39 Harrap, *Some Memories*, 80.
40 Stanley Bartlett to Walter Harrap, 22 September 1938, MSS 3269/322 ML.
41 Stanley Bartlett to Walter Harrap, 22 September 1938, MSS 3269/322 ML.
42 Walter Harrap to Stanley Bartlett, 2 September 1938, MSS 3269/322 ML.
43 Walter Harrap to George Ferguson, 23 June 1939, MSS 3269/322 ML.
44 Walter Harrap to Stanley Bartlett, 2 September 1938, MSS 3269/322 ML.
45 Walter Harrap to Stanley Bartlett, 2 September 1938, MSS 3269/322 ML.
46 Walter Harrap to Stanley Bartlett, 2 September 1938, MSS 3269/322 ML.
47 George Ferguson to Walter Harrap, 26 October 1938, MSS 3269/322 ML.
48 Walter Harrap to Stanley Bartlett, 2 September 1938, MSS 3269/322 ML.
49 S. F. Ferguson, Director, Australian Association of British Manufacturers, Melbourne, in 'Tariff Board Inquiry', *Ideas: Booksellers, Stationers and Fancy Goods (1946)*, 130.

50 Frank Tate, President of Library Association of Victoria, in Australian Tariff Board, *Report of Evidence at Tariff Board Inquiries into Proposal of Duty on Books, Magazines and Fashion Plates held in Adelaide, Brisbane, Sydney and Melbourne* (Melbourne: Australian Booksellers Association, 1930), 61.
51 John Morley Bath, South Australian Branch of the Australian Booksellers Association, quoting a conversation with George Robertson, in Australian Tariff Board, *Report of Evidence (1930)*, 10.
52 George Ferguson to Walter Harrap, 26 October 1938, MSS 3269/322 ML.
53 Stanley Bartlett to Walter Harrap, 22 September 1938, MSS 3269/322 ML.
54 Stanley Bartlett to Walter Harrap, 22 September 1938, MSS 3269/322 ML.
55 Stanley Bartlett to Walter Harrap, 22 September 1938, MSS 3269/322 ML.
56 Stanley Bartlett to Walter Harrap, 22 September 1938, MSS 3269/322 ML.
57 George Robertson to H. G. Albert, 29 November 1927, MSS 314/2 ML. Angus & Robertson would eventually purchase Alberts Bookshop Pty Ltd in order to take advantage of educational bookselling opportunities in Western Australia.
58 Lothian Publishing Company, Melbourne to Stella Miles Franklin, 11 September 1930, MSS 364/80 ML.
59 Lothian Publishing Company, Melbourne to Stella Miles Franklin, 11 September 1930, MSS 364/80 ML.
60 George Ferguson to Dwye Evans, 6 February 1948, MSS 3269/330 ML.
61 George Ferguson to Dwye Evans, 6 February 1948, MSS 3269/330 ML.
62 George Ferguson to Dwye Evans, 6 February 1948, MSS 3269/330 ML.
63 George Robertson to H. G. Albert, 29 November 1927, MSS 314/2 ML.
64 Aubrey Cousins to Walter Harrap, 1 June 1953, MSS 3269/322 ML.
65 George Robertson to H. G. Albert, 29 November 1927, MSS 314/2 ML.
66 Stanley Bartlett to Walter Harrap, 22 September 1938, MSS 3269/322 ML.
67 Stanley Bartlett to Walter Harrap, 22 September 1938, MSS 3269/322 ML.
68 Stanley Bartlett to Walter Harrap, 22 September 1938, MSS 3269/322 ML.
69 H. L. White, Acting Commonwealth Librarian, National Library, Canberra, in 'Tariff Board Inquiry', *Ideas: Booksellers, Stationers and Fancy Goods (1946)*, 24.
70 George Ferguson to Walter Harrap, 26 October 1938, MSS 3269/322 ML.
71 George Ferguson to Walter Harrap, 26 October 1938, MSS 3269/322 ML.
72 George Ferguson to Walter Harrap, 26 October 1938, MSS 3269/322 ML.
73 Walter Harrap to A. A. Ritchie, 16 October 1946, MSS 3269/322 ML.
74 Harrap, *Some Memories*, 42.
75 Norrie, *Mumby's Publishing*, 143.
76 George Ferguson to Walter Harrap, 11 July 1939, MSS 3269/322 ML.
77 Walter Harrap to George Ferguson, 23 June 1939, MSS 3269/322 ML.
78 George Ferguson to Walter Harrap, 11 July 1939, MSS 3269/322 ML.
79 Walter Harrap to George Ferguson, 25 July 1939, MSS 3269/322 ML.
80 Hector MacQuarrie to George Ferguson, 19 October 1949, MSS 3269/440 ML.
81 Rees, 'Australian Books In London'.
82 George Ferguson to Walter Harrap, 19 October 1948, MSS 3269/322 ML.
83 George Ferguson, interview with Suzanne Lunney, 11 May 1976, TRC 452, National Library of Australia, 40–41.
84 George Ferguson, interview with Suzanne Lunney, 11 May 1976, TRC 452, National Library of Australia, 40–41.
85 Angus & Robertson's net profit for the full pre-war and post-war period was: 1937 £18,663; 1938 £19,943; 1939 £17,590; 1940 £16,652; 1941 £19,445; 1942 £14,135; 1943 £17,594; 1944 £22,657; 1945 £22,930; 1946 £25,341; 1947 £25,067; 1948 £30,035; 1949 £27,894; 1950 £26,857; 1951 £24,464; and 1952 £23,650. These figures are derived from the financial pages of: *Mercury*, 4 October 1940; *Sydney Morning Herald*, 17 January 1941; *Argus*, 4 October

1941; *Sydney Morning Herald*, 8 October 1942; *Sydney Morning Herald*, 20 October 1944; *Argus*, 20 October 1945; *Argus*, 17 October 1949; *Argus*, 10 April 1951; *Argus*, 25 October 1951; *Argus*, 24 October 1952; and *Sydney Morning Herald*, 24 October 1952.

86 J. Hagan, *Printers and Politics: A History of the Australian Printing Unions 1850–1950* (Canberra: Australian National University Press, 1966), 266.

87 Hagan, *Printers and Politics*, 266.

88 'Fiction Ban: Conserving Dollar Exchange', *Canberra Times*, 12 April 1940.

89 'Restriction of Imports: Publications on New List', *Sydney Morning Herald*, 12 April 1940.

90 'Fiction Ban: Conserving Dollar Exchange', *Canberra Times*, 12 April 1940.

91 'Millions of Books: Australian Issues', *Sydney Morning Herald*, 2 December 1941.

92 'Millions of Books: Australian Issues', *Sydney Morning Herald*, 2 December 1941.

93 'War Books: Demand Falls Sharply', *Sydney Morning Herald*, 30 June 1944.

94 'Millions of Books: Australian Issues', *Sydney Morning Herald*, 2 December 1941.

95 'Millions of Books: Australian Issues', *Sydney Morning Herald*, 2 December 1941.

96 Ernest Gunn in 'Tariff Board Inquiry', *Ideas: Booksellers, Stationers and Fancy Goods (1946)*, 139.

97 'Millions of Books: Australian Issues', *Sydney Morning Herald*, 2 December 1941.

98 'Book Exports to Britain: Australia's Trade', *Sydney Morning Herald*, 15 January 1946.

99 S. F. Ferguson, Director, Australian Association of British Manufacturers quoted in 'Britain's Book Imports', *Sydney Morning Herald*, 5 April 1947.

100 'Millions of Books: Australian Issues', *Sydney Morning Herald*, 2 December 1941.

101 Graeme Johanson, *Colonial Editions in Australia 1843–1972* (Wellington: Elibank Press, 2000), 32.

102 'Bottleneck in Book Production: Publishers and Authors Miss Unique Opportunity', *Sydney Morning Herald*, 7 October 1944.

103 L. L. Woolacott in 'Tariff Board Inquiry', *Ideas: Booksellers, Stationers and Fancy Goods (1946)*, 30.

104 H. L. White in 'Tariff Board Inquiry', *Ideas: Booksellers, Stationers and Fancy Goods (1946)*, 40.

105 H. J. Johnston in 'Tariff Board Inquiry', *Ideas: Booksellers, Stationers and Fancy Goods (1946)*, 10.

106 George Ferguson to A. J. Day (Department of Commerce and Agriculture), 1 July 1948, MSS 3269/580 ML.

107 Hector MacQuarrie to George Ferguson, 6 October 1949, MSS 3269/440 ML. When Angus & Robertson was eventually able to import Australian children's books into the UK, the company underwent some criticism for the 'old-fashioned' presentation and general poor production quality. See AM Haldine Ltd (Library Book Supply Company) to Barry Rowland, 5 March 1958, MSS 3269/646 ML and Barry Rowland to AM Haldine Ltd (Library Book Supply Company), 18 March 1958, MSS 3269/646 ML.

108 'Bottleneck in Book Production: Publishers and Authors Miss Unique Opportunity', *Sydney Morning Herald*, 7 October 1944.

109 'Bottleneck in Book Production: Publishers and Authors Miss Unique Opportunity', *Sydney Morning Herald*, 7 October 1944.

110 W. G. Cousins, Angus & Robertson, in 'Tariff Board Inquiry', *Ideas: Booksellers, Stationers and Fancy Goods (1946)*, 35.

111 Douglas Stewart, interview with Suzanne Lunney, 1975, TRC 336, National Library, 5.

112 W. G. Cousins, Angus & Robertson, in 'Tariff Board Inquiry', *Ideas: Booksellers, Stationers and Fancy Goods (1946)*, 35.

113 Hubert Wilson, quoted from the *Bookseller*, 2 January 1941, in Norrie, *Mumby's Publishing*, 87–8.

114 Stanley Unwin, *The Truth about a Publisher* (London: George Allen & Unwin, 1960), 278.

115 Stanley Unwin to Miles Franklin, 20 February 1953, Franklin Miles AUC 591 London Vol. 17, University of Reading.

116 Norrie, *Mumby's Publishing*, 88.

117 John Feather, *A History of British Publishing* (London: Routledge, 1988), 220.

118 'Britain Sends All available Books Here', *Argus*, 30 January 1946.

119 Michael Joseph, 'Publishing Slump', *New Statesman and Nation*, 25 September 1948.
120 Gael Cresp, *The British Publishers' Traditional Market Agreement* (Melbourne: Royal Melbourne Institute of Technology, 1977), 4.
121 'British Bid to Hold Book Market', *Sydney Morning Herald*, 9 August 1945.
122 Feather, *British Publishing*, 220.
123 Hagan, *Printers and Politics*, 266.
124 Walter Harrap to George Ferguson, 11 August 1939, MSS 3269/322 ML.
125 George Ferguson to Walter Harrap, 1 September 1939, MSS 3269/322 ML.
126 Walter G. Harrap, representing George G. Harrap and the Publishers Association, London, in 'Tariff Board Inquiry', *Ideas: Booksellers, Stationers and Fancy Goods (1946)*, 116.
127 Walter Harrap to A. A. Ritchie, 16 October 1946, MSS 3269/322 ML.
128 'Book Exports to Britain: Australia's Trade', *Sydney Morning Herald*, 15 January 1946.
129 Walter Harrap to George Ferguson, 23 November 1953, MSS 3269/322 ML.
130 George Ferguson to Walter Harrap, 23 November 1950, MSS 3269/322 ML. It is worth noting that 'books based on one test match series are ephemeral', Walter Harrap to George Ferguson, 1 December 1950, MSS 3269/322 ML
131 Walter Harrap to George Ferguson, 29 April 1954, MSS 3269/322 ML.
132 George Ferguson to Walter Harrap, 22 April 1954, MSS 3269/322 ML.
133 The titles are drawn from a search of the British Library and the National Library of Australia catalogues.
134 George Ferguson to Dwye Evans, 21 November 1960, MSS 3269/330 ML.
135 George Ferguson to Dwye Evans, 21 November 1960, MSS 3269/330 ML.
136 George Ferguson to Walter Harrap, 21 February 1958, MSS 3269/322 ML.
137 George Ferguson to Dwye Evans, 21 November 1960, MSS 3269/330 ML.
138 Dwye Evans to George Ferguson, 29 June 1961, MSS 3269/330 ML.
139 G. Fielding to Angus & Robertson, 13 June 1932, MSS 3269/330 ML.
140 George Ferguson to Dwye Evans, 6 February 1948, MSS 3269/330 ML.
141 George Ferguson to Dwye Evans, 6 February 1948, MSS 3269/330 ML.
142 George Ferguson to Dwye Evans, 6 February 1948, MSS 3269/330 ML.
143 Dwye Evans to George Ferguson, 27 April 1948, MSS 3269/330 ML.
144 Dwye Evans to George Ferguson, 27 April 1948, MSS 3269/330 ML.
145 George Ferguson to Dwye Evans, 5 May 1948, MSS 3269/330 ML.
146 Alan Hill, *In Pursuit of Publishing* (London: John Murray, 1988), 99.
147 Hill, *In Pursuit*, 100.
148 F. D. Sanders, *British Book Trade Organisation: A Report on the Work of the Joint Committee with an Introduction by Stanley Unwin* (London: George Allen & Unwin 1939), 13.
149 Nile and Walker, 'The "Paternoster"', 9.
150 Stanley Unwin to Rev. W. B. Hay, 30 March 1950, Allen & Unwin AUC 20, Vol. 13, University of Reading.
151 Unwin, *The Truth*, 115.
152 Stanley Unwin to W. G. Hay, 21 November 1928, Allen & Unwin AUC 20, Vol. 13, University of Reading.
153 Stanley Unwin to W. G. Hay, 26 February 1918, Allen & Unwin AUC 20, Vol. 13, University of Reading.
154 Stanley Unwin to W. G. Hay, 20 December 1928, Allen & Unwin AUC 20, Vol. 13, University of Reading.
155 Stanley Unwin to Rev. W. B. Hay, 30 March 1950, Allen & Unwin AUC 20, Vol. 13, University of Reading.
156 Luke Trainor, 'Australian Writers, British Publishers, 1870–1902: Talking to the Nation?', *Australian Historical Studies* 127 (2006): 140.
157 Walter Harrap to Stanley Bartlett, 2 September 1938, MSS 3269/322 ML.

158 Walter Harrap to George Ferguson, 30 December 1953, MSS 3269/322 ML.
159 Walter Harrap to George Ferguson, 4 October 1954, MSS 3269/322 ML.
160 Walter Harrap to George Ferguson, 4 October 1954, MSS 3269/322 ML.
161 Walter Harrap to A. A. Ritchie, 16 October 1946, MSS 3269/322 ML.
162 Walter Harrap to George Ferguson, 4 October 1954, MSS 3269/322 ML.
163 Walter Harrap to Stanley Bartlett, 2 September 1938, MSS 3269/322 ML.
164 Laura J. Miller, *Reluctant Capitalists: Bookselling and the Culture of Consumption* (London: University of Chicago Press, 2006), 8.
165 Nile and Walker, 'The "Paternoster"', 9.
166 Miller, *Reluctant Capitalists*, 9.

Chapter 4 The World is Made of Paper Restrictions

1 Roger Page, *Australian Bookselling* (Melbourne: Hill of Content, 1970), 113.
2 A. C. Moore to Walter G. Cousins, 6 April 1943, MSS 3269/92 ML.
3 Walter G. Cousins to E. P. Hamilton (US Consulate, Auckland), 12 July 1945, MSS 3269/316 ML.
4 'Imported Fiction: Ban Operates from Today', *Mercury*, 2 April 1940. Article is dated 1 April 1940.
5 Walter G. Cousins to E. P. Hamilton (US Consulate, Auckland), 12 July 1945, MSS 3269/316 ML.
6 'Grave Overseas Threat to Australian Writers', *Fellowship: Official Organ of the Fellowship of Australian Writers* 1.1 (June 1944): 1.
7 A. C. Moore to Walter G. Cousins, 28 November 1942, MSS 3269/92 ML.
8 Ben Courtice to H. V. Evatt, Attorney-General, 18 December 1946, MSS 3269/92 ML.
9 A. C. Moore to Walter G. Cousins, 28 November 1942, MSS 3269/92 ML.
10 A. C. Moore to Walter G. Cousins, 9 March 1943, MSS 3269/92 ML.
11 A. C. Moore to Walter G. Cousins, 9 March 1943, MSS 3269/92 ML.
12 A. C. Moore to Walter G. Cousins, 6 April 1943, MSS 3269/92 ML.
13 A. C. Moore to Walter G. Cousins, 9 March 1943, MSS 3269/92 ML.
14 George Ferguson to Hector MacQuarrie, 18 March 1952, MSS 3269/443 ML.
15 Hector MacQuarrie to George Ferguson, 24 October 1949, MSS 3269/440 ML.
16 George Ferguson to Hector MacQuarrie, 11 October 1949, MSS 3269/440 ML.
17 Hector MacQuarrie to George Ferguson, 18 December 1957, MSS 3269/448 ML.
18 Hector MacQuarrie to George Ferguson, 5 March 1958, MSS 3269/449 ML.
19 George Ferguson to Hector MacQuarrie, 1 November 1950, MSS 3269/441 ML.
20 See also Frank Sanders (The Publishers Association, London) to George Ferguson, 19 June 1953, MSS 3269/556.
21 See Hector MacQuarrie to George Ferguson, 8 December 1953, MSS 3269/444 ML and George Ferguson to Hector MacQuarrie, 18 December 1953, MSS 3269/444 ML.
22 George Ferguson to Hector MacQuarrie, 18 September 1951, MSS 3269/442 ML. See also Hector MacQuarrie to Bennett Cerf (Random House New York), 9 July 1954, MSS 3269/445 ML.
23 See Aubrey G. Cousins to Hector MacQuarrie, 27 August 1952, MSS 3269/443 ML and George Ferguson to Hector MacQuarrie, 7 December 1956, MSS 3269/447 ML. It is worth noting that in 2009 the relative worth of £96 sterling from 1951 ranges between £2,250 using the retail price index to £9,060 using the share of GDP index. See calculators at http://www.measuringworth.com/ukcompare/result.php for more details.
24 George Ferguson to Hector MacQuarrie, 14 December 1951, MSS 3269/442 ML.
25 Luke Trainor, 'Australian Writers, British Publishers, 1870–1902: Talking to the Nation?', *Australian Historical Studies* 127 (2006): 140.
26 Walter G. Cousins to E. P. Hamilton (US Consulate, Auckland), 12 July 1945, MSS 3269/316 ML.

27 Walter G. Cousins to Miles Franklin, 15 June 1944, MSS 314/35 ML.
28 Walter G. Cousins to A. J. Day (Australian Department of Trade and Customs), 25 March 1943, MSS 3269/92 ML
29 Walter G. Cousins to George Farwell, 8 August 1944, MSS 3269/258 ML; George Farwell to Walter G. Cousins, 15 August 1944, MSS 3269/258 ML.
30 George Farwell to Walter G. Cousins, 4 August 1944, MSS 3269/258 ML.
31 'Grave Overseas Threat to Australian Writers', *Fellowship: Official Organ of the Fellowship of Australian Writers* 1.1 (June 1944): 1.
32 George Ferguson to W. T. Kirwan, 6 August 1945, MSS 3269/311 ML.
33 Angus & Robertson to Halstead Press, 13 January 1947, MSS 3269/312 ML.
34 Halstead Press to Paul Tracey, 3 October 1947, MSS 3269/312 ML.
35 J. Farram, Halstead Press, to Angus & Robertson, 9 September 1943, MSS 3269/311 ML.
36 J. Farram, Halstead Press, to Angus & Robertson, 9 September 1943, MSS 3269/311 ML.
37 Walter G. Cousins to Commonwealth Prices Commissioner, 23 September 1943, MSS 3269/311 ML.
38 George Ferguson to Municipal Council of Sydney, 30 March 1948, MSS 3269/313 ML.
39 Walter G. Cousins to Commonwealth Prices Commissioner, 23 September 1943, MSS 3269/311 ML.
40 J. Farram, Halstead Press, to Angus & Robertson, 9 September 1943, MSS 3269/311 ML.
41 The figures that follow are taken from the report 'A Comparison of the Output of Departments and Machines at Halstead', 29 January 1948, MSS 3269/312 ML.
42 S. W. Graham, Halstead Press, to J. F. Wilson, Printing Industry Employees Union, 22 April 1948, MSS 3269/312 ML.
43 Hector MacQuarrie to George Ferguson, 6 October 1949, MSS 3269/440 ML.
44 The Goodheart-Willcox Company, Chicago, to Walter G. Cousins, 14 August 1946, MSS 3269/312 ML.
45 Department of Trade and Customs, Sydney, to Halstead Press, 7 March 1947, MSS 3269/348 ML.
46 'Export Difficulty Stressed', *Mercury*, 29 March 1944.
47 W. E. Dedrick to George Ferguson, 18 June 1946, MSS 3269/348 ML.
48 George Ferguson to W. E. Dedrick, 22 August 1946, MSS 3269/348 ML.
49 W. E. Dedrick to George Ferguson, 4 September 1946, MSS 3269/348 ML.
50 W. E. Dedrick to George Ferguson, 3 October 1946, MSS 3269/348 ML.
51 W. E. Dedrick to George Ferguson, 30 October 1946, MSS 3269/348 ML.
52 Department of Trade and Customs, Sydney, to Halstead Press, 7 March 1947, MSS 3269/348 ML.
53 Walter G. Cousins to Halstead Press, 24 October 1947, MSS 3269/314 ML.
54 George Ferguson to W. E. Dedrick, 11 April 1950, MSS 3269/348 ML.
55 George Ferguson to Walter Harrap, 8 June 1948, MSS 3269/322 ML.
56 George Ferguson to Walter Harrap, 8 November 1948, MSS 3269/322 ML.
57 George Ferguson to Stanley Unwin, 31 March 1948, MSS 3269/10 ML.
58 Walter Harrap to A. A. Ritchie, 16 October 1946, MSS 3269/322 ML.
59 Marjorie Plant, *The English Book Trade: An Economic History of the Making and Sale of Books* (London: George Allen & Unwin, 1939), 441.
60 Laura J. Miller, *Reluctant Capitalists: Bookselling and the Culture of Consumption* (London: University of Chicago Press, 2006), 143.
61 R. E. Barker and G. R. Davis, eds, *Books Are Different: An Account of the Defence of the Net Book Agreement before the Restrictive Practices Court in 1962* (London: Macmillan, 1966), 479.
62 Barker and Davis, *Books Are Different*, 467.
63 Barker and Davis, *Books Are Different*, 472.
64 Barker and Davis, *Books Are Different*, 467.
65 Miller, *Reluctant Capitalists*, 25.

66 Barker and Davis, *Books Are Different*, 84.
67 Barker and Davis, *Books Are Different*, 84.
68 Inger L. Stole, 'Advertising', in *Culture Works: The Political Economy of Culture*, ed. Richard Maxwell (Minnesota: University of Minnesota Press, 2001), 84.
69 The Coalition for Cheaper Books, http://www.cheaperbooks.com.au.
70 Miller, *Reluctant Capitalists*, 158.
71 Stole, 'Advertising', 84.
72 Miller, *Reluctant Capitalists*.
73 Stole, 'Advertising', 85.
74 John Feather, *A History of British Publishing* (London: Routledge, 1988), 183.
75 Feather, *A History*, 192.
76 Barker and Davis, *Books Are Different*, 467.
77 Barker and Davis, *Books Are Different*, 466.
78 Barker and Davis, *Books Are Different*, 466.
79 Barker and Davis, *Books Are Different*, 467.
80 Barker and Davis, *Books Are Different*, 467.
81 Barker and Davis, *Books Are Different*, 481.
82 George Ferguson to Hector MacQuarrie, 22 February 1950, MSS 3269/440.
83 George Ferguson to Walter Harrap, 19 October 1948, MSS 3269/322 ML.
84 Walter Harrap to George Ferguson, 26 June 1948, MSS 3269/322 ML.
85 Frank Sanders, Publishers Association to RE Jones, Australian Booksellers Association, 17 April 1952, MSS 3269/556 ML.
86 Walter Harrap to George Ferguson, 26 June 1948, MSS 3269/322 ML.
87 Walter Harrap to George Ferguson, 26 June 1948, MSS 3269/322 ML.
88 Walter Harrap to George Ferguson, 26 June 1948, MSS 3269/322 ML.
89 Walter Harrap to George Ferguson, 26 June 1948, MSS 3269/322 ML.
90 George Ferguson to Walter Harrap, 19 October 1948, MSS 3269/322 ML.
91 George Ferguson to Walter Harrap, 10 May 1949, MSS 3269/322 ML.
92 George Ferguson to Walter Harrap, 6 July 1948, MSS 3269/322 ML.
93 Walter Harrap to George Ferguson, 14 July 1948, MSS 3269/322 ML.
94 George Ferguson to A. J. Day, 1 July 1948, MSS 3269/580 ML.
95 Vera Wellings to George Ferguson, 29 October 1953, MSS 3269/18 ML.
96 George Ferguson to A. J. Day, 1 July 1948, MSS 3269/580 ML.
97 'Restriction on Books', *Mercury*, 21 March 1947.
98 George Ferguson to A. J. Day, 1 July 1948, MSS 3269/580 ML.
99 George Ferguson to A. J. Day, 1 July 1948, MSS 3269/580 ML.
100 Hector MacQuarrie to George Ferguson, 6 October 1949, MSS 3269/440 ML.
101 'British Restrictions on Book Imports', *Argus*, 17 March 1947.
102 George Ferguson to A. J. Day, 1 July 1948, MSS 3269/580 ML.
103 'Restriction on Books', *Mercury*, 21 March 1947.
104 'Restriction on Books', *Mercury*, 21 March 1947.
105 George Ferguson to Miles Franklin, 6 April 1949, MSS 314/35 ML.
106 George Ferguson to Miles Franklin, 6 April 1949, MSS 314/35 ML.
107 Robert Victor Smith, Librarian, Workers' Educational Association, Brisbane, in Australian Tariff Board, *Report of Evidence at Tariff Board Inquiries into Proposal of Duty on Books, Magazines and Fashion Plates held in Adelaide, Brisbane, Sydney and Melbourne* (Melbourne: Australian Booksellers Association, 1930), 16.
108 George Ferguson to Colin Roderick, 1 July 1958, MSS 3269/19 ML.
109 S. F. Ferguson, Director, Australian Association of British Manufacturers, in 'Tariff Board Inquiry into the Publishing Industry in Australia', *Ideas: Booksellers, Stationers and Fancy Goods Journal of Australia and New Zealand* (Melbourne: D. W. Thorpe, February 1946), 130.

110 Walter Harrap, in 'Tariff Board Inquiry', *Ideas: Booksellers, Stationers and Fancy Goods (1946)*, 120.
111 George Ferguson to A. J. Day, 1 July 1948, MSS 3269/580 ML.
112 George Ferguson to Walter Harrap, 10 May 1949, MSS 3269/322 ML; See also 'Australian Book Ban in Britain', *Age*, 7 February 1947, 2.
113 George Ferguson to A. J. Day, 1 July 1948, MSS 3269/580 ML.
114 George Ferguson to A. J. Day, 1 July 1948, MSS 3269/580 ML.
115 George Ferguson to A. J. Day, 1 July 1948, MSS 3269/580 ML.
116 George Ferguson to Walter Harrap, 10 May 1949, MSS 3269/322 ML; See also 'Australian Book Ban in Britain', *Age*, 7 February 1947, 2.
117 George Ferguson to A. J. Day, 1 July 1948, MSS 3269/580 ML.
118 Barker and Davis, *Books Are Different*, 501.
119 George Ferguson to A. J. Day, 7 July 1948, MSS 3269/580 ML.
120 George Ferguson to H. E. Parr (Publishing Industry Committee), 15 July 1949, MSS 3269/580 ML.
121 George Ferguson to H. E. Parr (Publishing Industry Committee), 15 July 1949, MSS 3269/580 ML.
122 Walter Harrap to George Ferguson, 5 October 1948, MSS 3269/322 ML.
123 Beatrice Davis to Hector MacQuarrie, 8 October 1949, MSS 3269/440 ML.
124 Sheila Hodges (Victor Gollancz) to George Ferguson, 10 February 1949, MSS 3269/293 ML.
125 George Ferguson to Sheila Hodges (Victor Gollancz), 15 February 1949, MSS 3269/293 ML.
126 George Ferguson to Sheila Hodges (Victor Gollancz), 24 February 1949, MSS 3269/293 ML.
127 Hector MacQuarrie to Colin Roderick, 13 October 1949, MSS 3269/440 ML.
128 Hector MacQuarrie to Colin Roderick, 13 October 1949, MSS 3269/440 ML.
129 George Ferguson to Hector MacQuarrie, 14 October 1949, MSS 3269/440 ML.
130 Samuel French to Hector MacQuarrie, 2 November 1949, MSS 3269/440 ML.
131 Patrick Anderson to George Ferguson, 15 October 1949, MSS 3269/164 ML.
132 George Ferguson to A. E. Turnbull (W. & R. Chambers, Edinburgh), 14 July 1949, MSS 3269/172 ML.
133 George Ferguson to Sheila Hodges, 21 November 1949, MSS 3269/293 ML.
134 George Ferguson to Walter Harrap, 8 September 1949, MSS 3269/322 ML.
135 Walter Harrap to George Ferguson, 26 September 1949, MSS 3269/322 ML.
136 George Ferguson to Walter Harrap, 8 September 1949, MSS 3269/322 ML.
137 George Ferguson to Hector MacQuarrie, 8 May 1950, MSS 3269/440 ML.
138 Hector MacQuarrie to George Ferguson, 6 October 1949, MSS 3269/440 ML.
139 Hector MacQuarrie to George Ferguson, 6 October 1949, MSS 3269/440 ML.
140 Hector MacQuarrie to George Ferguson, 6 October 1949, MSS 3269/440 ML.
141 George Ferguson to Hector MacQuarrie, 11 October 1949, MSS 3269/440 ML.
142 Beatrice Davis to Hector MacQuarrie, 8 October 1949, MSS 3269/440 ML.
143 George Ferguson to Hector MacQuarrie, 11 October 1949, MSS 3269/440 ML.
144 George Ferguson to Hector MacQuarrie, 11 October 1949, MSS 3269/440 ML.
145 Hector MacQuarrie to George Ferguson, 27 July 1950, MSS 3269/441 ML.
146 George Ferguson to Hector MacQuarrie, 8 November 1949, MSS 3269/440 ML.
147 George Ferguson to Hector MacQuarrie, 17 May 1950, MSS 3269/440 ML.
148 J. V. B. to Hector MacQuarrie, 17 November 1949, MSS 3269/440 ML.
149 Walter Harrap to Hector MacQuarrie, 21 November 1949, MSS 3269/440 ML.
150 George Ferguson to Hector MacQuarrie, 17 November 1949, MSS 3269/440 ML.
151 George Ferguson, interview with Suzanne Lunney, 11 May 1976, TRC 452, National Library of Australia, 53.

152 Bill Ashcroft, 'Home and Horizon', in *Diaspora: The Australasian Experience*, ed. Cynthia vanden Driesen and Ralph Crane (New Delhi: Prestige Books, 2006), 48.
153 George Ferguson, interview with Suzanne Lunney, 11 May 1976, TRC 452, National Library of Australia, 56.
154 George Ferguson to Hector MacQuarrie, 14 March 1950, MSS 3269/440 ML.
155 George Ferguson to Frederick Melcher, Publishers' Weekly, New York, 21 September 1950, MSS 3269/580 ML.
156 George Ferguson to Hector MacQuarrie, 28 January 1950, MSS 3269/440 ML.
157 George Ferguson, interview with Suzanne Lunney, 11 May 1976, TRC 452, National Library of Australia, 39.
158 George Ferguson, interview with Suzanne Lunney, 11 May 1976, TRC 452, National Library of Australia, 39.
159 Aubrey Cousins to Hector MacQuarrie, 28 June 1950, MSS 3269/440 ML.
160 J. V. B. to Hector MacQuarrie, 17 November 1949, MSS 3269/440 ML.
161 George Ferguson, interview with Suzanne Lunney, 11 May 1976, TRC 452, National Library of Australia, 51.
162 Hector MacQuarrie to George Ferguson, 24 November 1949, MSS 3269/440 ML.
163 'Australia in London', *Sydney Morning Herald*, 24 April 1920.
164 Hector MacQuarrie to George Ferguson, 29 November 1949, MSS 3269/440 ML.
165 Hector MacQuarrie to George Ferguson, 29 November 1949, MSS 3269/440 ML.
166 Hector MacQuarrie to George Ferguson, 29 November 1949, MSS 3269/440 ML.
167 Hector MacQuarrie to George Ferguson, 29 November 1949, MSS 3269/440 ML.
168 George Ferguson to Ian Collins, 19 December 1949, MSS 3269/172 ML.
169 Victor Gollancz to George Ferguson, 13 January 1950, MSS 3269/293 ML.
170 Hector MacQuarrie to George Ferguson, 28 February 1950, MSS 3269/440 ML.
171 Hector MacQuarrie to George Ferguson, 10 January 1950, MSS 3269/440 ML.
172 George Ferguson to Victor Gollancz, 7 February 1950, MSS 3269/293 ML.
173 Hector MacQuarrie to George Ferguson, 29 March 1950, MSS 3269/440 ML.
174 Hector MacQuarrie to George Ferguson, 9 December 1949, MSS 3269/440 ML.
175 George Ferguson to Hector MacQuarrie, 22 December 1949, MSS 3269/440 ML.
176 Hector MacQuarrie to George Ferguson, 25 April 1950, MSS 3269/440 ML.
177 George Ferguson to Hector MacQuarrie, 28 January 1950, MSS 3269/440 ML.
178 George Ferguson to Hector MacQuarrie, 22 December 1949, MSS 3269/440 ML.
179 Hector MacQuarrie to George Ferguson, 10 January 1950, MSS 3269/440 ML.

Chapter 5 The First Salesman in London

1 George Ferguson, 'Publishing in London by Angus & Robertson Limited: A Paper for the guidance of the Board', unpublished, August 1970, MSS 3269/34 ML.
2 An earlier version of this chapter was first published in Jason Ensor, 'Angus & Robertson and the Case of the Bombshell Salesman', *Script & Print* 35.2 (Burwood, Victoria: Bibliographical Society of Australia and New Zealand, 2011): 69–79.
3 George Ferguson to Hector MacQuarrie, 28 February 1950, MSS 3269/440 ML.
4 George Ferguson to Hector MacQuarrie, 6 April 1950, MSS 3269/440 ML.
5 George Ferguson to Hector MacQuarrie, 22 February 1950, MSS 3269/440 ML.
6 Hector MacQuarrie to James Askew & Son, 6 December 1950, MSS 3269/441 ML.
7 Hector MacQuarrie to George Ferguson, 9 March 1950, MSS 3269/440 ML.
8 Hector MacQuarrie to George Ferguson, 30 June 1950, MSS 3269/440 ML.
9 Hector MacQuarrie to T. E. Smith (W. & R. Holmes Books Ltd), 17 October 1950, MSS 3269/441 ML.
10 George Ferguson to Hector MacQuarrie, 28 July 1950, MSS 3269/441 ML.

11 Hector MacQuarrie to George Ferguson, 29 March 1950, MSS 3269/440 ML.
12 George Ferguson to Hector MacQuarrie, 6 April 1950, MSS 3269/440 ML.
13 Hector MacQuarrie to George Ferguson, 13 April 1950, MSS 3269/440 ML.
14 R. E. Barker and G. R. Davis, eds, *Books Are Different: An Account of the Defence of the Net Book Agreement before the Restrictive Practices Court in 1962* (London: Macmillan, 1966), 411.
15 Hector MacQuarrie to George Ferguson, 13 April 1950, MSS 3269/440 ML.
16 George Ferguson to Hector MacQuarrie, 13 September 1950, MSS 3269/441 ML.
17 Hector MacQuarrie to George Ferguson, 3 October 1950, MSS 3269/441 ML.
18 George Ferguson to Hector MacQuarrie, 22 November 1950, MSS 3269/441 ML.
19 George Ferguson to Hector MacQuarrie, 12 October 1950, MSS 3269/441 ML.
20 George Ferguson to Hector MacQuarrie, 8 May 1950, MSS 3269/440 ML.
21 George Ferguson to Hector MacQuarrie, 27 October 1950, MSS 3269/441 ML.
22 Mrs Woods to George Ferguson, 12 October 1950, MSS 3269/441 ML.
23 Hector MacQuarrie to George Ferguson, 30 June 1950, MSS 3269/440 ML.
24 George Ferguson to Hector MacQuarrie, 28 June 1950, MSS 3269/440 ML.
25 Hector MacQuarrie to George Ferguson, 20 July 1950, MSS 3269/441 ML.
26 Mrs Woods to George Ferguson, 12 October 1950, MSS 3269/441 ML.
27 George Ferguson to Hector MacQuarrie, 27 October 1950, MSS 3269/441 ML.
28 Hector MacQuarrie to George Ferguson, 10 January 1951, MSS 3269/442 ML.
29 Hector MacQuarrie to George Ferguson, 9 May 1951, MSS 3269/442 ML.
30 Hector MacQuarrie to George Ferguson, 20 July 1950, MSS 3269/441 ML.
31 Hector MacQuarrie to George Ferguson, 27 September 1950, MSS 3269/441 ML.
32 Hector MacQuarrie to George Ferguson, 12 September 1950, MSS 3269/411 ML.
33 Hector MacQuarrie to George Ferguson, 17 October 1950, MSS 3269/441 ML.
34 George Ferguson to Hector MacQuarrie, 31 August 1950, MSS 3269/441 ML.
35 George Ferguson to Hector MacQuarrie, 20 September 1950, MSS 3269/441 ML.
36 Hector MacQuarrie to George Ferguson, 27 September 1950, MSS 3269/441 ML.
37 'Angus & Robertson will distribute for Cheshire and Ure Smith', *Bookseller*, 7 April 1951.
38 George Ferguson to Hector MacQuarrie, 6 October 1950, MSS 3269/441 ML.
39 George Ferguson to Hector MacQuarrie, 4 December 1950, MSS 3269/441 ML.
40 Hector MacQuarrie, quoted in Neil James, 'Spheres of Influence: Angus and Robertson and Australian Literature from the Thirties to the Sixties' (PhD diss., unpublished, University of Sydney, 2000), 258.
41 James, 'Spheres of Influence', 258.
42 Hector MacQuarrie to T. E. Smith (W. & R. Holmes Books Ltd), 17 October 1950, MSS 3269/441 ML.
43 Hector MacQuarrie to T. E. Smith (W. & R. Holmes Books Ltd), 17 October 1950, MSS 3269/441 ML.
44 Hector MacQuarrie to T. E. Smith (W. & R. Holmes Books Ltd), 17 October 1950, MSS 3269/441 ML.
45 Hector MacQuarrie to Bernard Robinson, 17 October 1950, MSS 3269/441 ML.
46 Hector MacQuarrie to George Ferguson, 18 October 1950, MSS 3269/441 ML.
47 T. E. Smith to Hector MacQuarrie, 24 October 1950, MSS 3269/441 ML.
48 Hector MacQuarrie to James Askew & Son, 6 December 1950, MSS 3269/441 ML.
49 Hector MacQuarrie to Bernard Robinson, 25 October 1950, MSS 3269/441 ML.
50 Hector MacQuarrie to George Ferguson, 2 November 1950, MSS 3269/441 ML.
51 George Ferguson to Bernard Robinson, 19 December 1950, MSS 3269/441 ML.
52 Hector MacQuarrie to George Ferguson, 17 October 1950, MSS 3269/441 ML.
53 George Ferguson to Hector MacQuarrie, 15 November 1950, MSS 3269/441 ML.
54 George Ferguson to Hector MacQuarrie, 1 November 1950, MSS 3269/441 ML.
55 George Ferguson to Walter Butcher, 18 December 1956, MSS 3269/447 ML.

56 Hector MacQuarrie to George Ferguson, 7 December 1950, MSS 3269/441 ML.
57 George Ferguson to Hector MacQuarrie, 1 November 1950, MSS 3269/441 ML.
58 Hector MacQuarrie to George Ferguson, 21 November 1950, MSS 3269/441 ML.
59 George Ferguson to Hector MacQuarrie, 1 November 1950, MSS 3269/441 ML.
60 Hector MacQuarrie to George Ferguson, 21 November 1950, MSS 3269/441 ML.
61 George Ferguson to Hector MacQuarrie, 16 May 1951, MSS 3269/442 ML.
62 George Ferguson to Hector MacQuarrie, 15 December 1953, MSS 3269/445 ML.
63 George Ferguson to Hector MacQuarrie, 1 November 1950, MSS 3269/441 ML.
64 George Ferguson to Hector MacQuarrie, 15 November 1950, MSS 3269/441 ML.
65 George Ferguson to Hector MacQuarrie, 22 November 1950, MSS 3269/441 ML.
66 Hector MacQuarrie to James Askew & Son, 6 December 1950, MSS 3269/441 ML.
67 George Ferguson to Hector MacQuarrie, 18 December 1950, MSS 3269/441 ML.
68 George Ferguson to Bernard Robinson, 19 December 1950, MSS 3269/441 ML.
69 Hector MacQuarrie to George Ferguson, 22 January 1951, MSS 3269/442 ML.
70 George Ferguson to Hector MacQuarrie, 4 January 1951, MSS 3269/442 ML.
71 Hector MacQuarrie to Bernard Robinson, 20 February 1951, MSS 3269/442 ML.
72 Hector MacQuarrie to George Ferguson, 8 January 1951, MSS 3269/442 ML.
73 Hector MacQuarrie to Bernard Robinson, 20 February 1951, MSS 3269/442 ML.
74 Hector MacQuarrie to George Ferguson, 17 October 1950, MSS 3269/441 ML.
75 Hector MacQuarrie to George Ferguson, 22 January 1951, MSS 3269/442 ML.
76 George Ferguson to Hector MacQuarrie, 20 April 1951, MSS 3269/442 ML.
77 Robert Haupt, 'The Book Rebellion', *Age*, 5 November 1988.
78 Hector MacQuarrie to Bernard Robinson, 26 January 1951, MSS 3269/442 ML.
79 Hector MacQuarrie to Bernard Robinson, 20 February 1951, MSS 3269/442 ML.
80 Bernard Robinson to Hector MacQuarrie, 15 February 1951, MSS 3269/442 ML.
81 Hamish Hamilton to Aubrey Cousins, 15 January 1952, MSS 3269/316 ML.
82 George Ferguson to Hamish Hamilton, 7 February 1952, MSS 3269/316 ML.
83 Hamish Hamilton to Aubrey Cousins, 15 January 1952, MSS 3269/316 ML.
84 Hamish Hamilton to Aubrey Cousins, 15 January 1952, MSS 3269/316 ML.
85 Vera Wellings to Aubrey Cousins, 4 April 1952, MSS 3269/18 ML.
86 George Ferguson to Hector MacQuarrie, 15 January 1951, MSS 3269/442 ML.
87 George Ferguson to Hector MacQuarrie, 15 January 1951, MSS 3269/442 ML.
88 Hector MacQuarrie to Bernard Robinson, 24 January 1951, MSS 3269/442 ML.
89 George Ferguson to Hector MacQuarrie, 15 January 1951, MSS 3269/442 ML.

Chapter 6 The Getting of Bookselling Wisdom

1 George Ferguson to Hector MacQuarrie, 6 April 1950, MSS 3269/440 ML.
2 Hector MacQuarrie to George Ferguson, 10 January 1951, MSS 3269/442 ML.
3 George Ferguson to Hector MacQuarrie, 8 May 1950, MSS 3269/440 ML.
4 Hector MacQuarrie to CL Hewitt, 9 August 1950, MSS 3269/441 ML.
5 Hector MacQuarrie to CL Hewitt, 9 August 1950, MSS 3269/441 ML.
6 'The History of Australia House', Australian High Commission: United Kingdom, http://www.uk.embassy.gov.au/lhlh/History.html, accessed 16 February 2010.
7 'The History of Australia House', Australian High Commission: United Kingdom, http://www.uk.embassy.gov.au/lhlh/History.html, accessed 16 February 2010.
8 Hector MacQuarrie to George Ferguson, 23 November 1951, MSS 3269/442 ML.
9 Hector MacQuarrie to CL Hewitt (Australia House), 9 August 1950, MSS 3269/441 ML.
10 Hector MacQuarrie to CL Hewitt (Australia House), 9 August 1950, MSS 3269/441 ML.
11 Hector MacQuarrie to George Ferguson, 21 August 1950, MSS 3269/441 ML.
12 Hector MacQuarrie to George Ferguson, 3 January 1951, MSS 3269/442 ML.

13 Hector MacQuarrie to George Ferguson, 27 October 1950, MSS 3269/441 ML.
14 George Ferguson to Hector MacQuarrie, 10 October 1951, MSS 3269/442 ML.
15 Hector MacQuarrie to George Ferguson, 21 August 1950, MSS 3269/441 ML.
16 George Ferguson to Hector MacQuarrie, 31 August 1950, MSS 3269/441 ML.
17 George Ferguson to Hector MacQuarrie, 25 September 1950, MSS 3269/441 ML.
18 George Ferguson to Hector MacQuarrie, 25 September 1950, MSS 3269/441 ML.
19 Hector MacQuarrie to George Ferguson, 29 January 1951, MSS 3269/442 ML.
20 Walter Butcher to George Ferguson, 31 March 1965, MSS 3269/23 ML.
21 George Ferguson to Hector MacQuarrie, 14 February 1951, MSS 3269/442 ML.
22 George Ferguson to Hector MacQuarrie, 25 January 1951, MSS 3269/442 ML.
23 Hector MacQuarrie to George Ferguson, 29 August 1951, MSS 3269/442 ML.
24 Hector MacQuarrie to George Ferguson, 1 November 1951, MSS 3269/442 ML.
25 Hector MacQuarrie to George Ferguson, 17 October 1951, MSS 3269/442 ML.
26 Hector MacQuarrie to George Ferguson, 1 November 1951, MSS 3269/442 ML.
27 Hector MacQuarrie to George Ferguson, 1 November 1951, MSS 3269/442 ML.
28 'Refusal to Lift Ban on American Novel', *Sydney Morning Herald*, 26 October 1951.
29 'Minister Lifts Ban on Novel', *Argus*, 2 November 1951.
30 Hector MacQuarrie to George Ferguson, 1 November 1951, MSS 3269/442 ML.
31 Hector MacQuarrie to George Ferguson, 25 April 1952, MSS 3269/443 ML.
32 Hector MacQuarrie to George Ferguson, 28 August 1952, MSS 2369/443 ML.
33 Aubrey Cousins to Vera Wellings, 24 December 1952, MSS 3269/18 ML.
34 George Ferguson to Hector MacQuarrie, 9 July 1951, MSS 3269/442 ML.
35 Neil James, 'Spheres of Influence: Angus & Robertson and Australian Literature from the Thirties to the Sixties' (PhD diss., University of Sydney, 2000), 260.
36 George Ferguson to Hector MacQuarrie, 18 September 1951, MSS 3269/442 ML.
37 George Ferguson to Aubrey Cousins, 17 December 1951, MSS 3269/442 ML.
38 George Ferguson to Hector MacQuarrie, 18 September 1951, MSS 3269/442 ML.
39 Aubrey Cousins to Vera Wellings, 20 June 1952, MSS 3269/18 ML.
40 George Ferguson to Hector MacQuarrie, 19 July 1951, MSS 3269/442 ML.
41 George Ferguson to Hector MacQuarrie, 13 September 1950, MSS 3269/441 ML.
42 Hector MacQuarrie to George Ferguson, 17 October 1951, MSS 3269/442 ML.
43 Hector MacQuarrie to Captain Taylor, 28 August 1953, MSS 3269/444 ML.
44 George Ferguson to Hector MacQuarrie, 19 July 1951, MSS 3269/442 ML.
45 George Ferguson to Hector MacQuarrie, 19 July 1951, MSS 3269/442 ML.
46 George Ferguson to Aubrey Cousins, 17 December 1951, MSS 3269/442 ML.
47 George Ferguson to Hector MacQuarrie, 19 July 1951, MSS 3269/442 ML.
48 George Ferguson to Hector MacQuarrie, 2 January 1952, MSS 3269/443 ML.
49 Aubrey Cousins to George Ferguson, 7 December 1951, MSS 3269/442 ML.
50 Aubrey Cousins to George Ferguson, 29 November 1951, MSS 3269/442 ML.
51 Vera Wellings to Paul Tracy, 26 February 1952, MSS 3269/18 ML.
52 Vera Wellings to Hector MacQuarrie, 3 April 1952, MSS 3269/18 ML.
53 Aubrey Cousins to Vera Wellings, 17 April 1952, MSS 3269/18 ML.
54 Aubrey Cousins to Vera Wellings, 17 April 1952, MSS 3269/18 ML.
55 R. E. Barker and G. R. Davis, eds, *Books Are Different: An Account of the Defence of the Net Book Agreement before the Restrictive Practices Court in 1962* (London: Macmillan, 1966), 467.
56 Hector MacQuarrie to George Ferguson, 11 February 1952, MSS 3269/443 ML.
57 Aubrey Cousins to Vera Wellings, 20 June 1952, MSS 3269/18 ML.
58 Aubrey Cousins to George Ferguson, 7 December 1951, MSS 3269/442 ML.
59 George Ferguson to Vera Wellings, 10 November 1952, MSS 3269/18 ML.
60 George Ferguson to Hector MacQuarrie, 2 January 1952, MSS 3269/443 ML.
61 George Ferguson to Hector MacQuarrie, 17 January 1952, MSS 3269/443 ML.

62 George Ferguson to Hector MacQuarrie, 2 January 1952, MSS 3269/443 ML.
63 Tariff Board Australia, *Report of Evidence at Tariff Board Inquiries into Proposal of Duty on Books, Magazines and Fashion Plates Held in Adelaide, Brisbane, Sydney and Melbourne* (Melbourne: Australian Booksellers Association, 1930), 64.
64 George Ferguson to Hector MacQuarrie, 14 February 1952, MSS 3269/443 ML.
65 Aubrey Cousins to George Ferguson, 7 December 1951, MSS 3269/442 ML.
66 George Ferguson to Aubrey Cousins, 17 December 1951, MSS 3269/442 ML.
67 Barker and Davis, eds, *Books Are Different*, 480.
68 George Ferguson to Hector MacQuarrie, 15 July 1952, MSS 3269/443 ML.
69 Aubrey Cousins to Hector MacQuarrie, 11 July 1952, MSS 3269/443 ML.
70 Aubrey Cousins to Mrs Wood, 11 July 1952, MSS 3269/443 ML.
71 Aubrey Cousins to Mrs Wood, 11 July 1952, MSS 3269/443 ML.
72 George Ferguson to Vera Wellings, 10 November 1952, MSS 3269/18 ML.
73 Aubrey Cousins to John Jarrold, Jarrolds Publishers, London, 17 July 1952, MSS 3269/364 ML.
74 George Ferguson to Hector MacQuarrie, 14 February 1952, MSS 3269/443 ML.
75 George Ferguson to Hector MacQuarrie, 14 December 1951, MSS 3269/442 ML.
76 George Ferguson to Hector MacQuarrie, 19 July 1951, MSS 3269/442 ML.
77 George Ferguson to Walter Butcher, 26 September 1951, MSS 3269/442 ML.
78 George Ferguson to Hector MacQuarrie, 14 December 1951, MSS 3269/442 ML.
79 Walter Butcher to George Ferguson, 16 September 1953, MSS 3269/444 ML.
80 George Ferguson to Hector MacQuarrie, 2 March 1954, MSS 3269/445 ML.
81 George Ferguson to Hector MacQuarrie, 3 December 1951, MSS 3269/442 ML.
82 Hector MacQuarrie to George Ferguson, 11 December 1951, MSS 3269/442 ML.
83 George Ferguson to Hector MacQuarrie, 3 December 1951, MSS 3269/442 ML.
84 George Ferguson to Frank Eyre, Oxford University Press, 5 March 1951, MSS 3269/525 ML.
85 George Ferguson to Hector MacQuarrie, 2 January 1952, MSS 3269/443 ML.
86 George Ferguson to Hector MacQuarrie, 18 September 1951, MSS 3269/442 ML.
87 Hector MacQuarrie to George Ferguson, 17 October 1951, MSS 3269/442 ML.
88 George Ferguson to Hector MacQuarrie, 25 October 1951, MSS 3269/442 ML.
89 George Ferguson to Hector MacQuarrie, 18 September 1951, MSS 3269/442 ML.
90 Aubrey Cousins to Vera Wellings, 24 December 1952, MSS 3269/18 ML.
91 Hector MacQuarrie to George Ferguson, 16 November 1951, MSS 3269/442 ML.
92 Vera Wellings to George Ferguson, 12 January 1952, MSS 3269/18 ML.
93 George Ferguson to Vera Wellings, 17 January 1952, MSS 3269/18 ML.
94 Hector MacQuarrie to George Ferguson, 27 February 1952, MSS 3269/443 ML.
95 Hector MacQuarrie to George Ferguson, 14 March 1952, MSS 3269/443 ML.
96 Hector MacQuarrie to George Ferguson, 29 March 1952, MSS 3269/443 ML.
97 Hector MacQuarrie to George Ferguson, 16 April 1952, MSS 3269/443 ML.
98 Profit and Loss Statement, 31 March 1952, MSS 3269/443 ML.
99 Aubrey Cousins to Vera Wellings, 2 September 1952, MSS 3269/443 ML.
100 Aubrey Cousins to Hector MacQuarrie, 27 August 1952, MSS 3269/443 ML.
101 Hector MacQuarrie to George Ferguson, 7 March 1952, MSS 3269/443 ML.
102 Aubrey Cousins to Hector MacQuarrie, 11 July 1952, MSS 3269/443 ML.
103 Aubrey Cousins to Hector MacQuarrie, 27 August 1952, MSS 3269/443 ML.
104 Vera Wellings to Hector MacQuarrie, 23 July 1952, MSS 3269/18 ML.
105 Vera Wellings to Aubrey Cousins, 7 January 1953, MSS 3269/18 ML.
106 Vera Wellings to Hector MacQuarrie, 24 July 1952, MSS 3269/18 ML.
107 Hector MacQuarrie to George Ferguson, 20 September 1952, MSS 3269/18 ML.
108 Hector MacQuarrie to George Ferguson, 25 April 1952, MSS 3269/443 ML.
109 Hector MacQuarrie to George Ferguson, 25 April 1952, MSS 3269/443 ML.
110 Hector MacQuarrie to George Ferguson, 8 April 1952, MSS 3269/443 ML.

111 Hector MacQuarrie to George Ferguson, 28 August 1952, MSS 3269/443 ML.
112 Hector MacQuarrie to George Ferguson, 7 May 1952, MSS 3269/443 ML.
113 Vera Wellings to Aubrey Cousins, 30 April 1952, MSS 3269/18 ML.
114 Aubrey Cousins to Vera Wellings, 9 May 1952, MSS 3269/18 ML.
115 Aubrey Cousins to Vera Wellings, 19 May 1952, MSS 3269/18 ML.
116 Aubrey Cousins to Vera Wellings, 2 September 1952, MSS 3269/443 ML.
117 George Ferguson to Vera Wellings, 10 November 1952, MSS 3269/18 ML.
118 Aubrey Cousins to Vera Wellings, 24 December 1952, MSS 3269/18 ML.
119 Aubrey Cousins to Vera Wellings, 2 September 1952, MSS 3269/443 ML.
120 Aubrey Cousins to Vera Wellings, 2 September 1952, MSS 3269/443 ML.
121 Hector MacQuarrie to George Ferguson, 17 November 1952, MSS 3269/443 ML.
122 George Ferguson to Hector MacQuarrie, 2 January 1952, MSS 3269/443 ML.
123 George Ferguson to Hamish Hamilton, 7 February 1952, MSS 3269/316 ML.

Chapter 7 Preparing for 'Operation London'

1 George Ferguson to Vera Wellings, 17 January 1952, MSS 3269/18 ML.
2 George Ferguson, interview with Suzanne Lunney, 11 May 1976, TRC 452, National Library of Australia, 70–71.
3 Hector MacQuarrie to Aubrey Cousins, 6 January 1953, MSS 3269/444 ML.
4 Calculated according to the costs of production only. Hector MacQuarrie to George Ferguson, 4 February 1953, MSS 3269/444 ML.
5 Vera Wellings to Aubrey Cousins, 6 February 1953, MSS 3269/18 ML.
6 Aubrey Cousins to Hector MacQuarrie, 8 May 1953, MSS 3269/444 ML.
7 Hector MacQuarrie to George Ferguson, 23 September 1953, MSS 3269/444 ML.
8 Frank Sanders to George Ferguson, 19 June 1953, MSS 3269/556 ML.
9 Robert Haupt, 'The Book Rebellion', *Age*, 5 November 1988.
10 George Ferguson to Hector MacQuarrie, 3 September 1953, MSS 3269/444 ML.
11 Hector MacQuarrie to George Ferguson, 9 September 1953, MSS 3269/444 ML.
12 Hector MacQuarrie to George Ferguson, 29 October 1953, MSS 3269/444 ML.
13 Hector MacQuarrie to George Ferguson, 8 December 1953, MSS 3269/444 ML.
14 Hector MacQuarrie to George Ferguson, 8 December 1953, MSS 3269/444 ML.
15 Hector MacQuarrie to George Ferguson, 18 January 1955, MSS 3269/446 ML.
16 Hector MacQuarrie to George Ferguson, 8 December 1953, MSS 3269/444 ML.
17 Hector MacQuarrie to George Ferguson, 8 December 1953, MSS 3269/444 ML.
18 George Ferguson to Hector MacQuarrie, 18 December 1953, MSS 3269/444 ML.
19 George Ferguson to Hector MacQuarrie, 18 December 1953, MSS 3269/444 ML.
20 George Ferguson to Hector MacQuarrie, 7 January 1955, MSS 3269/446 ML.
21 Walter Harrap to George Ferguson, 30 December 1953, MSS 3269/322 ML.
22 Frank Sanders, Publishers Association Members' Circular, 18 January 1954, MSS 3269/556 ML.
23 Frank Sanders, Publishers Association Members' Circular, 12 May 1958, MSS 3269/557 ML.
24 R. E. Barker and G. R. Davis, eds, *Books Are Different: An Account of the Defence of the Net Book Agreement before the Restrictive Practices Court in 1962* (London: Macmillan, 1966), 907.
25 Leonard Mann, Fellowship of Australian Writers, in "Tariff Board Inquiry into the Publishing Industry in Australia", *Ideas: Booksellers, Stationers and Fancy Goods Journal of Australia and New Zealand* (Melbourne: D. W. Thorpe, January 1946), 70.
26 George Ferguson to Hector MacQuarrie, 4 November 1953, MSS 3269/444 ML.
27 Hector MacQuarrie to George Ferguson, 8 December 1953, MSS 3269/444 ML.
28 George Ferguson to Hector MacQuarrie, 20 April 1954, MSS 3269/445 ML.
29 Barker and Davis, *Books Are Different*, 467.

30 Richard Nile, 'Cartels, Capitalism and the Australian Booktrade,' *Continuum: The Australian Journal of Media and Culture* 4.1 (1990): 71–91.
31 Hector MacQuarrie to Captain Taylor, 28 August 1953, MSS 3269/444 ML.
32 Neil James, 'Spheres of Influence: Angus & Robertson and Australian Literature from the Thirties to the Sixties' (PhD diss., unpublished, University of Sydney, 2000), 260.
33 Hector MacQuarrie to Stanley Rinehart, 4 November 1954, MSS 3269/445 ML.
34 George Ferguson to Hector MacQuarrie, 6 October 1954, MSS 3269/445 ML.
35 Hector MacQuarrie to Captain Taylor, 28 August 1953, MSS 3269/444 ML.
36 Hector MacQuarrie to J. A. Jones, *The Evening News*, 9 September 1953, MSS 3269/444 ML.
37 Hector MacQuarrie to Stanley Rinehart, 4 November 1954, MSS 3269/445 ML.
38 Hector MacQuarrie to Captain Taylor, 28 August 1953, MSS 3269/444 ML.
39 Hector MacQuarrie to Captain Taylor, 28 August 1953, MSS 3269/444 ML.
40 James, 'Spheres of Influence', 262.
41 Hector MacQuarrie to J. A. Jones, *The Evening News*, 9 September 1953, MSS 3269/444 ML.
42 Hector MacQuarrie to George Ferguson, 12 November 1953, MSS 3269/444 ML.
43 George Ferguson to Hector MacQuarrie, 6 August 1953, MSS 3269/444 ML.
44 George Ferguson to Hector MacQuarrie, 22 November 1954, MSS 3269/445 ML.
45 George Ferguson, 'Publishing in London by Angus & Robertson Limited: A Paper for the guidance of the Board', unpublished, August 1970, MSS 3269/34 ML.
46 George Ferguson to Hector MacQuarrie, 7 March 1958, MSS 3269/448 ML.
47 Hector MacQuarrie to George Ferguson, 10 October 1953, MSS 3269/444 ML.
48 Angus and Robertson Limited, *Report of the Directors*, Sydney, 1 November 1954.
49 George Ferguson to Hector MacQuarrie, 15 December 1953, MSS 3269/444 ML.
50 George Ferguson to Hector MacQuarrie, 15 September 1953, MSS 3269/444 ML.
51 Hector MacQuarrie to George Ferguson, 10 November 1953, MSS 3269/445 ML.
52 This document was not discovered in the Mitchell Library collections after extensive research. This is an important gap in the documentary evidence for any history of Angus & Robertson's London office; its procedures however can be reasonably interpreted from the company's activities. George Ferguson to Hector MacQuarrie, 19 November 1953, MSS 3269/445 ML.
53 Hector MacQuarrie to George Ferguson, 10 November 1953, MSS 3269/445 ML.
54 Hector MacQuarrie to George Ferguson, 2 August 1953, MSS 3269/444 ML.
55 Hector MacQuarrie to George Ferguson, 2 August 1953, MSS 3269/444 ML.
56 Hector MacQuarrie to Vera Wellings, 30 September 1952, MSS 3269/18 ML.
57 Hector MacQuarrie to Vera Wellings, 30 September 1952, MSS 3269/18 ML.
58 George Ferguson to Hector MacQuarrie, 20 October 1952, MSS 3269/443 ML.
59 George Ferguson to Vera Wellings, 20 October 1952, MSS 3269/18 ML.
60 Hector MacQuarrie to George Ferguson, 28 October 1952, MSS 3269/443 ML.
61 George Ferguson to Hector MacQuarrie, 15 September 1953, MSS 3269/444 ML.
62 Barry Rowland to George Ferguson, 15 September 1954, MSS 3269/645 ML.
63 Hector MacQuarrie to George Ferguson, 16 August 1956, MSS 3269/447 ML.
64 George Ferguson to Hector MacQuarrie, 12 December 1955, MSS 3269/446 ML.
65 James, 'Spheres of Influence', 262.
66 George Ferguson to Hector MacQuarrie, 22 November 1954, MSS 3269/445 ML.
67 George Ferguson to Hector MacQuarrie, 15 September 1953, MSS 3269/444 ML.
68 Hector MacQuarrie to George Ferguson, 23 September 1953, MSS 3269/444 ML.
69 Hector MacQuarrie to George Ferguson, 5 August 1954, MSS 3269/445 ML.
70 Vera Wellings to George Ferguson, 25 September 1953, MSS 3269/18 ML.
71 Aubrey Cousins to Vera Wellings, 20 October 1953, MSS 3269/18 ML.
72 Vera Wellings to George Ferguson, 25 September 1953, MSS 3269/18 ML.

73 George Ferguson to Vera Wellings, 2 October 1953, MSS 3269/18 ML.
74 Hector MacQuarrie to George Ferguson, 8 December 1953, MSS 3269/445 ML.
75 Hector MacQuarrie to George Ferguson, 9 October 1953, MSS 3269/444 ML.

Chapter 8 The Shiralee in the North

1 Hector MacQuarrie to Stanley Rinehart, 4 November 1954, MSS 3269/445 ML.
2 Hector MacQuarrie to George Ferguson, 5 October 1954, MSS 3269/445 ML.
3 George Ferguson to Hector MacQuarrie, 19 November 1953, MSS 3269/444 ML.
4 George Ferguson to Barry Rowland, 30 April 1954, MSS 3269/645 ML.
5 Bill Ashcroft, 'Home and Horizon', in *Diaspora: The Australasian Experience*, eds, Cynthia vanden Driesen and Ralph Crane (New Delhi: Prestige Books, 2006), 52.
6 George Ferguson to Hector MacQuarrie, 19 November 1953, MSS 3269/444 ML.
7 Hector MacQuarrie, 'Operation London', December 1954, 16, quoted in Neil James, 'Spheres of Influence: Angus and Robertson and Australian Literature from the Thirties to the Sixties' (PhD diss., unpublished, University of Sydney, 2000), 260–61.
8 Hector MacQuarrie to George Ferguson, 10 November 1953, MSS 3269/445 ML.
9 Hector MacQuarrie to George Ferguson, 10 November 1953, MSS 3269/445 ML.
10 Sheila MacKay Russell to Hector MacQuarrie, 23 March 1955, MSS 3269/446 ML.
11 Hector MacQuarrie to George Ferguson, 14 May 1954, MSS 3269/445 ML.
12 Hector MacQuarrie to George Ferguson, 3 March 1954, MSS 3269/445 ML.
13 George Ferguson to Hector MacQuarrie, 28 October 1954, MSS 3269/645 ML.
14 George Ferguson to Sydney Sewell, 15 March 1955, MSS 3269/446 ML.
15 Hector MacQuarrie to George Ferguson, 5 October 1954, MSS 3269/445 ML.
16 Barry Rowland to George Ferguson, 19 October 1954, MSS 3269/645 ML.
17 See, for example, the discussion of London office sales in James, 'Spheres of Influence', 261.
18 George Ferguson to Hector MacQuarrie, 16 March 1954, MSS 3269/445 ML.
19 Barry Rowland to George Ferguson, 7 October 1958, MSS 3269/646 ML.
20 Barry Rowland to George Ferguson, 30 March 1960, MSS 3269/648 ML.
21 Hector MacQuarrie to George Ferguson, 4 November 1954, MSS 3269/445 ML.
22 George Ferguson to Hector MacQuarrie, 18 December 1953, MSS 3269/444 ML.
23 Hector MacQuarrie to Stanley Rinehart, 4 November 1954, MSS 3269/445 ML.
24 George Ferguson to Barry Rowland, 30 April 1954, MSS 3269/645 ML.
25 Hector MacQuarrie to Stanley Rinehart, 4 November 1954, MSS 3269/445 ML.
26 Hector MacQuarrie to George Ferguson, 4 November 1954, MSS 3269/445 ML.
27 Hector MacQuarrie, quoted in James, 'Spheres of Influence', 260. It also appears in Hector MacQuarrie to George Ferguson, 4 November 1954, MSS 3269/445 ML.
28 Hector MacQuarrie to George Ferguson, 20 August 1953, MSS 3269/444 ML.
29 George Ferguson to Hector MacQuarrie, 18 December 1953, MSS 3269/444 ML.
30 Author's full name is not cited in any correspondence regarding this work.
31 Hector MacQuarrie to D'Arcy Niland, 7 December 1954, MSS 3269/445 ML.
32 Hector MacQuarrie to George Ferguson, 5 October 1954, MSS 3269/445 ML.
33 Hector MacQuarrie to George Ferguson, 15 February 1954, MSS 3269/445 ML.
34 Hector MacQuarrie to George Ferguson, 24 November 1954, MSS 3269/445 ML.
35 Barry Rowland to George Ferguson, 21 January 1954, MSS 3269/645 ML.
36 George Ferguson to Hector MacQuarrie, 17 September 1954, MSS 3269/445 ML.
37 Hector MacQuarrie to Stanley Rinehart, 4 November 1954, MSS 3269/445 ML.
38 George Ferguson to Barry Rowland, 28 October 1954, MSS 3269/645 ML.
39 Barry Rowland to George Ferguson, 19 October 1954, MSS 3269/645 ML.
40 Hector MacQuarrie to George Ferguson, 15 November 1954, MSS 3269/445 ML.
41 George Ferguson to Barry Rowland, 28 October 1954, MSS 3269/645 ML.

42 George Ferguson to Hector MacQuarrie, 17 September 1956, MSS 3269/447 ML.
43 George Ferguson to Hector MacQuarrie, 8 November 1955, MSS 3269/446 ML.
44 Hector MacQuarrie to George Ferguson, 12 April 1955, MSS 3269/446 ML.
45 George Ferguson to Hector MacQuarrie, 27 August 1954, MSS 3269/445 ML.
46 Hector MacQuarrie to George Ferguson, 12 April 1955, MSS 3269/446 ML.
47 Barry Rowland to George Ferguson, 19 October 1954, MSS 3269/645 ML.
48 George Ferguson to Hector MacQuarrie, 12 December 1955, MSS 3269/446 ML.
49 Hector MacQuarrie to George Ferguson, 18 January 1955, MSS 3269/446 ML.
50 Hector MacQuarrie to George Ferguson, 10 January 1956, MSS 3269/447 ML.
51 Hector MacQuarrie to George Ferguson, 7 April 1954, MSS 3269/445 ML.
52 Barry Rowland to George Ferguson, 13 September 1955, MSS 3269/645 ML.
53 George Ferguson to Barry Rowland, 30 April 1956, MSS 3269/646 ML.
54 Barry Rowland to George Ferguson, 19 October 1954, MSS 3269/645 ML.
55 George Ferguson to Sydney Sewell, 15 March 1955, MSS 3269/446 ML.
56 Hector MacQuarrie to George Ferguson, 23 September 1956, MSS 3269/447 ML.
57 Laura J. Miller, *Reluctant Capitalists: Bookselling and the Culture of Consumption* (London: University of Chicago Press, 2006), 7.
58 Hector MacQuarrie to George Ferguson, 23 September 1956, MSS 3269/447 ML.
59 George Ferguson to Hector MacQuarrie, 7 January 1955, MSS 3269/446 ML.
60 Hector MacQuarrie to George Ferguson, 22 February 1956, MSS 3269/447 ML.
61 Hector MacQuarrie to George Ferguson, 15 November 1954, MSS 3269/445 ML.
62 Hector MacQuarrie to George Ferguson, 14 February 1955, MSS 3269/446 ML.
63 George Ferguson to Hector MacQuarrie, 12 December 1955, MSS 3269/446 ML.
64 Hector MacQuarrie to George Ferguson, 16 August 1956, MSS 3269/447 ML.
65 George Ferguson to Hector MacQuarrie, 18 January 1956, MSS 3269/447 ML.
66 George Ferguson to Hector MacQuarrie, 12 December 1955, MSS 3269/446 ML.
67 George Ferguson to Hector MacQuarrie, 15 August 1956, MSS 3269/447 ML.
68 George Ferguson to Hector MacQuarrie, 17 September 1956, MSS 3269/447 ML.
69 John Feather, *A History of British Publishing* (London: Routledge, 1988), 195.
70 Quote from the dust jacket of D'arcy Niland, *The Shiralee* (London, England and Sydney, New South Wales: Angus & Robertson, 1955).
71 Hector MacQuarrie to George Ferguson, 5 October 1954, MSS 3269/445 ML.
72 George Ferguson to Hector MacQuarrie, 20 October 1954, MSS 3269/445 ML.
73 George Ferguson to Hector MacQuarrie, 20 October 1954, MSS 3269/445 ML.
74 George Ferguson to Hector MacQuarrie, 20 October 1954, MSS 3269/445 ML.
75 George Ferguson to Hector MacQuarrie, 19 October 1955, MSS 3269/446 ML.
76 Hector MacQuarrie to Beatrice Davis, 1 November 1954, MSS 3269/445 ML.
77 Hector MacQuarrie to George Ferguson, 29 October 1954, MSS 3269/445 ML.
78 Hector MacQuarrie to George Ferguson, 1 March 1955, MSS 3269/446 ML.
79 George Ferguson, interview with Suzanne Lunney, 11 May 1976, TRC 452, National Library of Australia, 51.
80 Hector MacQuarrie to George Ferguson, 14 December 1955, MSS 3269/446 ML.
81 George Ferguson to Hector MacQuarrie, 18 November 1954, MSS 3269/445 ML.
82 George Ferguson to Hector MacQuarrie, 23 November 1954, MSS 3269/445 ML.
83 Barry Rowland to Aubrey Cousins, 25 July 1955, MSS 3269/645 ML.
84 George Ferguson to Hector MacQuarrie, 19 April 1955, MSS 3269/446 ML.
85 Niland, *The Shiralee*, 1.
86 Barry Rowland to Aubrey Cousins, 25 July 1955, MSS 3269/645 ML.
87 Hector MacQuarrie to George Ferguson, 20 April 1955, MSS 3269/446 ML.
88 Hector MacQuarrie to George Ferguson, 11 February 1955, MSS 3269/446 ML.
89 Barry Rowland to George Ferguson, 15 August 1955, MSS 3269/446 ML.

90 Barry Rowland to George Ferguson, 26 September 1955, MSS 3269/645 ML.
91 C. L. Shard to Barry Rowland, 16 September 1955, MSS 3269/446 ML.
92 Hector MacQuarrie to George Ferguson, 12 April 1955, MSS 3269/446 ML.
93 H. E. Alexander to Hector MacQuarrie, 25 March 1955, MSS 3269/446 ML.
94 Hector MacQuarrie to George Ferguson, 2 October 1957, MSS 3269/448 ML.
95 Jacqueline Kent, *A Certain Style: Beatrice Davis A Literary Life* (Camberwell, Victoria: Penguin, 2001), 140.
96 Barry Rowland to George Ferguson, 19 June 1959, MSS 3269/19 ML.
97 John Ferguson to George Ferguson, 5 April 1962, MSS 3269/20 ML.
98 Hector MacQuarrie to George Ferguson, 23 November 1955, MSS 3269/446 ML.
99 Hector MacQuarrie to George Ferguson, 1 November 1955, MSS 3269/446 ML.
100 George Ferguson to Hector MacQuarrie, 19 October 1955, MSS 3269/446 ML.
101 George Ferguson to Barry Rowland, 20 October 1955, MSS 3269/645 ML.
102 Hector MacQuarrie to George Ferguson, 11 October 1955, MSS 3269/446 ML.
103 Barry Rowland to George Ferguson, 14 March 1960, MSS 3269/648 ML.
104 Barry Rowland to George Ferguson, 10 March 1960, MSS 3269/648 ML.
105 George Ferguson to Hector MacQuarrie, 27 June 1956, MSS 3269/447 ML.
106 Hector MacQuarrie to George Ferguson, 22 February 1955, MSS 3269/446 ML.
107 George Ferguson to Hector MacQuarrie, 11 October 1949, MSS 3269/440 ML.
108 James, 'Spheres of Influence', 260.
109 Hector MacQuarrie to George Ferguson, 7 April 1954, MSS 3269/445 ML.
110 Barry Rowland to George Ferguson, 20 May 1954, MSS 3269/645 ML.
111 Hector MacQuarrie to George Ferguson, 4 May 1954, MSS 3269/445 ML.
112 George Ferguson to Barry Rowland, 21 May 1954, MSS 3269/645 ML.
113 Barry Rowland to George Ferguson, 24 April 1954, MSS 3269/645 ML.
114 George Ferguson to Hector MacQuarrie, 20 April 1954, MSS 3269/445 ML.
115 Hector MacQuarrie to George Ferguson, 21 May 1954, MSS 3269/445 ML.
116 George Ferguson to Barry Rowland, 29 January 1955, MSS 3269/645 ML.
117 Barry Rowland to George Ferguson, 21 December 1955, MSS 3269/645 ML.
118 George Ferguson to Hector MacQuarrie, 23 February 1956, MSS 3269/447 ML.
119 Hector MacQuarrie to George Ferguson, 4 January 1957, MSS 3269/448 ML.
120 Barry Rowland to George Ferguson, 26 September 1955, MSS 3269/645 ML.
121 George Ferguson to Hector MacQuarrie, 7 August 1956, MSS 3269/447 ML.
122 George Ferguson to Hector MacQuarrie, 21 May 1956, MSS 3269/447 ML.
123 George Ferguson to Hector MacQuarrie, 1 March 1956, MSS 3269/447 ML.
124 Barry Rowland to George Ferguson, 10 March 1960, MSS 3269/648 ML.

Chapter 9 A Commercial and Cultural Relationship

1 George Ferguson to Walter Harrap, 3 January 1961, MSS 3269/322 ML.
2 George Ferguson to Walter Harrap, 3 January 1961, MSS 3269/322 ML.
3 Craig Munro, 'Case-Study: A&R's Takeover Crisis', in *A History of the Book in Australia 1946–2005: Paper Empires*, ed. Craig Munro and Robyn Sheahan-Bright (St Lucia: University of Queensland Press, 2006), 16.
4 George Ferguson to Barry Rowland, 5 May 1959, MSS 3269/647 ML.
5 George Ferguson to Barry Rowland, 5 May 1959, MSS 3269/647 ML.
6 Hector MacQuarrie to George Ferguson, 10 January 1956, MSS 3269/447 ML.
7 Hector MacQuarrie to George Ferguson, 9 December 1959, MSS 3269/449 ML.
8 Hector MacQuarrie to George Ferguson, 4 January 1957, MSS 3269/448 ML.
9 Barry Rowland to George Ferguson, 9 December 1959, MSS 3269/647 ML.
10 George Ferguson to Hector MacQuarrie, 17 September 1956, MSS 3269/447 ML.

11 R. E. Barker and G. R. Davis, eds, *Books Are Different: An Account of the Defence of the Net Book Agreement before the Restrictive Practices Court in 1962* (London: Macmillan, 1966), 472.
12 Hector MacQuarrie to George Ferguson, 25 June 1957, MSS 3269/448 ML.
13 George Ferguson to Hector MacQuarrie, 9 July 1957, MSS 3269/448 ML.
14 George Ferguson to Hector MacQuarrie, 18 January 1956, MSS 3269/447 ML.
15 George Ferguson to Barry Rowland, 30 July 1959, MSS 3269/647 ML.
16 George Ferguson to Hector MacQuarrie, 4 December 1959, MSSW 3269/449 ML.
17 George Ferguson to Hector MacQuarrie, 4 December 1959, MSSW 3269/449 ML.
18 Stephen Alomes, *When London Calls: The Expatriation of Australian Creative Artists to Britain* (Cambridge: Cambridge University Press, 1999), 92.
19 George Ferguson to Stanley Unwin, 3 January 1961, MSS 3269/10 ML.
20 George Ferguson (from the London office) to Aubrey Cousins, 18 March 1958, MSS 3269/646 ML.
21 Sir Keith Sinclair, quoted in Stephen Alomes, 'Colonial to Global: Paradoxes of Expatriation in Australia's Diasporic Story', in *Diaspora: The Australasian Experience*, ed. Cynthia vanden Driesen and Ralph Crane (New Delhi: Prestige Books, 2006), 134.
22 Hector MacQuarrie to George Ferguson, 14 August 1957, MSS 3269/448 ML.
23 Bill Ashcroft, 'Home and Horizon', in *Diaspora: The Australasian Experience*, ed. Cynthia vanden Driesen and Ralph Crane (New Delhi: Prestige Books, 2006), 52.
24 Ashcroft, 'Home and Horizon', 52.
25 The figure is quoted by Frank Sanders in Barker and Davis, *Books Are Different*, 411.
26 Barker and Davis, *Books Are Different*, 472.
27 Tim Dolin, 'Fiction and the Australian Reading Public, 1888–1914', Australian Common Reader, http://www.australiancommonreader.com/?p=15, accessed 26 March 2010.
28 Alomes, 'Colonial to Global', 137.
29 George Ferguson to Walter Harrap, 1 December 1949, MSS 3269/440 ML.
30 Hector MacQuarrie to George Ferguson, 14 November 1957, MSS 3269/448 ML.
31 George Ferguson to Hector MacQuarrie, 9 July 1957, MSS 3269/448 ML.
32 Neil James, 'Spheres of Influence: Angus & Robertson and Australian Literature from the Thirties to the Sixties' (PhD diss., unpublished, University of Sydney, 2000), 261.
33 Barry Rowland to George Ferguson, 21 December 1955, MSS 3269/645 ML; and George Ferguson to Hector MacQuarrie, 23 February 1956, MSS 3269/447 ML.
34 George Ferguson to Barry Rowland, 15 July 1957, MSS 3269/646 ML.
35 George Ferguson to Hector MacQuarrie, 30 April 1957, MSS 3269/448 ML.
36 'Landed Costs of Angus & Robertson London Titles', Paul Tracy to George Ferguson, circa December 1957, MSS 3269/745 ML.
37 Hector MacQuarrie to George Ferguson, 4 January 1957, MSS 3269/448 ML.
38 Barry Rowland to George Ferguson, 28 January 1957, MSS 3269/646 ML.
39 Hector MacQuarrie to George Ferguson, 14 November 1957, MSS 3269/448 ML.
40 Hector MacQuarrie to George Ferguson, 2 October 1957, MSS 3269/448 ML.
41 Barry Rowland to George Ferguson, 15 January 1960, MSS 3269/648 ML.
42 George Ferguson to Hector MacQuarrie, 4 December 1957, MSS 3269/448 ML.
43 Hector MacQuarrie to George Ferguson, 30 January 1958, MSS 3268/448 ML.
44 George Ferguson to Barry Rowland, 4 February 1959, MSS 3269/647 ML.
45 George Ferguson to Hector MacQuarrie, 8 April 1957, MSS 3268/448 ML.
46 Beatrice Davis to Hector MacQuarrie, 27 March 1957, MSS 3269/448 ML.
47 George Ferguson to Hector MacQuarrie, 29 April 1957, MSS 3269/448 ML.
48 George Ferguson to Hector MacQuarrie, 6 March 1957, MSS 3269/448 ML.
49 Barry Rowland to George Ferguson, 17 April 1957, MSS 3269/646 ML.
50 Beatrice Davis to Hector MacQuarrie, 14 March 1957, MSS 3269/448 ML.
51 Barry Rowland to George Ferguson, 17 April 1957, MSS 3269/646 ML.

52 Barry Rowland to George Ferguson, 17 April 1957, MSS 3269/646 ML.
53 James, 'Spheres of Influence', 262.
54 Barry Rowland to George Ferguson, 15 May 1957, MSS 3269/646 ML, and George Ferguson to Barry Rowland, 5 June 1957, MSS 3269/646 ML.
55 George Ferguson to Barry Rowland, 15 January 1958, MSS 3269/646 ML.
56 George Ferguson to Hector MacQuarrie, 17 December 1958, MSS 3269/449 ML.
57 Hector MacQuarrie to George Ferguson, 21 October 1957, MSS 3269/448 ML.
58 George Ferguson to Hector MacQuarrie, 4 March 1958, MSS 3269/448 ML.
59 George Ferguson to Hector MacQuarrie, 12 February 1958, MSS 3269/449 ML.
60 Hector MacQuarrie to George Ferguson, 16 April 1958, MSS 3269/449 ML.
61 Barry Rowland to George Ferguson, 10 March 1960, MSS 3269/648 ML.
62 George Ferguson to Hector MacQuarrie, 17 December 1958, MSS 3269/449 ML.
63 Barry Rowland to George Ferguson, 3 December 1958, MSS 3269/646 ML.
64 Barry Rowland to George Ferguson, 10 March 1960, MSS 3269/648 ML.
65 George Ferguson to Hector MacQuarrie, 17 December 1958, MSS 3269/449 ML.
66 Barry Rowland to George Ferguson, 1 March 1960, MSS 3269/648 ML.
67 Barry Rowland to George Ferguson, 27 January 1959, MSS 3269/647 ML.
68 Barry Rowland to George Ferguson, 3 December 1958, MSS 3269/646 ML.
69 Barry Rowland to George Ferguson, 18 January 1959, MSS 3269/648 ML.
70 Barry Rowland to George Ferguson, 27 January 1959, MSS 3269/647 ML.
71 George Ferguson to Barry Rowland, 4 February 1959, MSS 3269/647 ML.
72 George Ferguson to Barry Rowland, 4 February 1959, MSS 3269/647 ML.
73 Barry Rowland to George Ferguson, 15 July 1959, MSS 3269/647 ML.
74 Barry Rowland to George Ferguson, 4 March 1959, MSS 3269/647 ML.
75 Barry Rowland to George Ferguson, 19 February 1960, MSS 3269/648 ML.
76 Barry Rowland to George Ferguson, 19 June 1959, MSS 3269/19 ML.
77 George Ferguson to Barry Rowland, 4 February 1959, MSS 3269/647 ML.
78 Barry Rowland to George Ferguson, 21 April 1959, MSS 3269/647 ML.
79 Barry Rowland to George Ferguson, 21 July 1959, MSS 3269/647 ML.
80 Barry Rowland to George Ferguson, 27 October 1959, MSS 3269/647 ML.
81 Barry Rowland to George Ferguson, 29 December 1959, MSS 3269/647 ML.
82 Barry Rowland to George Ferguson, 15 January 1960, MSS 3269/648 ML.
83 Barry Rowland to George Ferguson, 2 October 1959, MSS 3269/647 ML.
84 Barry Rowland to George Ferguson, 9 December 1957, MSS 3269/647 ML.
85 'Overseas Production', Paul Tracy to George Ferguson, 30 September 1959, MSS 3269/745 ML.
86 George Ferguson to Barry Rowland, 20 January 1960, MSS 3269/648 ML.
87 Barry Rowland to George Ferguson, 9 December 1957, MSS 3269/647 ML.
88 'Overseas Production', Paul Tracy to George Ferguson, 30 September 1959, MSS 3269/745 ML.
89 'Overseas Production', Paul Tracy to George Ferguson, 30 September 1959, MSS 3269/745 ML.
90 George Ferguson to Barry Rowland, 15 June 1960, MSS 3269/648 ML.
91 George Ferguson to Barry Rowland, 15 June 1960, MSS 3269/648 ML.
92 Barry Rowland to George Ferguson, 7 January 1960, MSS 3269/648 ML.
93 Barry Rowland to George Ferguson, 25 June 1959, MSS 3269/647 ML.
94 Barry Rowland to George Ferguson, 25 February 1960, MSS 3269/648 ML.
95 Barry Rowland to George Ferguson, 10 March 1960, MSS 3269/648 ML.
96 Barry Rowland to George Ferguson, 10 March 1960, MSS 3269/648 ML.
97 Barry Rowland to George Ferguson, 25 February 1960, MSS 3269/648 ML.
98 Barry Rowland to George Ferguson, 19 December 1959, MSS 3269/647 ML.

99 Barry Rowland to George Ferguson, 20 June 1960, MSS 3269/648 ML.
100 Barry Rowland to George Ferguson, 20 June 1960, MSS 3269/648 ML.
101 Barry Rowland to George Ferguson, 20 June 1960, MSS 3269/648 ML.
102 George Ferguson (in London) to RWD Delucey (Sydney), 25 July 1958, MSS 3269/19 ML.
103 Hector MacQuarrie to George Ferguson, 7 May 1957, MSS 3269/448 ML.

Chapter 10 Tomorrow, When London Publishing Ended

1 Douglas Stewart, interview with Suzanne Lunney, 21 March 1975, TRC 336, National Library of Australia.
2 Alec Bolton, interview with Heather Rusden, 11 October 1996–7 November 1996, TRC 3523, National Library of Australia.
3 Craig Munro, 'Case-Study: A&R's Takeover Crisis', in *A History of the Book in Australia 1946–2005: Paper Empires*, ed. Craig Munro and Robyn Sheahan-Bright (St Lucia: University of Queensland Press, 2006), 15. George Ferguson, however, does not mention this in a 1975 interview when questioned about Walter Burns. George Ferguson, interview with Suzanne Lunney, 11 May 1976, TRC 452, National Library of Australia, 59.
4 Regarding Burns' appointment as managing director, see George Ferguson to Barry Rowland, 5 February 1960, MSS 3269/648 ML; Craig Munro, 'A&R's Takeover'; and 'Bringing the Pirates on Board: The Battles for Angus and Robertson', in Jacqueline Kent, *A Certain Style: Beatrice Davis A Literary Life* (Camberwell, Victoria: Penguin, 2001), 222–36.
5 George Ferguson to Barry Rowland, 12 August 1959, MSS 3269/647 ML.
6 A 'bridge-head' is a military fortification that protects the end of a bridge that is closest to the enemy. Hector MacQuarrie to George Ferguson, 19 March 1958, MSS 3269/449 ML.
7 Richard Hauser, Institute for Group and Society Development, to Stanley Amor, 20 February 1961, MSS 3269/19 ML.
8 George Ferguson to Hector MacQuarrie, 21 February 1958, MSS 3269/449 ML.
9 George Ferguson to Hector MacQuarrie, 26 November 1958, MSS 3269/449 ML.
10 George Ferguson to Hector MacQuarrie, 21 February 1958, MSS 3269/449 ML.
11 George Ferguson to Hector MacQuarrie, 2 March 1960 MSS 3269/449 ML.
12 Hector MacQuarrie to George Ferguson, 17 March 1960, MSS 3269/449 ML.
13 Walter Harrap to George Ferguson, 15 February 1966, MSS 3269/322 ML.
14 Walter Burns, 'A. & R. In London', letter to the financial editor, *Sydney Morning Herald*, 24 November 1960.
15 Allan Swain to Richard Hauser, 13 May 1960, MSS 3269/19 ML.
16 George Ferguson to Hector MacQuarrie, 21 June 1957, MSS 3269/448 ML.
17 George Ferguson to RE Aubrey, 18 March 1958, MSS 3269/646 ML.
18 Hector MacQuarrie to George Ferguson, 14 November 1957, MSS 3269/448 ML.
19 George Ferguson to Hector MacQuarrie, 28 February 1957, MSS 3269/448 ML.
20 'Overseas Production', Paul Tracy to George Ferguson, 30 September 1959, MSS 3269/745 ML.
21 George Ferguson to Hector MacQuarrie, 7 November 1957, MSS 3269/448 ML.
22 George Ferguson to Barry Rowland, 29 January 1955, MSS 3269/645 ML Independent comparisons by a *Sydney Morning Herald* journalist between Australian and English prices for the same 1954 edition of a British title singled out the Australian price as being 'needlessly high', though not without a reasonable attempt at explaining import overheads which contributed to inflated prices in Australia. 'Are Prices Fixed Needlessly High on Imported Books?', *Sydney Morning Herald*, 26 June 1954.
23 George Ferguson to Hector MacQuarrie, 28 February 1957, MSS 3269/448 ML.
24 The original quote is that 'it may be the fate of countries shaped by diasporas to produce their own diaspora'. Stephen Alomes, 'Colonial to Global: Paradoxes of Expatriation in Australia's

Diasporic Story', in *Diaspora: The Australasian Experience*, ed. Cynthia vanden Driesen and Ralph Crane (New Delhi: Prestige Books, 2006), 135.
25 George Ferguson to Hector MacQuarrie, 23 February 1955, MSS 3269/446 ML.
26 George Ferguson to Barry Rowland, 29 January 1955, MSS 3269/645 ML.
27 George Ferguson to Barry Rowland, 29 January 1955, MSS 3269/645 ML.
28 R. E. Barker and G. R. Davis, eds, *Books Are Different: An Account of the Defence of the Net Book Agreement before the Restrictive Practices Court in 1962* (London: Macmillan, 1966), 472.
29 George Ferguson to Barry Rowland, 29 January 1955, MSS 3269/645 ML.
30 Hector MacQuarrie to George Ferguson, 8 February 1955, MSS 3269/446 ML.
31 Barry Rowland to George Ferguson, 23 March 1960, MSS 3269/648 ML.
32 George Ferguson to Hector MacQuarrie, 16 February 1955, MSS 3269/446 ML.
33 'Are Prices Fixed Needlessly High on Imported Books?', *Sydney Morning Herald*, 26 June 1954.
34 Hector MacQuarrie to George Ferguson, 8 February 1955, MSS 3269/446 ML.
35 George Ferguson to Barry Rowland, 4 February 1959, MSS 3269/647 ML.
36 Barry Rowland to George Ferguson, 2 April 1959, MSS 3269/647 ML.
37 George Ferguson to Barry Rowland, 4 February 1959, MSS 3269/647 ML.
38 Barry Rowland to George Ferguson, 2 April 1959, MSS 3269/647 ML.
39 George Ferguson to Barry Rowland, 14 April 1959, MSS 3269/647 ML.
40 Barry Rowland to George Ferguson, 10 April 1959, MSS 3269/647 ML.
41 George Ferguson to Barry Rowland, 14 April 1959, MSS 3269/647 ML.
42 George Ferguson to Barry Rowland, 21 April 1960, MSS 3269/648 ML.
43 See *Table H: Summary of London office expenses 1961* in the Figures and Tables.
44 George Ferguson to Barry Rowland, 23 December 1957, MSS 3269/646 ML.
45 Richard Hauser, Institute for Group and Society Development, to Stanley Amor, 20 February 1961, MSS 3269/19 ML.
46 Hector MacQuarrie, 'A. and R.'s London Publishing', letter to the financial editor, *Sydney Morning Herald*, 23 November 1960.
47 Neil James, 'Spheres of Influence: Angus and Robertson and Australian Literature from the Thirties to the Sixties' (PhD diss., unpublished, University of Sydney, 2000), 262.
48 George Ferguson to Hector MacQuarrie, 24 November 1960, MSS 3269/449 ML. See also Walter Burns, 'A. & R. In London', letter to the financial editor, *Sydney Morning Herald*, 24 November 1960.
49 George Ferguson to Stanley Unwin, 3 January 1961, MSS 3269/10 ML.
50 George Ferguson to Hector MacQuarrie, 21 February 1958, MSS 3269/449 ML.
51 Hector MacQuarrie to George Ferguson, 19 June 1956, MSS 3269/447 ML.
52 Hector MacQuarrie to George Ferguson, 19 June 1956, MSS 3269/447 ML.
53 George Ferguson to Hector MacQuarrie, 7 December 1956, MSS 3269/447 ML.
54 George Ferguson to Barry Rowland, 21 December 1956, MSS 3269/646 ML.
55 George Ferguson to Barry Rowland, 30 April 1957, MSS 3269/646 ML.
56 George Ferguson to Hector MacQuarrie, 30 April 1957, MSS 3269/448 ML.
57 Hector MacQuarrie to George Ferguson, 14 November 1957, MSS 3269/448 ML.
58 Hector MacQuarrie to George Ferguson, telegram, 20 June 1957, MSS 3269/448 ML.
59 George Ferguson to Hector MacQuarrie, 21 June 1957, MSS 3269/448 ML.
60 George Ferguson to Barry Rowland, 23 December 1957, MSS 3269/646 ML.
61 George Ferguson (from the London office) to R. W. D. Delucey, 1 September 1958, MSS 3269/646 ML.
62 See *Table B: London office sales annual income* in the Figures and Tables.
63 George Ferguson (from the London office) to Paul Tracy, 23 August 1958, MSS 3269/745 ML.
64 George Ferguson to Hector MacQuarrie, 21 February 1958, MSS 3269/449 ML.
65 See *Table B: London office sales annual income* in the Figures and Tables.
66 George Ferguson to Hector MacQuarrie, 19 March 1958, MSS 3269/449 ML.

67 George Ferguson to Hector MacQuarrie, 21 February 1958, MSS 3269/449 ML.
68 Barry Rowland to George Ferguson, 29 June 1959, MSS 3269/647 ML.
69 George Ferguson to Hector MacQuarrie, 8 September 1959, MSS 3269/449 ML.
70 George Ferguson to Hector MacQuarrie, 8 September 1959, MSS 3269/449 ML.
71 George Ferguson (from the London office) to Paul Tracy, 23 August 1958, MSS 3269/745 ML.
72 Hector MacQuarrie to George Ferguson, 5 March 1958, MSS 3269/449 ML.
73 Hector MacQuarrie to George Ferguson, 5 March 1958, MSS 3269/449 ML.
74 Hector MacQuarrie to George Ferguson, 5 March 1958, MSS 3269/449 ML.
75 George Ferguson to Hector MacQuarrie, 19 March 1958, MSS 3269/449 ML.
76 George Ferguson (from the London office) to R. W. D. Delucey, 1 September 1958, MSS 3269/646 ML.
77 George Ferguson to Hector MacQuarrie, 21 February 1958, MSS 3269/449 ML.
78 Barry Rowland to George Ferguson, 29 June 1959, MSS 3269/647 ML.
79 George Ferguson (from the London office) to R. W. D. Delucey, 25 July 1958, MSS 3269/646 ML.
80 See *Table E: Panther Books sales for paperback editions of 'Operation London' titles* in the Figures and Tables.
81 Barry Rowland to George Ferguson, 2 April 1959, MSS 3269/647 ML.
82 George Ferguson to Barry Rowland, 14 April 1959, MSS 3269/647 ML.
83 George Ferguson to Hector MacQuarrie, 6 April 1959, MSS 3269/449 ML.
84 George Ferguson to Barry Rowland, 7 July 1959, MSS 3269/647 ML.
85 George Ferguson to Hector MacQuarrie, 4 December 1959, MSS 3269/449 ML.
86 Richard Hauser, 'A. & R. Ltd. London: Sales & Publishing Department', MSS 3269/19 ML.
87 Richard Hauser, 'A. & R. Ltd. London: Sales & Publishing Department', MSS 3269/19 ML.
88 George Ferguson to Hector MacQuarrie, 4 December 1959, MSS 3269/449 ML.
89 George Ferguson to Hector MacQuarrie, 10 February 1958, MSS 3269/449 ML.
90 George Ferguson to Barry Rowland, 7 March 1958, MSS 3269/646 ML.
91 George Ferguson to Hector MacQuarrie, 7 March 1958, MSS 3269/449 ML.
92 George Ferguson (in London) to Colin Roderick, 1 July 1958, MSS 3269/19 ML.
93 George Ferguson to Hector MacQuarrie, 7 March 1958, MSS 3269/449 ML.
94 George Ferguson to Hector MacQuarrie, 7 March 1958, MSS 3269/449 ML.
95 Hector MacQuarrie to George Ferguson, 7 May 1958, MSS 3269/449 ML.
96 George Ferguson to A. A. Ritchie, 1 July 1958, MSS 3269/19 ML.
97 George Ferguson to Hector MacQuarrie, 19 December 1957, MSS 3269/448 ML.
98 George Ferguson to Paul Tracy, 1 September 1958, MSS 3269/745 ML.
99 Hector MacQuarrie to George Ferguson, 7 May 1958, MSS 3269/449 ML.
100 Hector MacQuarrie to George Ferguson, 7 May 1958, MSS 3269/449 ML.
101 John Feather, *A History of British Publishing* (London: Routledge, 1988), 201.
102 George Ferguson to Barry Rowland and Hector MacQuarrie, 5 February 1960, MSS 3269/648 ML.
103 George Ferguson to Barry Rowland and Hector MacQuarrie, 5 February 1960, MSS 3269/648 ML.
104 George Ferguson to Hector MacQuarrie, 8 September 1959, MSS 3269/449 ML.
105 George Ferguson to Barry Rowland, 24 February 1960, MSS 3269/648 ML.
106 George Ferguson to Barry Rowland, 4 December 1959, MSS 3269/647 ML.
107 George Ferguson to Barry Rowland, 21 April 1960, MSS 3269/648 ML.
108 George Ferguson to Hector MacQuarrie, 2 March 1960, MSS 3269/449 ML.
109 George Ferguson to Barry Rowland, 4 December 1959, MSS 3269/647 ML.
110 George Ferguson to Barry Rowland, 24 February 1960, MSS 3269/648 ML.
111 Walter Burns, 'A. & R. in London', Letter to the financial editor, *Sydney Morning Herald*, 24 November 1960.

112 George Ferguson to Hector MacQuarrie, 2 March 1960, MSS 3269/449 ML.
113 George Ferguson to Hector MacQuarrie, 27 June 1956, MSS 3269/447 ML.
114 George Ferguson to Barry Rowland, 31 March 1960, MSS 3269/648 ML.
115 George Ferguson, 'Publishing in London by Angus & Robertson Limited: A Paper for the guidance of the Board', unpublished, August 1970, MSS 3269/34 ML.
116 George Ferguson to Barry Rowland, 21 April 1960, MSS 3269/648 ML.
117 George Ferguson to Barry Rowland, 21 April 1960, MSS 3269/648 ML.
118 George Ferguson to Barry Rowland, 21 April 1960, MSS 3269/648 ML.
119 Richard Hauser to Walter Burns, 18 May 1960, MSS 3269/19 ML.
120 Richard Hauser to Stanley Amor, 20 February 1961, MSS 3269/19 ML.
121 Richard Hauser to Walter Burns, 18 May 1960, MSS 3269/19 ML; and Richard Hauser to Walter Burns, 26 May 1960, MSS 3269/19 ML.
122 Richard Hauser to Walter Burns, 18 May 1960, MSS 3269/19 ML.
123 Richard Hauser to Walter Burns, 26 May 1960, MSS 3269/19 ML.
124 Richard Hauser to Walter Burns, 18 May 1960, MSS 3269/19 ML.
125 Richard Hauser to Walter Burns, 26 May 1960, MSS 3269/19 ML.
126 Richard Hauser to Walter Burns, 26 May 1960, MSS 3269/19 ML.
127 Richard Hauser to Walter Burns, 26 May 1960, MSS 3269/19 ML.
128 Richard Hauser to Walter Burns, 18 May 1960, MSS 3269/19 ML.
129 Walter Burns, 'A. & R. in London', Letter to the financial editor, *Sydney Morning Herald*, 24 November 1960.
130 Richard Hauser to Walter Burns, 18 May 1960, MSS 3269/19 ML.
131 Allan Swain to Richard Hauser, 13 May 1960, MSS 3269/19 ML.
132 Richard Hauser to Walter Burns, 26 May 1960, MSS 3269/19 ML;
133 Richard Hauser to Walter Burns, 26 May 1960, MSS 3269/19 ML;
134 Richard Hauser to Walter Burns, 26 May 1960, MSS 3269/19 ML;
135 Richard Hauser to Walter Burns, 26 May 1960, MSS 3269/19 ML;
136 George Ferguson to Stanley Unwin, 3 January 1961, MSS 3269/10 ML.
137 George Ferguson, 'Publishing in London by Angus & Robertson Limited: A Paper for the guidance of the Board', unpublished, August 1970, MSS 3269/34 ML.
138 George Ferguson to Walter Harrap, 16 November 1960, MSS 3269/322 ML.
139 Richard Hauser to Walter Burns, 18 May 1960, MSS 3269/19 ML.
140 George Ferguson to Walter Butcher, 27 July 1966, MSS 3269/26 ML.
141 The 1956 figure.
142 Richard Hauser to Walter Burns, 18 May 1960, MSS 3269/19 ML.
143 George Ferguson to Cliff Rust, 10 December 1964, MSS 3269/22 ML.
144 Angus & Robertson, *Report of the Directors*, NQ 332, 0994 ANG, National Library of Australia, 1959.
145 George Ferguson to Hector MacQuarrie, 4 December 1959, MSSW 3269/449 ML.
146 Hector MacQuarrie to George Ferguson, 19 March 1958, MSS 3269/449 ML.
147 George Ferguson to Hector MacQuarrie, 19 December 1957, MSS 3269/446 ML.
148 George Ferguson to Stanley Unwin, 3 January 1961, MSS 3269/10 ML.
149 George Ferguson to Stanley Unwin, 3 January 1961, MSS 3269/10 ML.
150 Walter Harrap to George Ferguson, 22 November 1960, MSS 3269/322 ML.
151 George Ferguson to Walter Harrap, 3 January 1961, MSS 3269/322 ML.
152 George Ferguson to Desmond Briggs, 4 July 1961, MSS 3269/19 ML.
153 George Ferguson to Barry Rowland, 20 December 1961, MSS 3269/648 ML.

Chapter 11 A House is Rebuilt

1 Walter Butcher to George Ferguson, 1 May 1962, MSS 3269/20 ML.
2 Hector MacQuarrie to George Ferguson, 24 October 1949, MSS 3269/440 ML.

3 George Ferguson to Walter Harrap, 18 October 1962, MSS 3269/322 ML.
4 George Ferguson to Hector MacQuarrie, 21 March 1963, MSS 3269/449 ML.
5 Walter Harrap to George Ferguson, 25 July 1961, MSS 3269/322 ML.
6 George Ferguson to Dwye Evans, 4 July 1961, MSS 3269/330 ML.
7 George Ferguson to Hector MacQuarrie, 21 March 1963, MSS 3269/449 ML.
8 George Ferguson to Hector MacQuarrie, 21 March 1963, MSS 3269/449 ML.
9 Helen Frizell, 'British Hold on Book Publishing', *Sydney Morning Herald*, 31 May 1969.
10 Walter Butcher to George Ferguson, 2 July 1964, MSS 3269/22 ML.
11 George Ferguson to Ron Barker (Publishers Association, UK), 23 January 1962, MSS 3269/557 ML.
12 George Ferguson to Sam Ure Smith, 11 January 1962, MSS 3269/20 ML.
13 George Ferguson to Barry Rowland, 2 May 1962, MSS 3269/648 ML.
14 George Ferguson to Barry Rowland, 23 October 1963, MSS 3269/648 ML.
15 Walter Butcher to George Ferguson, 2 July 1964, MSS 3239/22 ML.
16 George Ferguson to Brian Clouston (Jacaranda Press, Brisbane), 4 January 1962, MSS 3269/20 ML.
17 George Ferguson to Walter Butcher, 23 February 1963, MSS 3269/20 ML.
18 Walter Butcher to George Ferguson, 2 July 1964, MSS 3269/22 ML.
19 George Ferguson to Walter Butcher, 10 June 1965, MSS 3269/23 ML.
20 George Ferguson to Stanley Amor, 16 March 1961, MSS 3269/19 ML.
21 George Ferguson to Walter Butcher, 23 February 1962, MSS 3269/20 ML.
22 George Ferguson to Walter Butcher, 18 March 1964, MSS 3269/22 ML.
23 George Ferguson to Walter Butcher, 16 January 1962, MSS 3269/20 ML.
24 George Ferguson to Arthur Brooker, 22 May 1961, MSS 3269/19 ML.
25 George Ferguson to Barry Rowland, 23 October 1963, MSS 3269/648 ML.
26 George Ferguson to Cliff Rust, 10 December 1964, MSS 3269/22 ML.
27 Walter Butcher to George Ferguson, 18 December 1963, MSS 3269/22 ML.
28 Cliff Rust to George Ferguson, 25 February 1964, MSS 3269/22 ML.
29 George Ferguson to Cliff Rust, 30 April 1964, MSS 3269/22 ML.
30 George Ferguson to Cliff Rust, 17 July 1964, MSS 3269/22 ML.
31 Sam Ure Smith to John Brown, Publishers Association, London, draft, circa November 1963, MSS 3269/106 ML.
32 Sam Ure Smith to Walter Butcher, 26 May 1964, MSS 3269/22 ML.
33 O'Neil quoted in Helen Frizell, 'British Hold on Book Publishing', *Sydney Morning Herald*, 31 May 1969.
34 George Ferguson to Hector MacQuarrie, 14 December 1951, MSS 3269/442 ML.
35 Hector MacQuarrie to George Ferguson, 29 March 1950, MSS 3269/440 ML.
36 George Ferguson to Walter Butcher, 11 July 1963, MSS 3269/21 ML.
37 George Ferguson to Walter Butcher, 20 July 1966, MSS 3269/26 ML.
38 George Ferguson to Walter Butcher, 5 April 1968, MSS 3269/31 ML.
39 Walter Butcher to George Ferguson, 27 July 1966, MSS 3269/26 ML.
40 John Brown, Publishers Association, to Sam Ure Smith, Australian Book Publishers Association, 1 January 1964, MSS 3269/106 ML.
41 Andrew Fabinyi, F. W. Cheshire Ltd, to Sam Ure Smith, Australian Book Publishers Association, 14 February 1964, MSS 3269/106 ML.
42 Andrew Fabinyi, F. W. Cheshire Ltd, to Sam Ure Smith, Australian Book Publishers Association, 14 February 1964, MSS 3269/106 ML.
43 John Abernethy to Alec Bolton, 2 February 1967, MSS 3269/28 ML.
44 George Ferguson to Walter Butcher, 30 April 1964, MSS 3269/22 ML.
45 Walter Butcher to George Ferguson, 6 July 1964, MSS 3239/22 ML.
46 Hector MacQuarrie to George Ferguson, 29 March 1950, MSS 3269/440 ML.

47 George Ferguson to Stanley Amor, 28 March 1961, MSS 3269/19 ML.
48 Hector MacQuarrie to Stanley Rinehart, 4 November 1954, MSS 3269/445 ML.
49 George Ferguson to Sam Ure Smith, 11 January 1962, MSS 3269/20 ML.
50 Walter Butcher to George Ferguson, 2 July 1964, MSS 3269/22 ML.
51 George Ferguson to Walter Harrap, 3 January 1961, MSS 3269/322 ML.
52 Ron Barker and Walter Harrap had much advice to offer too. See Ron Barker to George Ferguson, 11 January 1961, MSS 3269/557; Walter Harrap to George Ferguson, 13 January 1961, MSS 3269/322 ML; and George Ferguson to Walter Harrap, 3 March 1961, MSS 3269/322 ML.
53 George Ferguson to Walter Harrap, 3 January 1961, MSS 3269/322 ML.
54 George Ferguson to Stanley Amor, 28 March 1961, MSS 3269/19 ML.
55 George Ferguson to Walter Harrap, 3 March 1961, MSS 3269/322 ML.
56 George Ferguson to Walter Harrap, 3 March 1961, MSS 3269/322 ML.
57 Cliff Rust to George Ferguson, 25 February 1964, MSS 3269/22 ML.
58 George Ferguson to Sanford J. Greenburger, New York, 21 February 1964, MSS 3269/22 ML.
59 Walter Harrap to George Ferguson, 13 January 1961, MSS 3269/322 ML.
60 George Ferguson to Walter Harrap, 3 January 1961, MSS 3269/322 ML.
61 George Ferguson to John Ferguson, 28 August 1961, MSS 3269/19 ML.
62 George Ferguson to Walter Harrap, 3 March 1961, MSS 3269/322 ML.
63 George Ferguson to Walter Harrap, 16 November 1960, MSS 3269/322 ML.
64 George Ferguson to Arthur Brooker, 22 May 1961, MSS 3269/19 ML.
65 George Ferguson to Barry Rowland, 2 May 1962, MSS 3269/648 ML.
66 George Ferguson to Stanley Amor, 28 March 1961, MSS 3269/19 ML.
67 'List of Stock Required from Sydney by A. & R. London', Walter Butcher to George Ferguson, 10 February 1961, MSS 3269/19 ML.
68 George Ferguson to Walter Butcher, 29 August 1961, MSS 3269/19 ML.
69 George Ferguson to Hector MacQuarrie, 28 August 1961, MSS 3269/449 ML.
70 Cliff Rust to George Ferguson, 11 August 1964, MSS 3269/22 ML.
71 George Ferguson to Walter Harrap, 3 March 1961, MSS 3269/322 ML.
72 Walter Butcher to George Ferguson, 24 July 1961, MSS 3269/19 ML.
73 Alec Bolton to George Ferguson, 18 March 1968, MSS 3269/31 ML.
74 George Ferguson to Hector MacQuarrie, 28 August 1961, MSS 3269/449 ML.
75 Walter Harrap to George Ferguson, 13 January 1961, MSS 3269/322 ML.
76 Walter Harrap to George Ferguson, 13 January 1961, MSS 3269/322 ML.
77 Walter Harrap to George Ferguson, 13 January 1961, MSS 3269/322 ML.
78 Walter Harrap to George Ferguson, 13 January 1961, MSS 3269/322 ML.
79 Walter Harrap to George Ferguson, 13 January 1961, MSS 3269/322 ML.
80 George Ferguson to Alan White, Publishers Association, London, 15 April 1955, MSS 3269/556 ML.
81 George Ferguson to John Ferguson, 22 September 1961, MSS 3269/19 ML.
82 George Ferguson to Walter Butcher, 10 June 1965, MSS 3269/23 ML.
83 George Ferguson to John Ferguson, 28 August 1961, MSS 3269/19 ML.
84 George Ferguson to Walter Butcher, 14 November 1961, MSS 3269/19 ML.
85 John Ferguson to George Ferguson, 13 October 1961, MSS 3269/19 ML.
86 George Ferguson to John Ferguson, 23 October 1961, MSS 3269/19 ML.
87 Walter Butcher to George Ferguson, 27 October 1961, MSS 3269/19 ML.
88 George Ferguson to Walter Butcher, 14 November 1961, MSS 3269/19 ML.
89 George Ferguson to Walter Butcher, 23 February 1962, MSS 3269/20 ML.
90 George Ferguson to Walter Butcher, 16 January 1962, MSS 3269/20 ML.
91 George Ferguson to Walter Butcher, 23 February 1962, MSS 3269/20 ML.

92 George Ferguson to Walter Butcher, 23 February 1962, MSS 3269/20 ML.
93 George Ferguson to Walter Butcher, 14 February 1964, MSS 3269/22 ML.
94 Barry Rowland to George Ferguson, 10 December 1961, MSS 3269/648 ML.
95 George Ferguson to Walter Butcher, 10 June 1965, MSS 3269/23 ML.
96 Walter Butcher to George Ferguson, 23 November 1962, MSS 3269/20 ML.
97 George Ferguson to Walter Butcher, 23 January 1963, MSS 3269/20 ML.
98 John Ferguson to George Ferguson, 17 January 1962, MSS 3269/20 ML.
99 George Ferguson to Walter Butcher, 6 December 1962, MSS 3269/20 ML.
100 George Ferguson to Walter Butcher, 23 February 1962, MSS 3269/20 ML.
101 George Ferguson to Barry Rowland, 2 May 1962, MSS 3269/648 ML.
102 George Ferguson to Walter Butcher, 10 April 1962, MSS 3269/20 ML.
103 George Ferguson to Cliff Rust, 11 December 1961, MSS 3269/19 ML.
104 George Ferguson to Stanley Amor, 28 March 1961, MSS 3269/19 ML.
105 Robert Haupt, 'The Book Rebellion', *Age*, 5 November 1988.
106 George Ferguson to Stanley Amor, 28 March 1961, MSS 3269/19 ML.
107 George Ferguson to Walter Butcher, 23 February 1962, MSS 3269/20 ML.
108 John Ferguson to Ian Novak, Ian Novak Publishing, Sydney, 6 September 1961, MSS 3269/19 ML.
109 George Ferguson to Walter Butcher, 23 October 1961, MSS 3269/19 ML.
110 George Ferguson to Walter Butcher, 14 February 1964, MSS 3269/22 ML.
111 Walter Butcher to George Ferguson, 1 May 1962, MSS 3269/20 ML.
112 Walter Butcher to George Ferguson, 16 October 1961, MSS 3269/19 ML.
113 George Ferguson to Walter Butcher, 10 April 1962, MSS 3269/20 ML.
114 John Ferguson to Ian Novak, Ian Novak Publishing, Sydney, 6 September 1961, MSS 3269/19 ML.
115 Walter Butcher to Don Hardy, 1 March 1968, MSS 3269/31 ML.
116 George Ferguson to Walter Butcher, 23 February 1962, MSS 3269/20 ML.
117 'Colonial Attitude of U.K. Resented', *Sydney Morning Herald*, 26 September 1963.
118 Sam Ure Smith to John Brown, 18 October 1963, MSS 3269/106 ML.
119 Sam Ure Smith to Walter Butcher, 26 May 1964, MSS 3269/22 ML.
120 Hector MacQuarrie to George Ferguson, 23 September 1953, MSS 3269/444 ML.
121 Sydney George (Sam) Ure Smith, interview with Hazel de Berg, 7 December 1976, ORAL TRC 1/980, National Library of Australia.
122 Sam Ure Smith to John Brown, 15 November 1963, MSS 3269/106 ML.
123 Sam Ure Smith to John Brown, 15 November 1963, MSS 3269/106 ML.
124 Andrew Fabinyi to Sam Ure Smith, 7 October 1963, MSS 3269/106 ML.
125 Sam Ure Smith to John Brown, 18 October 1963, MSS 3269/106 ML.
126 Sam Ure Smith to John Brown, 18 October 1963, MSS 3269/106 ML.
127 'Colonial Attitude of U.K. Resented', *Sydney Morning Herald*, 26 September 1963.
128 John Feather, *A History of British Publishing* (London: Routledge, 1988), 192.
129 Sam Ure Smith to John Brown, 15 November 1963, MSS 3269/106 ML.
130 John Brown to Sam Ure Smith, 10 July 1964, MSS 3269/106 ML.
131 John Brown to Sam Ure Smith, 10 July 1964, MSS 3269/106 ML.
132 John Brown to Sam Ure Smith, 10 July 1964, MSS 3269/106 ML.
133 John Brown to Sam Ure Smith, 10 July 1964, MSS 3269/106 ML.
134 R. C. Gowers, Publishers Association (UK), Members Circular, 26 June 1964, MSS 3269/106 ML.
135 Sam Ure Smith to Walter Butcher, 26 May 1964, MSS 3269/22 ML.
136 Walter Butcher to George Ferguson, 2 July 1964, MSS 3269/22 ML.
137 Sam Ure Smith to Walter Butcher, 26 May 1964, MSS 3269/22 ML.
138 George Ferguson to Walter Butcher, 18 March 1964, MSS 3269/22 ML.

139 Sam Ure Smith to Walter Butcher, 26 May 1964, MSS 3269/22 ML.
140 George Ferguson to Walter Butcher, 18 March 1964, MSS 3269/22 ML.
141 Sam Ure Smith to Walter Butcher, 26 May 1964, MSS 3269/22 ML.
142 Walter Butcher to George Ferguson, 2 July 1964, MSS 3269/22 ML.
143 George Ferguson to Walter Butcher, 11 July 1963, MSS 3269/21 ML.
144 George Ferguson to Walter Butcher, 17 January 1966, MSS 3269/24 ML.
145 George Ferguson to Walter Butcher, 25 August 1969, MSS 3269/34 ML.
146 Alec Bolton to George Ferguson, 4 December 1968, MSS 3269/32 ML.
147 Walter Butcher to George Ferguson, 11 March 1968, MSS 3269/31 ML.
148 Walter Butcher to George Ferguson, 11 March 1968, MSS 3269/31 ML.
149 George Ferguson to Bill Treble, 6 January 1967, MSS 3269/28 ML.
150 John Ferguson to Walter Butcher, 25 May 1965, MSS 3269/23 ML.
151 George Ferguson to Brian Batsford, 20 January 1966, MSS 3269/131 ML.
152 John Abernethy to Alec Bolton, 17 March 1967, MSS 3269/28 ML.
153 John Abernethy to Alec Bolton, 17 March 1967, MSS 3269/28 ML.
154 Alec Bolton to George Ferguson, 6 June 1968, MSS 3269/31 ML.
155 George Ferguson to Walter Butcher, 2 August 1966, MSS 3269/26 ML.
156 Alec Bolton to George Ferguson, 6 June 1968, MSS 3269/31 ML.
157 Alec Bolton to George Ferguson, 6 June 1968, MSS 3269/31 ML.
158 Alec Bolton to George Ferguson, 18 March 1968, MSS 3269/31 ML.
159 George Ferguson to Walter Butcher, 5 March 1965, MSS 3269/23 ML.
160 George Ferguson to Sam Ure Smith, 11 January 1962, MSS 3269/20 ML.
161 Stephen Alomes, 'Colonial to Global: Paradoxes of Expatriation in Australia's Diasporic Story', in *Diaspora: The Australasian Experience*, ed. Cynthia vanden Driesen and Ralph Crane (New Delhi: Prestige Books, 2006), 144.
162 Alomes, 'Colonial to Global', 137.
163 'The Frankfurt Book Fair: A Memorandum by the Export Research Committee', The Publishers Association, 14 December 1955, MSS 3269/556 ML.
164 George Ferguson, interview with Suzanne Lunney, 11 May 1976, TRC 452, National Library of Australia, 57.
165 George Ferguson, interview with Suzanne Lunney, 11 May 1976, TRC 452, National Library of Australia, 57.
166 For example, 'Frankfurt Book Fair, 18–23 October 1961', members' circular, Publishers Association, 18 April 1961, MSS 3269/19 ML.
167 Hector MacQuarrie to J. S. Meulenhoff, 16 September 1952, MSS 3269/443 ML.
168 Richard Hauser to Walter Burns, 18 May 1960, MSS 3269/19 ML.
169 Stanley Amor to George Ferguson, 24 April 1961, MSS 3269/19 ML.
170 George Ferguson to John Ferguson, 28 August 1961, MSS 3269/19 ML.
171 William St Clair, *The Reading Nation in the Romantic Period* (New York: Cambridge University Press, 2004), 423.
172 George Ferguson to John Ferguson, 28 August 1961, MSS 3269/19 ML.
173 John Ferguson to George Ferguson, 14 November 1961, MSS 3269/19 ML.
174 John Ferguson to George Ferguson, 14 November 1961, MSS 3269/19 ML.
175 George Ferguson to John Ferguson, 28 August 1961, MSS 3269/19 ML.
176 R. E. Barker to George Ferguson, 17 January 1962, MSS 3269/557 ML.
177 John Ferguson to George Ferguson, 12 September 1962, MSS 3269/20 ML.
178 George Ferguson to John Ferguson, 8 October 1962, MSS 3269/20 ML.
179 George Ferguson to Walter Butcher, 4 January 1963, MSS 3269/20 ML.
180 Walter Butcher to George Ferguson, 25 September 1962, MSS 3269/20 ML.
181 George Ferguson to Judy Fisher, 24 May 1962, MSS 3269/20 ML.
182 George Ferguson to A. A. Ritchie, 1 July 1958, MSS 3269/19 ML.

183 Paul Tracy, 'Notes on a Discussion of the Far East Sales Territory with Thomas Brash', 18 September 1958, MSS 3269/745 ML.
184 Paul Tracy, 'Notes on a Discussion of the Far East Sales Territory with Thomas Brash', 18 September 1958, MSS 3269/745 ML.
185 George Ferguson to Colin Roderick, 1 July 1958, MSS 3269/19 ML.
186 John Ferguson to George Ferguson, 17 January 1962, MSS 3269/20 ML.
187 Desmond Briggs to Brian Lamberth, 26 October 1959, MSS 3269/647 ML.
188 Walter Butcher to George Ferguson, 9 March 1962, MSS 3269/20 ML.
189 Contract between Angus & Robertson, London, and Leo Beek, 30 January 1952, MSS 3269/443 ML.
190 Hector MacQuarrie to George Ferguson, 15 August 1952, MSS 3269/443 ML.
191 Barry Rowland to George Ferguson, 23 February 1959, MSS 3269/19 ML.
192 Walter Butcher to George Ferguson, 2 July 1964, MSS 3269/22 ML.
193 George Ferguson to Walter Butcher, 18 March 1964, MSS 3269/22 ML.
194 George Ferguson, interview with Suzanne Lunney, 11 May 1976, TRC 452, National Library of Australia, 38.
195 Walter Butcher to George Ferguson, 2 July 1964, MSS 3269/22 ML.
196 Walter Butcher to George Ferguson, 2 July 1964, MSS 3269/22 ML.
197 John Abernethy to Alec Bolton, 23 January 1967, MSS 3269/28 ML. David Higham represented Denzil Batchelor, Donald Bradman, Nancy Cato, Charmian Clift, Kay Dick, Pat Flower, Catherine Gaskin, James Gleeson, John Gunn, Rodney Hall, Keith Hancock, George Johnston, Christopher Koch, John McGhee, John Manifold, Phillip Grenville Mann, James Vance Marshall, R. G. Menzies, Charles Osborne, Mary Patchett and Geoff Taylor.
198 Walter Butcher to George Ferguson, 2 July 1964, MSS 3269/22 ML.
199 Graham Huggan, *Australian Literature: Postcolonialism, Racism, Transnationalism* (Oxford: Oxford University Press, 2007), 46. Huggan makes two observations regarding the search for foundational works in Australian literature, but, paraphrased here, these points can also apply to the search for foundational events in Australian publishing history.
200 Horace Bohmer Newman, New South Wales section, British Book Publishers' Representatives Association of Australia and New Zealand, in Tariff Board Australia, *Report of Evidence at Tariff Board Inquiries into Proposal of Duty on Books, Magazines and Fashion Plates Held in Adelaide, Brisbane, Sydney and Melbourne* (Melbourne: Australian Booksellers Association, 1930), 56.
201 Walter Harrap to George Ferguson, 13 January 1961, MSS 3269/322 ML.
202 Huggan, *Australian Literature*, 46.
203 George Ferguson to Walter Butcher, 28 September 1970, MSS 3269/34 ML.
204 Lars Jensen, *Unsettling Australia: Readings in Australian Cultural History* (New Delhi: Atlantic Publishers, 2005), 18.
205 George Ferguson to Walter Butcher, 5 March 1965, MSS 3269/22 ML.
206 Alec Bolton to George Ferguson, 25 April 1969, MSS 3269/33 ML.
207 Walter Butcher to John Ferguson, 29 November 1966, MSS 3269/27 ML.
208 George Ferguson to Stanley Unwin, 27 October 1967, MSS 3269/10 ML.
209 George Ferguson to Walter Butcher, 26 November 1969, MSS 3269/34 ML.
210 Walter Butcher to George Ferguson, 16 November 1969, MSS 3269/34 ML.

Chapter 12 The Hidden Parts of Publishing Fortune

1 George Ferguson to Alec Bolton, 16 May 1968, MSS 3269/31 ML.
2 George Ferguson to Walter Butcher, 18 February 1970, MSS 3269/34 ML.
3 George Ferguson to Alec Bolton, 14 January 1970, MSS 3269/34 ML.
4 George Ferguson to Walter Butcher, 18 February 1970, MSS 3269/34 ML.
5 Alec Bolton to George Ferguson, 31 December 1969, MSS 3269/34 ML.

6 George Ferguson to Walter Butcher, 18 February 1970, MSS 3269/34 ML.
7 Quoted in Walter Butcher to John Abernethy, 26 September 1969, MSS 3269/34 ML.
8 Walter Butcher to George Ferguson, 16 October 1969, MSS 3269/34 ML.
9 Walter Butcher to George Ferguson, 1 August 1969, MSS 3269/34 ML.
10 Walter Butcher to George Ferguson, 12 February 1970, MSS 3269/34 ML.
11 George Ferguson, 'Publishing in London by Angus & Robertson Limited: A Paper for the guidance of the Board', unpublished, August 1970, MSS 3269/34 ML.
12 George Ferguson to Walter Butcher, 18 February 1970, MSS 3269/34 ML.
13 Walter Burns, 'A. & R. in London', letter to the financial editor, *Sydney Morning Herald*, 24 November 1960.
14 George Ferguson to Alec Bolton, 14 January 1970, MSS 3269/34 ML.
15 George Ferguson to Walter Butcher, 18 February 1970, MSS 3269/34 ML.
16 George Ferguson to Alec Bolton, 14 January 1970, MSS 3269/34 ML.
17 George Ferguson to Hector MacQuarrie, 11 June 1968, MSS 3269/449 ML.
18 George Ferguson to Louis Lothian, 19 January 1971, MSS 3269/34 ML.
19 George Ferguson to Alec Bolton, 14 January 1970, MSS 3269/34 ML.
20 Ferguson, 'Publishing in London', MSS 3269/34 ML.
21 Ferguson, 'Publishing in London', MSS 3269/34 ML.
22 See Gavin Souter, 'A and R Signs Wizard of Oz', *Sydney Morning Herald*, 28 March 1972.
23 Alec Bolton, interview with Heather Rusden, 11 October 1996–7 November 1996, TRC 3523, National Library of Australia.
24 Sam Everingham, *Gordon Barton: Australia's Maverick Entrepreneur* (Crow's Nest: Allen & Unwin, 2009), 188. See also Gavin Souter, 'A and R Signs Wizard of Oz', *Sydney Morning Herald*, 28 March 1972.
25 George Ferguson to Alec Bolton, 21 September 1967, MSS 3269/30 ML.
26 Ferguson, 'Publishing in London', MSS 3269/34 ML.
27 Walter Butcher to George Ferguson, 16 October 1969, MSS 3269/34 ML.
28 Walter Butcher to George Ferguson, 11 March 1968, MSS 3269/31 ML.
29 Alec Bolton to George Ferguson, 7 October 1969, MSS 3269/34 ML.
30 Alec Bolton to George Ferguson, 7 October 1969, MSS 3269/34 ML.
31 George Ferguson to Alec Bolton, 7 August 1969, MSS 3269/34 ML.
32 George Ferguson to Walter Butcher, 26 November 1969, MSS 3269/34 ML.
33 George Ferguson to Walter Butcher and Alec Bolton, 16 February 1968, MSS 3269/31 ML.
34 George Ferguson to Walter Butcher, 29 March 1968, MSS 3279/31 ML.
35 George Ferguson to Walter Butcher, 29 March 1968, MSS 3279/31 ML.
36 George Ferguson, interview with Suzanne Lunney, 11 May 1976, TRC 452, National Library of Australia, 38.
37 George Ferguson to Walter Butcher, 26 November 1969, MSS 3269/34 ML.
38 Walter Butcher to George Ferguson, 16 October 1969, MSS 3269/34 ML.
39 George Ferguson to Walter Butcher, 26 November 1969, MSS 3269/34 ML.
40 'Percentage of Turnover', March 1968, MSS 3269/32 ML.
41 George Ferguson to Hector MacQuarrie, 11 June 1968, MSS 3269/449 ML.
42 George Ferguson to Hector MacQuarrie, 11 June 1968, MSS 3269/449 ML.
43 George Ferguson to Walter Butcher, 29 March 1968, MSS 3269/31 ML.
44 Walter Butcher to George Ferguson, 13 October 1966, MSS 3269/27 ML.
45 George Ferguson to Alec Bolton, 16 May 1968, MSS 3269/31 ML.
46 Walter Butcher to George Ferguson, 26 September 1967, MSS 3269/30 ML.
47 Hansard (United Kingdom), Commons Sitting of 21 November 1967, series 5 vol. 754, 907.
48 Hansard (United Kingdom), Commons Sitting of 21 November 1967, series 5 vol. 754, 908.
49 Annual Report and Notice of Annual General Meeting, Angus & Robertson Ltd (1968), 25 October 1968, NQ 322.0994 ANG, National Library of Australia.
50 Walter Butcher to George Ferguson, 16 October 1969, MSS 3269/34 ML.

51 Alec Bolton to George Ferguson, 31 December 1969, MSS 3269/34 ML.
52 George Ferguson to Hector MacQuarrie, 11 June 1968, MSS 3269/449 ML.
53 Ferguson, 'Publishing in London', MSS 3269/34 ML.
54 Ferguson, 'Publishing in London', MSS 3269/34 ML.
55 Hector MacQuarrie to Stanley Rinehart, 4 November 1954, MSS 3269/445 ML.
56 Walter Butcher to George Ferguson, 16 November 1969, MSS 3269/34 ML.
57 John Ferguson to Walter Butcher, 25 May 1965, MSS 3269/23 ML.
58 Walter Butcher to George Ferguson, 13 May 1965, MSS 3269/23 ML.
59 Walter Butcher to Alec Bolton, 19 July 1966, MSS 3269/26 ML.
60 Alec Bolton, interview with Heather Rusden, 11 October 1996–7 November 1996, TRC 3523, National Library of Australia.
61 Alec Bolton, interview with Heather Rusden, 11 October 1996–7 November 1996, TRC 3523, National Library of Australia.
62 Alec Bolton, interview with Heather Rusden, 11 October 1996–7 November 1996, TRC 3523, National Library of Australia.
63 George Ferguson to Walter Butcher, 7 December 1966, MSS 3269/27 ML.
64 George Ferguson to Walter Butcher, 2 October 1967, MSS 3269/30 ML.
65 Ferguson, 'Publishing in London', MSS 3269/34 ML.
66 W. J. Treble to George Ferguson, 18 December 1966, MSS 3269/27 ML.
67 George Ferguson to Walter Butcher, 2 August 1966, MSS 3269/26 ML.
68 Ferguson, 'Publishing in London', MSS 3269/34 ML.
69 George Ferguson to Alec Bolton, 16 May 1968, MSS 3269/31 ML.
70 George Ferguson to Alec Bolton, 21 September 1967, MSS 3269/30 ML.
71 Walter Butcher to George Ferguson, 12 January 1967, MSS 3269/28 ML.
72 George Ferguson to Walter Butcher, 10 June 1965, MSS 3269/23 ML.
73 George Ferguson to Walter Butcher, 10 June 1965, MSS 3269/23 ML.
74 Alec Bolton, interview with Heather Rusden, 11 October 1996–7 November 1996, TRC 3523, National Library of Australia.
75 Alec Bolton to George Ferguson, 6 June 1968, MSS 3269/31 ML.
76 Alec Bolton, interview with Heather Rusden, 11 October 1996–7 November 1996, TRC 3523, National Library of Australia.
77 Alec Bolton, interview with Heather Rusden, 11 October 1996–7 November 1996, TRC 3523, National Library of Australia.
78 Alec Bolton, interview with Heather Rusden, 11 October 1996–7 November 1996, TRC 3523, National Library of Australia.
79 Ferguson, "Publishing in London', MSS 3269/34 ML.
80 George Ferguson to Walter Butcher and Alec Bolton, 16 February 1968, MSS 3269/31 ML.
81 Ferguson, 'Publishing in London', MSS 3269/34 ML.
82 George Ferguson to Walter Butcher and Alec Bolton, 16 February 1968, MSS 3269/31 ML.
83 George Ferguson to Walter Butcher, 20 July 1966, MSS 3269/26 ML.
84 George Ferguson to Walter Butcher, 2 August 1966, MSS 3269/26 ML.
85 Walter Butcher to Don Hardy, 1 March 1968, MSS 3269/31 ML.
86 George Ferguson to Walter Butcher, 20 July 1966, MSS 3269/26 ML.
87 George Ferguson to Walter Butcher, 2 August 1966, MSS 3269/26 ML.
88 George Ferguson to Walter Butcher, 2 August 1966, MSS 3269/26 ML.
89 Walter Butcher to George Ferguson, 10 August 1967, MSS 3269/30 ML.
90 Walter Butcher to George Ferguson, 12 July 1966, MSS 3269/26 ML.
91 Walter Butcher to George Ferguson, 12 July 1966, MSS 3269/26 ML.
92 Walter Butcher to George Ferguson, 13 October 1966, MSS 3269/27 ML.
93 George Ferguson to Walter Butcher, 2 August 1966, MSS 3269/26 ML.
94 Walter Butcher to George Ferguson, 27 July 1966, MSS 3269/26 ML.
95 George Ferguson to Cliff Rust, 25 January 1967, MSS 3269/28 ML.

96 George Ferguson to Walter Butcher, 14 March 1968, MSS 3269/31 ML.
97 George Ferguson to Cliff Rust, 9 June 1967, MSS 3269/29 ML.
98 Alec Bolton to George Ferguson, 22 May 1967, MSS 3269/29 ML.
99 Walter Butcher to George Ferguson, 22 March 1968, MSS 3269/31 ML.
100 George Ferguson to Walter Butcher, 29 March 1968, MSS 3269/31 ML.
101 George Ferguson to Cliff Rust, 9 June 1967, MSS 3269/29 ML.
102 Walter Butcher to George Ferguson, 10 August 1967, MSS 3269/30 ML.
103 George Ferguson to Walter Butcher, 29 March 1968, MSS 3269/31 ML.
104 George Ferguson to Walter Butcher, 29 March 1968, MSS 3269/31 ML.
105 Cliff Rust to Don Hardy, 6 September 1968, MSS 3269/32 ML.
106 George Ferguson to Cliff Rust, 9 June 1967, MSS 3269/29 ML.
107 George Ferguson to Walter Butcher, 13 March 1968, MSS 3269/31 ML.
108 Ferguson, 'Publishing in London', MSS 3269/34 ML.
109 Ferguson, 'Publishing in London', MSS 3269/34 ML.
110 Cliff Rust to John Ferguson, 11 May 1970, MSS 3269/34 ML.
111 George Ferguson to Walter Butcher and Alec Bolton, 16 February 1968, MSS 3269/31 ML.
112 George Ferguson to Walter Butcher, 3 October 1967, MSS 3269/30 ML.
113 George Ferguson to Walter Butcher, 1 November 1967, MSS 3269/106 ML.
114 Ferguson, 'Publishing in London', MSS 3269/34 ML.
115 Kathleen McLean, 'Culture, Commerce and Ambivalence: A Study of Australian Federal Government Intervention in Book Publishing' (PhD diss., unpublished, Monash University, 2002), 182.
116 *The Economic Development of the Territory of Papua and New Guinea: Report of an Economic Survey Mission to the Territory of Papua and New Guinea Organized by the International Bank for Reconstruction and Development at the Request of the Commonwealth of Australia* (Canberra: Department of Territories, 1964), 209.
117 Brian Pinkstone, *Global Connections: A History of Exports and the Australian Economy* (Canberra: Australian Government Publishing Service, 1992), 192, quoted in McLean, 'Culture, Commerce and Ambivalence', 182.
118 McLean, 'Culture, Commerce and Ambivalence', 183.
119 George Ferguson to Walter Butcher, 23 May 1963, MSS 3269/21 ML.
120 John Ferguson to Export Awards Committee, Canberra, 25 September 1968, MSS 3269/106 ML.
121 John Ferguson to Export Awards Committee, Canberra, 25 September 1968, MSS 3269/106 ML.
122 John Ferguson to Export Awards Committee, Canberra, 25 September 1968, MSS 3269/106 ML.
123 Walter Butcher to George Ferguson, 3 February 1965, MSS 3269/23 ML.
124 Walter Butcher to George Ferguson, 29 September 1967, MSS 3269/106 ML.
125 W. M. Tennant to Angus & Robertson, 26 October 1967, MSS 3269/106 ML.
126 Walter Butcher to W. M. Tennant, 27 November 1967, MSS 3269/30 ML.
127 W. M. Tennant to Walter Butcher, 3 November 1967, MSS 3269/106 ML.
128 W. M. Tennant to Angus & Robertson, 26 October 1967, MSS 3269/106 ML.
129 George Ferguson to Walter Butcher, 1 November 1967, MSS 3269/106 ML.
130 George Ferguson to Walter Butcher, 1 November 1967, MSS 3269/106 ML.
131 W. M. Tennant to Walter Butcher, 3 November 1967, MSS 3269/106 ML.
132 W. M. Tennant to Angus & Robertson, 26 October 1967, MSS 3269/106 ML.
133 George Ferguson to Walter Butcher and Alec Bolton, 16 February 1968, MSS 3269/31 ML.
134 George Ferguson to Walter Butcher, 1 November 1967, MSS 3269/106 ML.
135 Walter Butcher to W. M. Tennant, 15 November 1967, MSS 3269/30 ML.
136 Walter Butcher to George Ferguson, 14 November 1967, MSS 3269/30 ML.
137 George Ferguson to Walter Butcher, 1 December 1967, MSS 3269/30 ML.
138 George Ferguson to Walter Butcher, 1 December 1967, MSS 3269/30 ML.

139 George Ferguson to Alec Bolton, 1 July 1968, MSS 3269/32 ML.
140 Walter Butcher to W. M. Tennant, 28 June 1968, MSS 3269/32 ML.
141 George Ferguson to Walter Butcher, 1 July 1968, MSS 3269/33 ML.
142 George Ferguson to Walter Butcher, 11 July 1969, MSS 3269/34 ML.
143 George Ferguson to Walter Butcher, 4 December 1967, MSS 3269/30 ML.
144 George Ferguson to Walter Butcher, 8 January 1968, MSS 3269/31 ML.
145 George Ferguson to Walter Butcher, 2 October 1970, MSS 3269/34 ML.
146 Walter Butcher to George Ferguson, 29 January 1969, MSS 3269/33 ML.
147 Ferguson, 'Publishing in London', MSS 3269/34 ML.
148 Angus & Robertson, London, Sales Figures, MSS 3269/28 ML.
149 Angus & Robertson, London, Sales Figures, MSS 3269/30 ML.
150 Walter Butcher to George Ferguson, 15 May 1968, MSS 3269/31 ML.
151 George Ferguson to Hector MacQuarrie, 11 June 1968, MSS 3269/449 ML.
152 Walter Butcher to George Ferguson, 7 July 1969, MSS 3269/34 ML.
153 Angus & Robertson, London, Sales Figures, MSS 3269/34 ML.
154 Alec Bolton to George Ferguson, 18 March 1968, MSS 3269/31 ML.
155 Alec Bolton to George Ferguson, 18 March 1968, MSS 3269/31 ML.
156 George Ferguson to Alec Bolton, 7 August 1969, MSS 3269/34 ML.
157 George Ferguson to Alec Bolton, 7 August 1969, MSS 3269/34 ML.
158 George Ferguson to Alec Bolton, 7 August 1969, MSS 3269/34 ML.
159 Ferguson, 'Publishing in London', MSS 3269/34 ML.
160 Alec Bolton to George Ferguson, 31 December 1969, MSS 3269/34 ML.
161 Alec Bolton to George Ferguson, 31 December 1969, MSS 3269/34 ML.
162 Alec Bolton to George Ferguson, 31 December 1969, MSS 3269/34 ML.
163 Alec Bolton to George Ferguson, 31 December 1969, MSS 3269/34 ML.
164 Alec Bolton to George Ferguson, 31 December 1969, MSS 3269/34 ML.
165 Alec Bolton to George Ferguson, 31 December 1969, MSS 3269/34 ML.
166 Walter Butcher to George Ferguson, 16 October 1969, MSS 3269/34 ML.
167 Walter Butcher to George Ferguson, 16 October 1969, MSS 3269/34 ML.
168 Walter Butcher to George Ferguson, 16 October 1969, MSS 3269/34 ML.
169 George Ferguson to Alec Bolton, 14 January 1970, MSS 3269/34 ML.
170 Ferguson, 'Publishing in London', MSS 3269/34 ML.
171 Ferguson, 'Publishing in London', MSS 3269/34 ML.
172 Richard Hauser to Walter Burns, 26 May 1960, MSS 3269/19 ML.
173 *The Economic Development of the Territory of Papua and New Guinea* (Canberra: Department of Territories, 1964), 209.
174 George Ferguson to Walter Butcher, 18 February 1970, MSS 3269/34 ML.
175 George Ferguson to Alec Bolton, 14 January 1970, MSS 3269/34 ML.
176 George Ferguson to Walter Butcher, 2 October 1970, MSS 3269/34 ML.
177 Ferguson, 'Publishing in London', MSS 3269/34 ML.
178 The ANZ financial dictionary defines this term to mean: 'The use of lawful means to minimise a tax bill. In contrast to tax evasion, avoidance legally exploits loopholes in tax legislation, interpreting the letter rather than the spirit of the law, to reduce tax liability'.

Chapter 13 Learning from a Distance

1 Peter C. Pugsley, 'Literary Text as Cross-Cultural Exchange: The Selection of Australian Literature for the Chinese Book Market', *Asian Studies Review* 29 (December 2005): 383–93.
2 R. E. Barker to George Ferguson, 11 January 1961, MSS 3269/557 ML.
3 George G. Harrap, *Some Memories, 1901–1935: A Publisher's Contribution to the History of Publishing* (London: Harrap, 1935), 145.
4 Harrap, *Some Memories*, 145.

5 Pierre Bourdieu, *The Field of Cultural Production* (Cambridge: Polity Press, 1993).

6 Carol Hetherington, 'London Calling? Long Distance Connections in Australian Literature' in *London was Full of Rooms*, ed. Tully Barnett, et al. (Adelaide: Lythrum Press, 2006), 244.

7 Alistair McCleery, 'The Return of the Publisher to Book History: The Case of Allen Lane', *Book History* 5 (2002): 161–85.

8 Tim Reiffenstein, Roger Hayter and David W. Edgington, 'Crossing Cultures, Learning to Export: Making Houses in British Columbia for Consumption in Japan', *Economic Geography* 78.2 (April 2002): 198.

9 Summarised by John Attenborough in 'three well-defined phases'. R. E. Barker and G. R. Davis, eds, *Books Are Different: An Account of the Defence of the Net Book Agreement before the Restrictive Practices Court in 1962* (London: Macmillan, 1966), 467.

10 Barker and Davis, *Books Are Different*, 467.

11 Barker and Davis, *Books Are Different*, 467.

12 D. F. McKenzie, *Bibliography and the Sociology of Texts* (Cambridge: Cambridge University Press, 1999).

13 George Ferguson to Ron Barker (Publishers Association, UK), 23 January 1962, MSS 3269/557 ML.

14 Richard Nile, 'Cartels, Capitalism and the Australian Booktrade,' *Continuum: The Australian Journal of Media and Culture* 4.1 (1990): 71–91.

15 Reiffenstein, Hayter and Edgington, 'Crossing Cultures', 198.

16 Reiffenstein, Hayter and Edgington, 'Crossing Cultures', 198.

17 'Are Prices Fixed Needlessly High on Imported Books?', *Sydney Morning Herald*, 26 June 1954.

18 George Ferguson to Walter Butcher, 18 December 1956, MSS 3269/447 ML.

19 Walter Harrap to George Ferguson, 13 January 1961, MSS 3269/322 ML.

20 R. E. Barker , Members Circular, The Publishers Association, 18 January 1963, MSS 3269/557 ML.

21 George Ferguson to Hector MacQuarrie, 4 November 1953, MSS 3269/444 ML.

BIBLIOGRAPHY

Angus & Robertson Archives
Mitchell Library, State Library of New South Wales

[The following volumes represent over 14,000 documents in total.]

Subject	Period	Volume
Albert and Son Ltd (Perth)	1924–30	MSS 314/2
Allen & Unwin, London, England	1933–67	MSS 3269/10
Angus & Robertson London Office	1948–58	MSS 3269/18
Angus & Robertson London Office	1958–61	MSS 3269/19
Angus & Robertson London Office	1961–62	MSS 3269/20
Angus & Robertson London Office	1963	MSS 3269/21
Angus & Robertson London Office	1964	MSS 3269/22
Angus & Robertson London Office	1965	MSS 3269/23
Angus & Robertson London Office	1966	MSS 3269/24
Angus & Robertson London Office	1966	MSS 3269/25
Angus & Robertson London Office	1966	MSS 3269/26
Angus & Robertson London Office	1966	MSS 3269/27
Angus & Robertson London Office	1967	MSS 3269/28
Angus & Robertson London Office	1967	MSS 3269/29
Angus & Robertson London Office	1967	MSS 3269/30
Angus & Robertson London Office	1968	MSS 3269/31
Angus & Robertson London Office	1968	MSS 3269/32
Angus & Robertson London Office	1969	MSS 3269/33
Angus & Robertson London Office	1969–71	MSS 3269/34
Australian Book Trade Advisory Committee	1964–69	MSS 3269/109
Australian Book Trade Council	1949	MSS 3269/110
Australian Book Trade Organisations	1947–49	MSS 3269/110
Australian Booksellers Association	1933–70	MSS 3269/110
Australian Department of Trade and Customs	1942–63	MSS 3269/92
Batsford Booksellers (London)	1955–69	MSS 3269/131
Book Export Development Committee Australia	1967–68	MSS 3269/106
Burns Oates and Washbourne Publishers (London)	1949–54	MSS 3269/164
Central News Agency (South Africa)	1950–56	MSS 3269/172
Clune, Frank	1931	MSS 314/19
Department of War Organisation of Industry	1943	MSS 6656/1

Fellowship of Australian Writers	1929	MSS 314/30
Fellowship of Australian Writers	1933–69	MSS 3269/258
Gollancz Publishers (London)	1949–68	MSS 3269/293
Gordon & Gotch (Australasia) Ltd, Sydney, NSW	1924–25	MSS 314/34
Green, Henry Mackenzie	1922–31	MSS 314/34
Halstead Printing Co. Ltd, Sydney, NSW	1929–31	MSS 314/35
Halstead Press Australia, Sydney, NSW	1938–46	MSS 3269/311
Halstead Press Australia, Sydney, NSW	1947–48	MSS 3269/312
Halstead Press Australia, Sydney, NSW	1947–49	MSS 3269/313
Halstead Press Australia, Sydney, NSW	1949–60	MSS 3269/314
Halstead Press Australia, Sydney, NSW	1960–70	MSS 3269/315
Hamilton Hamish	1963–68	MSS 3269/316
Harrap, George G. & Co. Ltd, London, England	1916–27	MSS 314/36
Harrap, George G. & Co. Ltd, London, England	1949–69	MSS 3269/322
Heinemann, London, England	1932–73	MSS 3269/330
Hook C. Townsend and Co. Papermakers, London	1939–51	MSS 3269/348
Idriess, Ion Llewellyn	1926–30	MSS 314/39
Jarrolds Publishers, London, England	1939–53	MSS 3269/364
Lippincott, J. P. Co., Philadelphia, USA	1918	MSS 314/53
Lothian, Thomas C. Pty Ltd	1905–29	MSS 314/53
Macmillan & Co. Ltd, London, England	1898–29	MSS 314/57
MacQuarrie, Hector	1929–31	MSS 314/58
MacQuarrie, Hector	1949–50	MSS 3269/440
MacQuarrie, Hector	1950	MSS 3269/441
MacQuarrie, Hector	1951	MSS 3269/442
MacQuarrie, Hector	1952	MSS 3269/443
MacQuarrie, Hector	1953	MSS 3269/444
MacQuarrie, Hector	1954	MSS 3269/445
MacQuarrie, Hector	1955	MSS 3269/446
MacQuarrie, Hector	1956	MSS 3269/447
MacQuarrie, Hector	1957	MSS 3269/448
MacQuarrie, Hector	1958–69	MSS 3269/449
Oxford University Press, London, England	1919	MSS 314/65
Oxford University Press (Australia)	1937–52	MSS 3269/525
Publishers Association Committee in Australia	1943–64	MSS 3269/580
Publishers Association Committee in Australia	1958–64	MSS 3269/581
Publishers Association, London, England	1946–57	MSS 3269/556
Publishers Association, London, England	1958–69	MSS 3269/557
Rigby Ltd, Adelaide, SA	1919–27	MSS 314/70
Rowland, Barry	1953–55	MSS 3269/645
Rowland, Barry	1956–58	MSS 3269/646
Rowland, Barry	1959	MSS 3269/647
Rowland, Barry	1960–63	MSS 3269/648
Tracey, Paul	1951–68	MSS 3269/745

Online Bibliographic Databases

AustLit: The Australian Literary Resource
http://www.austlit.edu.au/
The Australian National Bibliographic Database
http://www.nla.gov.au/librariesaustralia/anbd.html
The British Library
http://www.bl.uk/

National Library of Australia Canberra, Australian Capital Territory

Angus & Robertson. Correspondence (Sydney) 1919–1931, 314/256.

Angus & Robertson. *Report of the Directors*. Sydney: The Company, 1928–60.

Angus & Robertson. *Directors' Report and Balance Sheet*. Sydney: The Company, 1961.

Angus & Robertson. *Annual Report and Notice of Annual General Meeting*. Sydney: The Company, 1963–9.

Bolton, Alec. 'Interview with Heather Rusden'. TRC 3523. National Library of Australia, 11 October 1996–7 November 1996.

Cresp, Gael. *The British Publishers' Traditional Market Agreement: A Study*. Melbourne: Royal Melbourne Institute of Technology, Department of Librarianship, 1977.

Cultural Defence Committee. *Mental Rubbish from Overseas: A Public Protest*. Sydney: Cultural Defence Committee, 1935.

Ferguson, George. 'Interview with Suzanne Lunney'. TRC 452. National Library of Australia, 11 May 1976.

Harrap, George G. *Some Memories, 1901–1935: A Publisher's Contribution to the History of Publishing*. London: Harrap, 1935.

History of Australia's Import Licensing Measures, December 1939 to December 1958. Import Policy Branch, Department of Trade, Canberra: The Department, 1959.

Kapusta, Caroline. 'British Influence on the Development of the Australian Booktrade'. Masters thesis, Monash University, 1983.

Stewart, Douglas. 'Interview with Suzanne Lunney'. TRC 336. National Library of Australia, 1975.

Ure Smith, Sydney George (Sam). 'Interview with Hazel de Berg'. ORAL TRC 1/980. National Library of Australia, 7 December 1976.

Tariff Board Australia. *Report of Evidence at Tariff Board Inquiries into Proposal of Duty on Books, Magazines and Fashion Plates Held in Adelaide, Brisbane, Sydney and Melbourne*. Melbourne: Australian Booksellers Association, 1930.

Tariff Board Australia. *Tariff Board's Report on Publishing Industry*. Canberra: Commonwealth Government Printer, 1946.

'Tariff Board Inquiry into the Publishing Industry in Australia'. In *Ideas: Booksellers, Stationers and Fancy Goods Journal of Australia and New Zealand*. Melbourne: D. W. Thorpe, January 1946.

'Tariff Board Inquiry into the Publishing Industry in Australia'. In *Ideas: Booksellers, Stationers and Fancy Goods Journal of Australia and New Zealand*. Melbourne: D. W. Thorpe, February 1946.

'Tariff Board Inquiry into the Publishing Industry in Australia'. In *Ideas: Booksellers, Stationers and Fancy Goods Journal of Australia and New Zealand*. Melbourne: D. W. Thorpe, March 1946.

White, H. L. *The Future of Australian Publishing*. Canberra: Commonwealth National Library, 1946.

Williams, Ernie. 'Interview with Suzanne Lunney'. ORAL TRC 387. National Library of Australia, 2 December 1975.

The University of Reading

Allen & Unwin Vol. 13 AUC 20
John Hetherington Vol. 9 AUC 194

Unpublished Theses

Alison, Jennifer. 'Angus & Robertson as Publishers 1888–1900: A Business History'. PhD diss., University of New South Wales, 1997.

Brown, Diane. 'Publishing Culture: Commissioning Books in Australia, 1970–2000'. PhD diss., Victoria University, 2003.

Galligan, Anne. 'The Textual Condition: Negotiating Change in the Australian Literary Field'. PhD diss., University of Southern Queensland, 2001.

Hegarty, Emma. 'The Calculated Risk: Bestsellers and Trends in Australian Trade Publishing 1983–1999'. Masters thesis, Monash University, 2001.

Henningsgaard, Per. 'Outside Traditional Book Publishing Centres: The Production of a Regional Literature in Western Australia'. PhD diss., University of Western Australia, 2008.

James, Neil. 'Spheres of Influence: Angus and Robertson and Australian Literature from the Thirties to the Sixties'. PhD diss., University of Sydney, 2000.

Jones, Caroline Vera. 'Australian Imprint: The Influence of George Robertson on a National Narrative 1890–1935'. PhD diss., University of Sydney, 2004.

McLean, Kathleen. 'Culture, Commerce and Ambivalence: A Study of Australian Federal Government Intervention in Book Publishing'. PhD diss., Monash University, 2002.

Nile, Richard. 'The Rise of the Australian Novel'. PhD diss., University of New South Wales, 1987.

Pagliaro, Teresa. 'Arthur Wilberforce Jose (1863–1934): An Anglo-Australian. A Study of his Contribution to Australian Literary Culture from the 1890s to the 1930s'. PhD diss., University of Sydney, 1990.

Sheahan-Bright, Robyn. 'To Market to Market: The Development of the Australian Children's Publishing Industry'. PhD diss., Griffith University, 2005.

Newspaper Articles (Trove)

'Are Prices Fixed Needlessly High on Imported Books?' *Sydney Morning Herald*, 26 June 1954.

'Art was Lost on the Soil'. *Argus*, 25 September 1954.

'Australia in London'. *Sydney Morning Herald*, 24 April 1920.

'Australia is Britain's Best Market for Books'. *Mercury*, 28 December 1948.

'Australia, it seems, is a Bookish Place'. *Sydney Morning Herald*, 22 May 1953.

'Australian Book Ban in Britain'. *Age*, 7 February 1947.

'Australian Book Industry Needed'. *Argus*, 31 January 1946.

'Australian Writing and Local Prejudice'. *Mercury*, 29 July 1950.

'Book Exports to Britain: Australia's Trade'. *Sydney Morning Herald*, 15 January 1946.

'Bottleneck in Book Production: Publishers and Authors Miss Unique Opportunity'. *Sydney Morning Herald*, 7 October 1944.

'Britain's Book Imports'. *Sydney Morning Herald*, 5 April 1947.

'Britain Sends All available Books Here'. *Argus*, 30 January 1946.

'British Bid to Hold Book Market'. *Sydney Morning Herald*, 9 August 1945.

'British Restrictions on Book Imports'. *Argus*, 17 March 1947.

Burns, Walter. 'A. & R. In London'. *Sydney Morning Herald*, 24 November 1960.

Cardus, Neville. 'The Pen and the Sword: Perils and Pleasures of Reading'. *Sydney Morning Herald*, 26 April 1941.

'Colonial Attitude of U.K. Resented'. *Sydney Morning Herald*, 26 September 1963.

'Fiction Ban: Conserving Dollar Exchange'. *Canberra Times*, 12 April 1940.

'Four in Every Ten Australians Never Read a Book'. *Argus*, 20 June 1953.

Frizell, Helen. 'British Hold on Book Publishing'. *Sydney Morning Herald*, 31 May 1969.

'Grave Overseas Threat to Australian Writers'. In *Fellowship: Official Organ of the Fellowship of Australian Writers* 1.1 (June 1944).

Haupt, Robert. 'The Book Rebellion'. *Age*, 5 November 1988.
'Imported Fiction: Ban Operates from Today'. *Mercury*, 2 April 1940.
MacQuarrie, Hector. 'A. and R.'s London Publishing'. *Sydney Morning Herald*, 23 November 1960.
'Millions of Books: Australian Issues'. *Sydney Morning Herald*, 2 December 1941.
'Minister Lifts Ban on Novel'. *Argus*, 2 November 1951.
Neill, Rosemary. 'Is This the Most Feared Man in Australian Literature? – The Biblio Files'. *Australian*, 22 July 2006.
Neill, Rosemary. 'Who is Killing the Great Books of Australia? Lits Out'. *Australian*, 18 March 2006.
'Refusal to Lift Ban on American Novel'. *Sydney Morning Herald*, 26 October 1951.
'Restriction of Imports: Publications on New List'. *Sydney Morning Herald*, 12 April 1940.
'Restriction on Books'. *Mercury*, 21 March 1947.
Souter, Gavin. 'A and R Signs Wizard of Oz'. *Sydney Morning Herald*, 28 March 1972.
'Sydney was Tough in those Days', *Argus*, 19 January 1952.
'War Books: Demand Falls Sharply'. *Sydney Morning Herald*, 30 June 1944.
Wellings, Vera. 'Australians are Bookworms: Literary Influence'. *Sydney Morning Herald*, 21 December 1940.

General Reading

Akerlof, George A. and Rachel E. Kranton. 'Economics and Identity'. *Quarterly Journal of Economics* 65.3 (August 2000): 715–53.
Alison, Jennifer. 'Publishers and Editors: Angus & Robertson, 1888–1945'. In *A History of the Book in Australia 1891–1945: A National Culture in a Colonised Market*, edited by Martyn Lyons and John Arnold, 27–35. St Lucia: University of Queensland Press, 2001.
Alomes, Stephen. 'Colonial to Global: Paradoxes of Expatriation in Australia's Diasporic Story'. In *Diaspora: The Australasian Experience*, edited by Cynthia vanden Driesen and Ralph Crane, 130–45. New Delhi: Prestige Books, 2006.
Alomes, Stephen. *When London Calls: The Expatriation of Australian Creative Artists to Britain*. Cambridge: Cambridge University Press, 1999.
Anderson, Benedict. *Imagined Communities*. London: Verso, 2006.
Arnold, John. 'Australian Books, Publishers and Writers in England, 1900–1940'. In *Australians in Britain: The Twentieth-Century Experience*, edited by Carl Bridge, Robert Crawford and David Dunstan, 10.1–19. Clayton: Monash University ePress, 2009.
Ashcroft, Bill. 'Home and Horizon'. In *Diaspora: The Australasian Experience*, edited by Cynthia vanden Driesen and Ralph Crane, 425–8. New Delhi: Prestige Books, 2006.
Australia Council. *Economic Analysis of Literary Publishing in Australia: Final Report September 2008*. Sydney: SGS Economics and Planning, 2008.
Ayers, David. 'Materialism and the Book'. *Poetics Today* 24.4 (2003): 759–80.
Baranay, Inez. 'Multiculturalism, Globalisation and Worldliness: Origin and Destination of the Text'. *Journal of the Association for the Study of Australian Literature* 3 (2004): 117–32
Barker, Anthony. *George Robertson: A Publishing Life in Letters*. St Lucia: University of Queensland Press, 1993.
Barker, R. E. and G. R. Davis, eds. *Books Are Different: An Account of the Defence of the Net Book Agreement before the Restrictive Practices Court in 1962*. London: Macmillan, 1966.
Barnes, John. '"Heaven Forbid that I Should Think of Treating with an English Publisher": The Dilemma of Literary Nationalists in Federated Australia'. In *Literary Cultures and the Material Book*, edited by Simon Eliot, Andrew Nash and Ian Willison, 399–412. London: The British Library, 2007.
Barnes, Katherine and Jan Lloyd Jones. *Words for Their Own Sake: The Pursuit of Literature in an Economic Rationalist World*. Melbourne: Australian Scholarly Publishing, 2004.
Barnett, Tully, Nena Bierbaum, Syd Harrex, Rick Hosking and Graham Tulloch, eds. *London Was Full of Rooms*. Adelaide: Lythrum Press, 2006.

Beacham, Richard. 'An Introduction to the London Charter'. Paper presented at the Joint CIPA / VAST / EG / EuroMed Event, The E-volution of IC Technology in Cultural Heritage, 2006.

Beckmann, Roger. 'Literature, Science and Economic Rationalism'. In *Words for their Own Sake: The Pursuit of Literature in an Economic Rationalist World*, edited by Katherine Barnes and Jan Lloyd-Jones, 58–69. Melbourne: Australian Scholarly Publishing, 2004.

Bennett, Bruce and Jennifer Strauss, eds. *The Oxford Literary History of Australia*. Melbourne: Oxford University Press, 1998, 130–46.

Bennett, Tony, Michael Emmison and John Frow. *Accounting for Tastes: Australian Everyday Cultures*. Cambridge: Cambridge University Press, 1999.

Bhabha, Homi K., ed. *Nation and Narration*. London: Routledge, 1990.

Bhabha, Homi K. *The Location of Culture*. London: Routledge, 2004.

Bird, Delys, Robert Dixon and Christopher Lee, eds. *Authority and Influence: Australian Literary Criticism 1950–2000*. St Lucia: University of Queensland Press, 2001.

Bird, Delys, Robert Dixon and Susan Lever, eds. 'CanonOzities: The Making of Literary Reputations in Australia'. *Southerly* 57.3 (1997).

Black, Fiona, Bertrum MacDonald and J. Malcolm Black. 'Geographic Information Systems: A New Research Method for Book History'. *Book History* 1.1 (1998): 11–31.

Blainey, Geoffrey. *The Tyranny of Distance*. Melbourne: Sun Books, 1966.

Bode, Katherine. 'Beyond the Colonial Present: Quantitative Analysis, "Resourceful Reading" and Australian Literary Studies'. *Journal of the Association for the Study of Australian Literature* [online], 2 May 2008.

Bode, Katherine. 'From British Domination to Multinational Conglomeration? A Revised History of Australian Novel Publishing, 1950 to 2007'. In *Resourceful Reading: The New Empiricism, eResearch and Australian Literary Culture*, edited by Katherine Bode and Robert Dixon, 194–222. Sydney: Sydney University Press, 2009.

Bode, Katherine and Robert Dixon, eds. *Resourceful Reading: The New Empiricism, eResearch and Australian Literary Culture*. Sydney: Sydney University Press, 2009.

Bolton, Alec. 'Publishing in an Age of Innocence: Angus and Robertson in the 1950s'. *Publishing Studies* 1 (Spring 1995): 12–20.

Bourdieu, Pierre. *The Field of Cultural Production: Essays on Art and Literature*. Cambridge: Polity Press, 1993.

Bridge, Carl, Robert Crawford and David Dunstan, eds. *Australians in Britain: The Twentieth-Century Experience*. Clayton: Monash University ePress, 2009.

Brown, Stephen. *Consuming Books: The Marketing and Consumption of Literature*. London: Routledge, 2004.

Buckridge, Patrick and Belinda McKay, eds. *By the Book: A Literary History of Queensland*. St Lucia: University of Queensland Press, 2007.

Carey, Steve. 'Between Two Worlds: Australian Publishing on the Horns of an Import Dilemma'. *Publishing Research Quarterly* 24.3 (2008): 156–64.

Carter, David. 'Going, Going, Gone? Britishness and Englishness in Contemporary Australian Culture'. *Overland* 169 (2001): 81–6.

Carter, David. 'Literary Canons and Literary Institutions'. *Southerly* 57.3 (1997): 16–37.

Carter, David and Anne Galligan, eds. *Making Books: Contemporary Australian Publishing*. St Lucia: University of Queensland Press, 2007.

Cetina, Karin Knorr. 'Sociality with Objects: Social Relations in Postsocial Knowledge Societies'. *Theory, Culture and Society* 14.4 (1997): 1–30.

Cheah, Pheng and Jonathan Culler, eds. *Grounds of Comparison: Around the Work of Benedict Anderson*. London: Routledge, 2003.

Curtain, John. 'Distance Makes the Market Fonder: The Development of Book Publishing in Australia'. *Media, Culture & Society* 15 (1993): 233–44.

Curtain, John. 'How Australian Publishing Won its Way against the Odds'. *Logos: Journal of the World Book Community* 9.3 (1998): 141–7.

Darnton, Robert. *The Kiss of the Lamourette*. London: Faber & Faber, 1990.

Department of Territories. *The Economic Development of the Territory of Papua and New Guinea: Report of an Economic Survey Mission to the Territory of Papua and New Guinea Organized by the International Bank for Reconstruction and Development at the Request of the Commonwealth of Australia*. Canberra: Department of Territories, 1964.

Dixon, Robert. 'Australian Fiction and the World Republic of Letters, 1890–1950'. In *The Cambridge History of Australian Literature*, edited by Peter Pierce, 223–54. Melbourne: Cambridge University Press, 2009.

Dixon, Robert. 'Australian Literary Studies and Post-Colonialism'. *AUMLA: Journal of the Australasian Universities Language and Literature Association* 100 (2003): 108–21.

Dixon, Robert. 'Australian Literature – International Contexts'. *Southerly* 67.1–2 (2007): 15–27.

Dixon, Robert. 'Boundary Work: Australian Literary Studies in the Field of Knowledge Production'. In *Australian Studies Centre 25th Anniversary Collection*, edited by David Carter and Martin Crotty, 20–37. St Lucia: University of Queensland Press, 2005.

Dixon, Robert. 'Home or Away? The Trope of Place in Australian Literary Criticism and Literary History'. *Westerly* 54.1 (July 2009): 12–17.

Dixon, Robert. 'Making Oz Lit'. *Australian Book Review* (February 2003): 45–6.

Dolin, Tim. 'Fiction and the Australian Reading Public, 1888–1914', Australian Common Reader Project [online], 1 September 2008.

Dolin, Tim. 'First Steps toward a History of the Mid-Victorian Novel in Colonial Australia'. *Australian Literary Studies* 32.3 (2006): 273–93.

Dolin, Tim. 'The Secret Reading Life of Us'. In *Readers, Writers, Publishers: Essays and Poems*, edited by Brian Matthew, 115–34. Canberra: Australian Academy of the Humanities, 2004.

Dutton, Geoffrey. *Snow on the Saltbush: The Australian Literary Experience*. Victoria: Penguin, 1985.

Eagleton, Terry. *Marxism and Literary Criticism*. London: Routledge, 2002.

Edwards, Justin D. *Postcolonial Literature*. London: Palgrave Macmillan, 2008.

Eggert, Paul. 'Australian Classics and the Price of Books: The Puzzle of the 1890s'. *Journal of the Association for the Study of Australian Literature* [online] (May 2008): 130–57.

Eggert, Paul. 'The Colonial Market, Imperial Publisher, and the Demise of the Three-Decker Novel'. *Book History* 6 (2006): 127–46.

Eliot, Simon. 'Very Necessary but Not Quite Sufficient: A Personal View of Quantitative Analysis in Book History'. *Book History* 5 (2002): 283–93.

Eliot, Simon, Andrew Nash and Ian Willison, eds. *Literary Cultures and the Material Book*. London: The British Library, 2007.

Ensor, Jason. 'A Policy of Splendid Isolation: Angus & Robertson, George G. Harrap and the Politics of Co-operation in the Australian Book Trade During the Late 1930s'. In *Script & Print* 34.1, 34–42. Victoria: Bibliographical Society of Australia and New Zealand, 2010.

Ensor, Jason. 'Is a Picture Worth 10,175 Australian Novels?' In *Resourceful Reading: The New Empiricism, eResearch and Australian Literary Culture*, edited by Katherine Bode and Robert Dixon, 240–73. Sydney: Sydney University Press, 2009.

Ensor, Jason. 'Reprints, International Markets and Local Literary Taste: New Empiricism and Australian Literature'. *Journal of the Association for the Study of Australian Literature* [online] (May 2008): 198–218.

Ensor, Jason. 'Still Waters Run Deep: Empirical Methods and the Migration Patterns of Regional Publishers' Authors and Titles within Australian Literature'. In *Antipodes: A North American Journal of Australian Literature*, 197–208. New York: American Association of Australian Literary Studies, 2009.

Everingham, Sam. *Gordon Barton: Australia's Maverick Entrepreneur*. Crow's Nest: Allen & Unwin, 2009.

Fabinyi, Andrew. 'Australian Book Perspective, 1961'. *Meanjin Quarterly* 20.2 (1961): 212–16.

Feather, John. *A History of British Publishing*. London: Routledge, 1988.

Feenberg, Andrew. 'From Critical Theory of Technology to the Rational Critique of Rationality'. *Social Epistemology* 22.1 (January–March 2008): 5–28.

Feltes, N. N. *Modes of Production of Victorian Novels*. Chicago: University of Chicago Press, 1986.

Ferguson, George and Neil James. 'Flagship Angus & Robertson'. In *A History of the Book in Australia 1946–2005: Paper Empires*, edited by Craig Munro and Robyn Sheahan-Bright, 10–12. St Lucia: University of Queensland Press, 2006.

Finkelstein, David and Alistair McCleery, eds. *The Book History Reader*. London: Routledge, 2002.

Flanders, Julia. 'Data and Wisdom: Electronic Editing and the Quantification of Knowledge'. *Literary and Linguistic Computing* 24.1 (2009): 53–62.

Floridi, Luciano. 'What is the Philosophy of Information?' *Metaphilosophy* 33.1/2 (January 2002): 123–45.

Frow, John. *Genre*. London: Routledge, 2006.

Garrioch, David, ed. *The Culture of the Book: Essays from Two Hemispheres in Honour of Wallace Kirsop*. Melbourne: Bibliographical Society of Australia and New Zealand, 1999.

Gelder, Ken. 'Notes on the Research Future of Australian Literary Studies'. *Australian Humanities Review* 37 [online] (2005).

Gelder, Ken. *Popular Fiction: The Logics and Practices of a Literary Field*. London: Routledge, 2004.

Gelder, Ken. 'Recovering Australian Popular Fiction: Towards the End of Australian Literature'. Paper presented at the Proceedings of the 2000 ASAL Conference, *Australian Literary Studies in the 21st Century*, 2001.

Grainger, Gareth. 'Protection of Cultural Sovereignty in a Free-Trade Environment'. *Media and Culture Review* [online] (July 1998).

Green, Dorothy. *H. M. Green's History of Australian Literature, Volume 1, 1789–1923*. Sydney: Angus & Robertson, 1984.

Green, Dorothy. *H. M. Green's History of Australian Literature, Volume 2, 1923–1950*. Sydney: Angus & Robertson, 1985.

Guide to the Angus & Robertson archives in the Mitchell Library, State Library of New South Wales, Mitchell Library, Sydney, 1990.

Hagan, J. *Printers and Politics: A History of the Australian Printing Unions 1850–1950*. Canberra: Australian National University Press, 1966.

Haraway, Donna. 'Situated Knowledges: The Science Question in Feminism and the Privilege of Partial Perspective'. *Feminist Studies* 14.3 (1988): [575–99].

Hassam, Andrew. 'From Ned Kelly to Don Bradman: India, Australia and the Incongruities of Globalisation'. In *New Bearings in English Studies: A Festschrift for C.T. Indra*, edited by C. Vijayasree, R. Azhagarasan, Bruce Bennett, Mohan Ramanan, R. Palanivel and T. Sriraman, 137–51. Hyderabad: Orient Longman, 2008.

Hassam, Andrew. 'How British Are We?' *Meanjin* 63.3 (2004): 123–30.

Hetherington, Carol. 'AustLit: A Resource for Print Culture Research'. *Journal of Publishing* 1 (October 2005): 115–27.

Hetherington, Carol. 'Little Australians? Some Questions about National Identity and the National Literature'. *Antipodes* 21.1 (June 2007): 11–15.

Hetherington, Carol. 'London Calling? Long-Distance Connections in Australian Literature'. In *London Was Full of Rooms*, edited by Tully Barnett, Nena Bierbaum, Syd Harrex, Rick Hosking and Graham Tulloch, 244–52. Adelaide: Lythrum Press, 2006.

Hill, Alan. *In Pursuit of Publishing*. London: John Murray, 1988.

Huggan, Graham. *Australian Literature: Postcolonialism, Racism, Transnationalism*. Oxford: Oxford University Press, 2007.

Hutchinson, Robert. 'Knowledge and Control: A Marxian Perspective on the Productivity Paradox of Information Technology'. *Rethinking Marxism* 20.2 (April 2008): 288–304.

Hunter, Lynette. *Critiques of Knowing: Situated Textualities in Science, Computing and the Arts*. New York: Routledge, 1999.

James, Neil. 'A Paperback Canon: The Australian Pocket Library'. *Australian Literary Studies* 19.3 (May 2000): 295–305.

James, Neil. '"Basically We Thought About Books" – An Interview with George Ferguson'. *Publishing Studies* 5 (Spring 1997): 8–16.

James, Neil. 'Breaching the Absolute Gap: Angus and Robertson in Asia'. *Meanjin* 57.3 (1998): 553–63.

James, Neil. '"The Fountainhead": George Ferguson and Angus & Robertson'. *Publishing Studies* 7 (Autumn 1999): 6–16.

James, Neil and Elizabeth Webby. 'Canon Around the Hub: Angus and Robertson and the Post-War Literary Canon'. *Southerly* 57.3 (Spring 1997): 51–66.

Jameson, Frederic. *Postmodernism or, the Cultural Logic of Late Capitalism*. Durham: Duke University Press, 1991.

Jensen, Lars. *Unsettling Australia: Readings in Australian Cultural History*. New Delhi: Atlantic Publishers & Distributors, 2005.

Jessop, Martyn. 'Digital Visualisation as a Scholarly Activity'. *Literary and Linguistic Computing* 23.3 (2008): 281–93.

Johanson, Graeme. *A Study of Colonial Editions in Australia, 1843–1972*. Wellington: Elibank Press, 2000.

Johnson-Woods, Toni. 'The Mysterious Case of Carter Brown: Or, Who Really Killed the Australian Author?' *Australian Literary Studies* 21.4 (2004): 74–88.

Johnson-Woods, Toni. 'The Promiscuous Carter Brown'. *Journal of the Association for the Study of Australian Literature* [online] (2 May 2008).

Johnson-Woods, Toni. *Pulp: A Collector's Book of Australian Fiction Covers*. Canberra: National Library of Australia, 2004.

Johnson-Woods, Toni. '"Pulp" Fiction Industry in Australia 1949–1959'. *Antipodes* 20.1 (2006): 63–7.

Jones, Caroline Vera. 'The Influence of Angus and Robertson on Colonial Knowledge'. *Journal of the Royal Australian Historical Society* 89.1 (2003): 26–37.

Jones, Caroline Vera. 'Historical Midwifery: The Editorial Birth of an Australian Narrative'. *Journal of Publishing* 2 (July 2007): 26–45.

Jose, Nicholas. 'A Shelf of Our Own: Creative Writing and Australian Literature'. *Australian Book Review* [online] (November 2005): 25–9.

Joseph, Michael. 'Publishing Slump'. *New Statesman and Nation* [online], 25 September 1948.

Joshi, Priya. 'Quantitative Methods, Literary History'. *Book History* 5 (2002): 263–74.

Kent, Jacqueline. *A Certain Style: Beatrice Davis, a Literary Life*. Victoria: Penguin, 2001.

Kilner, Kerry. 'A Fool's Errand? Or, Ten Thousand Authors and the Madness of a National Bibliography'. *AustLit* [online] (2006). http://www.austlit.edu.au:7777/presentations/index.html, accessed April 2009.

Kingsford, Reginald John Lethbridge. *The Publishers Association, 1896–1946: With An Epilogue*. London: Cambridge University Press, 1970.

Kirsop, Wallace. *Towards a History of the Australian Book Trade*. Sydney: Wentworth Books, 1969.

Leavis, Q. D. *Fiction and the Reading Public*. London: Chatto & Windus, 1965.

Lee, Jenny. 'Against the Odds: Australian Book Publishers Become Global'. *Logos: Journal of the World Book Community* 15.3 (2004): 154–60.

Lee, Jenny. 'War and Peace in the Australian Book Trade'. Unpublished paper.

Lewis, Glen. '"It's Academic": Imperialism and the Australian Tertiary Book Industry'. *Continuum: The Australian Journal of Media and Culture* 4.1 (1990): 92–108.

Lloyd, Peter. '100 Years of Tariff Protection in Australia'. *Australian Economic History Review* 48.2 (July 2008): 99–145.

Lyons, Martyn. 'Britain's Largest Export Market'. In *A History of the Book in Australia 1891–1945: A National Culture in a Colonised Market*, edited by Martyn Lyons and John Arnold, 19–26. St Lucia: University of Queensland Press, 2001.

Macherey, Pierre. *A Theory of Literary Production*. London: Routledge, 2006.

Magner, Brigid. 'Anglo-Australian Relations in the Book Trade'. In *A History of the Book in Australia 1946–2005: Paper Empires*, edited by Craig Munro and Robyn Sheahan-Bright, 7–10. St Lucia: University of Queensland Press, 2006.

Malouf, David. 'Made in England: Australia's British Inheritance'. In *4 Classic Quarterly Essays on the Australian Story*, 3–70. Melbourne: Black Inc.

Matthews, Brian. *Readers, Writers, Publishers: Essays and Poems*. Canberra: Australian Academy of the Humanities, 2004.

Maxwell, Richard, ed. *Culture Works: The Political Economy of Culture*. Minneapolis: University of Minnesota Press, 2001.

Mayall, Margery. 'Attached to their Style: Traders, Technical Analysis and Postsocial Relationships'. *Journal of Sociology* 43.4 (2008): 421–37.

McCarty, Willard. 'Humanities Computing'. In *Encyclopaedia of Library and Information Science*, edited by Miriam Drake, 1224–35. London: CRC Press, 2003.

McCleery, Alistair. 'The Return of the Publisher to Book History: The Case of Allen Lane'. *Book History* 5 (2002): 161–85.

McDonald, Peter. *British Literary Culture and Publishing Practice: 1880–1914*. Cambridge: Cambridge University Press, 1997.

McGregor, Russell. 'The Necessity of Britishness: Ethno-cultural Roots of Australian Nationalism'. *Nations and Nationalism* 12.3 (2006): 493–511.

McKenzie, D. F. *Bibliography and the Sociology of Texts*. Cambridge: Cambridge University Press, 1999.

McLean, Kathleen. 'Books and Tariffs: An Australian Story'. *Journal of Publishing* 1 (October 2005): 17–36.

Mead, Philip. *Australian Literary Studies in the 21st Century: Proceedings of the 2000 ASAL Conference*. Maryborough: Association for the Study of Australian Literature, 2001.

Mead, Philip. 'Nation, Literature, Location'. In *The Cambridge History of Australian Literature*, edited by Peter Pierce, 549–67. Melbourne: Cambridge University Press, 2009.

Miller, E. Morris. *Australian Literature, Volume 1: From its Beginnings to 1935*. Sydney: Sydney University Press, 1975.

Miller, E. Morris. *Australian Literature, Volume 2: From its Beginnings to 1935*. Sydney: Sydney University Press, 1975.

Miller, Laura J. *Reluctant Capitalists: Bookselling and the Culture of Consumption*. London: University of Chicago Press, 2006.

Moretti, Franco. *Atlas of the European Novel 1800–1900*. London: Verso, 1999.

Moretti, Franco. *Graphs, Maps, Trees: Abstract Models for Literary History*. London: Verso, 2007.

Moretti, Franco. 'Graphs, Maps, Trees. Abstract Models for Literary History'. *New Left Review* 24 (November–December 2003): 67–93.

Moretti, Franco. *Signs Taken For Wonders*. London: Verso, 1988.

Moretti, Franco. *The Novel, Volume 1: History, Geography and Culture*. Princeton: Princeton University Press, 2006.

Moretti, Franco. *The Novel, Volume 2: Forms and Themes*. Princeton: Princeton University Press, 2007.

Morton, Peter. 'Australia's England, 1880–1950'. In *The Cambridge History of Australian Literature*, edited by Peter Pierce, 255–81. Melbourne: Cambridge University Press, 2009.

Munro, Craig. 'The A & R War: Profits, Personalities, and Paperbacks'. In *Publishing Studies* 1 (Spring 1995): 21–8.

Munro, Craig. 'Case-Study: A&R's Takeover Crisis'. In *A History of the Book in Australia 1946–2005: Paper Empires*, edited by Craig Munro and Robyn Sheahan-Bright, 13–18. St Lucia: University of Queensland Press, 2006.

Munro, Craig and Robyn Sheahan-Bright, eds. *A History of the Book in Australia 1946–2005: Paper Empires*. St Lucia: University of Queensland Press, 2006.

Nile, Richard, ed. *Australian Civilisation*. Melbourne: Oxford University Press, 1994.

Nile, Richard. *The Australian Legend and Its Discontents*. St Lucia: University of Queensland Press, 2000.

Nile, Richard. 'Cartels, Capitalism and the Australian Booktrade'. *Continuum: The Australian Journal of Media and Culture* 4.1 (1990): 71–91.

Nile, Richard. 'Literary Democracy and the Politics of Reputation'. In *The Oxford Literary History of Australia*, edited by Bruce Bennett and Jennifer Strauss, 130–46. Melbourne: Oxford University Press, 1998.

Nile, Richard. *The Making of the Australian Literary Imagination*. St Lucia: University of Queensland Press, 2002.

Nile, Richard. 'Pulp Fiction: Popular Culture and Literary Reputation'. *Journal of Australian Studies* 58 (1998): 66–73.

Nile, Richard and Jason Ensor. 'The Novel, the Implicated Reader and Australian Literary Cultures, 1950–2008'. In *The Cambridge History of Australian Literature*, edited by Peter Pierce, 517–48. Melbourne: Cambridge University Press, 2009.

Nile, Richard and David Walker. 'Marketing the Literary Imagination: Production of Australian Literature, 1915–1965'. *Australian Literary Studies* 13.4 (1988): 284–302.

Nile, Richard and David Walker. 'The "Paternoster Row Machine" and the Australian Book Trade, 1890–1945'. In *A History of the Book in Australia 1891–1945: A National Culture in a Colonised Market*, edited by Martyn Lyons and John Arnold, 3–18. St Lucia: University of Queensland Press, 2001.

Norrie, Ian. *Mumby's Publishing and Bookselling in the Twentieth Century*. London: Bell & Hyman, 1982.

Olivier, Jacques, Mathias Thoenig and Thierry Verdier. 'Globalisation and the Dynamics of Cultural Identity'. *Journal of International Economics* 76 (2008): 356–70.

Osborne, Roger. 'A National Interest in an International Market: The Circulation of Magazines in Australia during the 1930s'. *History Australia* 5.3 (2008): 75.1–75.16.

Page, Roger. *Australian Bookselling*. Melbourne: Hill of Content, 1970.

Pagliaro, Teresa. 'Case-Study: A. W. Jose & the *Australian Encyclopaedia*'. In *A History of the Book in Australia 1891–1945: A National Culture in a Colonised Market*, edited by Martyn Lyons and John Arnold, 42–8. St Lucia: University of Queensland Press, 2001.

Petrucci, Amanda. 'Reading to Read: A Future for Reading'. In *A History of Reading in the West*, edited by Guglielmo Cavallo and Roger Chartier, 345–67. Cambridge: Polity Press, 1999.

Pierce, Peter, ed. *The Cambridge History of Australian Literature*. Melbourne: Cambridge University Press, 2009.

Plant, Marjorie. *The English Book Trade: An Economic History of the Making and Sale of Books*. London: Allen & Unwin, 1965.

Poland, Louise. 'Publishing for Posterity: Beatrice Davis and Angus & Robertson, 1937–1973'. *Journal of Publishing* 2 (July 2007): 114–42.

Poster, Mark. 'Consumption and Digital Commodities in the Everyday'. *Cultural Studies* 18.2/3 (March and May 2004): 409–23, 421.

Productivity Commission. *Restrictions on the Parallel Importation of Books*. Canberra: Research Report, 2009.

Pugsley, Peter C. 'Literary Text as Cross-Cultural Exchange: The Selection of Australian Literature for the Chinese Book Market'. *Asian Studies Review* 29 (December 2005): 383–93.

Raley, Rita. 'eEmpires'. *Cultural Critique* 57 (Spring 2004): 111–50.

Ramsay, S. 'In Praise of Pattern'. *Text Technology* 2 (2005):177–90.

Ranciere, Jacques. *The Politics of Aesthetics*. London: Continuum International Publishing Group, 2006.

Rees, Leslie. 'Australian Books In London: Attacking British Apathy'. *West Australian* [online] (2 May 1936).

Reiffenstein, Tim, Roger Hayter and David W. Edgington. 'Crossing Cultures, Learning to Export: Making Houses in British Columbia for Consumption in Japan'. *Economic Geography* 78.2 (April 2002): 195–219.

Richards, I. A. *Principles of Literary Criticism.* London: Routledge, 2001.

Roe, Jill. *Stella Miles Franklin: A Biography*. London: Fourth Estate, 2008.

Rooney, Bridget, ed. *Literary Activists: Writer-Intellectuals and Australian Public Life*. St Lucia: University of Queensland Press, 2009.

Said, Edward W. *Culture and Imperialism.* London: Chatto & Windus, 1993.

Sanders, Frank, ed. *British Book Trade Organisation: A Report on the Work of the Joint Committee*. London: Allen & Unwin, 1939.

Sassoon, Donald. 'On Cultural Markets'. *New Left Review* 17 (2002): 113–26.

Scholes, Kirsten. 'Parallel Importing'. *Canterbury Law Review* 6 (1997): 564–92.

Sculley, D. and Bradley M Pasanek. 'Meaning and Mining: The Impact of Implicit Assumptions in Data Mining for the Humanities'. *Literary and Linguistic Computing* 23.4 (2008): 409–24.

St Clair, William. *The Reading Nation in the Romantic Period.* New York: Cambridge University Press, 2004.

Stole, Inger L. 'Advertising'. In *Culture Works: The Political Economy of Culture*, edited by Richard Maxwell, 83–106. Minnesota: University of Minnesota Press, 2001.

Taraporevala, Russi Jal. *Competition and Its Control in the British Book Trade 1850–1939.* London: Pitman Publishing, 1973.

Thomas, Julian. 'CDs and the Politics of Intellectual Property'. *Media and Culture Review* (July 1998): 1–2.

Thrift, Nigel. 'The Material Practices of Glamour'. *Journal of Cultural Economy* 1.1 (2008): 9–23.

Trainor, Luke. 'Australian Writers, British Publishers, 1870–1902'. *Australian Historical Society* 37.127 (April 2006): 140–55.

Turkle, S. *Life on the Screen.* London: Weidenfeld & Nicolson, 1996.

Turner, Graeme. *National Fictions: Literature, Film and Construction of Australian Narrative*. Sydney: Allen & Unwin, 1989.

Unwin, Stanley. *The Truth about a Publisher.* London: Allen & Unwin, 1960.

Van Maanen, J. *Tales of the Fields.* Chicago: University of Chicago Press, 1998.

Vanden Driesen, Cynthia and Ralph Crane, eds. *Diaspora: The Australasian Experience.* New Delhi: Prestige Books, 2006.

Walsh, Richard. 'Case-Study: The New A & R'. In *A History of the Book in Australia 1946–2005: Paper Empires*, edited by Craig Munro and Robyn Sheahan-Bright, 57–62. St Lucia: University of Queensland Press, 2006.

White, H. L. *The Future of Australian Publishing.* Sydney: Australian Institute of Political Science, 1946.

Wooldridge, Tessa. 'Ensuring the Best – AustLit: The Resource for Australian Literature'. Paper presented at a conference, Melbourne: Australian and New Zealand Society of Indexers, 20 March 2005.

Yates, Alan. *Carter Brown, Ready When You Are, C.B.! The Autobiography of Alan Yates Alias Carter Brown.* Melbourne: Macmillan, 1983.

Zifcak, Michael. 'The Evolution of Australian Publishing'. *Logos: Journal of the World Book Community* 1.3 (1990): 18–25.

Zwick, Detlev and Nikhilesh Dholakia. 'Bringing the Market to Life: Screen Aesthetics and the Epistemic Consumption Object'. *Marketing Theory* 6 (2006): 41–62.

INDEX